Greenhill Books

BATTLESHIPS OF THE WORLD

RENÉ GREGER

Battleships of the World

Translated from the original German by Geoffrey Brooks

Greenhill Books, London

Rivadavia in dry dock in the USA.

Preface

A number of factors were instrumental in persuading me to write this book about big-gun capital ships, despite the existence of numerous works on the subject. Unfortunately, many 'standard works' omit important information, or contradict other publications on technical or historical points, and, in addition, most of their authors arrange their data in such a manner as to render ship comparison difficult or even impossible.

I have compiled a book for naval historians, ship lovers and model-makers which, besides incorporating the most recent research, is illustrated with many rare photographs and accurate scale drawings and it has not been my objective merely to provide reliable detail, but also to attempt to explain the underlying circumstances which caused each individual ship to come into existence.

I have described herein all the big-gun capital ships built after 1905 and the large pre-dreadnoughts building in that year. I have excluded monitors with heavy guns, coast defence battleships and heavy armoured cruisers, to which latter category belong the three so-called 'pocket battleships' of the German Navy, which are not normally considered to be capital ships. I have similarly disregarded unfulfilled projects while including all capital ships which were laid down but for various reasons never completed.

To all those who have contributed towards the publication of this book, and especially to my editor J. Schödler, I would like to express my thanks.

René Greger

Battleships of the World
First published 1997 by Greenhill Books, Park House, 1 Russell Gardens, London NW11 9NN

Copyright © by Motorbuch Verlag, Postfach 10 37 43, 70032 Stuttgart
English translation © Lionel Leventhal Limited, 1997
Drawings by M. Polák

British Library Cataloguing in Publication Data
Greger, Rene
Battleships of the World
  1.Battleships – History 2. Battleships – Identification
  I.Title
  623.8'252'09

ISBN 1-85367-275-0

Publishing History
Battleships of the World is translated from *Schlachtschiffe der Welt* first published by Motorbuch Verlag, Stuttgart, 1993.

Edited by Roger Chesneau

Printed and bound in Great Britain by The Bath Press

Frontispiece: HMS *Barham* in 1934.

Contents

Abbreviations and Explanatory Notes

AA	anti-aircraft (guns)
cal	calibre
CT	conning tower
DP	dual-purpose
ft	feet
ft/sec	feet per second
hp	horsepower (1 horsepower = 0.74kW)
ihp	indicated horsepower
in	inches
kt	knot(s) (one nautical mile per hour = 1.852km/hr)
L	barrel length (expressed in multiples of the gun calibre)
lb	pound
MG	machine gun(s)
mm	millimetres
m/sec	metres per second
min	minute
nm	nautical miles (1nm = 1.15 statute miles = 1.852km)
shp	shaft horsepower
t	tonne(s)
yd	yard(s)

Displacement: The first figure gives the normal displacement and the second figure the maximum (or deep load) displacement for the ship. The operational displacement is the weight of the fully equipped ship carrying approximately 90 per cent of the maximum fuel supply. The standard displacement was laid down by the 1922 Washington Treaty as being the weight of the fully equipped ship, including ammunition, armament, crew, provisions and drinking water but minus fuel and the reserve fresh water supply; it is referred to in long tons. The normal displacement was calculated differently by different navies, but in respect of ships built up to 1921 was uniformly interpreted as being 'the fully equipped ship but carrying only one-third of the fuel and one-half of the fresh water supply'. For later battleships, details provided by the official naval departments concerned have been used.

Dimensions: Length x beam x draft in metres. Length generally means waterline length, and beam the maximum beam including any anti-torpedo bulges and casemates.

Machinery: The maximum output is stated either in indicated horsepower (in the case of reciprocating steam engines) or in shaft horsepower (for turbines and diesel engines).

Fuel: Unless otherwise stated, the maximum capacity of the fuel bunkers is quoted. Supplies of aviation fuel for shipboard aircraft and fuel for motor launches, auxiliary machinery etc are not included.

Speed/range: In general, the official maximum designed speed in knots is stated, the actual maximum speed reached on trials being indicated in the text. The range, that is, the maximum travelling distance possible without refuelling, is stated, together with the most economic cruising speed necessary to achieve it. Range is not synonymous with radius of action, which is half the range less about 15 per cent reserve.

Armour: Generally, the greatest thickness of armour (in millimetres) is given. In the case of the horizontal armour of older ships which were built with several armoured decks, the thickness quoted represents the aggregate of the individual thicknesses; in the case of main turrets the greatest thickness (which was generally at the turret face) is again indicated.

Weight of armour: This is expressed as a percentage of the normal displacement. Where the latter is given in long tons, the armour weight is also shown as long tons.

Armament: Given as the number of guns x calibre and barrel length (barrel length being the gun calibre multiplied by the given figure, e.g. 305mm 45-cal is a barrel length of 13,725mm). Information is restricted to heavy and medium guns and excludes single-purpose light naval guns. For the sake of clarity, gun ranges have been expressed in kilometres (and not in hectometres, i.e. tenths of a kilometre, which is the German practice). *Editor's note: Information concerning British and US guns is expressed in Imperial measurements, in line with contemporary practice.*

Anti-aircraft weapons: Given as the number of barrels x calibre above 25mm; in most cases 20mm AA guns and machine guns are omitted. Underwater torpedo tubes have not been included as they proved to be of little value aboard capital ships and were removed from all units undergoing modernisation in the inter-war period. The same applies to shipboard aircraft and catapults for similar reasons (although they were favoured for scouting purposes by heavy commerce-raiding ships of the German Navy during the Second World War).

Building data: The actual date of keel-laying is given, not the official date. The commissioning date is the date when the ship was actually received into service in a battle-ready condition. This date is often confused with the date of completion, or the date the vessel was accepted from the builder. These different events might be separated by a period ranging from several months to a full year. Individual navies (for example, that of Russia) also interpreted the term differently. Therefore a commissioning date quoted in this book is that when the unit joined the Fleet to which it had been assigned.

Line drawings: Most are to a uniform scale in order to facilitate comparisons, but in a few cases, generally for reasons of space, this has not been possible.

Introduction

At the beginning of the twentieth century it was the opinion of military strategists and politicians that, as future wars would be decided on land, a battleship 'race' would be a waste of money. Nevertheless, the total number of dreadnoughts in the national fleet was the crucial factor by which the political muscle of the larger states of Europe, Asia and America came to be assessed. Before the outbreak of the First World War a battleship of the dreadnought type was practically a symbol of state because it embodied military might. Accordingly, battleship construction was the subject of long-standing diplomatic negotiations and, between the two world wars, of international naval conferences. Yet during the First World War capital ships failed to live up to expectations as super-weapons. Even when committed in battle *en masse* they failed to prove decisive either as regards the outcome of the war itself or even in a particular theatre.

One must suppose that the sight of a big-gun capital ship had a spellbinding effect on governments, for little else can explain why they continued to invest stupendous amounts of taxpayers' money in the construction of ever larger leviathans armed with ever more gigantic guns when the usefulness of submarines and aircraft for naval warfare had been made ominously clear to them. No matter how modern or how heavy its guns, it gradually became clear that the battleship alone could no longer decide the outcome of a naval operation. Air power gradually assumed the predominant role in the war at sea, and the available battleships and battlecruisers were eventually relegated to secondary tasks. After the Second World War, however, a handful of modernised US battleships were retained for the specialised role of bombarding enemy coasts from offshore while sheltering under their own air umbrella.

Steam-Powered Ships of the Line

Great men o' war under sail, armed with dozens of cannon, were the dominant warships in every navy at the end of the sixteenth century. The English battle instructions of 1653 prescribed the line as the most desirable battle formation, and it was in such lines (of reasonable length) that belligerent fleets clashed.

In 1754 the British Admiralty standardised warships into six classes, and any vessel armed with 64 cannon or more was classed as a ship of the line (or 'line-of-battle ship'). As time progressed the size of these sailing ships increased (in the mid-1700s the largest ships displaced 3,500 tonnes) and the number of cannon carried rose to around 140.

Kaiser Wilhelm II sailed on board the first German armoured cruiser *Prinz Heinrich II* on the occasion of his visit to the Russian Czar.

This involved a steep rise in building costs, and so fewer ships of the line participated in the naval battles at the turn of the eighteenth century. Nevertheless, at the time of the Crimean War in 1854, the three strongest fleets in the world (those of Britain, France and Russia) possessed a considerable number of ships of the line, although few of them had steam engines. The introduction of the steam engine, initially as an auxiliary means of propulsion, began aboard ships of the line from about 1847, and by the time of the Crimean War 29 of the Royal Navy's fleet of 81 wooden ships, one of the French Fleet of 27 and four of the enemy Russian Fleet of 47 carried a steam plant for propulsion in addition to sail.

The Crimean War provided the impetus for many technical advances in warship construction. In gunnery, the high-explosive shell, invented by the Frenchman Paixhans, and the rifled breech-loading gun built by the Swede Wahrendorf, were widely known, although the devastating effect of the HE shell was only recognised in November 1853 when the Russians destroyed a Turkish squadron in the anchorage at Sinope. The threat posed by the new shells led to the idea of protecting wooden hulls with wrought iron plates, and the epoch of the armoured ship began with the wooden-hulled French *Gloire* in 1858, followed a year later by two British iron-hulled ships of the *Warrior* class. The smaller navies, notably the Italian and Austrian, followed the lead in armoured ship construction surprisingly quickly, and in many respects contrib-

uted substantially to the development of the armoured ship. However the military situation offered little opportunity to examine the actual merits of individual armoured ships or their weapons, and the one major sea battle of the time, that at Lissa on 20 July 1866, had a negative

The hulls of numerous armoured ships of the 1860s were of wood overlain with iron plates.

The Russian *Pervenets*, a typical battery ship of 1864.

influence on armoured ship construction and naval tactics, for the sinking of the *Re d'Italia*, and the victory of the inferior Austrian Fleet over the Italians, seemed to confirm the validity of the long-outdated theory of sinking ships by ramming.

By 1875 most battleships had iron hulls and a steam plant as the principal method of propulsion (while retaining sails as a means of extending their cruising range), and they were generally larger than their predecessors of ten to fifteen years previously. They had thick iron plating for protection and carried guns which were frequently upgraded in calibre. Britain had 16in (406mm) guns and Italy even had a 450mm (17.7in) weapon, but although these were obviously larger and more powerful than the 8in (203mm) pieces of the early 1860s they were difficult to work. However, by 1875 the importance of the big gun as the decisive weapon in naval warfare was no longer in dispute, and armoured ships, whether intended for operations on the high seas or for coast defence, remained the yardstick by which the strength of a particular fleet was measured. The following table shows the growth in armoured ship construction from 1858:

Year	Britain	France	Italy	Russia
1865	12 of 77,700t	12 of 68,200t	9 of 37,500t	2 of 9,200t
1870	35 of 224,700t	29 of 146,000t	12 of 48,500t	10 of 42,400t
1875	43 of 280,000t	35 of 176,500t	14 of 60,600t	11 of 45,100t

In 1875 Austria had nine and Germany six newly built armoured ships. Japan had none and the United States was not interested in building them.

Towards a Standard Battleship

Combined with the technical problems inherent in warship construction in the 1870–1890 period, the relatively stable political situation in Europe after 1878 brought about a degree of stagnation in battleship construction. Up to 1875 France had begun 26 such ships, including *Gloire*, and Britain 58, including *Warrior*. Over the next fourteen years these numbers had shrunk to 12 and 17 respectively. Confusion was the rule, for shipbuilding and gunnery technology was progressing so swiftly that in order to keep pace new ships were having to be modernised even before they could be completed. Enormously long building periods of seven to eleven years were not uncommon. Even Britain was no exception: the turret ship *Colossus* left the yards at the end of October 1886 after more than seven years under construction. It took even longer to build large warships in France, nine years and more being needed to complete the barbette ships of the *Terrible* class. New tactical concepts based on the introduction of new weapons brought further complications for naval architects. Experimentation was rife, and most broadside ironclads, central battery ships, barbette ships, turret ships, armoured rams and sea-going monitors were produced singly or in small series. Accordingly, the squadrons of armoured ships on the inventories of the naval powers at the end of the 1880s were a hotch-potch of the most diverse designs and sizes, equipped with every imaginable calibre of gun and poorly endowed

with sea-keeping qualities. The commanding admiral of the British squadron which bombarded the Egyptian port of Alexandria in July 1882 had at his disposal eight dissimilar armoured ships. Each had its own individual calibres of gun, and six knots separated the fastest and slowest units of the force. Whereas these differences were not significant in that particular action, in a full-scale naval battle they would probably have been disastrous, as the 1888 Royal Navy summer exercises were to confirm.

The experience gained led to the demand for homogeneous groups comprised only of ships with similar manoeuvrability and fighting power, including a uniform armament, and the Naval Defence Act of 1889 was the response. The legislation provided for eight similar first class battleships, two smaller battleships, 42 cruisers of three classes and 18 torpedo gunboats to be built within a period of five years, and most important innovation was the creation of the homogeneous battleship squadron.

A large proportion of the armoured ships built about 25 years previously, and even a number of more recent vessels, had become so obsolete as to warrant decommissioning, and it was recognised that much activity was required to make up the leeway in warship construction. The political philosophy behind the British naval legislation is known historically as the 'Two Power Standard', which decreed that the strength of the Royal Navy should exceed the combined strengths of any two of its rivals. In a review of all battleships with a displacement of at least 5,000 tons and up to 15 years old, the Royal Navy is clearly seen to be numerically superior to its two nearest rivals at this time, the more so since three of the four Russian ships could always be expected to be bottled up on station in the Black Sea:

Numbers of Battleships

Year	Britain	France	Russia	Germany
1880	52	46	13	9
1890	43	30	12	13
of which less than 15 years old:				
1890	21	15	4	5

In comparison with the figures in 1875, the average size of British and French armoured ships increased quickly from 1890 and the differences in size of new ships, which still existed in 1880, visibly diminished:

Year	Britain	France	Russia	Germany
1890	7,620t	7,010t	4,850t	6,830t
of which less than 15 years old:				
1890	9,580t	9,400t	10,200t	7,270t

However, to draw a comparison between two Fleets on the basis of the number of ships each possessed, or of the aggregate tonnage only (as was frequently done before the Great War), is misleading if the age of the vessels is not taken into account as a significant factor.

◀ The turret ship *Petr Velikiy*, built between 1869 and 1876, was the first Russian battleship.

◀▼ *Chesma* was one of three large barbette ships in the Black Sea completed between 1889 and 1890.

▼ The 10,500-tonne turret ship *Navarin* was sunk at Tsushima.

▶ *Oslabiya* was one of three units of a class designed for commerce-raiding.

▶▶ *Pantelimon* (ex *Kniaz Potemkin*) at Sevastopol in 1916.

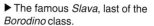

▶ The famous *Slava*, last of the *Borodino* class.

◄ Pagoda-like fighting tops were characteristic of French battleships of the 1880–1900 period. Pictured here is *Charles Martel*, built 1891–97.

◄ ▼ *Massena*, completed in 1898, was the first battleship with three-shaft propulsion. She also had very poor sea-keeping qualities.

▶ *Patrie*, completed in 1906, was typical of the last generation of French pre-dreadnoughts. Despite possessing some good features, she was obsolete at the end of her six-year building period.

▼ Completed in June 1898, *Bouvet* was the last large French battleship to be equipped with 305mm (12in) guns in circular turrets. On 18 March 1915 she struck a mine off the Dardanelles and sank in 90 seconds with the loss of 660 of her crew.

121 MARINE DE GUERRE. — "*Masséna*" (*Cuirassé d'Escadre*). — LL.

The Standard Battleship

The era of the standard battleship began in 1889, when the eight *Royal Sovereign* class units authorised under the Naval Defence Act of that year were laid down, and lasted until the end of 1904. The differences between a battleship of the early 1890s and one built in 1904 were fairly minor despite some technical improvements, and, as in that fifteen-year period a relatively large number were built to replace units which had become obsolete, these formed the backbone of every fleet.

The 'carving up' of the world had been more or less decided around 1890, but this left the major powers with the task of protecting their colonies and other spheres of influence. In these imperial matters the Fleet was the most important instrument for carrying through the national interest, and this gave rise to the term 'navalism' to describe the activities of the period.

In the 1890s new and existing tensions began to burgeon and the consequence of this was a general armaments race. National military budgets rose constantly, especially the allocations for naval expenditure. At the turn of the century the annual naval expenditure of the major powers (in millions of German marks) was: Britain 622, France 286, Russia 196, USA 272 and Germany 176. Compared with 1880, naval expenditure had increased in Britain by 290 per cent, in France by 180, in Russia by 210, in the USA by 430 and in Germany by 410 per cent.

For the protection of its colonies and seaborne trade, each naval power needed large numbers of cruisers whose usefulness was ultimately dependent on naval supremacy—which could only be established in battle. For this, battleships were indispensable, and it was therefore logical that the building of battleships should take precedence in every naval building programme.

As all battleships (at the time still often referred to as armoured cruisers or ships of the line) between 1890 and 1904 were generally of the same size and speed, and similarly armed and protected, the important thing was not so much the level of technology but rather battle tactics, and around 1890 the tactics of the line of battle had been reasserted in the light of technical advances in gun and torpedo

armament. Most line-of battle ships displaced from 13,000 to 16,000 tonnes in terms of size, although in some navies (particularly the Austro-Hungarian and German Navies), units of between 9,000 and 11,000 tonnes, specifically intended for use in enclosed European waters, were to be found.

In the field of propulsion, the triple-expansion reciprocating engine was ubiquitous before the introduction of the marine turbine, and, despite trials with oil-firing, coal remained the principal fuel. As a result, average speeds were in the region of 18 knots, although 'fast battle-ships' such as those of the Italian *Regina Elena* class exceptionally reached 22 knots.

The invention of new, lighter steel alloys led to a real reduction in armour thicknesses, and as the resistant power of armour grew, the areas under protection were extended. Each navy went its own way in the design of armour protection, which from about 1895 began to embrace the submerged portions of the ship.

There had been a similar divergence for some time in the choice of calibre for the main and medium armament, while the number and arrangement of heavy guns, mostly 12in (305mm), was uniform, four barrels being paired in twin turrets fore and aft. The German, Austro-Hungarian and, for a short time, Russian Navies experimented with heavy guns of a smaller calibre (9.45in, 240mm, and 10in, 254mm) on the grounds of their higher rate of fire and good ballistic performance in comparison with the 12in. Thus all ten battleships launched in Germany between 1896 and 1901, and the three coast defence ships and six battleships launched by Austria-Hungary between 1895 and 1905, carried only 240mm guns. The Battle of Tsushima in 1905 put paid to any future idea of using such units in a naval engagements, and an appreciation of the need for an increase in hitting power finally led to the demise of the standard battleship.

Initially the medium gun calibres of 7.5in (190mm) and 8in (203mm) were replaced with 'medium-heavy' guns of 9.2in (234mm) and 9.45in (240mm) and 'intermediate-calibre' 10in (254mm) weapons, but it was soon found that dividing a ship's main armament into several calibres caused problems with fire control. As demands were growing universally for ships of a similar size and armed with a uniform main battery, the era of the standard battleship—henceforth generally referred to as the 'pre-dreadnought'—and the transitional 'semi-dreadnought' came swiftly to its close.

◀◀▲ *Repulse*, completed in 1894, was a *Royal Sovereign* class vessel and the first battleship designed by the renowned British naval architect Sir William White.

◀▲ The *Majestic* class of 1895 evolved from the *Royal Sovereigns* and carried the new 12in (305mm) gun in place of the earlier 13.5in (343mm) calibre. *Majestic* herself is pictured.

◀◀ *Canopus* and her five sister ships, completed between 1900 and 1902, were smaller and faster versions of the *Majestic* class.

◀ *Britannia*, completed in October 1906, was a unit of the *King Edward VII* class, the last and largest of the British pre-dreadnoughts.

◀◀ *Kurfürst Friedrich Wilhelm*, a unit of the German *Brandenburg* class, was one of the most heavily armed battleships in the world at the end of the nineteenth century.

◀ In May 1906 *Lothringen*, the final unit of the *Brandenburg* class, joined the German Fleet. These well protected ships, with their moderate gun battery, were comparable in fighting efficiency to British ships of equivalent size.

◀◀▼ *Kaiser Wilhelm II* was added to the German Fleet in February 1900. The five ships of this class were the slowest and most poorly armed battleships of the period.

◀▼ The three units of the Austro-Hungarian *Erzherzog Karl* class, completed in 1907, were not only fine ships but were well armed for their size.

Building Programmes 1890–1905

The construction of a large fleet required long-term planning and the availability of capital. The traditional practice was to ask Parliament to grant the means of finance annually, but the path was fraught with uncertainty. The political composition of Parliament might change; government ministers were prone to frequent reshuffles, so that the timely provision of battleships for the formation of a homogeneous squadron could not be guaranteed. The only solution was naval legislation and fleet programmes, the approval for which was almost always obtained by exploiting the international political situation and public opinion so as to ensure that the necessary funds were secured in advance.

The first such naval law was not the British Act of 1889 but a naval construction programme drafted in 1881 and signed by Czar Alexander III on 20 May 1882, which provided for the construction of twenty battleships—more even than projected under the later British legislation, although a longer period, twenty years, was allowed for its completion. However, the Russian programme was soon revised and the number of ships authorised was reduced in 1885.

The extent to which a naval construction programme could influence world politics was demonstrated by Admiral Tirpitz's Navy Laws. The various powers reacted surprisingly quickly to the British naval legislation of 1889, and in November 1890 a five-year building programme was drafted for the Russian Baltic Fleet which allowed for the building of six smaller 7,500-tonne battleships, four heavily armed coast defence ships and three large armoured cruisers. At the end of 1891 a programme was decided upon by France (and named after its creator, Gervais) which set plans in motion for ten battleships, a coast defence ship and 45 cruisers by 1901.

Britain responded quickly both to these developments and to the Franco-Russian military agreement of 17 August 1892. Although the Naval Defence Act was not planned to take effect until the end of 1893, approval for the construction of two additional battleships and for a draft construction plan for the years 1894 to 1898 was given in the Naval Estimates for 1892–93. In December 1893 the Spencer Programme provided for the construction of seven large battleships and 30 cruisers.

► The USS *Oregon*, completed in July 1898, was a successor to the US battleship *Indiana*. She carried four 13in (330mm) and eight 8in (203mm) guns.

►► *Maine* (BB10) was completed in October 1904 and was the name-ship of a new class featuring 12in (305mm) guns.

▼ *Georgia* (BB15) was one of five battleships of the *Virginia* class. She carried a proportion of her 8in (203mm) medium battery in two-tiered turrets.

►►▼ *New Hampshire* was the last US pre-dreadnought to be authorised. She was very powerfully armed, with four 12in (305mm), eight 8in (203mm) and twelve 7in (178mm) guns.

Russia was the first of the major powers to respond, although the official reasons for this reply cited the rapid growth in German naval power as the principal concern. Under the 1895 building programme, the Russian Baltic Fleet would receive five large battleships, four coast defence ships and six large armoured cruisers by the end of 1901. Only two years later, at the end of 1897, another building programme was drafted; it was approved the following year and provided for five very large battleships and sixteen cruisers within seven years, for use in the Far East. However, in contrast to the progress made in Germany (where the Navy Laws of 1898 and 1900 were carried through) and Britain, delays blighted the Russian and more particularly the French programmes; in the latter case, the French Fleet had actually shrunk in size by the turn of the century.

The growth in size of the US Fleet proceeded in a systematic manner although no long-term naval construction programme was put into effect. Sixteen battleships and thirteen armoured cruisers were launched during President Theodore Roosevelt's term of office (1901–1909). He of course was a former Navy Minister.

Naval construction on the basis of a long-term programme was a rare occurrence before 1900 amongst the smaller navies, the exceptions being Holland and, especially, Japan, which within the seven years up to the end of 1903 created a considerable battle fleet from her 1897 building programme.

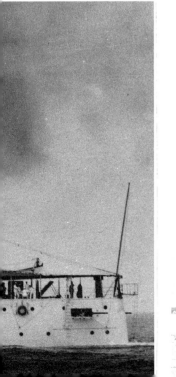

Construction of Battleships exceeding 7,000 tons

Nation	1890–94	1895–99	1900–04	Total
Britain (GB)	11	20	16	47
France (F)	5	8	4	17
Germany (G)	4	4	12	20
Russia (R)	6	4	4	19
USA	3	6	10	19
Japan (J)	–	5	1	6
Italy (It)	2	2	4	8
Austria-Hungary (AH)	–	–	5	5

In the following three years (1905–07) a considerable number of battleships and semi-dreadnoughts were launched, but only six French and three Austro-Hungarian semi-dreadnoughts subsequent to 1907:

Nation	1905–06	1907	1908–10	Total (from 1890)
Britain	4	–	–	51
France	1	1	6	25
Germany	4	–	–	24
Russia	3	1	–	23
USA	6	–	–	25
Japan	3	1	–	10
Italy	1	1	–	10
Austria-Hungary	1	–	3	9

The last ten of the British ships, the last six of the French, the last four of the Japanese and the last three of the Austro-Hungarian were of the transitional type with two heavy calibres of guns. Only these were considered battleworthy enough for operations in the opening phases of the First World War, the older units being relegated to secondary duties or to minor theatres. At the end of the 'ship of the line' era, these units formed the backbone of every fleet, and naval strength was measured by their numbers and tonnage. In February 1905 the British battle fleet was unequivocally superior to any possible combination of two or (in terms of tonnage) even three combined rivals.

According to Weyer, the naval strengths of the various powers as of 1 January 1905 (excluding losses in the Russo-Japanese war) were:

Fleet	GB	F	R	G	USA	J
Ships	56	28	23	17	14	7
Tonnage (x 1,000t)	742.0	280.0	269.9	186.8	151.6	92.0

A different picture of the true operational strengths of the various navies emerges, however, when a list is compiled only of those ships over 7,000 tons and under 15 years old, and this confirms the British in their convictions of 1905:

Fleet	GB	F	R	G	USA	J
Ships	42	12	12	16	12	4
Average disp. (t)	14,000	11,400	12,100	12,000	11,500	14,300

It is hardly surprising that, after the Battle of Tsushima, the British Special Commission recommended a pause in British battleship construction, but the completion of HMS *Dreadnought* and the swift transition to the construction of dreadnought-type ships in Germany altered the situation almost at a stroke, for the formation of homogeneous squadrons of capital ships within a few years rendered even the most recently completed pre-dreadnoughts obsolete. Those of the latter less than 15 years in age went into reserve, while those over 20 years old were scrapped immediately. However, for a period of time after *Dreadnought* and her equivalents in other navies had entered commission, the older battleships still constituted the backbone of the fleet and, with the increasing risk of war in Europe (for example, the 'scares' of 1908 and 1911), their large-scale employment could not be avoided. Even in 1914, the most powerful of the recent pre-dreadnoughts were expected to be used in naval squadrons, if predominantly in the rear of the line.

Effective fleet strengths in terms of pre-dreadnoughts (less than 15 years since launching) and semi-dreadnoughts are shown in the following table:

Date	GB	F	R	It	G	AH	USA	J
01.01.1908	40	11	4	5	18	6	19	6
01.01.1912	31	13	4	6	18	9	21	11
01.09.1914	20	11	7	6	14	8	14	5

From this it can be seen how quickly after 1911 the inventory of pre-dreadnoughts in the major fleets was reduced while an effective increase in strength was enjoyed by other navies, especially those which had begun building semi-dreadnoughts too late. The Japanese figures include older Russian ships put into service after capture or salvage. It is also worth noting the relative strengths of the fleets of Austria-Hungary and Italy. The statistics go a long way towards explaining the entirely passive role played by the Italian battle fleet in the Adriatic during the First World War.

Armoured Cruiser Programmes

In the first years of the era of 'navalism' great attention was paid to the concept of the armoured cruiser, which had evolved some fifteen years earlier from the small but fast second-rate ship of the line. During its development, the desire was expressed for a speed superior to that of the normal battleship: the French wanted a vessel with a long range for a possible commerce-raiding role against British shipping, while the British responded with a faster 'heavy cruiser' carrying medium-calibre guns but relatively lightly protected. Armoured cruisers were also attractive to the smaller navies, which could employ them as substitutes for battleships.

In Britain, the value of a large, fast and relatively well-armoured ship attached to a battle squadron for scouting purposes had been recognised at the end of the nineteenth century, and the British built armoured cruisers precisely for that purpose. The German Navy followed this example, whilst the French were building ever larger versions for the

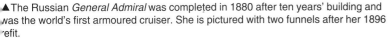

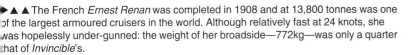

▲The Russian *General Admiral* was completed in 1880 after ten years' building and was the world's first armoured cruiser. She is pictured with two funnels after her 1896 refit.

▶▲▲ The French *Ernest Renan* was completed in 1908 and at 13,800 tonnes was one of the largest armoured cruisers in the world. Although relatively fast at 24 knots, she was hopelessly under-gunned: the weight of her broadside—772kg—was only a quarter that of *Invincible*'s.

▶▲ The German armoured cruiser *Gneisenau* was not completed until early 1908. In the engagement with British battlecruisers off the Falkland Islands in 1914 she had no chance.

▶ *Sankt Georg*, the last Austro-Hungarian armoured cruiser, was very well armed for her size.

commerce-raiding role. Since armoured cruisers were not considered capital ships, they have not been described in this book, although admittedly before the First World War it was the custom to include armoured cruisers in the totals of major ships and aggregate tonnage as a means of documenting naval strength.

Speculation that this type of ship might be a match for a battleship under favourable conditions proved to be baseless. It was clearly proved at Jutland that even the largest armoured cruisers had very little prospect of achieving anything in battle against a capital unit. The construction of armoured cruisers in large series was expensive, and once the orders for the first dreadnoughts and battlecruisers had been placed, the class was abandoned worldwide.

The last heavily armed cruisers, such as the Russian *Ryurik* and the Japanese *Ikoma* and *Ibuki*, bore comparison with fast, well-armed capital ships and probably represented an embryonic stage in the development of the battlecruiser. How armoured cruiser construction progressed after 1890 is shown in the following table, which summarises units launched having a displacement of over 5,000 tons and armed with guns of a calibre greater than 152mm (6in):

Nation	1890–94	1895–99	1900–04	1905–08	Total
Britain	–	2	15	7	24
France	1	3	13	4	21
Russia	1	2	1	4	8
Italy	–	4	1	4	9
Germany	–	1	5	3	9
Austria-Hungary	1	1	1	–	3
USA	–	1	7	3	11
Japan	–	5	3	4	12

The importance attached to the role of the armoured cruiser, the second most powerful type of warship, in the fleets of individual naval powers is shown in the following table of the larger such units in commission and not exceeding ten years in age (it should be noted that this excludes ten units of the British *Monmouth* class, which after completion were generally employed as cruisers attached to overseas stations on account of their weak armament of 14 x 6in, 152mm, guns):

Date	GB	F	R	It	G	USA	J
01.01.1905	13	13	2	3	4	1	8
00.08.1914	15	6	4	4	6	10	4

The Evolution of the All-Big-Gun Ship

At the beginning of 1905 the Royal Navy advocated a pause in battleship construction, yet only a few months later it ordered the ship which was to become a milestone in the development of the capital ship. HMS *Dreadnought* was the first of the 'all-big-gun ships', and gave her name to the generic type of capital ship which she spawned.

There had earlier been calls for an increase in the speed of the battle squadron in order for it to achieve tactical advantages during engagements, while the tendency to upgrade the fighting power of the type had manifested itself some years earlier. The introduction of an intermediate, 'medium-heavy' gun calibre had quickly been recognised as erroneous because of doubts as to its effectiveness and the difficulty of achieving satisfactory gunnery control at longer ranges. Accordingly, the building of all 'semi-dreadnought' battleships was rapidly brought to a halt.

It had been realised in trials held by several navies that it was possible to increase the effective gunnery range from 3,000yd to 7,000yd; indeed, the new Barr & Stroud rangefinder installed aboard HMS *Venerable* in 1903–04 had demonstrated that there was an astonishingly high probability of a hit at ranges up to 7,300yd, although in a naval battle conducted at this distance only the heavy guns would be effective. The quick-firing guns advocated by some artillery experts performed very poorly in terms of their accuracy. Thus the development of a capital ship which was a little larger and faster than the standard battleship but much better armed was already in the air in 1904, and the British were the first to put the idea into effect.

The realisation of the *Dreadnought* project is closely associated with the person of Admiral Sir John Fisher, who was appointed First Sea Lord on 21 October 1904. Amongst the reforms he demanded for the Royal Navy in order to improve the fighting strength of the British Fleet was the introduction of the 'all-big-gun ship' and the scrapping of all outdated warships. This involved all battleships completed more than fourteen years previously.

Before his appointment, Fisher had been working with W. H. Gard, the Chief Constructor at Malta Dockyard, on the design of two ships with a uniform main calibre, and on 21 October the partnership presented its projects for a battleship, 'HMS Untakeable', and a large armoured cruiser, 'HMS Unapproachable'. The 21-knot battleship would be armed with sixteen 10in (254mm) guns in twin turrets. The 25-knot armoured cruiser was a less radical concept and with her armament of four 9.2in (234mm) and twelve 7.5in (190mm) guns bore a resemblance to the *Minotaur* type.

It has often been suggested that these ideas and designs were influenced by the work of Colonel Vittorio Cuniberti, the Constructor to the Italian Navy, but it would have been obvious to Gard at least that the details published by Cuniberti in the 1903 edition of *Jane's Fighting Ships* could never have been realised on a hull displacement of 17,000 tonnes, as the Russians were to discover to their cost with Cuniberti's specifications five years later.

Fisher came to the conclusion that the 12in (305mm) gun was undoubtedly superior to the 10in (254mm) Armstrong model preferred by the Admiralty, which had three times the rate of fire, and he instructed Gard to review their common project for 'HMS Untakeable'. Design B therefore provided for eight 12in guns in four twin turrets, of which three could combine for a broadside. A second condition stipulated a speed of 21 knots for the battleship and 25 knots for the armoured cruiser. The drawings proceeded on the basis of steam reciprocating propulsion, turbines not appearing until the final stages of the design following experiments conducted in January and February 1905 by the two light cruisers *Amethyst* and *Sapphire* in which the former, the first large turbine-driven ship of the Royal Navy, was found to be substantially more economical at higher speeds than her sister ship fitted with reciprocating engines.

On 22 December 1904 a Committee on Designs was formed under the chairmanship of Admiral Fisher and consisting of sixteen members including naval architects Philip Watts and W. H. Gard; J. H. Narbeth, later the chief architect of HMS *Dreadnought*, acted as secretary. The committee investigated the various projects for the new kind of battleship. The first designs envisaged a number of relatively small and short ships armed with eight 12in (305mm) guns. These were all rejected by the Committee. The Fisher-Gard partnership also failed to secure acceptance of its designs for larger and longer ships with five or six twin turrets (two or three turrets stepped one above the other forward, with three aft), although on 13 January 1905 the Committee did agree on the number of 12in guns and the arrangement of the turrets.

Next, a 21,000-tonne ship with six twin turrets arranged hexagonally was considered, then a shorter variant and finally a preliminary design, 'H', which was shorter still. The last had her main armament disposed in five twin turrets, of which four could be brought to bear for the broadside. After a number of meetings—and probably following the conclusion of the trials of the *Amethyst*—the Committee decided that the two shorter variants should have steam turbines. On 22 February 1905 the Committee drew up its report, to which the Admiralty gave its approval in March, and in May Narbeth began work on the detailed design for HMS *Dreadnought*.

The Committee had some difficulties regarding a choice of armoured cruiser since only two designs had been placed before it. The planned four (later three) units were included in the 1905–06 Estimates to be presented to Parliament before 1 April. Watts' design for a combination of 12in (305mm) and 9.2in (234mm) guns fell short of expectations, leaving only the Fisher-Gard design.

Before the Committee on Designs had come into existence, Fisher had asked for an armoured cruiser which, if possible, should carry eight 12in (305mm) guns and be capable of 25 knots. In a memorandum he described its principal purpose to be the pursuit and destruction of the classical large armoured cruiser preying on commerce on the high seas. In the past the cruiser had been allocated a role for which it was unsuited owing to its inadequate armour. Its high speed, which in Fisher's view afforded it the best means of protection, would also enable it to pursue a defeated squadron of enemy battleships and deal with any stragglers. It would be unwise for a capital ship with only 2in (51mm) of armoured deck to attempt this (as, indeed, experience during the First World War was to show).

Whilst the Fisher-Gard design, with its 12in (305mm) guns in four twin turrets stepped fore and aft, fitted the specification, it did not meet with the approval of the Committee, and in the absence of any other projects Watts and Narbeth produced four or five more outline designs. One of these had a diagonal midships arrangement for the central 12in turrets, and this awakened Fisher's interest. After a number of improvements, including the incorporation of turbine propulsion, this armoured cruiser project was accepted by the Committee and endorsed by the Admiralty later. The ship was termed a 'battlecruiser' in the final stages of the design. The particulars of the new battleship were kept strictly secret, and secrecy was maintained even in the case of the three *Invincible* class battlecruisers, which took more than twice as long building as HMS *Dreadnought*.

The Reaction of the Other Naval Powers

Although never stated in his memoranda, Fisher's efforts were aimed at maintaining the existing numerical and qualitative superiority of the Royal Navy over the steadily expanding German Fleet. It had been calculated in British naval circles that Germany would continue to lag behind on account of the considerable delays caused by the widening of the Kiel Canal and by the essential dockyard expansion work being carried out at the Wilhelmshaven naval base.

Some German authors have attempted to show that the *Dreadnought* came as no surprise to the German *Konstruktionsamt* (Design Office) and Admiral Tirpitz. This seems a perverse view, since no German battleship or dreadnought type was laid down in 1906 even though the construction of two ships was planned. These comprised one 14,000-tonne and one 15,000-tonne ship originally designed as 'transitional' battleships, the first armed with four 280mm (11in) and eight 240mm (9.45in) guns and the second having eight 280mm guns, the 240mm twin mountings being replaced by four 280mm single wing turrets. These two designs were approved by the *Kaiser* in 1905 but were cancelled, and the designers did not start drawing up a 19,000-tonne ship until the winter of 1905. An armoured cruiser was authorised in the 1906 Budget, and as the British had successfully concealed their plans for a battlecruiser, the German Navy had ordered a large and fast armoured cruiser, *Blücher*, which had 210mm (8.25in) guns and which was therefore no match for the British battlecruisers despite her stronger armour.

The Germans benefited from the more or less enforced pause in building work by concentrating on extending the armour plating and underwater protection of their major ships. They were completely unprepared for the revolution in capital ship propulsion, however, for Germany's marine engineers—as in the case of the Americans—had so far failed to develop a reliable and economical marine turbine. In common with five US and two Brazilian battleships, all eight German battleships launched in 1910 were still using reciprocating steam engines for their powerplants.

The other major naval powers did not find it necessary to react to the *Dreadnought* as quickly as Germany, and even at the end of 1907 most were biding their time. In the case of France, which started building six large 'transitional' battleships in 1907–08, even the next generation of capital ships planned for the summer of 1908 would still be equipped with two different calibres of heavy guns. This delay in reaction by the various naval powers is shown in the following table summarising all battleships and battlecruisers built from 1906 (not including the year of launching) and having a maximum gun calibre of 12in (305mm), excluding 'super-dreadnoughts' whose construction began later.

In looking at these figures, it should be remembered that Britain was the leading naval power and began to construct 'super-dreadnoughts' in 1909. It will be noticed that the other European powers, with the exception of Germany, did not respond to the *Dreadnought* until later, and it was not until the political climate in Europe quickly deteriorated following the 1908 Bosnian crisis that the intensive construction of capital ships began.

Nation	1906–07	1908	1909	1910	1911	1912	1913	1914	1915/16	Total
Britain	7	2	3	3	2	–	–	–	–	17
Germany	–	4	4	2	4	3	5	1	1	24
USA	–	3	2	1	2	2	–	–	–	10
Japan	–	–	–	1	1	–	–	–	–	2
Russia	–	–	–	–	4	–	1	2	1	8
France	–	–	–	–	2	2	–	–	–	4
Italy	–	–	–	1	3	–	2	–	–	6
Austria-Hungary	–	–	–	–	1	2	–	1	–	4
Spain	–	–	–	–	–	1	1	1	–	3
Others	–	1	1	–	2	–	1	–	–	5
Total	7	10	10	8	21	10	10	5	2	83

Battleship Strength in Europe, 1911

The mass building of dreadnoughts did not lead immediately to a radical increase in naval strengths, for in a possible conflict the pre-dreadnoughts would still have played the decisive role by virtue of their numerical superiority even though each had only 50 per cent of the hitting power of a dreadnought in terms of broadsides. This is indicated in the next table, which shows the Fleet composition of all the potential belligerents. All theoretically available dreadnoughts and pre-dreadnoughts launched after 1895 have been included. The hitting power is expressed as the total of heavy guns available for a broadside using a coefficient of 0.5 for all guns in the calibre range 9.2in–10in (234mm–254mm).

Britain (hitting power coefficient)

10 dreadnoughts:	86 x 12in	=	86
4 battlecruisers:	32 x 12in	=	32
35 pre-dreadnoughts:	132 x 12in	=	132
as well as	8 x 10in	=	4
and	36 x 9.2in	=	18

| Total | 14 capital ships and | |
| | 35 pre-dreadnoughts = 272 | |

Germany (hitting power coefficient)

4 dreadnoughts:	32 x 280mm =	32
1 battlecruiser:	8 x 280mm =	8
10 pre-dreadnoughts:	40 x 280mm =	40
10 further pre-dreadnoughts:	40 x 240mm =	20

| Total | 5 capital ships and | |
| | 20 pre-dreadnoughts = 100 | |

Pre-dreadnoughts are superior numerically and have considerable hitting power (57–60 per cent of the Fleet totals); 49 British ships would have opposed 25 German ships, a ratio of 2:1 but in terms of firepower an advantage of 2.7:1. The reason for this was both the British numerical superiority in dreadnoughts and the smaller calibre of gun equipping the German ships. In the Mediterranean, the 'semi-dreadnoughts' and pre-dreadnoughts would have played an even greater role as all the dreadnoughts destined to operate in that theatre were still on the stocks.

France

6 *Danton*s with 24 x 305mm and 36 x 240mm	= 42
8 pre-dreadnoughts with 28 x 305mm and 2 x 274mm	= 29
Total 14 units	= 71

Austria-Hungary

3 *Radetzky*s with 12 x 305mm and 12 x 240mm	= 18
6 pre-dreadnoughts with 21 x 240mm	= 10.5
Total 9 units	= 28.5

These figures clarify why *Kaiser* Wilhelm II finally drew back following the second Moroccan crisis of 1911.

Big Warships and Small Navies

Some nations of lesser political importance reacted quickly to the new trend in battleship construction despite the huge long-term financial burden with which it presented them. This involved not only the poorer Mediterranean nations but also the South American states. In 1905–06 a naval race developed between Brazil and Argentina. Brazil was enjoying a period of economic prosperity, and she aimed for a significant increase in naval strength with a view to achieving maritime supremacy in the South American region. Argentina, her rival, reacted by placing orders to give her at least an equivalent status in capital ship strength, and this in turn, in combination with Peruvian naval building policy, supplied Chile with a reason to arm herself along similar lines.

The Spanish decision in 1907 to build capital ships came as a surprise to many, but it was nevertheless a logical step. Although she had lost her richest colonies, Spain still required a powerful navy to protect her remaining overseas colonies as well as her long coastline.

Turkey, despite her parlous political and economic situation, was determined to retrieve the position in the Black Sea and eastern Mediterranean which she had lost during the previous century. That Greece, small and poor, should require capital ships at all, and actually went as far as ordering two, must be attributed to a form of war psychosis, but this was the way in which, before the First World War, thinking in battleship units' spilled over from the major powers to the lesser powers.

'Super-Dreadnought' Programmes to 1918

Developments in gunnery provided the impetus towards the construction of super-dreadnoughts. By 1908 British and American naval experts had come to the conclusion that success in a gunnery duel at long range depended on the effect of single hits. The advantages of the larger calibres were undisputed simply because a larger shell had more internal volume for an explosive charge, which automatically increased its destructive power. However, as any increase in the calibre of a ship's guns inevitably meant an increase in the weight of guns and turrets, and thus required more deck space, larger ships had to be built. As these were more expensive to construct, the number of dreadnoughts building had to be kept in check, but the transition to the super-dreadnought armed with a 13.5in (343mm) calibre gun or larger was the only possible way to establish naval supremacy over any

potential enemy. Britain, as the leading naval power, undertook this step, and on this occasion her advantage over the other powers, and in particular her rival Germany, increased more rapidly than had been the case following the introduction of the *Dreadnought* four years before, as a study of battleships and battlecruisers launched between 1910 and 1918 and armed with 13.5in guns or larger proves.

The rapid transition to building super-dreadnoughts guaranteed the Royal Navy a quantitative and qualitative superiority over the German and other fleets, and in fact towards the end of the First World War it was even greater in respect of firepower since half of the front-line super-dreadnoughts and battlecruisers were equipped with 15in (381mm) guns while the ships of foreign fleets (with the exception of the two German *Bayern* class units) were armed only with 13.5in (340mm) or 14in (356mm) guns.

The construction costs of the super-dreadnoughts exceeded those of the successors to the *Dreadnought* by a wide margin: for example, a *Queen Elizabeth* class ship cost £2.7 million whereas a *St Vincent* had cost £1.7 million. Between 1906 and 1914 Britain's expenditure on all new naval construction was £131 million, and the building costs for battleships and battlecruisers from the *Dreadnought* to the final unit of the *Queen Elizabeth* class accounted for £68 million, or 52 per cent, of this figure.

Ultimately the investment of such vast sums of money in building these enormous ships was wasted, for the French, Italian, Austrian and even the Russian Baltic units never emerged on operations. The only meeting between the two great European Fleets, at Jutland in 1916, concluded indecisively, and had no influence on the manner in which the naval war between Britain and Germany was to develop.

Construction of Super-Dreadnoughts up to 1918 (per year after launching)

Nation	1910	1911	1912	1913	1914	1915	1916	1917	1918	Total
Britain	2	6	5	5	3	4	6	0	1	32
Germany	0	0	0	0	0	2	1	3	0	6
Russia	0	0	0	0	0	3	1	0	0	4
France	0	0	0	3	3	1	0	0	0	7
USA	0	0	2	0	2	2	0	3	0	9
Japan	0	0	2	2	1	1	1	1	0	8
Others	0	0	0	2	1	0	0	0	0	3
Totals	2	6	9	12	10	13	9	7	1	69

▶ One of the 305mm (12in)/L35 Krupp guns mounted aboard the Austro-Hungarian barbette ship *Kronprinz Rudolph*, completed in 1889.

▶▶ An 8mm anti-aircraft machine gun atop the 240mm (9.45in) gun turret of an Austro-Hungarian pre-dreadnought—the first naval weapon designed for use against dive-bombers.

▼ The famous 305mm (12in) triple gun turret during assembly at the Skoda weapons factory.

▶▶▼ Anti-aircraft defences aboard a German battleship in 1942: a 105mm twin flak mounting (left), a single 20mm (centre) and a twin 37mm (right).

The Naval Question after the First World War

As the requirements for fighting North Sea and Baltic naval battles bore no comparison with what would be needed in the expanses of the Pacific, battleships, and super-dreadnoughts in particular, became the final arbiters in the strategic considerations of both Japanese and US naval planners. The race in naval construction between the United States and Japan developed for the purposes of pre-eminence in the Pacific, and Britain joined in for reasons of prestige and to bolster her ambitions in the Indo-Pacific region. At the end of 1919 the British Admiralty took a highly critical view of its fleet in comparison with those of Japan and the United States, which had both ordered even larger units for the future. Despite the precarious financial situation of the Empire, the Royal Navy sought approval for capital ships which would be the equals of those fielded by the two Pacific powers, and in March 1921 the Admiralty convinced Parliament that at least four large battlecruisers with nine 16in (406mm) guns were needed in order to maintain Britain's position at sea. Meanwhile Japan was being confronted by a serious economic crisis, and in the US the strength of the anti-battleship lobby, who considered that the money would be better invested in military aviation, was increasing.

Naval Agreements between the Wars

It was in this atmosphere that the US President, Warren Harding, sounded out the possibility of a Naval Disarmament Conference in July 1921 and, after positive responses from Britain, France, Japan and Italy, he invited representatives of these powers to a meeting in Washington on 12 November 1921. The Naval Conference was opened by US Secretary of State Hughes, who proposed drastic disarmament measures in which all battleship construction was to be stopped, the older capital ships and all pre-dreadnoughts were to be scrapped and a future strength ratio among the various fleets would be established by agreement. To the general surprise of world opinion all the delegates agreed in principle to the US proposal a few days later. The Washington Treaty, signed on 6 February 1922 and ratified by all five signatory states (Britain, the United States, Japan, France and Italy) by the summer of 1923, put a stop to the massive construction programmes in Britain, the US and Japan. It also contained numerical and qualitative limits for capital ships both afloat and building.

The London Naval Agreement of 1930 was mainly concerned with cruisers, but the provisions of the second London Conference, enshrined in the treaty signed on 25 March 1936 and supplemented on 30 June 1938, had great significance for battleship construction.

In Washington, the naval strength of the treaty partners was laid down as being roughly Britain 5, USA 5, Japan 3, France 1.75 and Italy 1.75. This ratio remained in force until the ratification of the second London Naval Treaty on 29 July 1937, when all numerical limits imposed

by previous Agreements were abolished. Under the limits imposed by the 1922 Washington Treaty corresponding to the respective fleet strengths, individual powers were prohibited from exceeding the following restrictions placed on their aggregate battleship tonnage: Britain and the USA 525,000 tons, Japan 315,000 tons, and France and Italy 175,000 tons each. These tonnage limits would not come into effect for twelve years (i.e. not until the end of 1934). On the other hand, limits on battleship numbers applied immediately and were specified as being Britain 22 (later 20), USA 18, Japan 10, France 7 and Italy 6. France and Italy exceptionally were permitted to retain three and four pre-dreadnoughts respectively, and to replace these units with three new vessels between 1927 and 1931.

After her two new battleships still building, West Virginia and Colorado, had been commissioned, the United States would then scrap two older units while Britain would scrap four older battleships when two new Nelson class battleships entered commission. Otherwise, no new battleships were to be constructed before 1931, and decommissioned units were to be scrapped, sunk or converted for use as target ships. However, each power could convert two battleships, completed or not, into aircraft carriers, and whereas the maximum displacement for an aircraft carrier was stipulated to be 27,000 tons by the Treaty, a battleship conversion was permitted to be of 33,000 tons.

The London Agreement, ratified by Britain, the United States and Japan on 27 October 1930, extended the moratorium on battleship construction until 31 December 1936 and brought forward the 5:5:3 numerical ratio in battleships laid down in the 1922 Washington Agreement by three years to the end of 1931. This meant the premature scrapping of five British, three US and one Japanese battleship. France and Italy declined to sign this treaty, and on the expiry of the London Agreement on 31 December 1936 all quantitative limits were abolished.

The influence of the numerical limits of the two naval agreements on the battleship strength of the individual major powers is shown in the following tables:

Capital Ships in Commission (older battleships in parentheses)

Nation	1920	1922	1931–36
Britain	30 (+ 12)	22	15
USA	20 (+ 11)	18	15
Japan	10 (+ 9)	10	9
France	7 (+ 4)	6 (+ 3)	6
Italy	6 (+ 4)	5 (+ 4)	4

Tonnage of Battleships Completed or Under Construction in 1920 (x 1,000 tons)

Nation	1920	1922	1931–36
Britain	1,296	559	475
USA	1,178	510	464
Japan	570	301	272
France	290	221	133
Italy	236	183	90

The Washington Naval Treaty fixed the upper tonnage displacement limit for battleships at 35,000 tons but the lower limit of 17,500 tons was first introduced in the 1936 London Treaty. The June 1938 supplement to the latter agreement increased the upper limit for standard displacement to 45,000 tons. The qualitative limit of a standard displacement (always in imperial tons) led to certain compromises as it favoured the naval powers whose capital ships were not intended to rove the world's oceans, and it was this limit, rather than the numerical and tonnage restrictions, which influenced the last stages of battleship design.

The definition of an upper age limit for battleships, which had been fixed at 20 years by the 1922 agreement, proved onerous and it was raised by six years in the 1936 London Treaty. The Washington Treaty had also prescribed that no battleship might carry guns of a larger calibre than 16in (406mm), and this restriction remained in force until the outbreak of the Second World War.

As the naval treaties had imposed the abandonment of battleship construction for more than a decade, the naval powers switched their attentions to cruiser building and developing their naval air arms. Since the First World War the biplane had not improved significantly in terms of either speed or load-carrying capability, and in order to use aircraft with a limited endurance over expanses of ocean, the aircraft carrier was seen as the only solution, yet the upper limits on tonnage impinged more heavily on the construction of these ships than on battleships. A report by the British Imperial Defence Committee dated 30 July 1936 stated the view that, in spite of its increased performance, the aircraft could not take over the role of the battleship, and that a stoutly built battleship with strong deck armour could still absorb severe punishment from bombing, whilst its effectiveness against enemy aircraft improved with the increasing firepower of the ship's anti-aircraft batteries.

Following the expiry of the London Naval Treaty on 31 December 1936 and the ending of the moratorium on capital ship construction, the naval powers embarked upon a fresh 'naval race', this time involving both battleship and aircraft carrier construction. However, except in the United States, the outbreak of the Second World War put an end to the feverish battleship building programmes.

The End of an Era

Despite such measures as the radical strengthening of its horizontal armour, the mounting of vast numbers of multi-barrelled anti-aircraft weapons of the latest design, improving its speed and, not least, increasing its size, it soon became obvious that even the most modern battleship was susceptible to a massed attack by bombers. Generally, by 1942 the aircraft had established itself as supreme over the world's oceans, and the naval powers now turned their attention to building aircraft carriers. In the new battle groups, the aircraft carrier would be protected by the battleships.

After the war, the numbers of battleships in the British and US navies were drastically cut back, and in Britain the older units soon went for scrap, mainly because of financial considerations. The US Navy still envisaged a possible sphere of activity for modernised battleships, for their heavy, radar-directed guns had proved of great value in the coastal bombardment ('fire support') role and their armour had even resisted atomic testing. After rebuilding it was planned to use the vessels as headquarters ships.

Several decades later this foresight was rewarded during the Vietnam War, when *Iowa* class battleships successfully pounded inland targets from positions offshore. In the 1990s four veterans may still be found on the US Navy's inventory, but the role of the battleship as the final arbiter—politically as well as physically—has been ceded to another type of vessel, the most powerful representatives of which today exceed in size even the original HMS *Dreadnought*: the nuclear-powered submarine armed with strategic missiles.

And it is the missile, not the gun, that has proved to be the real 'final arbiter'.

The US battleship *Missouri* in 1986.

Germany

Developments up to 1918

For the leaders of the Reich, the year 1906 saw an end to any illusion they had of destroying the political and military alliance, the Entente Cordiale, which threatened to encircle Germany. Despite all the efforts of *Kaiser* Wilhelm II, Czarist Russia had remained a true ally of France, and after a thaw in the relationship between the traditional enemies Britain and France in 1904, consultations had been held between the General Staffs of the two powers at the beginning of 1906 which had led to an agreement whereby permission was given for British troops to be stationed on the European continent in case of war with Germany. In Europe, therefore, Germany was isolated, and Austria-Hungary was her only reliable ally.

The cause of this had been the failure of the German leadership to predict the future development of the political situation. The powerful Fleet desired by the *Kaiser*, which had been systematically enlarged by his State Secretary at the *Reichsmarineamt* (RMA), Admiral Tirpitz, had not only failed to intimidate Britain, but had rather forced the world's leading naval power to adopt counter-measures such that Germany was now obliged to reckon with Britain as a third potential opponent, and one which was superior in strength at sea. The building up of the German Imperial Navy after 1898 had the effect of forcing Britain to alter her naval policy of 'splendid isolation'.

Admiral Tirpitz's 'Risk Theory', which was the justification for his Supplementary Navy Law of 1900, proved ineffective, particularly in retrospect in 1912 and 1914. Officially, the aim of naval construction was the protection of German overseas colonies and maritime trade by securing 'peace with honour', but its real aim was to bring pressure on Britain, as was intimated in the passage justifying the Navy Bill: 'In order to protect Germany's maritime trade and colonies under present circumstances, there is only one means: Germany must possess a battle fleet of such might that war would present so great a danger even for the most powerful adversary as to call into question his own position of strength. To this end, it is not absolutely essential that the German battle fleet should be equal in strength to the greatest naval power, for . . . in general they will not be in a position to concentrate their total force against us . . .' What Tirpitz was planning was a Fleet potentially able to inflict losses on the Royal Navy of such a scale as to ruin the 'Two Power Standard', the political maxim by which the strength of the Royal Navy must be greater than that of any two rivals combined. The first two of these Navy Laws boosted an Imperial Fleet, which until then had been primarily orientated towards coast defence, into the first rank of naval powers by the early twentieth century, and regularly augmented Germany's High Seas Fleet thereafter.

The launch of *Hindenburg*, the last Imperial German Navy battlecruiser to be completed.

s „Hindenburg" in Wilhelmshaven.

Mit Genehmigung der Illustrirten Zeitung, Leipzig

330

E.P. & Co. A.G.L.

What inventory of battleships and armoured cruisers did the early Navy Laws provide for? The first Navy Law, presented by Tirpitz in the winter of 1897 and agreed by the *Reichstag* on 10 April 1898, envisaged nineteen battleships, eight coast defence ships and twelve large cruisers. Three of the last were intended for overseas duty and represented no threat to the sea routes of the British Empire. Seven battleships, but only two large armoured cruisers, were scheduled for the end of the 1903–04 financial year (that is, by 31 March 1904). The active list was to consist of a single squadron of vessels, made up of eight battleships and a flagship.

What alarmed the British, however, was the second Bill, drafted in 1899 and passed on 14 June 1900, for this contemplated a further, radical strengthening of the German Fleet by adding another eleven battleships and two armoured cruisers by 1917; in this period, moreover, nine of the existing battleships and all eight coast defence ships were to be replaced by new battleships. The Germans were somewhat hampered in their attempts to realise a programme of this kind, for such shipyards as were suitable would need to be enlarged, which would substantially extend building schedules in comparison to those obtaining in Britain. Yet the 1900 Bill would have been unnecessary had the RMA not stipulated an active life of 25 years for battleships and 20 years for large cruisers. As Tirpitz stated in his memoirs, the limits had been set as a result of a parliamentary misunderstanding. This led to a situation in which old and obsolete ships such as the *Oldenburg* (a central battery ironclad built to an 1879 design) and the weakly armed *Kaiserin Augusta* (which had been originally designated a cruiser-corvette) had to be kept on the active list until 1907 and 1910 respectively because it was legally impossible to replace them. The eight worthless small coast defence battleships which the 1900 Act pronounced to be front-line vessels could not be replaced until 1913. Therefore, the *Kaiser*'s insistence in December 1905 that the age limit for battleships should be reduced from 25 to 18 years was justified, as the battleships and armoured cruisers which had been built only fifteen years previously were already hopelessly outdated. If these aspects had been taken into consideration by the 1898 Bill, then the 1908 Supplement could have been avoided.

The strength of the German battle fleet at the beginning of 1906 cannot be assessed by its stock of ships, nor by the principles of the naval legislation referred to, nor indeed by the number of ships of the active fleet in commission. It was the Fleet Distribution Plan that was definitive, since the prescribed strength in major ships in the active and reserve battle fleets was never achieved in the 1900–1906 period. According to the 1900 Navy Law, the battle fleet was supposed to consist of two fleet flagships plus four squadrons each composed of eight battleships, eight large cruisers and 24 small cruisers or scouts. The 1st and 2nd Squadrons were to be made up of all the battleships and cruisers in permanent service, while the other two squadrons were to form the reserve battle fleet, of which only half the ships were in commission. In addition to the fleet flagship, the reserve would thus comprise 16 + 8 battleships and 2 + 4 armoured cruisers. In the 1906 order of battle there were only fifteen battleships in the active fleet and two others in reserve, a deficiency of seven. The situation involving the large cruisers of the two scouting groups was worse, for there were only three of these altogether, with none in reserve. The overseas fleet consisted of one armoured cruiser instead of the three intended.

The exaggerated age limits for ships, and the problematic method of accounting for the six antiquated cruisers of no use except as training vessels, exemplify the flaws in the naval legislation. Two armoured cruisers were under construction, but these exhausted the quota. If the building tempo of the three large ships under construction was to be stepped up so as to achieve the required number of modern armoured cruisers, a Supplementary Law was now necessary to augment the Overseas Fleet by five large cruisers (and the material reserve by one). However, the Supplement passed on 26 May 1906 was interpreted by Britain as further evidence of Germany's aggressive intentions, which at the time did not exist. Tirpitz was now, as he was to confirm in 1908 and 1912, simply not capable of adapting himself to the rapid changes in the political and military situation. On the other hand, the naval legislation with its long-term warship building programme which had been enacted earlier had made possible the smooth transfer to dreadnought construction in Germany, since within the accepted practice of building three large ships annually these could be requested in the annual budget without reference to their tonnage. Thus on 26 May 1906 the *Reichstag* authorised two 18,000-tonne battleships and one 15,000-tonne large cruiser under the 1906–07 Budget.

The building of larger ships incurred higher capital expenditure within the naval legislation for the enlargement of port installations, the building of new docks and the widening of the Kiel Canal and its locks. This strategic investment amounted in total to 221 million marks (then equivalent to some £11 million). All the work was completed shortly before the outbreak of the First World War, and it made possible the rapid transit of all capital ships to and from the North Sea and the Baltic—a matter of great significance in view of the increasing strength of the Russian Baltic Fleet.

Following the 1906–07 Budget, naval expenditure began to rise sharply, but Tirpitz persevered with his policy of building a powerful High Seas Fleet which, he maintained, would force Britain to change her political alignment. It was entirely for this reason that the British proposals at the 1907 Hague Peace Conference, and the feelers put out by the British Foreign Ministry for a naval armament limitation agreement, were doomed from the outset.

The 1908 Supplement did not actually increase the fleet numerically, but it accelerated the construction of modern ships to replace the worthless coast defence battleships, and thereby substantially increased the fighting strength of the navy. The 1908 Supplement also reduced the active lifetime of a battleship to 20 years, and although this seems a matter of little importance at first glance, it had significant consequences for world politics, for it meant that within the period 1908–1917 three more battleships and one more large cruiser would be replaced than had hitherto been the case. Tirpitz succeeded in having the appropriate replacement vessels authorised for the 1908–1911 financial years, so that Germany would complete four instead of three capital ships annually.

In view of what the British perceived to be a threatening German naval superiority in local waters, the Royal Navy reacted by strengthening and restructuring those parts of the British Fleet which were based at home ports. After another round of negative soundings on the subject of naval limitation, Britain stepped up the pace of its capital ship building programme in the early part of 1909, and the 'naval race' began.

As the world political situation rapidly worsened, it became ever clearer that Tirpitz's 'Risk Theory' had damaged Germany. The second Moroccan crisis at Agadir provided the critics of the naval building programme amongst the German Army Staff with further fuel. The German General Staff had been requesting a strengthening of the Army since 1905, and this was now energetically repeated in the wake of the Moroccan crisis. It was alleged that the naval programme had swallowed up funds urgently needed for building up the Army. The War Minister put the case to the *Reichstag*, but all he got was two new army corps. The matter was raised again in 1913, when the General Staff demanded another three army corps; they were granted two, and an increase of seven per cent in expenditure. The naval budget was also increased. Criticisms were levelled at Tirpitz and the Navy, especially after the First World War, that they had deprived the Army of urgently needed funds in the pre-war years. However, it is clear that in the negotiations for the 1914 military budget the critics of Tirpitz's plans got their way, for in that year the proportion of funds allocated for naval expenditure decreased significantly in comparison to the previous years:

German Military Expenditure (millions of marks)

Year	Army		Navy	
1911	832	(65.2%)	444	(34.8%)
1912	944	(67.5%)	454	(32.5%)
1913	1,009	(68.2%)	471	(31.8%)
1914	1,770	(78.8%)	476	(21.2%)

Tirpitz, who had been against sending the cruiser *Panther* to Agadir, manipulated the diplomatic reversal which Germany had sustained in the 1911 Morocco crisis for his own purposes. In order to enhance the readiness of the High Seas Fleet, he decided to strengthen it by adding a further squadron of battleships. He required only three new ships to accomplish this, as the Navy was proposing to activate the fleet flagship, four battleships and four large cruisers then in reserve. In material terms this would increase the strength of the battle fleet from seventeen battleships and four large cruisers to 25 and eight respectively.

On 14 November 1911 Tirpitz received the assent of the *Kaiser* to present his Supplement to the *Reichstag* during the debate on the 1912 Budget proposals. The British quickly got wind of the new amendment and at the beginning of February 1912 the Minister for War, Haldane, visited Berlin, where he met first with the Chancellor, then with the *Kaiser* and finally with Tirpitz. He informed the German side about the enormous British naval construction programme and proposed a mutual limitation on naval armament. Haldane was seeking either an agreement not to proceed with the three new battleships, or a pause in the German building programme. Crucially, however, his Government was not prepared to offer Germany a neutrality treaty in return, and his mission failed. The 'naval race' continued, with all its fateful portents for the world political situation.

But was it solely the British plans which induced in Tirpitz his attitude of rigid inflexibility? Historians point to this, but they overlook the very relevant fact that since April 1911 the Russian Navy Ministry had been working on long-term naval legislation and a short-term building programme for the Baltic Fleet—matters which were vital to Germany's naval interests.

The draft Russian bill envisaged that, by 1930, Russian Baltic forces would consist of two active battle squadrons each with eight battleships and four battlecruisers—24 capital ships in all—and according to the programme for the period 1911–1915 the Russians proposed to make an immediate start with the battlecruisers. Four fast and well-armed battleships were launched at St Petersburg in 1911, and following the launching of the battlecruisers in 1914–15 the laying down of four more capital ships could be expected within the framework of the legislation enacted.

What the German Naval Staff had therefore to take into their calculations was the fact that by 1920 at the latest three modern Russian battle groups totalling twelve capital ships would be at large in the Baltic. Long-term German naval plans reached as far ahead as 1920, by which time the High Seas Fleet would consist of 22 dreadnought-type battleships and sixteen old pre-dreadnoughts. The 1912 amendment gave Tirpitz just three more new battleships, which fulfilled his requirement for three active squadrons equipped with modern units. The two reserve squadrons were composed of outdated pre-dreadnoughts, some of which were armed only with four 240mm (9.45in) guns. To what extent these ships would have been in a position to protect the German sea lanes in the Baltic and off the German Baltic coast against the powerful Russian battle groups is doubtful. It is therefore quite possible that Tirpitz and the *Reichsmarineamt* had the threat of Russian aggression in mind when they drafted the 1912 amendment. Ultimately, Tirpitz's naval plans achieved the required numbers, but not quality, of ships prescribed.

German Battleship Construction 1906–1918

Although the *Konstruktionsdepartement* of the *Reichsmarineamt* (K-RMA) had presented the design of a 14,000-tonne battleship armed with four 280mm (11in) and eight 240mm (9.45in) guns to the *Kaiser* in 1903, the four battleships laid down in 1903 and 1904 were based on 1901 designs. The reason for this was principally technical—the width of the Kiel Canal and harbour locks. The Imperial Navy had not accepted the concept of the transitional 'semi-dreadnought', and so the K-RMA worked to improve the 1903 design, producing a variant known as 'Project C', which had a uniform armament comprising eight 280mm (11in) guns arranged hexagonally in two twin and four single wing turrets. The design was laid before the *Kaiser* on 18 March 1905 but was rejected because such a heavy armament on a hull displacing 15,700 tonnes implied a weak armour system and too moderate a speed. On 4 October 1905 Tirpitz recommended that the displacement limit for battleships be raised from 13,000 tonnes to 19,000 tonnes and he obtained the *Kaiser*'s agreement to this, even though it would mean lengthening slipways, installing new equipment in all German yards and enlarging docks.

The increase in displacement enabled the K-RMA to improve the main armament on the proposed ship by disposing the 280mm guns in four twin turrets and to devote more attention to the system of armour protection. The naval architect Bürkner considered that the 'survivability' of the capital ship was of the first importance, and he placed special emphasis on an extensive system underwater protection, dividing the hull into a honeycomb of narrow, watertight compartments. This resulted in a broader beam than was favoured by other navies but also made the ships very stable.

'Project G-7b', completed in the first half of 1906, was the immediate forerunner of the Nassau class and embodied these characteristics. The displacement of 18,700 tonnes allowed for twelve 280mm (11in) 45-cal guns and a powerful secondary battery. The thickness of armour and the total armoured surface exceeded that on equivalent British ships, although the maximum thickness of the belt had only been 270mm (10.6in) at the design stage and was not increased to 300mm (11.8in) until later.

The choice of the relatively small 280mm (11in) gun has often been criticised, but the Waffenabteilung (Weapons Section) of the RMA was convinced that it was superior to the British 12in (305mm) weapon. Certainly in 1907 its ballistic performance was not inferior to that of the British gun. As the principal future battle area was presumed to be the North Sea, where, as a consequence of the usually poor visibility, gunnery exchanges at long range were not considered to be very likely, the fitting of guns of a calibre greater than 305mm was thought to be unnecessary even later. Within a short while, 'Project G-7b' was finalised into blueprints for the Nassau class, and the details were passed to the shipyards on 15 August 1906. The construction of two battleships—still officially referred to as Linienschiffe (literally, 'ships of the line')—was approved on 26 May 1906 under the 1906–07 Budget. Five days later the order for the first unit, Nassau herself, was placed at the Imperial Yard at Wilhelmshaven. The order for the second unit, Westfalen, was placed with AG Weser on 30 October 1906. Both shipyards experienced delays because of severe difficulties lengthening the slipways, and work was not begun on the first two German dreadnoughts until July and August 1907 respectively, two and three months respectively after the third and fourth ships of the class authorised under the 1907–08 Budget, Rheinland and Posen, had been laid down.

Under the 1908–09 Budget three battleships of the new Helgoland class were authorised (the fourth being approved in 1909 under the 1908 supplementary legislation), and these were designed to carry the new 305mm (12in) gun. Despite an increase in ship length, the arrangement of the twin turrets was not altered, and the Helgoland class ships were limited, as had been their predecessors, to a broadside of six barrels.

Because of its relative reliability, reciprocating machinery was retained, but this was also partially due to the Imperial Navy's lack of experience with marine turbines. The small cruiser Lübeck was the only turbine-powered German warship of the time, and the manufacturing plants required to produce steam turbines were still under construction. The four-cylinder piston engines were reliable and all units exceeded their designed speed. Oldenburg reached 21.3 knots at 34,394ihp at maximum output over the measured mile.

The first German battleship to be fitted with turbines was laid down at the Kiel Navy Yard in the autumn of 1909. The Parsons turbines for this vessel (Kaiser) and her two sister ships (Kaiserin and Prinzregent Luitpold, which were laid down in private yards at Kiel a year later), were supplied by the Navy Yard's turbine workshops. The fourth and fifth sister ships, Friedrich der Grosse and König Albert, received AEG Curtis and Schichau turbines respectively for trials.

The results over the measured mile showed that the ships fitted with Parsons turbines were faster (Kaiser made 23.4 knots at 55,187shp) than those with the other turbines (for example, König Albert achieved 22 knots at 39,183shp). Nevertheless, even the slowest ship of the class, Prinzregent Luitpold, which had only two turbines, with a 12,000hp Krupp diesel driving the central shaft, reached her designed speed of 21 knots on trials. Diesel propulsion increased the cruising range from 7,900 to 9,900 nautical miles at 12 knots for the ships under turbine drive, but diesel machinery was not considered ready for wholesale installation on board ships and it would seem that no further development occurred before the war. A new feature on the Kaiser class was the arrangement of the 305mm (12in) guns, where the midships pair were set diagonally relative to each other and the foremost twin turret aft was superimposed so as to fire over the other.

In the 1911–12 Budget the first instalment of funds was made available for the construction of three battleships of the new König class, which was essentially a development of the preceding Kaiser. Work on König herself, Grosser Kurfürst and Markgraf was begun in the autumn of 1911 and on the fourth ship, Kronprinz, which was authorised in the 1912–13 Budget, in the summer of 1912. All were completed between the summer and autumn of 1914.

It was originally planned that each vessel would mount a MAN 6-cylinder two-stroke 12,000hp diesel engine, but this was abandoned for the same reasons as in the case of Prinzregent Luitpold. The degree of protection was comparable to that incorporated in the Kaiser class, comprising very strong and extensive belt armour 350mm (13.8in) in thickness. The 305mm (12in) twin turrets were, however, arranged quite differently, despite the preference of the Reichsmarineamt for the diagonal layout adopted for the Kaiser class, and the positioning of the twin turrets along the fore-and-aft line of the ship was an innovation in German design which coincided with the arrangement on the battlecruiser Derfflinger. These architecturally demanding and very reliable ships were also fast (up to 24 knots in service), but they were weakly armed for their size at the time of commissioning.

Discussions followed once the Imperial Navy realised that it had to react to increases worldwide in capital ship armament. This could be achieved either by the use of triple turrets or by increasing the gun calibre. The question of the triple turret had been under review since 1907, and the Konstruktionsamt favoured it. The Waffendepartement (Weapons Department) believed that difficulties would be encountered in supplying ammunition to the central barrel, which would reduce the rate of fire, and in November 1910 they therefore advocated retaining twin turrets but with an increased calibre of 337mm (13.2in). It is interesting to note that shortly afterwards, in July 1911, Krupps presented plans for a turret to house 340mm (13.4in) guns. Tirpitz preferred the 400mm (15.75in) calibre, and the Kaiser agreed with this in principle on 26 September 1911. K-RMA, which wanted the 350mm (13.8in) calibre, voted against the short 400mm 35-cal gun and proposed the 380mm (15in) calibre for the 1913 round of battleships. In a meeting with the Kaiser on 9 January 1912 it was agreed that the new ships would receive eight 380mm 45-cal guns in four twin turrets.

The assertion frequently made in naval literature to the effect that the Imperial German Navy followed the British lead in calibres does not tally with the facts. On the contrary, rumours regarding the calibre increase to 356mm (14in) for the *König* class ships then building influenced the British Design Committee in the spring of 1912 to arm the three battleships awaiting authorisation in the 1912–13 Estimates with a calibre larger than the projected 13.5in (343mm). The Royal Navy was merely introducing the 15in (381mm) naval gun more quickly than the Germans.

The plans for the *Bayern* class for 1913 were approved by the *Kaiser* on 30 September 1912 and the orders for the first two units, *Bayern* and *Baden*, were placed on 1 and 3 April 1913 respectively after the *Reichstag* had agreed the 1913 Budget. Except for her heavy armament, *Bayern* was merely a larger version of the *König*s and had the same excellent manoeuvrability. During her trials she steamed at 21.5 knots for six hours at an output of 37,430shp, 0.5 knots above her designed speed. The first two ships were completed in 1916, but as a result of the war situation and the preference for battlecruiser construction the third and fourth ships, *Sachsen* and *Württemberg*, though launched in November 1916 and January 1917 respectively, were never completed. An extra knot of speed had been required of the latter pair, and it had been hoped that this could be achieved by lengthening the forecastle by 2.4m (8ft) and installing improved machinery. *Sachsen*, approved in the 1914 Budget, was fitted with a MAN diesel, under development for some time, for her centre propeller shaft. This would have provided her with an extra 2,000nm of range at 12 knots. *Württemberg* had all-turbine machinery and a higher performance.

No German battleship was laid down after January 1915, but capital ship designs continued to be drawn up and discussions concerning preferred ship types were revived. The K-RMA made numerous studies mainly of battlecruisers and fast battleships with gun calibres up to 420mm (16.5in), but the Naval Staff showed little enthusiasm for them. The *Kaiser* held a different view, and on 11 September 1918, two months before the Armistice, ordered the completion of a project designated 'L20', this being the class of ship which would form the backbone of the German battle fleet after the war. On a maximum displacement of 49,500 tonnes, she would have carried eight 420mm (16.5in) guns in four twin turrets and have had a speed of 26 knots. Her weakness, as was the case with all German battleships, was that her horizontal armour was inadequate for the conditions of modern naval warfare. The defeat of Germany brought all such projects to an end.

The Construction of Large Cruisers

The era of the German battlecruiser began with a ship that could be rated a capital ship on account of her size but not as regards the calibre of her main armament. Until 1918 the armoured cruiser *Blücher* was officially classified by the Imperial Navy as a 'large cruiser', as were the later battlecruisers. She was intended for deployment with the Fleet, operated in a Battle Cruiser Squadron, and was sunk in an action involving such a group. The 15,840-tonne armoured cruiser had been

designed in 1904–05 and was a prototype for the *Nassau* class; not only did she outwardly resemble these ships, but her main turrets were arranged to the same hexagonal layout. Compared to all other large armoured cruisers either complete or still building, *Blücher* was, at 25.8 knots on trials, faster despite her piston machinery, and also the most heavily armoured (for example, she carried 180mm, 7in, armour on the waterline), and her new model 210mm (8.3in) 45-cal guns were not ballistically inferior to the British 9.2in (234mm) weapon.

Blücher was, therefore, a fine ship, but she should never have been ordered, for six months before her keel was laid it was learned that the armoured cruisers ordered for the Royal Navy under the 1905 Estimates were to be equipped with eight 12in (305mm) guns and not with the 9.2in (234mm) calibre that the Germans had assumed early in 1906.

Blücher was no match for ships such as these, for her main artillery broadside was a mere 1,000kg (2,200lb) as opposed to the 3,080kg (6,790lb) of the British units. Therefore 'Large Cruiser F' (*Von der Tann*, which was approved in the 1907–08 Budget) was the real German answer to the British *Invincible* class, and work proceeded on the design after August 1906, when the principal details of *Invincible* became known. The *Kaiser* gave his approval to the first preliminary design on 24 November 1906, and the final design was completed in June 1907. The *Reichstag* authorised funds for the construction of the vessel in the 1907 Budget, and the ship was ordered from the Blohm & Voss yard at Hamburg, which in the years ahead would specialise in battlecruiser building. The completed vessel was delivered on 1 September 1910. She achieved a speed of 24.8 knots over the measured mile, exceeding her designed speed by 2.6 knots.

Von der Tann was a complete success: she was well armed and protected, despite her relatively light displacement, and she had excellent sea-keeping properties. She was also the first German capital ship to be fitted with turbines, and the system of spreading the output of two turbine sets over four shafts was followed in all successive German battlecruisers. The high-pressure turbine drove the outer shafts and the low-pressure plant drove the two inner shafts.

However, before building work on *Von der Tann* had even begun, on 27 May 1907 the *Kaiser* approved ten project sketches for 'Large Cruiser 08'. The design work on plans for a pair of battlecruisers was completed in September 1908, and once authorisation had been obtained in 1908 and 1909 respectively, a start was made on *Moltke* in January 1909 and on her sister ship *Goeben* in August of the same year. They displaced 3,600 tonnes more than *Blücher* and differed in the form of the hull. An increase in length had been made necessary by the

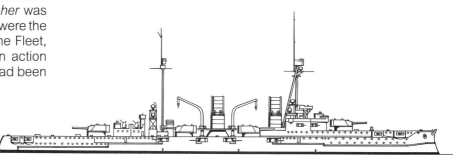

Blücher, 1914

Blücher in a 1912 photograph.

requirement to fit a fifth 280mm (11in) turret superimposed above the original aft turret, and the broader beam amidships was useful for consolidating the underwater protection. Although the battleships budgeted for in 1908 carried 305mm (12in) guns, the 280mm (11in) calibre weapons had been retained on the battlecruisers on account of the *Kaiser*'s predilection for them. *Moltke*, *Goeben* and the next ship, *Seydlitz*, were all fitted with these guns, albeit with lengthened barrels. On trials, all three vessels exceeded their designed speed of 25.5 knots by between 2.5 and 2.9 knots.

Despite her unchanged armament, 'Large Cruiser J', *Seydlitz*, authorised in the 1910 Budget, was not simply an enlarged *Moltke*. The designs completed in January 1910 provided for a longer but slimmer hull with an increased ability to absorb punishment. The belt armour was up to 300mm (11.8in) thick and was as effective as that customary at the time for the much slower battleships. An improvement in sea-keeping performance was achieved by raising the forecastle one deck higher. With her 280mm (11in) armament, however, *Seydlitz* was weakly armed for her size.

'Large Cruiser K', named *Derfflinger*, was the first of the type to receive four 305mm (12in) twin turrets following the decision taken by Admiral Tirpitz on 25 August 1910. The plans for this battlecruiser were completed in June 1911 and were subsequently repeated for *Lützow*, which was approved in 1912. *Derfflinger* was a transitional design not only in that her heavy turrets were aligned fore and aft down the centreline, but also for her flush-deck layout. Another innovation was partial oil-firing. Four of the eighteen boilers were oil-fired, which gave

her an increased range of 1,200 nautical miles over *Seydlitz*. For the same engine output, and notwithstanding their greater displacement, *Derfflinger* and *Lützow* were designed to match *Seydlitz*'s maximum speed of 26.5 knots, but in fact they were both faster and in service *Derfflinger* reached 28 knots.

Hindenburg, which was authorised in 1913, was built to a design presented in October 1912, but she was little more than a variation of *Derfflinger*: her hull was longer by 2m (6ft 6in) and she was provided with more horsepower and larger propellers which were designed to give her an extra knot in speed. Over the wartime measured mile she reached 26.6 knots at 95,777shp, which corresponded to 28.5 knots under normal conditions. The building of this battlecruiser took longer than that of her predecessors because of the demands of the war, and she was the last to be completed.

The 'large cruiser' *Ersatz Victoria Luise*, which was approved in the 1914 Budget and launched on 21 April 1917 with the name *Mackensen*, was never finished. The K-RMA had been working on the design of this ship since August 1912. At the forefront of its deliberations from the very beginning had been the question of the calibre of her main armament, but even so the last German battlecruisers still building, which were to be equipped with 305mm (12in) guns, would have been poorly matched against the fast British battleships with their eight 15in (381mm) guns.

Mackensen, the first of a class originally intended to comprise seven units, would have been a well-armed, well-protected and above all fast ship. Her output of 90,000shp was designed to give her a speed of 28 knots, and by fitting two additional cruising turbines it was intended that

Mackensen and her three sister ships (*Ersatz Freya*, *Graf Spee* and *Ersatz* 'A') would have a 20 per cent greater range at 16 knots.

In 1916 it was decided to convert the three least advanced *Mackensens* (*Ersatz Yorck*, *Ersatz Gneisenau* and *Ersatz Scharnhorst*) to mount 380mm (15in) guns. Their engine plant, armour and parts of the hull were in various stages of completion, and, whereas the requirement for an increase in calibre was met, that for increased performance was not, and the speed was estimated to be from 0.5 to 0.75 knots slower on account of the increased displacement. The boilers were the same as for *Mackensen* but the uptakes were trunked together to allow the smoke to be discharged through a single broad funnel.

The only ship of these three to be laid down, at Vulcan, Hamburg, in July 1916, was the vessel identified in the building programme as *Ersatz Yorck*, which is now the accepted class name. Hardly any work had been carried out on any of the three units by the end of the war, and the building material was broken up on the stocks in 1919.

During the war other battlecruiser projects ('GK I' to 'III'), which had the same armament as the *Ersatz Yorck* class but two knots' extra speed, were worked on. There was no prospect of these ever being built, and so *Mackensen* was the last capital ship of the Imperial German Navy to be brought to a stage approaching completion. She represented the zenith of German battlecruiser construction.

German *Linienschiffe* in 1914

In mid-August 1914 the High Seas Fleet consisted of 36 battleships in five squadrons. Fourteen of the newest battleships were attached to two squadrons, while the remaining three II, IV, and V, were made up of 22 *Linienschiffe* which, with two exceptions, had been laid down between 1895 and 1905, during the period of frantic German battleship building and, to their misfortune, just prior to the technological revolution in battleship design. Accordingly, their value as fighting units was not very high and, in the case of the ten ships armed with 240mm (9.45in) guns, hopeless should they become involved in an engagement with a superior force. In the course of 1915 the latter ships were disarmed and mostly relegated to harbour or accommodation ship duty. After Jutland nearly all the pre-dreadnoughts armed with 280mm (11in) guns were similarly treated, even though the majority were less than ten years old. Six actually took part at Jutland, although their presence there did little more than provide an theoretical strengthening of the High Seas Fleet. In battle, their weak armament could not have been brought into play and their limited ability to absorb punishment would have resulted in enormous loss of life—as in the case of *Pommern*, which disintegrated, leaving no survivors, after a torpedo hit.

After two years of war, therefore, more than half the stock of battleships had been paid off, and most of their medium and heavy guns were transferred to the Army for use on land, although some were installed in Navy coastal batteries.

Pommern, a *Deutschland* class pre-dreadnought, seen before the First World War.

Principal Details of *Linienschiffe*

Units	Class	Completed	Disp.	Speed	Main armament
2	*Wörth*	1893	10,000t	16.5kt	6 x 280mm
5	*Kaiser*	1898–1902	11,200t	17.5kt	4 x 240mm
5	*Wittelsbach*	1902–1903	11,800t	18.0kt	4 x 240mm
5	*Braunschweig*	1904–1906	13,200t	18.0kt	4 x 280mm
5	*Deutschland*	1906–1908	13,200t	18.0kt	4 x 280mm

German Dreadnoughts in the First World War

It was the wish of the *Kaiser* that the High Seas Fleet should not be gambled away, for he foresaw the need for a long hand in trumps to use at a future peace conference. Therefore the activities of the Fleet in the conflict with Britain were to be restricted primarily to short probes into the North Sea in the hope of reducing the numerical superiority of the Royal Navy preparatory to a future decisive encounter. This great battle would take place in the North Sea if possible, since German battleships were not built for wide-ranging operations in the Atlantic.

The Baltic, which was dominated by Germany throughout the war, was considered a secondary theatre, and up to the outbreak of war the deployment of capital ships there had not figured in the plans of the Admiralty Staff. With the exception of Tsingtao on the Chinese mainland, the provision of bases for the heavy cruisers of the *Auslandflotte* (literally, 'overseas fleet') had been neglected, and in the summer of 1914 there was only a single German battlecruiser on an overseas station, *Goeben* in the Mediterranean.

The great battleships engaged each other only on one occasion during the First World War, at Jutland on 31 May 1916. The newly appointed commander-in-chief, Vice-Admiral Scheer, had sixteen dreadnoughts and six older battleships in his force while the British C-in-C, Admiral Jellicoe, had 24 battleships and three battlecruisers. The British also had a substantial superiority in their scouting groups, with four fast *Queen Elizabeth* class battleships and six battlecruisers at their disposal against Admiral Hipper's five weaker battlecruisers. However, it was precisely this small German battlecruiser force which achieved the greatest successes at Jutland and made the major contribution to what Germany considered to be a satisfactory outcome to the battle.

Despite his numerical inferiority in ships, Admiral Scheer manoeuvred his force with skill and finally escaped from the clutches of the Grand Fleet and its battlecruisers. In the meantime his battleships had sunk two large British armoured cruisers (*Defence* and *Warrior*) in a rain of shells, and forced the newest 'super-dreadnought', *Warspite*, to break off and make for home with heavy damage. This proved the quality of the German naval gunners aboard the battleships, but it would probably have been a different story against a numerically superior enemy, which would have been encountered had the battle gone on for much longer.

Scheer was sufficiently bold to renew his attacks on the enemy fleet but soon recognised that he would be unable to defeat it. He succeeded in making his now famous *Gefechtskehrtwendung* ('battle turn-

away') manoeuvre under cover of a massed destroyer attack and the charge of the German battlecruisers towards the British line. None of Scheer's dreadnought battleships was lost. His force had maintained its maximum speed throughout the battle and manoeuvred very well, but the real heroes were Admiral Hipper's battlecruisers, which had borne the main burden of the fighting until the withdrawal.

Following overhauls involving nearly all the ships that took part at Jutland, the High Seas Fleet made three unsuccessful sorties into the North Sea between 19 August and 5 November 1916 in order to demonstrate its unimpaired strength. These exercises were not repeated in 1917, but for the first time the newest capital ships sortied into the Baltic.

In Operation 'Albion', the occupation of the islands off the Latvian and Estonian coasts carried out on 12 October 1917, eleven capital ships supported the large-scale landings. Their guns knocked out the much-feared coastal batteries, proving decisive for the success of the operation and also freeing the approaches to the Bay of Riga to allow the ships to tackle the two old but powerful Russian pre-dreadnoughts on station there. In a gunnery duel on 17 October, *König* and *Kronprinz* inflicted serious damage on both vessels, and *Slava* had to be scuttled later. At the beginning of the operation, the battleships *Grosser Kurfürst* and *Bayern* (the latter being one of the newest ships in the battle fleet) were mined in the early hours. *Bayern*'s forward torpedo rooms were flooded and the forecastle was soon awash. After two weeks under repair, *Bayern* headed for Germany at reduced speed, but was much delayed in reaching Kiel following a renewed inrush of water caused by another breach. The beam torpedo tubes were subsequently removed during a refit.

The swansong of the German High Seas Fleet was an uneventful sortie against the British Norwegian convoy routes in April 1918, and the mutinies at Kiel and Wilhelmshaven put paid to any idea of a last-ditch battle against the Grand Fleet in the final days of the war.

The armour of the German battlecruisers proved highly resistant to British 13.5in (343mm) and 15in (381mm) armour-piercing shells. The carefully designed subdivision of their hulls ensured that damage from torpedoes and mines would not interfere materially with their manoeuvrability, as experience with *Goeben* was to demonstrate.

After the successful bombardment of the English East Coast towns at the end of 1914, three battlecruisers, accompanied by the large but poorly armed cruiser *Blücher*, were intercepted for the first time at the Dogger Bank on 24 January 1915. The enemy force was superior in numbers and especially in terms of armament, as three of its five battlecruisers carried eight 13.5in (343mm) guns whilst only one German ship had a calibre as large as 305mm (12in).

The British commander used the greater speed of his battle group to good effect, and the engagement ended with the loss of the weakest German ship, caught out by her slower speed. *Blücher* was hit during the pursuit, fell away and was then overwhelmed in an unequal battle. While the three undamaged battlecruisers were able escape, *Seydlitz* had 165 dead and was in a badly damaged condition, but her gunners had found the large battlecruiser HMS *Lion* eighteen times and caused damage almost sufficient to sink her.

The Battle Cruiser Squadron was not at sea again until the end of April 1916 when, reinforced by the newly commissioned *Lützow*, it bombarded the East Coast town of Yarmouth.

All five battlecruisers fought at Jutland and bore the brunt of the exchanges. In a heroic engagement they sank three British battlecruisers and were later instrumental in saving their own battleships from annihilation. *Lützow*, hit by at least 24 shells, including four of 15in (381mm) calibre, and flooded with 7,500 tons of sea water, was kept afloat for many hours, and under more favourable circumstances might have been brought in to harbour. *Seydlitz* received hits from 21 shells and one torpedo but managed to make the German coast under her own steam with 7,000 tons of water aboard.

As can be seen from the following tables, the battlecruisers of the High Seas Fleet received worse damage than the battleships, and they were laid up undergoing repairs for longer. None was further involved in battle before the end of hostilities. The only battlecruiser not involved was *Goeben*, which was attached to the *Auslandflotte*, stationed in the Mediterranean in 1914, from where she operated successfully, and later in the Black Sea under the Turkish flag.

In addition to *Ostfriesland*, which was mined during the withdrawal and did not return to the Fleet until 26 July 1916, 56 days after putting in for repairs, the following German capital ships received shell damage during the Battle of Jutland:

Battleship	Hits received	Ready for action
Rheinland	1 medium	10 June
Helgoland	1	16 June
Oldenburg	1	16 June
Westfalen	1 medium	17 June
Nassau	2 medium	9 July
Grosser Kurfürst	8	17 July
Markgraf	5	20 July
König	10	21 July
Kaiser	2	Early August
Battlecruisers		
Moltke	4	30 July
Von der Tann	4	2 August
Seydlitz	21 heavy, 2 medium	16 September
Derfflinger	17 heavy, 4 medium	15 October

The End of the High Seas Fleet

The Armistice signed on 11 November 1918 decreed that Germany would surrender ten of her most modern battleships and six battlecruisers in addition to a number of cruisers and destroyers, and on 21 November the ships of the undefeated navy sailed into the Firth of Forth. *König* arrived on 4 December and *Baden*, which was sent as a replacement for the incomplete *Mackensen*, followed ten days later. A total of 74 German warships were interned in the great anchorage at Scapa Flow.

When the crews were informed that by the terms of the treaty a further eight battleships, eight cruisers and dozens of destroyers and torpedo boats were to be relinquished to the Allies, Rear-Admiral Reuter, who knew he could count on the loyalty of the crews, gave the order to scuttle all ships at Scapa Flow in protest against the terms. At a signal from the cruiser *Emden*, the seacocks on every unit were opened at 11.15 on the morning of 21 June 1919 and the entire Fleet began to sink.

The British were taken by surprise, and of the big ships only *Baden* could be towed into shallow water for beaching. Shortly afterwards the remnants of the Imperial Navy, which lay disarmed in German harbours, were distributed amongst the victorious powers. None was ever destined to serve a foreign flag and all were either scrapped or sunk as target ships. Only eight old pre-dreadnoughts remained under the German ensign.

Armament

All the heavy guns mounted by capital ships of the Imperial German Navy were manufactured by Krupp at Essen and in general were the best in the world. They took longer to produce than weapons made in British armaments factories and this led on occasion to delays in fitting out warships.

The German Navy preferred guns with a high muzzle velocity. Their greater range has been ascribed to the high degree of elevation of the barrel, which is incorrect: whilst the maximum elevation of British guns of the same calibre was usually greater, it did not endow them with a longer range than the equivalent German gun. The success of German naval gunnery was attributable to the excellence of the weapons and the quality of the shell casings and explosive charges.

German stereoscopic rangefinders were superior to the British split-image equipment, as is confirmed by a comparison of the performance of the capital ships of both fleets at Jutland: the Royal Navy fired 4,598 heavy shells and scored 100 hits (2.17 per cent) whilst the German Navy fired 3,597 shells and obtained 120 hits (3.33 per cent). However, it was in this battle that the superiority of their larger calibre guns began to tell in favour of the British in artillery duels. The effect of a hit by the British 15in (381mm) armour-piercing shell (in spite of its poor-quality detonator and explosive charge) as compared to a hit by a German 280mm (11in) or 305mm (12in) shell showed itself in the engagement between the fast battleships of the *Queen Elizabeth* class and the German battlecruisers.

Guns of 305mm (12in) calibre were too small for modern dreadnoughts of the time and the German transition to 350mm (13.8in) and 380mm (15in) calibres followed fairly late. The German Navy adhered far too long to the 280mm (11in) calibre on the grounds that, in the prevailing conditions of weather and visibility in the North Sea, a battle at long range was not likely, and also because it believed in the better ballistic properties of the 280mm weapon. This calibre had been found aboard ships of the *Wörth* class at the beginning of the 1890s, while the 240mm (9.45in) calibre made its appearance on pre-dreadnoughts completed at the turn of the century. The reasoning behind this was the conviction that a weapon of inferior calibre with three times the rate of fire would have a greater cumulative effect than a slower-firing larger one.

Details of Heavy Guns aboard German Capital Ships

Gun	Year	Wt of shell	Muzzle velocity	Range/elevation
380mm 45-cal	1913	750kg	800m/sec	20.4km/16°
350mm 45-cal	1914	600kg	815m/sec	23.2km/20°
305mm 50-cal	1908	405kg	855m/sec	18.0km/13.5°
280mm 50-cal	1909	302kg	880m/sec	18.1km/13.5°
280mm 45-cal	1907	302kg	855m/sec	18.9km/20°

Following the experiences gained during the Dogger Bank action and particularly at Jutland, the turret mountings on German ships were quickly modified in order to obtain greater elevation for the guns. This led to substantial increases in range, especially in cases where the elevation could be raised to 20 degrees. The range of the 380mm (15in) gun increased to 23.2km (25,350yd) and the 280mm (11in) 45-cal gun to 20.4km (22,300yd). In the case of the 280mm 50-cal and 305mm (12in) 50-cal weapons, where the elevation had been limited originally to 13.5 degrees, an increase of 2.5 degrees gave a range of 19.1km (20,900yd) and 20.4km (22,300yd) respectively. The elevation of *Goeben*'s guns was raised to 22.5 degrees, which increased their range to 21.4km (23,400yd).

There is some doubt about the actual size of the 350mm (13.8in) 45-cal gun. Numerous sources refer to a 350mm calibre, others to one of 355.6mm (14in). In a technical article by the well-informed 'Nauticus' in 1914, the performance figures for the Krupp 356mm 45-cal and 381mm 45-cal guns were compared with foreign models. The principal arguments in favour of the calibre having been 355mm are (a) an order by the *Reichsmarineamt* dated 26 August 1914 concerning a special mounting for the '35.5cm Gun No 1' with Krupp, and (b) a photograph taken on the Western Front in 1916 which clearly bears the inscription '35.5 cm Nr. 1' on the barrel. Whether this was a test gun, and the production weapons were to be bored down to 350mm, remains to be clarified.

In battleship projects which emerged immediately before the war, provision was made for 88mm (3.5in) anti-aircraft guns. The 88mm 45-cal gun developed by Krupp was the standard weapon against air attack. The total of four AA guns installed on battleships in the first years of the war was reasonably high for the period, but this was later reduced to two as AA weapons became desperately needed at the fronts. However, the number of AA guns aboard battlecruisers was not reduced because of the nature of the tasks these ships were required to fulfil. The 88mm 45-cal AA gun was the best weapon of its type throughout the First World War. It had a shell weight of 9.5kg (21lb), a muzzle velocity of 850 m/sec (2,800ft/sec) and an effective altitude of 9,000m (29,500ft) at 70 degrees' elevation.

Note: The Naval Yards were the Kaiserliche Werft at Kiel (KW Kiel) and Wilhelmshaven (KW Wilhelmshaven). The private yards were those of the Krupp Germania Werft at Kiel (Germania, Kiel); Howaldtswerke, Kiel (Howaldt, Kiel); AG Vulcan, Stettin; Friedrich Schichau, Danzig; AG Weser, Bremen; AG Vulcan, Hamburg; and Blohm und Voss, Hamburg (BuV). After the war the names of some of the shipyards were changed, and thus the Kaiserliche Werft at Kiel became the Deutsche Werke, Kiel AG, in 1925; the Kaiserliche Werft at Wilhelmshaven became the Reichsmarinewerft in 1919 (Kriegsmarinewerft Wilhelmshaven in 1935); AG Vulcan, Hamburg, became the Howaldtswerke, Hamburg, in 1930; and in the same year AG Weser, Bremen, became Deschimag, Bremen.

The after turrets of *Seydlitz*, showing the long barrels of her 280mm (11in) guns.

Nassau Class

Displacement: 18,900/20,535t
Dimensions: 145.6 x 26.9 x 8.8m
Machinery: 3 reciprocating
steam engines, 3 shafts,
22,000ihp
Fuel: 2,700t coal max. (+ 200t
oil from late 1915)
Speed/range: 19.5kt; 8,400nm at
10kt, 2,800nm at 19kt
Armour: Belt 290mm, deck
80mm, main armament 280mm,
CT 400mm
Weight of armour: 6,640t =
35.2% of normal displacement
Armament: 12 x 280mm 45-cal,
12 x 150mm 45-cal
Anti-aircraft guns: 2 x 88mm 45-
cal (from late 1915)
Complement: 1,130 (wartime)

Posen, representative of the first generation of German dreadnoughts.

Nassau, 1911.

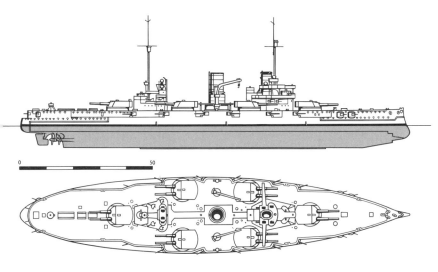

Ship	Builder	Laid down	Launched	Commissioned	In service
Nassau	Wilhelmshaven	22.07.1907	07.03.1908	01.10.1909	00.05.1910
Westfalen	Weser, Bremen	12.08.1907	01.07.1908	16.11.1909	00.05.1910
Rheinland	Vulcan, Stettin	01.06.1907	26.09.1908	30.04.1910	00.09.1910
Posen	Germania, Kiel	11.06.1907	12.12.1908	31.05.1910	00.09.1910

All four units received supplementary oil-firing in the winter of 1915–16 and all exceeded 20 knots on trials.

Nassau was surrendered to Japan as war reparation on 7 April 1920 and scrapped at Dordrecht later that year. *Posen* was surrendered to Britain on 13 May 1920 and scrapped at Dordrecht in 1922. *Westfalen* received a medium-calibre hit at Jutland and on 19 August 1916 was torpedoed by the British submarine *E23* during a sortie in the North Sea. She became a gunnery training ship on 1 September 1918, was surrendered to Britain on 5 August 1920 and scrapped at Birkenhead in 1924. *Rheinland* received a hit at Jutland. She participated in the liberation of Finland in spring 1918 but ran aground in the Aaland Sea on 11 April. She was later towed into Kiel and relegated to the role of accommodation ship after the decision was taken not to repair her. She was towed to Dordrecht on 29 July 1920 and scrapped from 1921.

Helgoland Class

Displacement: 22,800/24,700t
Dimensions: 166.5 x 28.5 x 8.9m
Machinery: 3 reciprocating steam engines, 3 shafts, 28,000ihp
Fuel: 3,200t coal max. (+ 200t oil from late 1915)
Speed/range: 20.5kt; 5,500nm at 10kt
Armour: Belt 300mm, deck 80mm, main armament 300mm, CT 400mm
Weight of armour: 8,350t = 36.6% of normal displacement
Armament: 12 x 305mm 50-cal, 14 x 150mm 45-cal
Anti-aircraft guns: 2 x 88mm 45-cal (from late 1915)
Complement: 1,300 (wartime)

Ostfriesland, 1914.

A wartime photograph of *Ostfriesland*.

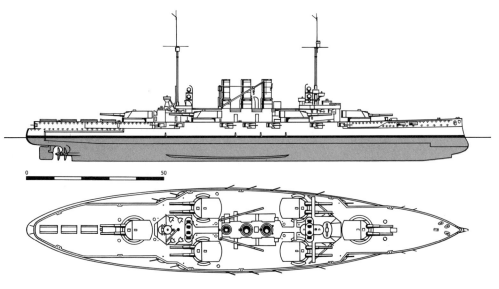

Ship	Builder	Laid down	Launched	Commissioned	In service
Helgoland	Howaldt, Kiel	24.11.1908	25.09.1909	23.08.1911	20.12.1911
Ostfriesland	Wilhelmshaven	19.10.1908	30.09.1909	01.08.1911	15.09.1911
Thüringen	Weser, Bremen	02.11.1908	27.11.1909	01.07.1911	10.09.1911
Oldenburg	Schichau, Danzig	01.03.1909	30.06.1910	01.05.1912	01.07.1912

The first three ships were authorised under the 1908–09 Budget and *Oldenburg* the following year. All reached speeds between 20.8 and 21.3 knots on trials.

Helgoland was surrendered to Britain on 5 August 1920 to replace a unit scuttled at Scapa Flow; she was scrapped there in 1924. *Ostfriesland* struck a mine and sustained damage while returning from Jutland on 1 June 1916. Surrendered to the United States as reparation, she was used as a target ship for American bomber aircraft and sank on 21 July 1921 after receiving seventeen bomb hits including four by bombs of between 500kg (1,100lb) and 1,000kg (2,200lb). *Thüringen* was allocated to France as war reparation, transferred to Cherbourg on 29 April 1920 and subsequently used as a target ship; she was scrapped in 1933. *Oldenburg* was surrendered to Japan as reparation on 13 May 1920 and immediately re-sold to a British shipbreaker; she was scrapped at Dordrecht from 1921.

Kaiser Class

Displacement: 24,720/27,000t
Dimensions: 171.86 x 29.0 x 9.1m
Machinery: 3 turbines, 3 shafts, 31,000shp (*Prinzregent Luitpold* 2 turbines, 2 shafts, 26,000shp)
Fuel: 3,600t coal + 200t oil
Speed/range: 21.0kt; 7,900nm at 12kt, 2,400nm at 21kt
Armour: Belt 350mm, deck 100mm, main armament 300mm, CT 300mm
Weight of armour: Approx. 10,100t = 40.1% of normal displacement
Armament: 10 x 305mm 50-cal, 14 x 150mm 45-cal
Anti-aircraft guns: 2 x 88mm 45-cal
Complement: 1,250 (wartime)

Friedrich der Grosse, 1918.

Kaiser, lacking torpedo nets.

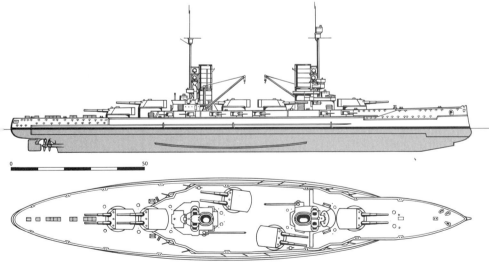

In addition to her Parsons turbines, *Prinzregent Luitpold* had an experimental Germania two-stroke diesel driving the centre shaft and producing 12,000shp. However, this was not considered to be fully developed and was therefore later omitted. *Prinzregent Luitpold* reached 21.7 knots on trials. The other four ships had three turbines, *Friedrich der Grosse*, *Kaiserin* and *König Albert* making between 22 and 22.4 knots without effort at an output of from 39,813 to 42,181shp and *Kaiser* 23.4 knots at 55,187shp.

Friedrich der Grosse was the fleet flagship from 22 January 1913 to 14 March 1917. All five ships fought at Jutland but only *Kaiser* received damage; she was repaired in August 1916.

After the Armistice all five were interned at Scapa Flow and were scuttled there on 21 June 1919. *Kaiser* was raised in March 1929, *Friedrich der Grosse* in April 1937, *Kaiserin* in May 1936, *Prinzregent Luitpold* in July 1931 and *König Albert* in July 1935; all were broken up at Rosyth.

Ship	Builder	Laid down	Launched	Commissioned	In service
Kaiser	KW Kiel	00.09.1909	22.03.1911	01.08.1912	07.12.1912
Friedrich der Grosse	Vulcan, Hamburg	26.01.1910	10.06.1911	15.10.1912	08.12.1912
Kaiserin	Howaldt, Kiel	00.07.1910	11.11.1911	14.05.1913	13.12.1913
König Albert	Schichau, Danzig	17.07.1910	27.01.1912	31.07.1913	08.11.1913
Prinzregent Luitpold	Germania, Kiel	00.10.1910	17.02.1912	19.08.1913	06.12.1913

König Class

Displacement: 25,800/28,600t
Dimensions: 174.7 x 29.5 x 9.2m
Machinery: 3 turbines, 3 shafts, 31,000shp
Fuel: 3,600t coal + 600t oil
Speed/range: 21.0kt; 8,000nm at 12kt, 4,000nm at 18kt
Armour: Belt 350mm, deck 100mm, main armament 300mm, CT 350mm
Weight of armour: 10,440t = 40.4% of normal displacement
Armament: 10 x 305mm 50-cal, 14 x 150mm 45-cal
Anti-aircraft guns: 4 x 88mm 45-cal
Complement: 1,300 (wartime)

König, 1918.

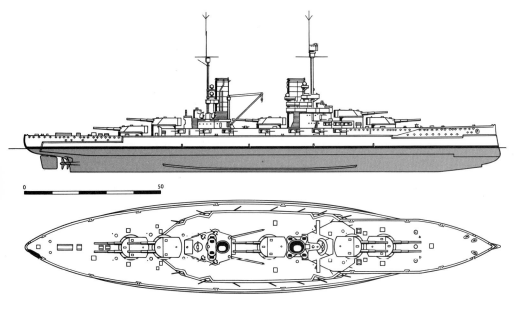

Ship	Builder	Laid down	Launched	Commissioned	In service
König	Wilhelmshaven	03.10.1911	01.03.1913	09.08.1914	23.11.1914
Grosser Kurfürst	Vulcan, Hamburg	03.10.1911	05.05.1913	30.07.1914	25.10.1914
Markgraf	Weser, Bremen	00.11.1911	04.06.1913	01.10.1914	10.01.1915
Kronprinz	Germania, Kiel	00.07.1912	21.02.1914	08.11.1914	02.01.1915

König was the first German capital ship to have a main gun turret sited amidships.

All units achieved their designed speed of 21 knots or trials, and two exceeded the requirement by between 0.2 to 0.3 knots, although substantially greater output (41,400–46,200shp) was necessary to achieve this. Al four units fought at Jutland and, with the exception of *Kronprinz*, received battle damage.

Grosser Kurfürst was torpedoed by the British submarine *J1* off the Danish west coast on 5 November 1916 but was returned to service on 10 February 1917; *J1* also torpedoed *Kronprinz* the same day but the damage was repaired within a month. On 5 March 1917 *Grosser Kurfürst* and *Kronprinz* collided in the Heligoland Bight but were back in service by the end of April. During Operation 'Albion' off the Russian coast in mid-October 1917, *Grosser Kurfürst* was mined while *König* and *Kronprinz* fought a gun battle against Russian units in the Bay of Riga. *Kronprinz* was renamed *Kronprinz Wilhelm* on 27 January 1918.

All four ships were interned at Scapa Flow after the Armistice and were scuttled there on 21 June 1919 *Grosser Kurfürst* was raised in April 1938 and scrapped at Rosyth.

Bayern Class

Displacement: 28,500/32,200t (second pair 28,800/32,500t)
Dimensions: 179.4 (second pair 181.8) x 30.0 x 9.3m
Machinery: 3 sets turbines, 3 shafts, 35,000shp
Fuel: 3,400t coal + 620t oil
Speed/range: 21.0kt; 5,000nm at 12kt, 2,400nm at 21kt
Armour: Belt 350mm, deck 70mm, main armament 350mm, CT 350mm
Weight of armour: 11,600t = 40.6% of normal displacement
Armament: 8 x 380mm 45-cal, 16 x 150mm 45-cal
Anti-aircraft guns: 4 x 88mm 45-cal
Complement: 1,220 to 1,270

The two unfinished units of the class were designed to be faster than their sisters with a substantially increased engine output: *Württemberg* would have made 22 knots at 48,000shp. *Sachsen* had two turbines plus a diesel driving the centre shaft, and an output of 42,000shp (12,000hp diesel) would have provided her with a speed of 22.5 knots (12 knots under diesel power alone). During six-hour forced-draught trials *Bayern* reached 21.5 knots at 37,430shp and 22 knots at a maximum output of 55,970shp.

Bayern missed Jutland as she was still undergoing trials at the time. During the occupation of the Baltic islands she struck a mine, causing flooding in her underwater torpedo rooms; during repairs all four beam torpedo tubes were removed. She was interned at Scapa Flow on 26 November 1918, scuttled there on 21 June 1919, raised in September 1934 and scrapped at Rosyth in 1935. *Baden* became the fleet flagship on entering service in March 1917. She was interned at Scapa Flow on 14 December 1918, but an attempt to scuttle her there on 21 June 1919 failed and she was beached by British tugs. She was used by the Royal Navy as a gunnery target from July 1919 and sunk off Portsmouth on 16 August 1921. The incomplete units were broken up at Hamburg and Kiel respectively in 1921.

Bayern, 1918.

Ship	Builder	Laid down	Launched	Commissioned	In service
Bayern	Howaldt, Kiel	22.01.1914	19.02.1915	18.03.1916	15.07.1916
Baden	Schichau, Danzig	22.12.1913	13.10.1915	19.10.1916	14.03.1917
Württemberg	Vulcan, Hamburg	07.04.1914	20.06.1917	–	–
Sachsen	Germania, Kiel	04.01.1915	21.11.1916	–	–

0   50

Baden, one of the two *Bayern* class units—the most powerful German battleships.

Baden with her main turrets
trained to fire a broadside.

Von der Tann

Displacement: 19,370/21,300t
Dimensions: 171.5 x 26.6 x 9.1m
Machinery: 2 sets turbines, 4
shafts, 42,000shp
Fuel: 2,800t coal
Speed/range: 24.8kt; 4,400nm at
24kt
Armour: Belt 250mm, deck
25mm, main armament 230mm,
CT 250mm
Weight of armour: 6,300t =
32.5% of normal displacement
Armament: 8 x 280mm 45-cal,
10 x 150mm 45-cal
Anti-aircraft guns: 4 x 88mm 45-
cal (from 1916)
Complement: 1,170 (wartime)
Builder: BuV, Hamburg (laid
down 25.03.1908; launched
20.03.1909; commissioned
01.09.1910; in service
19.02.1911)

Von der Tann as she appeared
in 1914.

Von der Tann at full speed.

Von der Tann was the first of the German battlecruisers.
A high-pressure turbine drove the two outer shafts and
a low-pressure turbine the two inner shafts. During her
six-hour forced-draught trials she reached 27.8 knots at
79,000shp.

The ship took part in nearly all the East Coast bombardments and fleet sorties and she distinguished herself at Jutland, where she sank the British battlecruiser
Indefatigable. Although she was later damaged by hits
from four 15in (381mm) and two 13.5in (343mm) shells,
she was repaired by 2 August 1916. She was interned at
Scapa Flow on 24 November 1918, scuttled there on 21
June 1919, raised in December 1930 and finally broken
up at Rosyth in 1934.

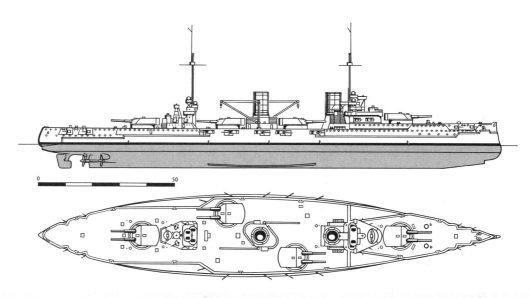

Moltke/Goeben

Displacement: 22,980/25,400t
Dimensions: 186.0 x 29.4 x 9.2m
Machinery: 2 sets turbines, 4 shafts, 52,000shp
Fuel: 3,100t coal
Speed/range: 25.5kt; 4,100nm at 14kt
Armour: Belt 270mm, deck 75mm, main armament 230mm, CT 350mm
Weight of armour: 7,600t = 33.1% of normal displacement
Armament: 10 x 280mm 50-cal, 12 x 150mm 45-cal (Goeben 10 x 150mm from 1915)
Anti-aircraft guns: 4 x 88mm 45-cal (from 1916)
Complement: 1,050 (Moltke 1,355 in May 1916)

Both ships exceeded their designed speed on trials, Goeben reaching 28 knots and Moltke 28.4 knots. The horizontal armour consisted of an armoured upper deck (23mm) and an armour deck (25mm with 50mm slopes).

Moltke took part in the North Sea sorties in the summer of 1915; torpedoed by the British submarine E1, she was repaired at Hamburg. She received four hits at Jutland and was under repair until the end of July 1916. She participated in operations off the East Baltic islands in

the autumn of 1917 and on 25 April 1918, during a fleet sortie into Norwegian waters, was torpedoed by the British submarine E42 but made port with 2,100 tons of sea water aboard. Interned at Scapa Flow on 24 November 1918, she was scuttled there on 21 June 1919. She was raised in June 1927 and finally scrapped at Rosyth by 1929.

Goeben was on duty in the Mediterranean from 1912 bombarding Philippeville (Algeria) on 4 August 1914

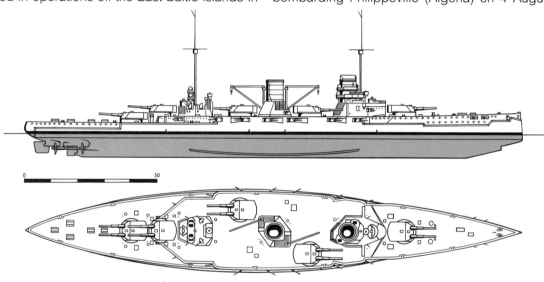

Goeben, 1913.

Ship	Builder	Laid down	Launched	Commissioned	In service
Moltke	BuV, Hamburg	23.01.1909	07.04.1910	30.09.1911	31.03.1912
Goeben	BuV, Hamburg	12.08.1909	28.03.1911	02.07.1912	28.08.1912

and fleeing from British ships to the then neutral Turkey where she was symbolically 'sold'. She subsequently served under the Turkish flag as Yavuz Sultan Selim with a German crew, and opened Russo-Turkish hostilities by bombarding Sevastopol. On 26 December 1914 she was mined in the approaches to the Bosphorus, but as no repair facilities were available at Constantinople she was temporarily patched up and, despite the damage, was engaged in a number of sorties in the Black Sea between April 1915 and January 1916. Following a successful attack on the island of Imbros, she struck two mines and was fortunate to make Constantinople under tow on 20 January 1918. For further career details see under Turkey.

Moltke before the First World War.

Seydlitz

Displacement: 25,000/28,550t
Dimensions: 200.0 x 28.5 x 9.3m
Machinery: 2 sets turbines, 4 shafts, 63,000shp
Fuel: 3,600t coal
Speed/range: 26.5kt; 4,200nm at 14kt
Armour: Belt 300mm, deck 55mm, main armament 250mm, CT 300mm
Weight of armour: ?
Armament: 10 x 280mm 50-cal, 12 x 150mm 45-cal
Anti-aircraft guns: 2 x 88mm 45-cal (from 1916)
Complement: 1,425 (May 1916)
Builder: BuV, Hamburg (laid down 04.02.1911; launched 30.03.1912; commissioned 22.05.1913; in service 17.08.1913)

During trials *Seydlitz* achieved 28.1 knots at 89,738shp. She was seriously damaged at on 24 January 1915 at Dogger Bank, where both after turrets were burnt out and the ship suffered heavy loss of life, and was mined on 25 April 1916 but reached the German coast with 1,400 tons of sea water aboard. She was involved in the sinking of the British battlecruiser *Invincible* at Jutland and, although receiving hits and being struck by a torpedo, managed to reach the Jade estuary under her own steam with 5,300 tons of sea water below decks. She was under repair at Wilhelmshaven until 16 September 1916. *Seydlitz* was interned at Scapa Flow on 24 November 1918 and scuttled there on 21 June 1919; raised in November 1928, she was scrapped at Rosyth.

Seydlitz, 1918.

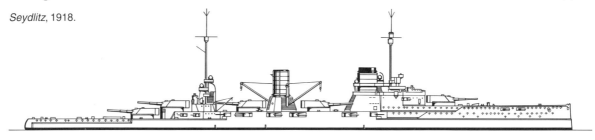

An aerial photograph of *Seydlitz* during the First World War.

Derfflinger/Lützow

Displacement: 26,600/31,200t (*Lützow* 26,740t normal)
Dimensions: 210.0 x 29.0 x 9.6m
Machinery: 2 sets turbines, 4 shafts, 63,000shp
Fuel: 3,500t coal (*Lützow* 3,700t) + 1,000t oil
Speed/range: 26.5kt; 5,600nm at 14kt
Armour: Belt 300mm, deck 80mm, main armament 270mm, CT 300mm
Weight of armour: 9,840t = 37.0% of normal displacement
Armament: 8 x 305mm 50-cal, 12 x 150mm 45-cal (*Lützow* 14 x 150mm)
Anti-aircraft guns: 4 x 88mm 45-cal
Complement: 1,390 (May 1916)

Lützow, 1916.

The first attempt to launch *Derfflinger* on 14 June 1913 failed and the ship became jammed on the stocks. On trials *Lützow* suffered sea water damage to her turbines and was not battleworthy for six months.

Derfflinger was involved in the sinking of the battlecruisers *Queen Mary* and *Invincible* at Jutland. During the battle she received 21 hits (17 from heavy shells) and returned to port with 157 dead and 3,000 tons of water aboard; temporary repairs were carried out at Wilhelmshaven, final repairs being completed at Howaldtswerke on 15 October 1916. The ship was interned at Scapa Flow at the end of November 1918, scuttled there on 21 June 1919, raised in 1939 and not finally broken up until 1956.

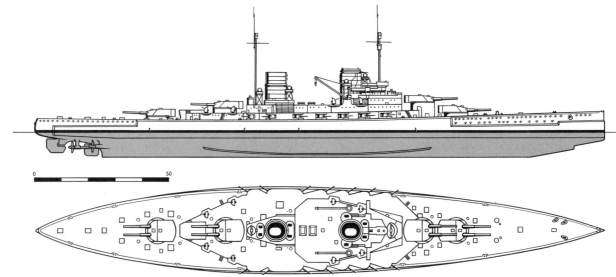

The battlecruiser *Derfflinger*, with tripod mast.

Derfflinger's 305mm (12in) twin turrets, photographed at Wilhelmshaven two days after Jutland on 2 June 1916.

Ship	Builder	Laid down	Launched	Commissioned	In service
Derfflinger	BuV, Hamburg	30.03.1912	12.07.1913	01.09.1914	08.11.1914
Lützow	Schichau, Danzig	00.07.1912	29.11.1913	08.08.1915	20.03.1916

Lützow was involved in sinking Invincible but later the same day was badly damaged by British battleships. She tried to return home with 7,500 tons of water in her hull but could not be kept afloat, and after her crew had been taken off she was scuttled by two torpedoes. In 1961–62 the wreck was partially broken up.

Hindenburg

Displacement: 26,950/31,500t
Dimensions: 212.5 x 29.0 x 9.6m
Machinery: 2 sets turbines, 4 shafts, 72,000shp
Fuel: 3,700t coal + 1,200t oil
Speed/range: 27.0kt; 6,100nm at 14kt
Armour: As *Derfflinger*, but side armour of main armament increased from 110 to 150mm
Weight of armour: 9,970t = 37.0% of normal displacement
Armament: 8 x 305mm 50-cal, 14 x 150mm 45-cal
Anti-aircraft guns: 4 x 88mm 45-cal
Complement: 1,180
Builder: Wilhelmshaven (laid down 30.06 1913; launched 01.08.1915; commissioned 10.05.1917; in service 25.10.1917)

Hindenburg was the last German battlecruiser to be completed: compared with *Derfflinger* and *Lützow*, the main armament was fitted on new mountings which gave the main guns an elevation of 16 degrees. The actual date of keel-laying was 1 October 1913. On her trials over the measured mile in a calm sea the ship achieved 26.6 knots at 95,777shp, but at least 2 knots more had been expected in normal sea conditions.

Hindenburg took part in two fleet sorties, into the western North Sea in November 1917 and the northern North Sea in April 1918. Interned at Scapa Flow on 24 November 1918, she was scuttled there on 21 June 1919. After a number of unsuccessful attempts at salvage, she was finally raised in 1930 and broken up at Rosyth from 1932.

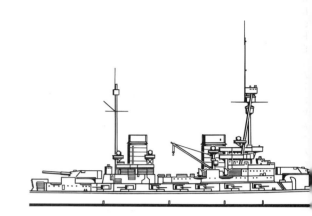

Hindenburg, 1918.

Hindenburg, the last battlecruiser to serve in the Imperial Navy.

Mackensen Class

Displacement: 31,000/35,300t
Dimensions: 223.0 x 30.4 x 9.3m
Machinery: 2 sets turbines, 4 shafts, 90,000shp
Fuel: 4,000t coal + 2,000t oil
Speed/range: 28.0kt; 8,000nm at 14kt
Armour: Belt 300mm, deck 75mm total, main armament 300mm, CT 350mm
Weight of armour: ?
Armament: 8 x 350mm 45-cal, 14 x 150mm 45-cal
Anti-aircraft guns: 4 x 88mm 45-cal
Complement: 1,188

Seven ships of the *Mackensen* class were originally planned and ordered but the three least advanced units ordered on 10 and 11 April 1915 were redesigned for 380mm (15in) guns and restyled the *Ersatz Yorck* class. At the end of the war *Mackensen* was twelve months short of her completion date and listed for surrender to the Allies, but *Baden* was handed over in her place and *Mackensen* was scrapped at Hamburg in 1924. The date for *Ersatz Yorck*'s keel-laying has been quoted as July 1916 but whether this means the re-laying of the keel to the amended design is not known. *Ersatz Freya* was broken up at Hamburg in 1922 when 21 months short of completion, having been launched in 1920. *Graf Spee*, 18 months short of completion, was broken up at Kiel by 1923. *Ersatz Yorck* and *Ersatz* 'A' were both laid down and then abandoned, and the material for these two ships, together with that for *Ersatz Scharnhorst* and *Ersatz Gneisenau*, was broken up on the slips.

Ship	Builder	Laid down	Launched
Mackensen	BuV, Hamburg	30.01.1915	21.04.1917
Ersatz Freya	BuV, Hamburg	01.05.1915	(13.03.1920)
Graf Spee	BuV, Hamburg	30.11.1915	15.09.1917
Ersatz 'A'	Wilhelmshaven	03.11.1915	–
Ersatz Yorck	Vulcan, Hamburg	04.11.1915	–
Ersatz Gneisenau	Germania, Kiel	–	–
Ersatz Scharnhorst	BuV, Hamburg	–	–

Simplified inboard profile of *Mackensen* (not to scale).

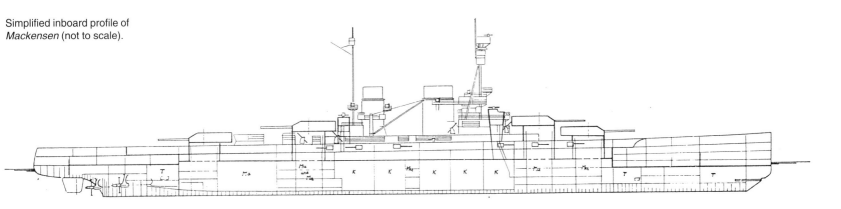

Developments up to 1945

The provisional *Reichsmarine*, formed in April 1919 following the German defeat, could do little more with its few available ships than begin training a new generation of naval officers and, most importantly, protect the German coasts of the central Baltic and East Prussia. For this it had no need for large battleships. The danger of conflict with Poland had not yet been completely averted, and the German Admiralty remained concerned at the possibility of a blockade. Poland's ally was France, a fact which loomed large when thought was given to planning new warships. The *Reich* Government was determined to abide by the provisions of the Versailles Treaty as regards warship construction, but nevertheless sharp opposition was encountered from socialist deputies in the *Reichstag* when the first 10,000-tonne armoured ship was approved in 1928, even though it was permitted under the terms of the treaty.

The first naval construction programme of the *Reichsmarine*, the *Schiffbau-Ersatzplan* (Ship Construction Replacement Plan), was initiated in 1929. Its first part proposed that during the years 1931–36 four new 10,000-tonne armoured ships should be built to replace the existing old battleships. This had implications for foreign policy, as France, with some justification, saw these so-called 'pocket battleships' as a threat to her trade routes.

Although the political situation in Europe appeared stable at the time, the system of collective security was soon to falter, to which Adolf Hitler's seizure of power in Germany in January 1933 obviously contributed. Following the French refusal to allow even a limited German rearmament programme, Germany withdrew from the League of Nations on 14 October 1933 and began to build up her military forces, at first secretly. Her naval planning was limited for the time being to project work, but this was undertaken without regard to the restrictions of the Treaty of Versailles.

After Germany concluded a non-aggression pact with Poland on 28 January 1934, France remained the only potential opponent at sea. In the opinion of the German Naval Staff, the ideological enemy in the East, the communist Soviet Union, did not present a serious threat in the Baltic at that time. The British, similarly, were not regarded as potential enemies, and in 1935 Hitler signalled his readiness to reach an arms agreement with them in order to avoid the possibility of any new naval rivalry.

By 1934 materials for the construction of two battleships, two heavy cruisers and a number of destroyers and U-boats had been secretly assembled. The Anglo-German Naval Agreement limited the German surface fleet to 35 per cent of the British strength (45 per cent in the case of submarines), but it also implicitly authorised Hitler to develop a fleet which could exceed the various limits imposed by the Treaty of Versailles. Thus the warships planned could now be completed. Under the provisions of the 1936 Programme, the *Kriegsmarine* (the term *Reichsmarine* was abolished on 21 May 1935) could now expect to receive two larger battleships, two aircraft carriers, three heavy cruisers and numerous smaller vessels.

A change in German naval policy occurred in 1938. After the annexation of Austria and the occupation of the Sudetenland, Hitler considered the world powers to be so weak that they would not seriously obstruct his military ambitions. As he now had to take into account the future opposition of the British, he ordered the building tempo for the two 35,000-tonne battleships and the U-boat programme to be accelerated.

The Naval Staff came to the conclusion that, in any future campaign against British sea-borne commerce, more effective results would be achieved by employing heavy surface units rather than U-boats, and this point of view was decisive for the wider naval construction policy of the *Kriegsmarine*. Hitler ordered Admiral Raeder, Commander-in-Chief of the Navy, to prepare a major building programme that could be put into effect rapidly.

Raeder presented two variations on his proposed programme. The first, for the construction of armoured ships and U-boats, would bear fruit more quickly. The second provided for a balanced fleet which would require greater finance and a period of ten years to accomplish. Raeder explained to the *Führer* that there would be only the rump of a fleet should hostilities begin with Britain before the programme could be completed, but Hitler assured him that the fleet would not be required for his political purposes until 1946. Without consulting his Naval Staff, on 28 April 1939 he repudiated the Anglo-German Naval Agreement.

In mid-January 1939 Hitler ordered that the completion date for the second variation of the Z-Plan (*Zielplan*, or Target Plan) should be the beginning of 1946, earlier than the Naval Staff had suggested to him. The plans authorised in March 1939 proposed that by that time the *Kriegsmarine* should have at its disposal eight battleships, five battlecruisers, three *Panzerschiffe* (armoured ships, i.e. 'pocket battleships'), four aircraft carriers, five heavy cruisers and 249 U-boats. A further six battleships, three battlecruisers, two aircraft carriers and 120 U-boats would then follow, together with numerous smaller units. The U-boats would have diesel-electric propulsion, in order to provide the greatest radius of action. Raeder's operational plan was aimed at the disruption of British seaborne trade by cruiser and U-boat warfare, while very powerful battle groups (carriers escorted by battleships) would finish off the convoy escorts.

The Z-Plan attracted a stream of critics who included the commander of the U-boat arm, the then Captain Dönitz, who argued that Britain would not simply stand by and watch a German naval armaments programme of this immensity; moreover, the *Kriegsmarine* had neither sufficient capital ships nor enough U-boats for an early naval conflict. He preferred the faster and less expensive proposal—a powerful U-boat arm.

Hitler persevered with his own ideas and on 27 January 1939 awarded absolute priority status to naval rearmament on the grounds that a powerful navy had a political role to play, but the outbreak of war in September 1939 killed off the Z-Plan. The orders placed for the heavy ships were cancelled forthwith, and naval construction was now concentrated on completing the most advanced large battleships already under construction and on the mass production of U-boats and small surface vessels.

If the Z-Plan had been realised, by 1946 the *Kriegsmarine* would have had at its disposal a string of technically obsolescent super-battleships. Moreover, the concept of conducting oceanic warfare with a relatively small number of aircraft carriers represented a poor alternative to the possibilities which a rapidly developed *Luftwaffe* could have offered.

German Battleship Construction 1934–1941

Under the Treaty of Versailles Germany was permitted to retain eight obsolete pre-dreadnoughts which she would be allowed to replace on the twentieth anniversary of the dates of their launching. For newly built *Panzerschiffe*, the class displacement had been set at a maximum of 10,000 tonnes, although the gun calibre was not limited. However, as it was impossible to construct a modern, combat-worthy battleship within the tonnage limitations, the first designs for the replacement ships appeared as coast defence battleships or heavy cruisers. The naval exercises of 1926 showed clearly that Germany would require armoured ships which were superior in firepower to a cruiser and faster than a battleship.

In mid-June 1927 the Chief of the Naval Staff, Admiral Zenker, decided that the future *Panzerschiff* 'A' would carry six 280mm (11in) guns and have a speed of 26 knots. However, its armour would be thin—thinner even than that of many of the Washington cruisers. After building work commenced on the first of the class (later to be named *Deutschland*), two others followed by 1932. These ships fall outside the scope of the present work since they were not capital ships but cruisers, albeit with an very powerful armament for their size. Indeed, after 1940 the *Kriegsmarine* officially redesignated them heavy cruisers.

The *Reichsmarine*'s *Schiffbau-Ersatzplan* of the autumn of 1929 envisaged the construction of eight armoured ships by 1940. The last four of these, to be built after 1934, would be larger versions of the first four, and in the reported view of the new Chief of the Naval Staff, Admiral Raeder, they should be of a similar displacement to the First World War battlecruiser *Von der Tann* (19,370 tonnes), although even at that time he was already thinking in terms of a further increase to 26,000 tonnes. As a result of the world economic crisis, the programme was modified in 1930 so that the keel-laying dates for the last four ships were postponed to 1936. The approval for a fast capital ship in France in 1931 (the battlecruiser *Dunkerque*) brought about the re-evaluation of all plans based on the concept of using German armoured ships against France's trade routes, for none of the German units was capable of handling a battlecruiser mounting eight 330mm (13in) guns.

The discussions about the size and armament of future armoured ships grew more heated within the Naval Staff following Hitler's accession to power. While construction work on the fourth armoured ship was still scheduled to commence in 1934 as originally planned, in March 1933 Raeder requested the Navy Design Office to provide a study project for two variants of a 26,500-tonne capital ship, armed with 305mm (12in) and 330mm (13in) guns respectively. After a conversation between Hitler and Raeder, the idea of an 'anti-*Dunkerque*' vessel was abandoned, but in June 1933 Raeder solicited the design of an armoured ship of approximately 18,000 tonnes, and two such units were ordered on 25 January 1934, although the finance for *Panzerschiff* 'E' was not approved for another month (on 28 February 1934). It is not known for certain when the keels were laid, although 1 April seems more likely than the date suggested in the most recent volume by Gröner (i.e. 14 February 1934), which would have been only three weeks after the placing of the orders. The ships were never launched, as all work was cancelled on 5 July that year following new thinking on the subject of their main armament. They would have been relatively large ships, planned for a maximum speed of 29 knots under turbines, but their high fuel consumption would have substantially limited their radius of action. Compared with the three earlier *Deutschland* class, ships 'D' and 'E' had better protection (for example, up to 220mm, 8.6in, belt armour) whilst mounting the same armament of six 283mm (11in) and eight 150mm (5.9in) guns.

The cancellation of the building work could be ascribed not only to the weaknesses of the ships but also to developments in the world political situation, for by 1934 it was recognised that it would only be a matter of time before Germany renounced the armament limitations. The Naval Staff had been thinking along these lines since 1932, and the Navy Design Office had already prepared a number of studies for true capital ships: the sixth *Panzerschiff*, 'F', which it was proposed to lay down in the autumn of 1935, reached the upper limit for tonnage imposed by the Washington Treaty, while Krupps had received orders to produce the 330mm (13in) guns for this unit in the spring of 1933. A year later the German Naval Staff came to the conclusion that the fleet of the future would need eight 35,000-tonne battleships.

During a conversation between Hitler and Raeder on 27 June 1934 it was decided that the next two *Panzerschiffe* under construction, 'D' and 'E', should carry nine instead of six heavy guns, but just eight days later building work was abandoned altogether because the slipways were required for two larger ships, although, in the event, the keels of these two units, later completed as *Scharnhorst* and *Gneisenau*, were not laid until May and June 1935 respectively. The Navy's designers had been working since 1932 on a project for two battleships, of 26,000 tonnes and 26,500 tonnes, but by the summer of 1934 no completed designs had yet been supplied. One of the main problems concerned the ships' machinery: diesel engines had been specified even for the larger *Panzerschiffe*, but the output necessary for the required speed exceeded the capacity of existing motors. Eventually it was decided to fit a high-pressure steam system which had been tested in the meantime.

The question of the ships' main armament was much more difficult to resolve, however. Because of its much higher rate of fire, it had been recommended that the newest model of the successful 283mm (11.1in) gun should be installed in three triple turrets, while other experts suggested the 330mm (13in) or 350mm (13.8in) calibres still under development. In view of the desire for a naval agreement with Britain, a compromise decision was made in which the smaller calibre would be mounted in triple turrets, but the installation would be carried out in such a way that 350mm guns could be substituted at a later date.

According to the original estimates, the ships would be ready by the end of December 1937 (*Gneisenau*) and May 1938 (*Scharnhorst*), but, because of the substantial delays in all warship building, *Gneisenau* did not run her trials until 21 May 1938. Her engines proved susceptible to breakdown, and although she failed to reach her designed speed of 32 knots the Naval Staff was satisfied with the actual figure of 31.3 knots at 165,930shp. The Navy took a dim view of the ship's sea-keeping properties: they were proposing to use her in Atlantic operations, but, partly as a result of her straight stem, the battlecruiser shipped green water over the forecastle as far aft as the bridge, and this affected the working of 'A' turret. That winter *Gneisenau* went to the dockyard for a refit and re-joined the Fleet in May 1939 with a new 'Atlantic bow'. This modification was also worked into *Scharnhorst*, which had reached 31.5 knots on her trials.

Following heavy bomb damage to *Gneisenau* at Kiel on 26 February 1942 (the forward half of the ship was destroyed), she was taken to Gdynia for repair, where it was planned to refit her with a new bow and with the 380mm (15in) guns first promised in 1935 and which were now available, partly from a stock built against an earlier unfulfilled Soviet order. The work commenced in the summer of 1942 but the worsening war situation led to the abandonment of the project in January 1943.

Panzerschiff 'F' was intended as a capital ship from the outset. The Naval Staff had virtually settled the size of the ship but the designers were constantly requested to supply variants showing different arrangements for three calibres of heavy armament. The original 330mm (13in) calibre had been rejected during the conversation between Raeder and Hitler on 27 June 1934. In March 1935 a 380mm (15in) gun was evaluated, and Raeder accepted this weapon on 9 May. On 18 June 1935 the '35 per cent' naval agreement was signed with Britain, which limited Germany to building only three 35,000-tonne battleships, and the completion date for these was set at October 1941. However, the nascent German warship building industry, overburdened with orders, was unable to keep pace with the planning and both ship 'F' (*Bismarck*) and ship 'G' (*Tirpitz*) were completed late, even though their keels had been laid in 1936. A third ship in the class failed to materialise, since Hitler was now in favour of larger and even more powerful ships. Therefore, in his eyes, *Bismarck* and *Tirpitz* were ships of an intermediate class, even though their technical characteristics in battle later showed them to be the best constructed battleships of the Second World War.

The quality of the newly developed 'Wotan' armour contributed to this superiority. The alloy 'Wh' (Wotan Hard) was used in thicknesses of up to 120mm (4.7in) for the horizontal armour and 'Ww' (Wotan Soft) in thicknesses up to 45mm (1.8in) for the torpedo bulkheads on all four German battleships. The *Bismarck* class, moreover, possessed excellent manoeuvrability and speed combined with outstanding sea-keeping qualities.

Unfulfilled Programmes

Concrete evidence that the last unit of the original eight *Panzerschiffe*, 'H', would be larger than the 35,000-tonne *Bismarck* class was supplied in February 1937. On 13 January 1937 Raeder gave the Naval High Command the task of evaluating further armament arrangements— twelve 350mm (13.8in), twelve 380mm (15in) and eight 406mm (16in)— for this ship. Two days previously he had ordered two new battleships to be laid down in 1938, and this was a clear breach of the Anglo-German Naval Agreement whichever way it was interpreted since the 35 per cent share would be exceeded by any new construction after ship 'H'. His instruction of 29 January, to pursue only the 380mm and 406mm options for the new battleships, proved that he was intending to respect the terms of the London Naval Treaty with regard to gun calibres but not tonnage limitations.

◀▲ *Gneisenau* as she appeared in 1938.

◀ *Scharnhorst*, fitted with the so-called 'Atlantic bow'.

Talk soon began to circulate in naval circles regarding the construction of a series of battleships of the 'H' class which had been forced on them by Hitler, although the proof of this was not forthcoming until the emergence of the *Werftbelegungsplan* (Shipyard Plan) of July 1937 specifying six 'Type 3' ships, 'H' to 'N', due for completion by 1 October 1944, and which proceeded on the assumption that Britain would be building a large class of battleships, automatically raising Germany's tonnage limit on the basis of her 35 per cent allowance.

It was hoped that construction work on the first two units of the 'H' to 'N' series might begin on 1 April 1939. These ships were the nucleus of the construction plan approved by Raeder on 21 December 1937, but special measures were necessary to ensure that it would be completed because all shipbuilding was subject to delays (*Bismarck* was 13 months late in completing). Hitler's decision on 5 November 1937 to guarantee the steel requirement ensured that all six units should be ready by the date he had stubbornly imposed (1 October 1944), but there was still a lack of shipyard capacity, despite a suggested cutback in merchant ship production. A variation known as 'New Construction Plan 7' came into force in December 1938 which allowed for the completion of four units by the relevant date, but on 17 January 1939 Hitler told Raeder that he expected his original demands to be implemented. The first orders for ships 'H' and 'J' were placed on 14 April 1939 and both were laid down a few weeks before the outbreak of war. The war situation led to the abandonment of the project on 21 September. The orders for ships 'K' to 'N', which had been placed on 25 May, were revoked in October 1939, although contracts for the manufacture of their 406mm (16in) guns, later to be installed in coastal batteries in Norway and France, remained in force.

While it was now no longer intended to build 'H' class battleships, the experience gained in the first two years of war was incorporated into the final drawings. The most important modification was an increase in the horizontal armour, and the armoured deck was designed to a maximum 200mm (7.9in). The main armament for the 'H-41' type ships to be laid down after the German victory would carry guns of 420mm (16.6in) calibre. As a result of these changes, the length of the projected vessel was extended to 275m (902ft 3in) and the standard displacement was increased by 10,400 tons.

Although there was a only a slim chance that the 'H-41' class would ever have been built, the Design Office was obliged by Hitler over the period 1942–1944 to draw up plans for several truly gigantic battleships which could never even have anchored in a German harbour. This was at a time when the future of the capital ship armed only with heavy guns had long been decided. Recent works on the subject have described these projects as purely academic, but the conversation of 26 August 1942 between Hitler and Raeder is significant. Despite all Raeder's arguments against the building of classical battleships, Hitler ordered him to find out from Krupps which calibre up to 530mm (20.8in) would offer the highest performance, technically and tactically, with regard to ship size. It should also not be overlooked that in January 1937 Hitler asked Raeder to prepare designs for a battleship of 100,000 tonnes. The horizontal and vertical armour of the 'H-44' design was substantially strengthened to a thickness of 330mm (13in) armour deck, which, with the projected 380mm (15in) belt armour, implies a very large displacement. The ships would have had diesel or diesel-turbine propulsion in order to achieve the required speed of 30 knots.

The main details of the individual designs were:

Design	Disp. (std)	Length	Beam	Main armament
'H-42'	83,268 tons	305m	42.8m	8 x 480mm
'H-43'	103,346 tons	330m	48.0m	8 x 480mm
'H-44'	122,047 tons	345m	51.5m	8 x 508mm

The possibility of a naval war against Britain was first intimated to the German Navy at the latest by 28 May 1938, when Hitler addressed the *Wehrmacht* chiefs on the subject of a possible Anglo-French-Czech coalition. It was appreciated that the only means of inflicting a mortal wound on this naval power was by means of cruiser warfare against her maritime trade, for which Germany had no need of huge battleships but rather numbers of fast *Panzerschiffe* with a large radius of action.

Raeder was an advocate of cruiser warfare, and on 19 August 1938 he put forward the proposal that, after battleships 'H' and 'J', attention should be redirected towards building battlecruisers which were better suited to Atlantic warfare. By September the Navy had made the first estimates of the size and number of ships required. The units, officially designated *Panzerschiffe* of approximately 20,000 tonnes displacement, would be built with all urgency, replacing a number of proposed light cruisers.

On 1 November 1938 Raeder suggested to Hitler the construction of twelve such *Panzerschiffe*, of which at least four were to be ready by the beginning of 1943. Hitler agreed, but remained adamant that all six large battleships should be completed by 1944 at the latest. The Z-Plan of 17 January 1939 provided for the completion by 1947 of ten of the twelve planned *Panzerschiffe*, offset by a reduction in the battleship programme. As this was not acceptable to Hitler, the *Panzerschiff* programme had to be curtailed in favour of battleship production.

Further problems arose regarding the question whether the 'P' class ships should be equipped with four 380mm (15in) guns in two twin turrets rather than the originally envisaged six 283mm (11in). On 9 June Raeder decided on a much bigger ship with three 380mm twin turrets; three units of the class would be brought into the Z-Plan at the beginning of July 1939 as battlecruisers 'O', 'P' and 'Q', while the *Panzerschiffe* 'P1' to 'P12' would be deleted from the programme the same month. With hindsight, Raeder's decision was correctly assessed, since the big *Panzerschiffe* of 22,145 tons standard displacement were weakly armed and had only eight 105mm AA weapons. This weakness was perpetuated in the design of the battlecruisers, the plans for which had been under development since 1938, initially without much prospect of their being realised. It is worth noting that the projects in the Z-Plan were still being referred to as Battleships 'O' to 'Q', and when they found a place in the Z-Plan in July nothing was known about them except their main armament.

Although orders for three of the ships were placed on 8 August 1939 and cancelled on 19 September, it remains uncertain whether the final designs ever existed. In standard reference works on German warships there is no consensus even on the standard displacement: Gröner quotes 28,900 tons, Breyer mentions 30,500 tons and Rohwer's Appendix in Dülffer gives 32,500 tons. However, it is clear that the armament was to be six 380mm (15in) and six 150mm (5.9in) guns, and the machinery a mixed system with four diesels for the outer shafts and

turbines for the central shaft. The ships would have been weakly protected for their size, as armour accounted for only 25 per cent of the displacement. Thus was represented the last stage of battlecruiser development in the *Kriegsmarine*.

Armament

The only heavy guns remaining aboard German battleships following the 1918 Armistice were antiquated 280mm (11in) models. It is an irony of history that the opening salvos in the Second World War, fired at Westerplatte, should have come from the ancient 280mm/L40 barrels of the pre-dreadnought cadet training ship *Schleswig-Holstein*.

The *Reichsmarine* received its first modern heavy guns about fifteen years after the end of the First World War. These were of 11in calibre to comply with the limitations imposed by the victorious powers. The new gun, designated 28cm SKC/28 and featuring an imposing barrel length, was fitted only to the first German 'pocket battleships' (*Deutschland* class), and in an improved version from 1934 for use on the proposed larger planned *Panzerschiffe* .

Krupps began the development of a 330mm (13in) gun and then in mid-1935 a 350mm (13.8in) weapon for the planned *Bismarck* class battleships, although these eventually received the 380mm (15in) guns which had been under development since 1934, while the improved 280mm (11in) SKC/34 gun became the provisional main armament for *Scharnhorst* and *Gneisenau*. The latter ships were, as we have noted, intended to carry a final armament of 380mm (15in) SKC/38 guns in three twin turrets. It was not realised either by Krupps or the *Kriegsmarine* until the autumn of 1939 that this particular model greatly interested the Soviet Navy, which ordered sixteen of them, although none was ever delivered.

Even the largest naval guns, which were manufactured for the 'H' class in small numbers, were eventually put to use in coastal batteries in northern Norway and along the English Channel. The careers of seven single-mounted 406mm (16in) SKC/34 weapons installed there are well documented.

German Heavy Naval Guns

Gun	Calibre	Wt of shell	Muzzle velocity	Range/ elevation
40.6cm SKC/34	406mm/L47	1,030kg	810 m/sec	36.4km/30°
38cm SKC/34	380mm/L47	800kg	820m/sec	35.6km/30°
28cm SKC/34	283mm/L54.5	330kg	890m/sec	40.9km/40°

All German capital ships received 105mm (4.1in) heavy and 37mm light AA guns as standard. The 105mm weapons (twin-mounted LC/31s aboard *Scharnhorst* and *Gneisenau* and LC/37s on *Tirpitz* and, partially, on *Bismarck*) were amongst the best in the world, although the same cannot be said of the smaller-calibre gun. Up to the time of the sinking of *Tirpitz*, there were no automatic anti-aircraft guns aboard any German capital ship other than the small and ineffective 20mm.

The rebuilt pre-dreadnought *Schleswig-Holstein*, flying the ensign of the *Reichsmarine*.

A 105mm flak mounting aboard *Gneisenau*.

Although the 3.7cm SKC/30 AA gun imparted an extraordinarily high muzzle velocity to the shell, its rate of fire of 30 rounds per minute could not provide an adequate defence against dive-bombers. An automatic 3.7cm AA gun which had been in service for some time with the Army would probably have averted the devastating attack mounted against *Bismarck* by slow British Swordfish torpedo bombers. The *Kriegsmarine* opted too late for the 3.7cm/M42 automatic, whilst the improved 3.7cm/M43 and the 4cm/Flak 28 Bofors were introduced (aboard a few cruisers) only during the final month of the war. Therefore the 20mm AA gun remained virtually the sole automatic weapon for use against dive-bombers, even though it had long been appreciated that only in exceptional instances could a single 20mm hit bring down an aircraft. The arrangement of the 2cm AA gun in the L38/43 quadruple grouping did nothing to improve the situation.

German Shipboard Anti-Aircraft Guns

Model	Calibre	Wt of shell	Muzzle velocity	Range/ elevation
10.5cm SKC/33	105mm/L65	15.10kg	900m/sec	12,500m/80°
3.7cm Flak M43	37mm/L57	0.64kg	820m/sec	4,800m/90°
3.7cm SKC/30	37mm/L65	0.75kg	1,000m/sec	6,700m/85°
2cm Flak 38	20mm L/65	0.12kg	875 m/sec	3,700m/85°

In the majority of cases the actual calibre length differed from that stated officially. The 40.6cm barrel was 52 calibres in length and the 38cm barrel was 51.7 calibres. The length of the bore was 48.6 and 48.4 calibres respectively. The barrel length of the 105mm gun was 65 calibres and the bore was 60.5 calibres. The 37mm Flak SKC/30 was 80 calibres in length.

German Battleships in the Second World War

Hitler's contemptuous attitude regarding the importance of the German naval forces and their handling during the course of the war, which he expressed to Raeder on 6 January 1943 after the failure of Operation 'Regenbogen' (the disastrous attack on the Russian convoy JW.51B by German surface forces), was unjustified. One month later he partially amended his view following a conversation with the newly appointed Commander-in-Chief, Grand Admiral Dönitz, who attempted to persuade him to concentrate all battleworthy heavy units in northern Norway for deployment from there. Hitler rescinded his order to scrap the heavy units, but reconstruction work on the damaged and disarmed Gneisenau was halted, and the once proud battlecruiser ended her days two years later as a blockship at Gdynia.

Following Hitler's order, the two remaining German capital ships made only two further sorties, the second of these resulting in the loss of Scharnhorst, which was operating alone. Until 13 February 1942 the two sister ships had achieved much success, and the use of Scharnhorst and Gneisenau in attacks on British convoys involving the sinking or capture of a large number of merchant vessels and an armed merchant cruiser (Rawalpindi in 1939) had been so effective that the British Admiralty was forced to employ battleships in the role of convoy escorts rather than in other operational areas where they were urgently needed. The foray between April and June 1940 as a diversion from the Norwegian campaign was also successful, and not merely because of the sinking of the aircraft carrier HMS Glorious and two destroyers on 8 June.

The death struggle of the battleship Bismarck on 27 May 1941 against a numerically superior force of British battleships is unique in the annals of naval warfare. Three days previously she had been in a German squadron which had also been matched against an enemy superior in firepower. The achievement of her gunners, not only in the engagement with Hood and Prince of Wales, but also in the final duel when confronted by the superior combined firepower of the battleships Rodney and King George V, instilled in the British such respect for the class that her sister ship Tirpitz was still profiting from it three years later. The mere presence of a large battleship in Norwegian waters had a powerful influence on British operations in the northern theatre up until the autumn of 1944. The measures taken by the Royal Navy in September 1943 (the attack by X-craft) and the Royal Air Force from September to November 1944 (massed attacks by heavy bombers carrying new 12,000lb 'Tallboy' bombs) are proof of this.

Scharnhorst/Gneisenau

Displacement: 35,540/38,700t;
32,000t standard
Dimensions: 226.0 x 30.0 x 9.9m
Machinery: 3 turbines, 3 shafts,
160,000shp
Fuel: 5,100t oil (6,000t including
reserve bunkers)
Speed/range: 31.0kt; 7,100nm at
19kt
Armour: Belt 350mm, 2 decks
155mm total, main armament
360mm, CT 350mm
Weight of armour: 14,245t =
40.2% of normal displacement
Armament: 9 x 283mm 54.5-cal,
12 x 150mm 55-cal
Anti-aircraft guns: 14 x 105mm
65-cal, 16 x 37mm 83-cal, 10
(later up to 38) x 20mm
Complement: 1,670 to 1,840

Scharnhorst, 1943.

Gneisenau following her 1939 refit.

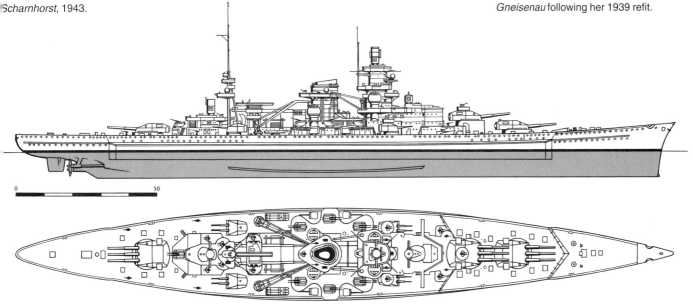

0   50

Ship	Builder	Laid down	Launched	Commissioned
Scharnhorst	Wilhelmshaven	16.05.1935	03.10.1936	07.01.1939
Gneisenau	DW-Kiel	06.05.1935	08.12.1936	21.05.1938

Soon after entering commission both ships returned to the builders for a refit, *Gneisenau*'s lasting until the spring of 1939 and *Scharnhorst*'s until September 1939; the so-called 'Atlantic bow' was fitted to both ships and *Scharnhorst*'s mainmast was moved 27m (88ft) aft. On trials both vessels exceeded their designed speed, *Gneisenau* by 0.3 knots and *Scharnhorst* by 0.5 knots.

During the Norwegian operation both units received serious damage when torpedoed by British submarines, repairs lasting until October (*Scharnhorst*) and November 1940 (*Gneisenau*). The ships acted together as commerce raiders between January and March 1941. During the Channel Dash on 12 February 1942 both were mined but reached German ports safely.

A Heinkel He 114 floatplane sits on *Gneisenau*'s catapult during the Naval Review of 22 August 1938.

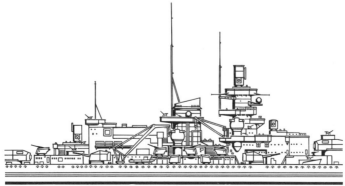

Gneisenau, 1942.

Scharnhorst underwent repairs at Kiel until October and transferred to northern Norway in March 1943. On 26 December 1943, on a commerce raiding expedition, she encountered a numerically superior naval force north-east of the North Cape and went down with 1,803 crew members after hits by numerous shells and fourteen torpedoes. *Gneisenau* was decommissioned after suffering serious bomb damage at Kiel on 27 February 1942. Following the original plans, she was removed to the newly built naval arsenal at Gdynia in Poland for rebuilding and re-arming, but work was abandoned in January 1943. The incomplete hull minus the forecastle was left at Gdynia and on 27 March 1945 was blown up in the harbour as the Soviet Army closed in. The wreck was raised and scrapped between 1947 and 1951.

Bismarck/Tirpitz

Displacement: 45,950/50,300t,
41,700t standard (*Tirpitz* –/
52,600t, 42,900t standard)
Dimensions: 241.6 x 36.0 x 9.9m
Tirpitz 10.6m)
Machinery: 3 turbines, 3 shafts,
138,000shp
Fuel: 6,450t oil (7,460t max.)
Speed/range: 29.0kt; 8,525nm at
19kt (*Tirpitz* 9,300nm at 16kt)
Armour: Belt 320mm, 2 decks
170mm total, main armament
360mm, CT 350mm
Weight of armour: 17,540t =
38.2% of normal displacement
Armament: 8 x 380mm 47-cal,
12 x 150mm 55-cal
Anti-aircraft guns: 16 x 105mm
65-cal, 16 x 37mm 83-cal, 12 x
20mm (*Tirpitz* 1944: 58 x 20mm)
Complement: 2,090 (*Tirpitz*
2,600)

Tirpitz in 1941.

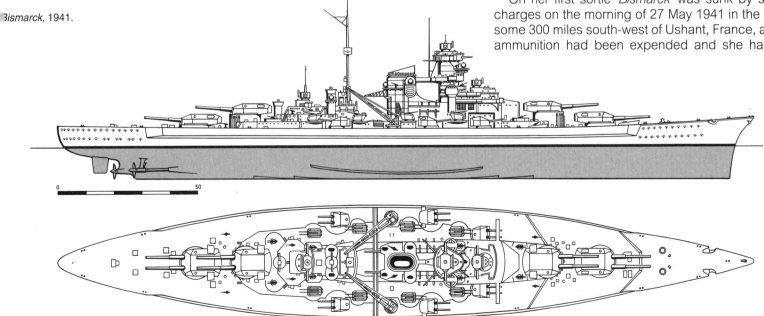

Bismarck, 1941.

Building work on *Bismarck* began on 16 November 1935. On trials *Bismarck* (Blohm & Voss turbines) reached 30.1 knots at 150,170shp and *Tirpitz* (Brown-Boveri turbines) 30.8 knots at 163,026shp.

On her first sortie *Bismarck* was sunk by scuttling charges on the morning of 27 May 1941 in the Atlantic some 300 miles south-west of Ushant, France, after her ammunition had been expended and she had been rendered *hors de combat*; 1,977 crew members were lost. *Tirpitz* was transferred to northern Norway in January 1942. On 22 September 1943 she was seriously

Ship	Builder	Laid down	Launched	Commissioned
Bismarck	BuV, Hamburg	01.07.1936	14.02.1939	24.08.1940
Tirpitz	Wilhelmshaven	02.11.1936	10.04.1939	25.02.1941

Bismarck after her commissioning in 1940.

damaged at Kaafjord by mines laid by the British midget submarines *X6* and *X7* and was not restored to a battleworthy condition until March 1944. On 3 April and 24 August that year she received numerous hits from British carrier aircraft and though damaged remained able to fight. Rendered unseaworthy on 15 September by a near-miss from a British heavy bomber (12,000lb, 5,440kg, 'Tallboy' bomb), she was brought to Tromsø on 17 October and anchored in shallow water, where she served as a floating battery. On 12 November 1944 she was hit by three 'Tallboys' and near-missed three times during a heavy air raid and capsized; 1,204 members of her crew were lost. The wreck was broken up piecemeal between 1948 and 1957.

H Class

Displacement: 56,440/63,600t; 52,600t standard
Dimensions: 266.0 x 37.0 x 11.0m
Machinery: 12 x MAN 9-cylinder diesels, 3 shafts, 165,000bhp
Fuel: 8,700t oil max.
Speed/range: 30.0kt; 19,200nm at 19kt
Armour: Belt 300mm, 2 decks 170mm total, main armament 385mm, CT 385mm
Weight of armour: 21,200t = 37.5% of normal displacement
Armament: 8 x 406mm 47-cal, 12 x 150mm 55-cal
Anti-aircraft guns: 16 x 105mm 65-cal in turrets, 16 x 37mm, 24 x 20mm
Complement: –

'H' was laid down by Blohm & Voss at Hamburg on 15 July 1939 and 'J' by Deschimag, Bremen, on 15 August 1939. Sister ships 'K' to 'N' were ordered on 25 April but the contracts were cancelled between 19 September and 10 October 1939; 'K' was scheduled to be laid down at Kiel on 1 October 1939. 30,000 tons of building material was ordered, of which 10,000 tons was delivered for the construction of the first two units. Building work was suspended on 21 September. The frequently quoted six 533mm (21in) underwater torpedo tubes were originally considered but not included in the final design.

France

Developments up to 1918

For decades the French Fleet lagged far behind that of Britain in terms of strength. This was certainly the case in 1905–06, when the dreadnought era began. In contrast to the orderly British squadrons of uniform battleships, the French possessed a miscellany of prototypes, the only common feature of which was their great age. Of 33 battleships, only 17 were less than fifteen years old. This was the consequence of a failed construction policy caused by the constant political changes in the Navy Ministry and the revamping of naval plans that accompanied them.

In 1906 Britain was no longer considered to be the enemy of France. The French had even acted for the British interest, basing the weight of the French naval presence in the Mediterranean; in 1906 the newest French capital ships were concentrated there despite a relaxation of tension in the relationship with their Italian rivals. What most concerned France was the expansion taking place of the German Navy, and a shift of emphasis from the Mediterranean to the Atlantic, and the building up of the bases at Cherbourg and Brest, was under consideration. It was for this reason that in 1905 the Navy Minister, Thomson, demanded a revision of the 1900 naval building programme to adjust the imbalance between the French and German Fleets. Thomson's plan was presented to the French Parliament in July 1905 and was approved on 9 April 1906 after long debate.

The authority for the new naval building programme and the debates on the 1906 naval estimates were of major importance for French capital ship construction. First, the number of battleships building was to be increased from three to six while a stop was to be put to the construction of armoured cruisers even though it had been planned to augment their numbers in the budget proposals. Secondly, the uselessness of the main armament both on existing units and proposed for the ships under construction was brought to light.

At the time the French had under construction two controversial units of the *Patrie* class and four of the *Verité* class, which had been laid down in 1901 and 1903 respectively and which, in spite of their size and their main armament of four 305mm (12in) guns, could fire a broadside of only nine 165mm (6.5in) and five 194mm (7.6in) shells. Accordingly, the approval sought in the 1906 budget proposals to order three comparable ships led to uproar.

The new ships would be armed with twelve 240mm (9.45in) guns in twin turrets in addition to the four 305mm (12in) main weapons and were therefore somewhat larger so as to carry them, but their armour would be the same as that adopted for the much-criticised *Patrie* class and the projected speed of 18 knots was below what had for some considerable time been accepted as the appropriate speed for a naval engagement.

The French battleship *Strasbourg* at Brest shortly before the Second World War.

The demand for turbine propulsion was rejected by the Minister as being a question 'too complicated and delicate', and in the event an 18,000-tonne ship was decided upon which could manage 19 knots, sacrificing some of the belt armour (reduced from 280mm, 11in, to 250mm, 9.85in) to gain the extra knot in speed. Not three but six of these ships were to be laid down in 1906. The French shipbuilding industry was at first unable to handle such demanding designs and it was not until mid-1907 that a start could be made on the class. When they were laid down, they were already more out of date than the *Patries*.

The name-ship, *Danton*, was completed within three years, but, being a battleship with two main calibres of gun, she was already technically obsolete. Following a study by French marine engineers with the assistance of the Royal Navy, the ships of the class were eventually to receive turbines, although when placed the orders had specified reciprocating engines. However, coal-firing was retained for the boilers, and the many weaknesses of the *Danton* class were compounded by the ships' high coal consumption.

By the end of 1907 four dreadnoughts were on the stocks in Germany and the German advantage in warship construction was increasing month by month. The French naval planners therefore proposed that the 1909–10 generation of battleships would displace 21,000 tonnes, be propelled by turbines and have a speed of 20 knots. The ships would carry four 305mm (12in) and twelve 240mm (9.45in) guns, subject to variations with a single calibre of heavy weapons. The calibres considered were 240mm and 305mm, and 274mm (10.8in). After consulting the planning offices of different shipyards, two projects were agreed upon in July 1908. Project 'A' was for a ship of 21,600 tonnes with four 305mm and twelve 240mm guns; Project 'B', a ship of 23,200 tonnes displacement, would have twelve 305mm guns in twin turrets. In October 1907 the Naval General Staff had instituted studies into the possible arrangements of heavy guns in triple or quadruple turrets, and a third project, 'C', emerged providing for twelve 305mm (12in) guns in two triple and three twin turrets.

Under the chairmanship of the Navy Minister, Picard (who had been in office since October 1908), Project 'A' (with two main calibres) was rejected as obsolete on 24 December 1908. A decision regarding the remaining two projects was not taken until the appointment as Navy Minister of the energetic Vice-Admiral Boué de Lapeyrère on 24 July 1909. He ordered the main armament of Project 'B' to be organised into twin turrets, and from Project 'C' incorporated the 138mm (5.4in) anti-torpedo guns and the system of armour protection. By December 1909 he had redesigned the circular gun turrets in the fashion of the British pattern and upgraded the medium battery from 18 to 22 barrels.

By the time approval was obtained for the first two units, the final designs had already been prepared, allowing a construction period of from 32 to 38 months. These first French dreadnoughts of the *Courbet* class contributed greatly to the modernisation of the Fleet, although after the four units had been completed they were found to have poor sea-keeping qualities, while the new model 305mm (12in) gun was a failure since it had a range of only 13.5km (14,750yd).

By July 1911 it was being assumed that a future naval war with Germany would be fought in the Cherbourg–Brest area, and this dictated that these bases, together with Toulon and Bizerta in the Mediterranean, should be further developed. Upgrading the latter two was necessary because of the increasing numbers of modern battle-ships entering service with the Italian and Austro-Hungarian fleets. At the end of September 1911 war broke out between Italy and Turkey, and Italian forces occupied Tripoli and a number of ports in Cyrenaica. Italy also captured two French freighters off the Cyrenaican coast, and as a result her relationships with France deteriorated rapidly. At the time the French Navy was almost paralysed as a consequence of the 'powder crisis' which had been in progress since 1907. On 25 September 1911 the three-year-old battleship *Liberté* blew up at Toulon after a powder explosion, killing 210 people. Most of France's stocks of powder had to be destroyed as a consequence.

The year 1912 was an important one for the French Navy. On 30 March the Second Chamber approved the new Navy Bill drawn up in February 1910 which proposed that by 1920 the Fleet should consist of four squadrons each with six active and four reserve battleships plus two scouts, the nature and size of which remained to be determined. The Navy Minister, Delcassé, knew that parity in naval strength with Germany could not be achieved and therefore concentrated his efforts in the Mediterranean in order to reduce the threat of Austro-Italian superiority there. The Anglo-French agreement regarding the division of operational areas between them assisted him in this, for Britain wanted to maintain only a single cruiser squadron in the Mediterranean at Malta, leaving France with a free hand to concentrate her Fleet there as from 12 September.

As a result of the growing Austro-Italian superiority in new battle-ships, the French Government decided to accelerate the implementation of the naval legislation of March 1912. In place of the original two there would now be three ships ordered in the same year, the unspeci-fied scouts were declared to be battlecruisers, and a new 340mm (13.4in) heavy naval gun which had become available would be fitted into the turrets of the battleships *Paris* and *France*. However, these intentions were frustrated by an enforced pause in the construction programme.

During the designing of the first French 'super-dreadnoughts' it was realised that the capacity of the repair docks at all French bases limited new ships to a size little larger than that of the *Courbet* class, and the construction of a larger class having six 340mm (13.4in) guns became impossible. However, by omitting the sixth 305mm (12in) turret from the amended Project 'B', a ship with five 340mm (13.4in) turrets was conceivable as the weight of the 340mm turret (1,200 tons as opposed to 970 tons) was within the specification. Thus was born the *Bretagne* class, three units of which were ordered from May to July 1912.

The Navy Law of 1912 provided that for each of the next two years two battleships would be laid down. Two ships were ordered in December 1912 and a further pair on 30 July 1913. The Naval Staff had also decided that from 1913 each squadron would consist of eight units instead of the previous six, so the three units of the *Bretagne* class would be supplemented by a fourth vessel, to be achieved by increasing the *Normandie* class, approved in 1913, to five units. The fifth unit was *Béarn*, ordered at the beginning of December that year and on which building started five weeks later.

The first preliminary design for a 25,000-tonne battleship in February 1912 had envisaged either three quadruple turrets of 340mm (13.4in) calibre or four quadruple 305mm (12in) turrets. The option of the quadruple turret represented a solution to a quandary as the Admiralty was demanding ever more powerful battleships which could not be accommodated in the small docks possessed by the French. By substituting quadruple turrets a saving of weight could be achieved concurrent with a reduction in the extent of the armoured citadel. The Admiralty approved Project 'A7 *bis*' on 26 October 1912.

The turbines installed in the *Danton* class ships were uneconomical and the consumption of coal by their boilers, especially when cruising, was enormous, and it was therefore decided that the ships still building would have a mixed propulsion of turbines for speed and reciprocating engines for cruising, although *Béarn* would be fitted with turbines only. Construction of all five units proceeded rapidly up to the outbreak of war, when building was suspended. In the event, this signalled an end to French battleship construction for almost two decades.

Unfulfilled Programmes

The naval legislation provided for the laying down of four more battleships in 1915. As it was clear by the end of 1913 that the dry docks at Brest, Lorient and Toulon would have to be enlarged by the summer of 1916, it became unnecessary to take into account the dimensions of the planned units. Their names were decided upon on 3 December 1913: the name-ship of the class would be *Lyon* and her sister ships *Lille*, *Duquesne* and *Tourville*. For some considerable time the armament of these ships remained unresolved: should the increase in hitting power be achieved by a greater gun calibre or by carrying more barrels?

Amongst the variations were designs with twenty 305mm (12in), several with fourteen to sixteen 340mm (13.4in) and finally those with eight to ten 380mm (15in) guns. The latter calibre met with approval and the 27,500-tonne variant armed with eight 380mm guns in four twin turrets might have been realised had the 380mm gun been developed. As it was, time was a commodity at a premium, and so it was decided to settle for an increase in the number of guns carried while retaining the 340mm (13.4in) calibre, of which two new models with a choice of two barrel lengths were available. The first, of 45 calibres, was a modification of the M12 model already under production for the *Bretagne* class. The longer passage of the projectile through the barrel promised an improved performance and the ballistics of the new, longer shell were expected to achieve a torpedo-like effect. The second gun had a barrel length of 50 calibres. The Naval Staff selected the first model, later designated M12M.

Two ship designs were discussed in detail. The smaller, 27,500-tonne vessel was designed to carry fourteen guns and the larger design, which was eventually adopted on 24 November 1913, sixteen guns in four quadruple turrets. The principal details of the latter ship were a displacement of 29,000 tons (full load), dimensions of 190 x 29 x 8.7m, a speed of 23 knots and an armament of 16 x 340 mm and 24 x 138mm (5.4in), plus anti-aircraft weapons. Armour was the same as that for the *Normandie* class, but there was a new system of underwater protection. Geared turbines which had been installed on the destroyer *Enseigne Gabolde* for trials were incorporated into a mixed propulsion system. Construction was intended to begin in the first quarter of 1915, but the war brought the project to a swift end; similarly, any intention of building battlecruisers in the future was also abandoned. Later designs were no more than diploma work by students at the Naval Academy: they were never discussed officially and so will not be reviewed here.

French Battleships in 1914

Pre-dreadnoughts predominated in the French Navy's order of battle of 1 August 1914. The Second Squadron consisted of the five *Patrie* and *Verité* class ships plus the incompletely armed *Paris* and *France* which had been out of active service for six and seven years respectively. Four older battleships, *Suffren*, *Bouvet*, *Saint Louis* and *Gaulois*, formed the Supplementary Division of the battle fleet and these were soon deployed in the Dardanelles. Finally, the elderly *Jaurequiberry* and *Charlemagne* were listed for home duties as the Special Division.

Bouvet, displacing 12,200 tons, completed in 1898 and mounting two 305mm (12in) and 2 x 274mm (10.8in) 1893-model guns, took part in the attack on Turkish emplacements but was mined and sunk on 18 March 1915. Her three sister ships of 11,300 tonnes, *Charlemagne*, *Saint Louis* and *Gaulois*, had been completed between 1899 and 1900 and carried four 305mm (12in) 1893-model guns. In 1914 they acted as convoy escorts and brought African troops to Marseilles. Transferred to the Dardanelles in 1915, *Gaulois* was mined and badly damaged there on 18 March. She was run aground and later salved, but was eventually sunk on 27 December 1916 in the Aegean by *U47*. The other two ships served in the eastern Mediterranean. *Saint Louis* was disarmed in April 1917.

Suffren, of 12,750 tons, completed in 1903 and mounting four 305mm 40-calibre guns, bombarded Turkish emplacements on a number of occasions in 1915. She was returning to Brest for repair on 26 November 1916 when she was torpedoed and sunk with all hands by *U52* off Lisbon.

The ships of the Second Squadron suffered no casualties. Between August and December 1914 they participated in attacks in the Adriatic and then remained in Greek waters and the Aegean, where they were never involved in fighting. After the war they were immediately disarmed; with the exception of *Patrie*, which served as a training ship until 1927, all had been scrapped by 1922 .

Armament

French naval gunnery had a poor reputation before the war. The explosions aboard *Iéna* in 1907 and *Liberté* in 1911 highlighted the poor quality of the nitro-cellulose powder in use in the French Navy. Most of it was eventually dumped at sea, but replacement supplies containing a new stabiliser were still found to be unsatisfactory. The quality of French armour-piercing shell, with its inadequate charge of melinite, also left much to be desired.

Beginning with the *Courbet* class, all French battleships were fitted with the roomy barbette-type turrets copied from the British design which permitted a higher rate of fire, although the range of the French 340mm (13.4in) and 305mm (12in) guns was inferior that obtaining in other navies. Not until 1916, when agents reported details of the range of modern Austrian naval guns, were the turrets modernised to increase the angle of elevation of the French barrels and so extend the range. Even so, these measures had not been implemented on all French capital ships by the time the war ended.

No French big-gun ship fought in a sea battle in the First World War. The action on 16 August 1914 involving French battleships which culminated in the sinking of the elderly Austro-Hungarian protected cruiser *Zenta*, in which 500 rounds were fired and eight hits observed, is not generally regarded as a classical sea engagement

Anti-aircraft defence was weak, but the French Fleet was not exposed to real aerial danger and the installation of a few adapted 47mm cannon on the roofs of the 204mm and 305mm turrets was deemed sufficient protection. These weapons were later replaced by modified 75mm M1897 35-calibre field guns which fired 6.2kg (13.7lb) shells and had a muzzle velocity of 570m/sec (1,870ft/sec).

Details of Heavy Guns aboard French Capital Ships

Gun	Model	Wt of shell	Muzzle velocity	Range/elevation (1915)	Range/elevation (1917)
340mm 45-cal	M.1912	540kg	795m/sec	14.5km/12°	18.0km/18°
305mm 45-cal	M.1910	432kg	783m/sec	13.5km/13°	16.0km/15°
305mm 45-cal	M.1906	418kg	780m/sec	13.0km/13°	–
240mm 50-cal	M.1900/06	220kg	800m/sec	13.0km/13°	18.0km/18°

Danton Class

Displacement: 18,350/19,800t
Dimensions: 144.9 x 25.8 x 9.2m
Machinery: 4 turbines, 4 shafts, 22,500shp
Fuel: 2,030t coal max.
Speed/range: 19.0kt; 3,370nm at 10kt
Armour: Belt 255mm, deck 93mm total, main armament 320mm, CT 300mm
Weight of armour: 4,950t = 27.0% of normal displacement
Armament: 4 x 305mm 45-cal, 12 x 240mm 50-cal
Anti-aircraft guns: 4 x 47mm naval guns added during the war
Complement: 900 to 920 (wartime)

On trials all units exceeded their designed speed, *Condorcet*, *Diderot* and *Vergniaud* (Niclausse boilers) by 0.2–0.5 knots and the rest (Belleville boilers) by 1.2–1.6 knots. At outbreak of war these ships formed the First Squadron, which was main component of the French Fleet. Forays into the Adriatic resulted in one success, the sinking of the small Austro-Hungarian cruiser *Zenta* on 16 August 1914. Four ships of the squadron took part in the action of 16 December 1916 forcing the Greek Government to alter its political alignment: when *Mirabeau* bombarded the Royal Palace at Athens, Greece conceded.

All the ships remained in Greek waters until the end of the war except *Danton*, which was torpedoed and sunk off Sardinia by *U64* on 19 March 1917. *Voltaire* was torpedoed and damaged by *U48* on 11 October 1918.

Following the capitulation of Turkey, the four remaining ships passed through the Turkish Narrows in November and were engaged against the Bolsheviks in the Black Sea. *Mirabeau* grounded on 13 February 1919 on the Crimean coast but was refloated in April. However, the damage was serious and the ship was towed away and disarmed at Toulon. She was stricken from the Fleet on 27 October 1921, then used as a target ship; she was scrapped in 1928. *Vergniaud* was used for experiments from October 1921 and was broken up in 1929. The three other vessels ships remained in commission after the war but only as training ships from 1927. *Diderot* was scrapped in 1937, *Voltaire* was broken up in 1938 and *Condorcet* was sunk at Toulon in 1944 and sold for scrapping in 1945.

Ship	Builder	Laid down	Launched	Commissioned
Danton	Arsenal de Brest	09.02.1908	04.07.1909	01.06.1911
Mirabeau	Arsenal de Lorient	04.05.1908	28.10.1909	01.08.1911
Diderot	St Nazaire	20.10.1907	19.04.1909	01.10.1911
Condorcet	St Nazaire	23.08.1907	20.04.1909	01.10.1911
Vergniaud	Bordeaux	00.07.1908	12.04.1910	02.01.1912
Voltaire	La Seyne	08.06.1907	16.01.1909	01.10.1911

Courbet Class

Displacement: 23,500/25,850–26,000t
Dimensions: 165.0 x 27.9 x 9.0m
Machinery: 4 Parsons turbines, 4 shafts, 28,000shp
Fuel: 2,700t coal + 300t oil
Speed/range: 21.0kt; 4,600nm at 10kt, 1,140nm at 20kt
Armour: Belt 270mm, deck 120mm total, main armament 320mm, CT 300mm
Weight of armour: 6,672t = 28.4% of normal displacement
Armament: 12 x 305mm 45-cal, 22 x 138.6mm 55-cal
Anti-aircraft guns: 1914–16: 4 x 47mm, later 4 x 75mm
Complement: 1,100

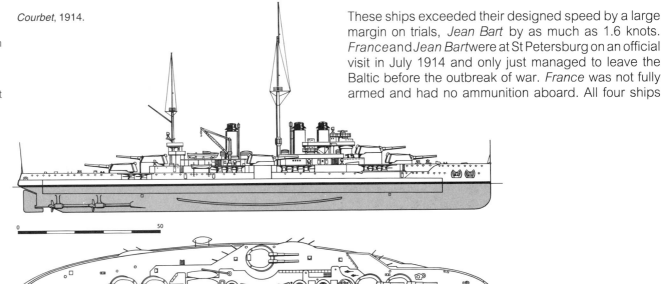

Courbet, 1914.

These ships exceeded their designed speed by a large margin on trials, *Jean Bart* by as much as 1.6 knots. *France* and *Jean Bart* were at St Petersburg on an official visit in July 1914 and only just managed to leave the Baltic before the outbreak of war. *France* was not fully armed and had no ammunition aboard. All four ships

Ship	Builder	Laid down	Launched	Commissioned
Courbet	Arsenal de Lorient	01.09.1910	23.09.1911	19.11.1913
Jean Bart	Arsenal de Brest	15.11.1910	22.09.1911	05.06.1913
Paris	La Seyne	10.11.1911	28.09.1912	01.08.1914
France	St Nazaire	30.11.1911	07.11.1912	00.08.1914

were transferred to the Mediterranean from August 1914. *Courbet* was the flagship of the *Armée Navale*. *Jean Bart* was the only ship of the class to be damaged, when she was torpedoed in the southern Adriatic by the Austro-Hungarian *U12*. The angle of elevation of all guns was

Paris at full speed.

Danton, the name-ship of a French semi-dreadnought class.

raised from 13 to 15 degrees. All ships survived the war. *France* was lost in Quiberon Bay on 26 August 1922 after grounding but the remaining three vessels were still in service at the outbreak of the Second World War.

Bretagne Class

Displacement: 23,700/26,000t
Dimensions: 165.0 x 26.9 x 9.1m
Machinery: 4 Parsons turbines, 4 shafts, 29,000shp
Fuel: 2,700t coal + 300t oil
Speed/range: 20.5kt; 2,800nm at 18.75kt
Armour: Belt 270mm, deck 120mm total, main armament 340/250mm, CT 314mm
Weight of armour: 7,683t = 32.5% of normal displacement
Armament: 10 x 340mm 45-cal, 22 x 138.6mm 55-cal
Anti-aircraft guns: 4 x 47mm (1918: 2 x 75mm 35-cal, 2 to 4 x 47mm)
Complement: 1,130

Bretagne, 1916.

Provence in 1918.

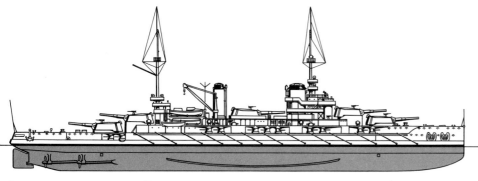

Ship	Builder	Laid down	Launched	Commissioned
Bretagne	Arsenal de Brest	22.07.1912	21.04.1913	10.02.1916
Provence	Arsenal de Lorient	21.05.1912	20.04.1913	01.03.1916
Lorraine	St Nazaire	07.11.1912	30.09.1913	10.03.1916

The ships were a development of the *Courbet* class but had larger calibre guns of 340mm which, despite their relatively poor range of 14,500m (15,850yd) at 12 degrees' elevation, were highly thought of. The increase in elevation to 18 degrees worked into *Lorraine*'s 'Q' turret by the war's end extended the range to 18,000m (19,680yd). The main turret armour varied between 400mm on the face of 'Q' turret to 250mm on the two superimposed turrets and 340mm on the others. All three ships remained in service after the war.

Normandie Class

Displacement: 25,230/27,500t
Dimensions: 175.6 x 27.0 x 8.7m
Machinery: 2 reciprocating steam engines + 2 Parsons turbines, 4 shafts, 40,000shp
Fuel: 2,700t coal + 300t oil for supplementary firing
Speed/range: 21.5kt; 6,500nm at 12kt, 1,800nm at 21kt
Armour: Belt 300mm, deck 120mm total, main armament 340mm, CT 300mm
Weight of armour: 7,637t = 30.3% of normal displacement
Armament: 12 x 340mm 45-cal, 24 x 138.6mm 55-cal
Anti-aircraft guns: 4 x 47mm
Complement: ?

In August 1914 it was decided to abandon construction on these ships after they had been launched, and with the exception of *Béarn* all were stricken on 18 April 1922; the hulls were sold for scrap in 1924. It was intended that the last ship approved, *Béarn*, would be fitted with four Parsons turbines driving four shafts. Her construction was resumed in December 1918 and she was launched in April 1920. After a specially erected flight deck was successfully used for take-offs and landings, full conversion of the ship to an aircraft carrier proceeded, taking from August 1923 to May 1927. *Béarn,* which was the only French carrier in existence at time of the capitulation in June 1940, was relegated to the role of training hulk in 1947 and scrapped in 1967.

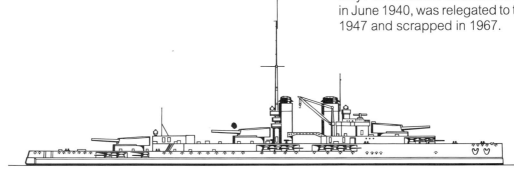

Normandie (original design)

Ship	Builder	Laid down	Launched	% complete
Normandie	St Nazaire	18.04.1913	19.10.1914	65
Lauguedoc	Bordeaux	18.04.1913	01.05 1915	49
Flandre	Arsenal de Brest	01.10.1913	20.10.1914	65
Gascogne	Arsenal de Lorient	01.10.1913	20.09.1914	60
Béarn	La Seyne	10.01.1914	–	25

Béarn, the sole French aircraft carrier prior to the Second World War.

75

Developments up to 1945

France was a victorious power after the First World War but had been left in ruins economically. The Navy was also affected by the country's increasing social problems. In military and political terms France had strengthened her position in the east and south-east of Europe and the Near East, but the old rivalry with Italy increased after the fascist take-over there in 1922. The strength of the Italian Fleet was the decisive factor in French naval building programmes up to 1939.

Building Programmes up to 1940

With the exception of seven capital ships, the postwar battleships and armoured cruisers of the French Navy were hopelessly outdated, but in spite of this many semi-dreadnoughts and large but poorly armed cruisers remained in service for years. Consideration was also given to finishing the five incomplete but obsolete *Normandie* class units on which work had been suspended in 1914. On 25 February 1919 the Naval Staff demanded a comprehensive modernisation of the project, and in particular the raising of the ships' speed by three knots to 24 knots, improvements to the internal protection by the addition of anti-torpedo bulges and an increase in the range of the 340mm (13.4) main armament. It would have demanded a national sacrifice of enormous proportions to satisfy these technical requirements, but work on the project was abandoned on 19 September when it was learnt that Italy had decided not to proceed with the completion of the *Caracciolo* class.

The Washington Treaty permitted France and Italy to maintain an aggregate battleship tonnage of 175,000 tons standard. As France was short of this limit, the treaty allowed her to replace old pre-dreadnoughts before 1931, for example by completing two new 35,000-ton battleships. On 19 April 1922 new French naval laws set down the battleship strength as 177,000 tonnes (175,000 tons standard); no new units were to be built before 1931 and the life of a battleship was deemed to be 20 years.

The terms of the Washington Treaty had laid down that most old battleships should be disarmed and, in most cases, scrapped forthwith, and France decided that, in addition to her seven dreadnoughts, three *Danton* class 'semi-dreadnoughts' would remain in service, *Condorcet* until 1931 and *Voltaire* and *Diderot* until 1936 (although in reserve). On 26 August 1922 the battleship *France* was lost through stranding, but even though this casualty could have been replaced by a new vessel it had become the preferred French policy (as was the case with the Italians) to build cruisers. Instead, the available battleships were given refits which included installing a tripod mast with new fire control equipment and increasing the range of the secondary armament by raising the maximum elevation of the guns.

In May 1925 the Navy Minister requested funds from Parliament for the construction of two ships each of 17,500 tonnes, armed with eight 305mm (12in) guns and capable of up to 35 knots. The Bill was not approved and he had to be content with a further modernisation of the six remaining battleships, mainly re-boilering them for oil-firing. The decision for a total reconstruction, or at least for a major refit, was not taken until much later.

Between 1931 and 1935 all three units of the *Bretagne* class received new narrow-tubed boilers for pure oil-firing; the underwater torpedo tubes were stripped out and the old model 340mm (13.4in) guns were replaced by the newer M1912 model manufactured for the *Normandie* class. The centre 340mm turret on *Lorraine* was unshipped and a catapult and hangar for four seaplanes were installed in its place. Despite all these improvements, the ships were not suitable for the new conflict which was already looming.

By the late 1920s the speedy construction of a large and modern Italian Fleet was leading to the eclipse of French naval superiority in the Mediterranean. As this state of affairs would have been sealed by the 1930 London Naval Treaty, France declined to sign the protocol and it was not until January 1931 that British diplomacy succeeded in uniting the two rivals in an agreement as to the number and size of their new capital ships up to 1936. However, the treaty was not ratified. Both powers were permitted to complete three battleships of 23,700 tonnes (23,333 tons standard) within the period.

A ship of this displacement and armed with eight 305mm (12in) guns appeared in the Parliamentary Bill of 18 June 1931 and was approved, but the keel laying was much postponed after April 1932 because of numerous revisions to the project and the choice of a 330mm (13in) calibre for the main armament. Although it was allegedly the German 10,000-tonne *Deutschland* class *Panzerschiffe* which dealt the French battleship project its death blow, it would seem more probable that the three Italian *Pola* class heavy cruisers then under construction, massively armoured and fast, were the real reason behind the decision to build a fast battlecruiser with 330mm (13in) guns: whereas the smaller units already suggested in June 1931 would have sufficed for the pursuit of the slower and lightly armoured 'pocket battleships', larger and more powerfully armed ships would have been needed to combat the new Italian cruisers. *Dunkerque*, on which work officially commenced on Christmas Eve 1932, fulfilled the latter requirements. No urgency was shown to build a sister ship until the reconstruction of two Italian battleships was made known in the autumn of 1933, and this led to approval being sought in 1934 for *Strasbourg*. Building was started the same year, but the Italians were quicker: a month earlier they had laid the keels of two 35,000-tonne battleships to be armed with 381mm (15in) guns.

The French, who were meanwhile designing a larger version of *Dunkerque* with three quadruple turrets housing 340mm (13.4in) guns were suddenly faced with the need for a ship with 380mm (15in) calibre weapons instead. In haste they settled for the *Dunkerque* profile, which had the main artillery grouped in two quadruple turrets on the forecastle. The armour to could thus be reduced by reason of the relatively smaller citadel. With armour accounting for 41 per cent of the ship's weight including normal armament, *Richelieu* belonged to the previous generation of battleships in this respect.

The fast tempo of Italian battleship construction, combined with the effects of the Anglo-German Naval Agreement, compelled the French Admiralty to act quickly, and in the 1935 Budget approval was obtained for one and later two 35,000-tonne battleships. The first of these was laid down in October 1935, but the second was long delayed because *Strasbourg* was occupying the building dock at St Nazaire. The limited building capacity was seriously to hinder later battleship construction. *Gascogne*, approved in 1938, had not even been laid down at the time of the capitulation in 1940 as the dock at St Nazaire was occupied by *Jean Bart* until March that year.

The second ship authorised in 1938, *Clémenceau*, was laid down at Brest immediately following *Richelieu*'s launch in January 1939, but building was interrupted for three months after the outbreak of the Second World War and when German forces arrived in June 1940 they discovered an incomplete hull on which little progress had been made.

Battleships not Completed

Richelieu was the only 35,000-tonne battleship to be completed in France during the Second World War. Despite the part she played in the battle at Casablanca, *Jean Bart* remained uncompleted throughout the war and first entered service in 1955 after numerous modifications had been made to her original design. The ships authorised in 1938 also underwent changes in design. *Clémenceau* was given twelve 152mm (6in) guns in four triple turrets in a different arrangement and a larger number of automatic anti-aircraft weapons, while *Gascogne* actually departed from the *Richelieu* class design as her 380mm (15in) guns were set one turret forward and one aft to enable the ship to fire directly astern.

Four 'super-battleships' were approved in a new naval construction programme on 15 April 1940, a few weeks before the German invasion. These ships would have had a standard displacement of 45,000 tons and have carried twelve 380mm (15in) guns in three quadruple turrets. Orders for these warships, which were known as the *Alsace* class, were never placed.

French Battleships in the Second World War

French battleships had little opportunity for action before the capitulation on 25 June 1940. Apart from the unsuccessful search by the two battlecruisers for the 'pocket battleship' *Admiral Graf Spee* in the autumn of 1939, the old *Lorraine*, supported by five British cruisers, bombarded the Italian-occupied port of Bardia in Cyrenaica on 21 June 1940. She was based at Alexandria and was disarmed there by the British after the capitulation. Her sister-ship, *Bretagne*, was lost on the same day, 3 July, when the British instituted Operation 'Catapult', which had as its objective, within the terms of the Armistice, the demobilisation of the French Mediterranean Fleet concentrated at Mers-el-Kebir. After declining a proposal to join forces against the Germans, the partially disarmed French ships were bombarded by three British battleships. *Bretagne* was sunk as a result of the attack with the loss of 1,129 of her crew, while her sister ship *Provence* and the modern *Dunkerque* were badly damaged. Only the damaged *Strasbourg* succeeded in escaping to Toulon. *Provence* and *Dunkerque* were later salvaged at Mers-el-Kebir and, following temporary repairs, were then towed to Toulon, where they were scuttled by their crews on 27 November 1942 to prevent them falling into the hands of the Germans. *Strasbourg* suffered the same fate.

On 8 November 1942 the Allies landed in North Africa. The incomplete *Jean Bart*, lying at Casblanca, returned fire with her one 380mm (15in) turret when attacked by the US battleship *Massachusetts* armed

with nine 16in (406mm) guns but was so badly damaged that she did not leave port until the war's end.

Only *Richelieu* escaped a fate similar to that of the other French battleships. Shortly before her completion she sailed from Brest on 18 June 1940 for Dakar, where she was attacked and damaged by British torpedo aircraft on 8 July. Her main armament remained intact, however, and intensive fire from her 380mm (15in) guns was used in an attempt to repel the heavy British attack on Dakar between 23 and 25 September. In this action she scored hits on the British battleship *Resolution*.

Richelieu remained at Dakar until 1942, when she was passed to the Free French without opposition. The ship was finally completed in New York between February and September 1943 and given a heavy anti-aircraft armament. From March 1944 she supported the British Eastern Fleet in numerous operations against Japanese-held bases in Indonesia and around the Andaman and Nicobar Islands.

The elderly *Lorraine* was also deployed operationally during the final phases of the Second World War. At the end of May 1943 she was placed at the disposal of the Free French and after having her anti-aircraft armament upgraded she was used to bombard German coastal installations in southern France and, from December 1944, in the Gironde estuary. On 15 April 1945 she took part in the attack against the German Atlantic fortifications at Royan. This was the last occasion on which French battleships were employed in European waters during the Second World War.

Armament

Having appreciated the shortcomings in range associated with their naval gunnery during the First World War, the French subsequently carried out a modernisation programme to increase the angle of elevation and the calibre of their guns from 305mm (12in) to 340mm (13.4in). Following the improvements, the 305mm gun had a range of 21km (23,000yd) and the 340mm gun could reach targets 24.2km (26,450yd) distant at an elevation of 23 degrees. Even better results were achieved using the newly developed, 1924-model long shells (1.5m, 4ft 11in, long as opposed to 1.25m, 4ft 1in), and with these the range of the 340mm gun was increased to 26.6km (29,000yd)

In the autumn of 1919 the French gun manufacturer Schneider acquired half of the share capital in the Bohemian firm of Skoda, and all the technical documentation for the latest Austro-Hungarian 350mm (13.8in) naval gun was removed to France and never returned. The Schneider experts openly admitted the superiority of the Skoda gun in comparison with all French heavy artillery, and they utilised the expertise of the Skoda gunmakers in the design and construction of the first French postwar weapons.

It is noticeable that the French showed little interest in the Skoda 305mm (12in) gun even though their battleship projects between 1925 and 1931 had been based solely around this calibre, and all the more surprising was the sudden appearance of a 1931-model 330mm (13in) weapon for *Dunkerque* approved that same year. The Navy was more satisfied with the old 340mm (13.4in) than the new 330mm (13in), but no experience of the latter weapon had been obtained under war conditions to allow it to be assessed properly. However, the perform-

Dunkerque's quadruple main turrets.

ance claimed for it was impressive. On the other hand, the 1935-model 380mm (15in) gun was given generally positive reviews.

The anti-aircraft weaponry of the French battleships remained one of the great weaknesses of the vessels' armament throughout. The Navy had adhered for too long to the 75mm gun, and even after their final refit the ships carried only seven or eight of them in single mountings. At this time modern 90mm calibre guns had been long available but had been installed only aboard cruisers. There was nothing exceptional about the 1932-model 100mm AA gun, but it was nevertheless fitted on the modernised *Lorraine* and on board *Richelieu*.

The 130mm AA guns installed on *Dunkerque* and later on *Strasbourg* were a thorough disappointment. This model, which had been conceived as a dual-purpose weapon, lacked any of the qualities desirable in an effective AA piece, and the fitting of two twin mountings in one turret proved an impracticality. It had been intended to arm *Richelieu* with automatic AA guns but these had not emerged from the develop-

ment stage by the outbreak of war. The 1933-model 37mm twin AA gun was not an automatic weapon (it fired 42 rounds a minute per barrel), and only the 13mm heavy machine gun fulfilled this function. *Richelieu* was not provided with an adequate defence against dive bombers until her refit in the United States.

Main Details of French Naval Guns

Gun	Model	Wt of shell	Muzzle velocity	Range/elevation
330mm 50-cal	1931	560kg	870m/sec	41.7km/35°
380mm 45-cal	1935	884kg	830m/sec	41.7km/35°
75mm 50-cal	1922	5.9kg	850m/sec	9,000m/90°
100mm 45-cal	1930	13.5kg	785m/sec	10,000m/80°
130mm 45-cal	1932	29.5kg	840m/sec	14,000m/75°
37mm 50-cal	1933	0.73kg	810m/sec	4,000m/80°

Courbet/Paris (as in 1939)

Displacement: 22,189 tons standard
Anti-aircraft guns: 7 x 75mm 50-cal
Other details as for earlier entry

▼▼ *Courbet* as she appeared in 1939.

Paris, 1940.

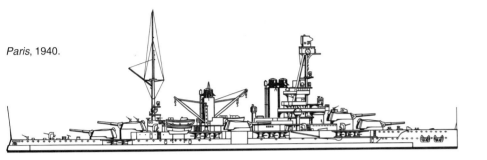

Ship	First reconstruction	Second reconstruction
Courbet	00.07.1923–00.04.1924	00.01.1927–00.01.1931
Paris	00.10.1922–00.11.1923	00.08.1927–00.01.1929
Jean Bart	00.10.1923–00.01.1925	00.08.1929–00.09.1931

All three vessels served as training ships from 1931, *Jean Bart* from 1938, under the name *Océan*, only as a hulk. In their first refit all received a tripod foremast, and the forward pair of funnels was replaced by a single, broad funnel on *Jean Bart* and *Courbet*. In the second refit the ships were partially re-boilered but it was decided not to reconstruct them totally.

These outdated units played no part in the war. *Courbet* withdrew from Cherbourg as the Germans advanced and was interned by Britain at Portsmouth after the French capitulation. She was run ashore off the Normandy coast as a breakwater on 10 June 1944 and broken up there after the war. *Paris* received light bomb damage off Le Havre on 11 June 1940. She put into Brest for repair, then escaped to Britain, where she used as an accommodation ship for personnel of the Polish Navy in exile. She was towed to Brest in 1945 and scrapped from 1956.

Bretagne Class (as in 1939)

Displacement: 23,700/25,200t; 21,838t standard (*Lorraine* 23,000/24,500t)
Machinery: 43,000shp after re-boilering
Fuel: 2,600t oil
Armament: From 1935, *Lorraine* 8 x 340mm 45-cal, all ships 14 x 138.6mm 55-cal
Anti-aircraft guns: 8 x 75mm 50-cal, 4 x 37mm 50-cal, 8 x 100mm 45-cal (*Lorraine*)
Other details as for earlier entry

In the first refit the angle of elevation of the 305mm (12in) guns was increased. *Provence* and *Bretagne* were bombarded by British battleships at Mers-el-Kebir on 3 July 1940. *Bretagne* exploded and capsized with heavy loss of life. She was raised in 1952 and broken up. *Provence*, on fire, was run aground but salved and towed to Toulon in November 1940. Scuttled there in November 1942, she was raised by the Germans but scuttled again as a blockship in 1944. The wreck was broken up 1949. *Lorraine* survived the war. Interned at Alexandria in July 1940, she was surrendered to the Free French on 31 May

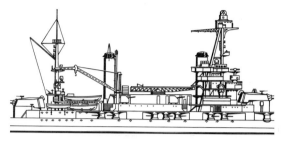

Lorraine, 1936.

Bretagne, 1940.

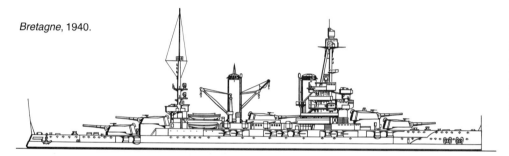

1943 and after a refit in which her catapult was removed and 14 x 40mm and 25 x 20mm automatic AA guns of US origin were installed was deployed initially in the Mediterranean and later in the Gironde estuary. She became a training ship in 1945, was stricken in 1953 and was broken up from January 1954.

Ship	First reconstruction	Second reconstruction	Third reconstruction
Provence	00.02.1922 to 00.07.1923	00.12.1925 to 00.07.1927	00.11.1931 to 00.08.1934
Bretagne	00.06.1919 to 00.10.1920	00.05.1924 to 00.09.1925	00.07.1932 to 00.11.1934
Lorraine	00.11.1921 to 00.12.1922	00.11.1924 to 00.08.1926	00.09.1934 to 00.11.1935

Lorraine after her third refit, showing the aircraft catapult amidships.

Dunkerque/Strasbourg

Displacement: 30,750/35,200t; 27,900 tons standard
Dimensions: 209.0 x 31.0 x 8.6m
Machinery: 4 turbines, 4 shafts, 112,500shp
Speed/range: 29.5kt; 7,500nm at 15kt, 3,600nm at 30kt
Armour: Belt 240mm, deck 175mm total, main armament 330mm, CT 355mm
Weight of armour: 10,665t = 34.5% of normal displacement
Armament: 8 x 330mm 50-cal
Anti-aircraft guns: 16 x 130mm 50-cal DP, 8 x 37mm 50-cal, 32 x MG
Complement: 1,430

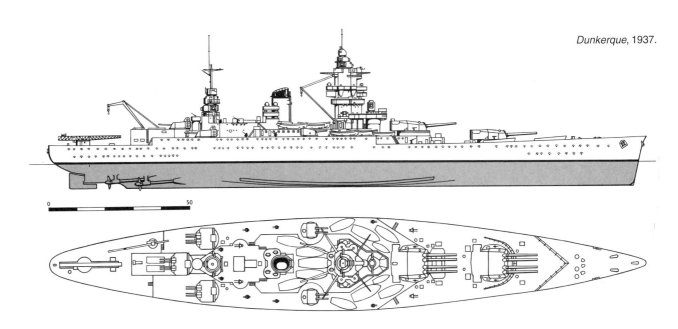

Dunkerque, 1937.

Ship	Builder	Laid down	Launched	Commissioned
Dunkerque	Arsenal de Brest	25.02.1933	02.10.1935	01.05.1937
Strasbourg	St Nazaire	25.11.1934	12.12.1936	00.12.1938

Strasbourg in 1939.

Work on Dunkerque commenced officially on 24 December 1932 although her keel was not laid until two months later. On trials the ships made up to 31kt.

Dunkerque's only wartime deployment before the French capitulation was an unsuccessful hunt for German 'pocket battleships' in the Atlantic in the autumn of 1939. Both ships were attacked by British battleships at Mers-el-Kebir on 3 July 1940. Dunkerque was badly damaged by shellfire and could not escape. Three days later she sustained further serious damage from carrier-borne aircraft even though not directly hit: a torpedo struck the submarine-chaser Terre Neuve lying alongside and the explosion of the latter's depth charges tore a long gash in the battlecruiser's hull. Dunkerque made for Toulon after temporary repairs on 20 February 1942; she left dry dock in August 1945 but did not enter service again and was scrapped thirteen years later.

Strasbourg escaped from Mers-el-Kebir to Toulon, where she was scuttled in shallow water on 27 November 1942. The hulk was raised by the Italians in April 1943 and hidden in remote bay, but the ship was discovered by the USAAF and bombed and sunk on 18 August 1944. Raised again in August 1945, she was used for explosives trials for several years before being scrapped in 1955.

Richelieu Class

Displacement: 40,900/46,000t; 37,960 tons standard
Dimensions: 242.0 x 33.1 x 9.6m
Machinery: 4 Parsons turbines, 4 shafts, 150,000shp
Fuel: 6,800t oil
Speed/range: 30.0kt; 8,500nm at 14kt
Armour: Belt 330mm, deck 150–170mm upper deck, 40–50mm lower deck, main armament 430mm, CT 340mm
Weight of armour: 16,800t = 41.1% of normal displacement
Armament: 8 x 380mm 45-cal, 15 x 152mm 55-cal designed (9 x 152mm actual in wartime)
Anti-aircraft guns: *Richelieu* 12 x 100mm 45-cal, 8 x 37mm 50-cal, 36 x 13mm MG; *Jean Bart* provisionally 4 x 90mm 50-cal, 6 x 37mm, 10 x MG
Complement: *Richelieu* 1,670

The commissioning date for *Richelieu* is nominal as the ship was forced to evacuate to Dakar on 18 June 1940 before completion. The keel-laying dates for *Jean Bart* and *Clémenceau* are official dates, and that for the latter corresponds to the date when *Richelieu* left her building dock. Building work on *Jean Bart* actually commenced during 1937. *Richelieu* made 32.5 knots on trials.

Richelieu remained at Dakar following the British attacks of July and September 1940. She sailed to the USA for repairs and a full refit in January 1943 where her radar and AA armament were upgraded, the ineffective French 37mm semi-automatics being removed and replaced by 57 x 40mm Bofors and 50 x 20mm Oerlikons from US stocks, and her aircraft catapult was landed. After six months of operations in South-East Asia, *Richelieu* returned Toulon on 1 October 1944 and was at Casablanca for refit until January 1945; she was then deployed with the British East Indies Fleet, returning to Europe in the spring of 1946. Placed in reserve until 1956, she was scrapped in Italy from 1968. The incomplete *Jean Bart* fled to Casablanca in June 1940 and with

her one operational 380mm turret offered heroic resistance to the US battleship *Massachusetts* on 8 November 1942. She was reconstructed from 1945 to early 1949 and was fully armed by 1952. Recommissioned in 1955, she was stricken in 1961, sold for scrapping in 1969 and broken up in Japan in 1970.

Note: The French Naval Dockyards were located at Brest (Arsenal de Brest) and Lorient (Arsenal de Lorient). The private yards were Forges et Chantiers de la Mediterranée; La Seyne, Toulon (La Seyne); Forges et Chantiers de la Gironde, Bordeaux (Bordeaux), Ateliers et Chantiers de la Loire; St Nazaire (St Nazaire); and Chantiers et Ateliers de St Nazaire (Penhoët).

Ship	Builder	Laid down	Launched	Commissioned
Richelieu	Arsenal de Brest	22.10.1935	17.01.1939	15.06.1940
Jean Bart	St Nazaire	12.12.1936	06.03.1940	After WW2
Clémenceau	Arsenal de Brest	17.01.1939	–	–

Richelieu, 1940.

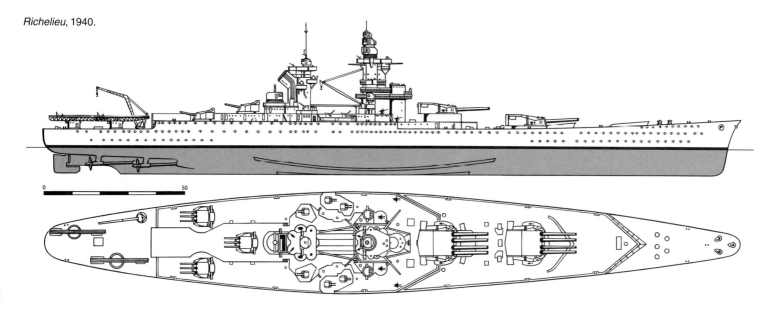

Richelieu in 1943, after her US refit.

Great Britain

Developments up to 1918

When the keel of the battleship *Dreadnought* was laid, world-political factors were extremely favourable for Britain. Her traditional rival, France, had been won over as an ally in March 1906 while Japan, which had been a close ally of the British Empire since January 1902, had handed out catastrophic defeats at sea and on land in the war with Russia, Britain's potential enemy to the east of Europe and in the Far East.

Only what it perceived as a challenge to its mastery in the North Sea caused the Royal Navy concern. Germany's fleet was still far inferior, but it was growing annually, and a great industrial power such as Germany was capable of forcing the pace of naval armament. Yet in 1905 the British Admiralty was convinced that the Navy could further increase its advantage in naval strength by building two pioneering battleship classes.

At the end of 1904 the British Mediterranean Fleet, with bases in Malta and Gibraltar, comprised twelve modern battleships. The Channel Fleet had more than eight battleships at its southern Irish base at Berehaven, with over ten armoured cruisers at Portland. Five battleships and three armoured cruisers were on the China Station, principally because of the continuing Russo-Japanese war.

By 1906 the situation had changed completely. The battleships in the Far East had been recalled to home waters and the Mediterranean Fleet at Malta had been reduced. In its place a new Atlantic Fleet had been formed at Gibraltar, from where its ships could easily reinforce the groups in the North Sea or the Mediterranean. The Channel Fleet, which included thirteen modern battleships, had moved its bases eastward to Portland, while three reserve divisions were stationed at Devonport and in the Thames Estuary.

Nevertheless, there was clearly a need for new bases along the North Sea coast, for the Berehaven–Devonport–Portsmouth–Chatham chain was still too far removed from the strategic area in question. In 1906, therefore, construction work began on a large naval base in the Firth of Forth, shipyards and dock installations being built at Rosyth. The use of Scapa Flow in the Orkneys as a fleet anchorage was not discussed until shortly before the First World War, when its possible usefulness was appreciated in connection with a new naval strategy, the 'distant blockade' of 1912.

At the end of 1908, the most powerful battleships and the first dreadnoughts were concentrated in the newly formed Home Fleet and Channel Fleet, whilst the number of older ships based at Malta and Gibraltar was gradually reduced. In April 1909 there was a significant

The Spithead Naval Reviews were used to demonstrate British naval power to the world. The photograph shows HMS *King George V* shortly before she was stricken in 1926.

redistribution when the Home Fleet became the nucleus of a battle fleet with four active squadrons, two of which would be based in the Firth of Forth.

The growing might of the German High Seas Fleet, together with unsuccessful diplomatic approaches to Germany concerning a possible naval limitation agreement, led to revised British naval concentrations announced in March 1912 by Winston Churchill, the new First Lord of the Admiralty. The manner in which the distribution changed between 1904 and 1912 is shown in the following table, which details assemblies of British battleships (no unit older than 15 years) and armoured cruisers (no unit older than 10 years):

Year	Malta, Gibraltar	Home waters	German Fleet
1904	12 + 4	14 + 10	12 + 2
1906	17 + 10	24 + 12	15 + 2
1908	14 + 8	28 + 17	18 + 4
1912	2 + 2	41 + 13	28 + 3

The figures for 1912 illustrate the new British naval strategy which allocated the Fleet two principal roles: the protection of the approaches to British ports, and the future distant blockade of Germany. The geographical position of Great Britain was most advantageous for the implementation of the second part of the plan. The powerful Grand Fleet was better able to control the North Sea from a string of bases along a lengthy coastline than the German High Seas Fleet, which possessed only one base, Wilhelmshaven, and that unfavourably positioned. By laying two mine barriers, one between Scapa Flow and Norway and the other across the mouth of the English Channel, enemy heavy units could be prevented from breaking out into the Atlantic for operations against British shipping, while the barriers would also greatly hinder any breakthrough by Germany's own blockade-runners.

Battleship Construction to 1914

In March 1905, when the Admiralty approved the project for the world's first dreadnought, six King Edward VII class battleships were building, two of which had yet to be launched. The construction of two Lord Nelson class ships had been approved in the 1904 Budget but the vessels had not yet been laid down. At the centre of attention in the higher echelons of the Navy was a new ship, the future Dreadnought, which would be completed just one year after her keel was laid. Her first trials did indeed take place precisely twelve months after work started on her, but a further six months was to elapse before she entered commission. She was a complete success, particularly as regards her new turbine propulsion—for Royal Navy capital ships, the reciprocating steam engine was henceforth a creature of the past.

In order to consolidate Britain's lead, Lord Fisher included four sister ships in the 1906 budget proposals. The figure was reduced to three, and these units, of a slightly modified design, were ordered that autumn. The Bellerophon class had thinner belt armour compared to Dreadnought but better watertight subdivision. The ineffective 3in (76mm) anti-torpedo guns were abandoned in favour of 4in (102mm) calibre weapons.

In 1907 the Admiralty encountered much stiffer opposition in its attempt to obtain capital for four more ships. The British Government, and Parliament, argued that the growth in capital shipbuilding in Germany had been less than expected, and eventually the Navy received approval for three ships that year, the fourth, Foudroyant, being postponed to 1908, when she was built as the singleton Neptune, and to an amended design. A new feature of the three ships authorised in the 1907 Budget was a 12in (305mm) gun of a new pattern (Mk XI) with a longer barrel and improved performance, although in other respects the St Vincent class was merely a somewhat enlarged and modified development of Dreadnought.

Only two capital ships, a battleship and a battlecruiser, were agreed in the 1908 Budget, although the total capital apportionment for the Navy was 3 per cent greater than the previous year on account of the financing of the Rosyth naval base.

In response to internal political pressure and the German Supplementary Naval Law of 1908, the construction of ten capital ships (six battleships and four battlecruisers) was authorised in 1909. The governments of Australia and New Zealand underwrote the cost of one battlecruiser each, and the capital resources for six battleships and two battlecruisers were provided in two halves by the 1909 Budget and a Supplementary Budget on 28 August that year.

Two of the six battleships were improved sister ships of the Neptune, originally planned as the fourth St Vincent class unit, which had diagonally positioned 12in (305mm) wing turrets in the so-called echelon arrangement, 'X' turret being stepped above 'Y' turret at the stern. Staggered turrets were also a feature of Colossus and Hercules, approved in 1909. The belt armour of these ships was thicker, but the designers took a retrograde step in underwater protection by omitting the transverse torpedo bulkheads. The staggered wing turrets fell short of expectations regarding a strengthening of the broadside, and they never appeared again on British capital ship designs.

The third ship authorised in 1909 was called a 'super-dreadnought' by the technical press and this term was subsequently applied to any vessel equipped with guns of a similar or larger calibre. Orion carried 13.5in (343mm) guns, the 12in (305mm) weapon having reached the end of its development: the necessary penetrative power at longer ranges could only be achieved by an increase in calibre at this stage of technical development. For battleships of the new generation, the midships installation of the 13.5in (343mm) turret was planned from the beginning. HMS Orion entered service after a 25-month construction period. On her trials it was found that she rolled very heavily, but otherwise the ship was a success, especially as regards her fighting qualities and improved armour.

The four King George V class battleships approved in 1910 were an improved version of Orion, as were the four larger and more heavily armed Iron Duke class units which were approved in the 1911 Budget. Iron Duke was equipped with a medium battery of 6in (152mm) calibre which had become essential as the size and efficacy of destroyers increased. This class was the last to have coal-fired boilers.

Approval for a new class of powerful, well armoured and fast capital ships was given in June 1912, and by February 1913 work was under way on four units. The Navy unexpectedly received a fifth ship as a gift from Malaya, and by the spring of 1916 the Grand Fleet had at its disposal a group of five mighty battleships of the Queen Elizabeth class

Five slower but more powerfully armed battleships with a mixed boiler firing system had been planned for the 1913 construction programme which fulfilled the Admiralty's need for a force for use in the North Sea, requiring a top speed of no more than 21 knots. However, as the question of fuel supply was an important matter, Sir Eustace Tennyson d'Eyncourt, the Director of Naval Construction, produced a design which was principally a further development of the *Iron Duke* with 15in (381mm) guns. The First World War had broken out in the meantime and Lord Fisher had returned to the Admiralty in October 1914. He at once put a temporary stop to building work on the new *Royal Sovereign* class and cannibalised the material being used for two of the hulls (*Repulse* and *Renown*) for the construction of two battlecruisers of the same name, as he needed fast ships for his North Sea strategy. This thinking also lay behind the important alterations to the concept of the *Royal Sovereign* class.

Royal Oak and *Resolution* had already been launched when the decision was taken to fit oil-fired boilers to all units in order to achieve a better performance (40,000shp instead of 31,000) and a top speed of 23 knots, although when the class was completed in 1916 it was discovered that none of the ships was actually able to make 22 knots. Nevertheless, they were strong and well armoured vessels with a new form of protection against hits below the waterline, the anti-torpedo bulge or 'blister'. This bulge ran for approximately two-thirds of the ship's length on both sides of the hull, and projected some 6ft (2m) from the outer hull beneath the waterline. It was designed to absorb the energy of an explosion in either an empty or flooded cell system. The new system was fitted to *Ramillies* as she was the only ship of the class still on the slipway, delaying her completion until the summer of 1917. From her trials in September of that year it was found that *Ramillies*' top speed of 21.5 knots was only 0.4 knots less than that of other units of the class. The addition of anti-torpedo bulges of an improved type was ordered for her sister ships, but only *Revenge* and *Resolution* had been fitted with them by the end of the war. With HMS *Ramillies* the building of battleships by Britain came to a temporary halt in 1918, as did designs for further battleships.

Battlecruiser Programmes

A new type of ship for the Royal Navy was born on 22 June 1905 when approval was given for the design of the super-powerful armoured cruiser advocated by Lord Fisher (the term 'battlecruiser' was not adopted by the Royal Navy until 1912). HMS *Inflexible* was laid down on 5 February 1906, and within eight weeks the keels of two sister ships were also on the stocks. In contrast to the genesis of the *Dreadnought*, no information respecting the true nature of the new design was allowed to seep out, and the Admiralty spread false rumours as to the armament and other details of the 'improved armoured cruiser of the *Minotaur* class'.

The news that Great Britain was building three super-fast capital ships armed with eight 12in (305mm) guns came as an even greater surprise to the world at large than did the launching of *Dreadnought*. Only during the war, however, did the appalling deficiencies of the new type, which had been developed according to the principle 'speed is the best protection', become manifest. By mid-1908 all three units had undergone their trials: they manoeuvred well, were not bad sea-keepers, had surprisingly good machinery and exceeded their projected speed. On the debit side, their building costs were extravagant.

For the 1908 Budget, Fisher requested a slightly enlarged version of the *Invincible*—the later *Indefatigable*—together with two further units of the class whose costs would be borne by the governments of Australia and New Zealand. These three ships were authorised and ordered in 1909. For the 1909 programme, the Admiralty contemplated ordering two more *Indefatigable* class ships until they heard that the new German *Moltke* class battlecruisers would be materially larger than the British units, and it was decided instead to reply with a battlecruiser version of *Orion*, with an armament of 13.5in (343mm) guns. *Lion* and *Princess Royal* were, accordingly, financed in the two Budgets of 1909 and building began at once, their keels being laid before those of the two *Indefatigable* class 'Dominions battlecruisers', whose weapons technology was surpassed by that of the new design. A propaganda campaign accompanied the new vessels, which were given the nickname 'The Splendid Cats'.

Princess Royal was designed for 34.7 knots on her trials and *Lion* was said to be able to maintain a speed of 31 knots. The actual top speed obtained was 3 knots less, although this was still faster than the German battlecruisers. Their protection was a different matter: although the belt armour of the British vessels was thicker, the horizontal armour was insufficient and fell below contemporary requirements. 'Super-battlecruisers' armed with eight 13.5in (343mm) guns would have to fight at long ranges, and a strong horizontal defence against plunging shells was more important than an impressive outward appearance. The shortcomings of the design were clearly demonstrated in the Dogger Bank action and at Jutland. Nowadays, even British technical authors tend to condemn 'The Splendid Cats' as fine looking battlecruisers but costly and inferior capital ships.

It was intended that the three ships of the *Lion* class —the third unit was named *Queen Mary*—should be augmented by a fourth in 1911, but when Japan ordered a better-armed and better-armoured battlecruiser of similar size from Armstrongs that year, Sir Philip Watts, then DNC, was asked to draw up something comparable. Accordingly, on 18 August 1911 the Design Committee was shown a proposal with an improved main turret layout compared to the *Lion* class, and with a secondary battery increased in calibre to 6in (152mm). A more extensive belt armour was incorporated, but protection was still insufficient. Coal-firing was retained, though on trials *Tiger*'s boilers were found to consume vast quantities of fuel and the ship failed to attain her projected speed of 30 knots. A sister-ship, *Leopard*, which was reportedly envisaged for the 1912 programme, was not proceeded with: the new regime at the Admiralty under Winston Churchill preferred fast battleships, and the new *Queen Elizabeth* class was ordered instead.

When Lord Fisher returned to office in October 1914 he pursued his pet theory about fast battlecruisers, and at the beginning of 1915 orders had been placed for the building of *Repulse* and *Renown*. Both ships showed good sea-keeping qualities in their trials in September 1916 and also reached the prescribed speed. Their horizontal armour was so inadequate, however, that, only four weeks after *Repulse* had been commissioned, Admiral Jellicoe, the Commander-in-Chief of the Grand Fleet, ordered the immediate reinforcement of the deck armour

The 15in (381mm) twin turrets of HMS *Queen Elizabeth*.

and stipulated that armoured bulkheads be built in below the conning tower. The refit was begun a month later at Rosyth and was completed in January 1917, when *Renown*, too, was taken in hand. The two ships of the *Courageous* class, on which construction was begun at Fisher's insistence during the first half of 1915, were more problematic, and these 'large light cruisers' were later converted into aircraft carriers.

As a result of the lessons learnt at Jutland, *Hood*, the name-ship of a new class—on which work began on the day of the battle, 31 May 1916—was much modified before her completion on 5 March 1920. She was then the most modern capital ship in the world, displacing 43,335/47,430t, armed with eight 15in (381mm) 42-calibre and twelve 5.5in (140mm) 50-calibre guns, with four single 4in (102mm) 50-calibre AA, and capable of a speed of 31 knots and a range of 7,500nm at 14 knots.

Ships Requisitioned by the Royal Navy

In August 1914 four capital ships were under construction in British yards for overseas buyers. Two of these vessels had been completed and were ready for delivery to Turkey. As a result of the swiftly deteriorating political situation and the dubious reliability of that particular country, however, the ships were impounded. The subsequent commissioning of *Erin* and *Agincourt* (see below, pages 252–4) under the White Ensign brought about a welcome increase in the strength of the Grand Fleet.

Chile had also ordered two fast and heavily armed ships. *Almirante Cochrane* had not yet left the slip, but *Almirante Latorre* was nearly complete, and the Royal Navy was very interested in taking possession of the latter, despite her non-standard 14in (356mm) main armament.

Because of her traditionally good relationships with Chile, Britain opted for the path of negotiation, and agreement was reached on 9 September 1914 for the purchase of the latter unit while building work on the other would be halted. *Almirante Latorre* was renamed *Canada*, and on completion she was attached to the 4th Battle Squadron of the Grand Fleet on 15 October 1915 (for further details see pages 248–9). The second hull was eventually completed in 1918 as the aircraft carrier *Eagle*.

▼ HMS *Agincourt*—formerly the Turkish *Sultan Osman I*—in 1918.

▼ ▼ HMS *Erin* (ex Turkish *Reshadieh*) in 1918.

British Battleships in the First World War

On 1 August 1914 the Home Fleet (renamed the Grand Fleet from 7 August) included two battle squadrons of pre-dreadnoughts, while the Channel Fleet had 23 of these ships distributed among four squadrons; two further units were stationed in the Bay of Bengal. None of these battleships was employed operationally during the war, although, particularly until 1916, they carried out secondary duties such as coastal bombardment and convoy protection. The majority were sunk in the process, eleven of them following torpedo hits or after striking mines. Other pre-dreadnoughts served as floating batteries in harbours overseas, stripped of much of their armament mainly because their 12in (305mm) guns were required for installation aboard the large monitors. Two of the ships became minelayers after their heavy guns had been

HMS *Canada* in 1918. This ship was originally built for Chile.

removed. By the end of the war very few pre-dreadnoughts were still in service.

With the exception of the elderly *Revenge* (allocated for scrapping before the war but which under the name *Redoubtable* bombarded the coast of German-occupied Flanders during the first year of hostilities), the following pre-dreadnought classes were still in service at the beginning of 1914:

No	Class	Launched	Disp.	Armament (normal)
9	*Majestic*	1894–96	15,000t	4 x 12in, 12 x 6in
6	*Canopus*	1897–99	13,400t	4 x 12in, 12 x 6in
3	*Formidable*	1898–99	14,700t	4 x 12in, 12 x 6in
5	*London*	1899–1902	14,500t	4 x 12in, 12 x 6in
5	*Duncan*	1901	13,700t	4 x 12in, 12 x 6in
8	*King Edward VII*	1903–05	16,000t	4 x 12in, 4 x 9.2in
2	*Swiftsure*	1903	12,100t	4 x 10in, 14 x 7.5in

Majestic was torpedoed and sunk by *U21* at Gallipoli in 1915. Of the *Canopus* class, *Goliath* (hit by three torpedoes) and *Ocean* (sunk by mine and gunfire) were lost the same year. *Formidable* was sunk by *U24* on 1 January 1915 and *Irresistible* was mined and sunk in the Dardanelles in March 1915. *Bulwark*, of the *London* class, sank in November 1914 after a magazine explosion. Of the *Duncan* class, *Russell* was mined and sunk in April 1916 and *Cornwallis* was torpedoed by *U73* on 9 January 1917. *King Edward VII* was mined and sunk in January 1916 and her sister ship *Britannia* was sunk by *UB50* on 9 November 1918. Of the *Swiftsure* class, *Triumph* was sunk by *U21* on 25 May 1915 off Gallipoli. By 1919 no pre-dreadnoughts remained in service, and by 1922 the survivors had all gone to the breakers' yards.

Apart from *Queen Elizabeth*, which bombarded Turkish fortresses in the Dardanelles, British dreadnoughts were used for their primary purpose only in the final phases of the Battle of Jutland, where their efforts were not decisive. As for the battlecruisers, after their triumphant baptism of fire against inferior opposition at the Falklands in 1914, their inability to take punishment led to the near-loss of *Lion* at Dogger Bank and to the destruction of three of their number at Jutland.

Armament

The standard 12in (305mm), 40-calibre naval gun of the British pre-dreadnoughts was superseded by a model with a longer barrel (45-calibre) originally intended for the two *Lord Nelson* class battleships but actually first fitted in *Dreadnought*. It was also fitted in the *Bellerophon* class battleships and the first three battlecruisers.

In 1907 the *St Vincent* class was fitted with a 12in (305mm) gun with an even longer barrel, followed two years later by the 13.5in (343mm) weapon. The British armaments industry not only supplied the Royal Navy but also manufactured new or improved models of various calibres for foreign navies which were never introduced in British service.

The largest gun fitted to ships of the Royal Navy was the 15in (381mm) piece introduced in 1912 by the Admiralty and installed in all subsequent capital ship designs, although Armstrongs also developed an 18in (457mm) gun in 1916 (for installation in HMS *Furious*), the only gun of such calibre to be fitted aboard a warship anywhere before the end of the First World War.

The Royal Navy persisted with the wire-wound barrel because of its lower cost of production and the possibility of re-use at the end of its life, although in comparison with the Krupps inner-cased barrel it had less han 40 per cent of the life of the latter. Moreover, the Admiralty opposed he installation of triple turrets, and their preference for twin turrets was o be confirmed throughout the First World War.

British heavy guns, and particularly the 305mm (12-inch), were not particularly outstanding developments, but the 15in (381mm) can lightly claim to be a major world achievement, and this weapon was also used successfully in the Second World War. The 13.5in (343mm) Mk VI gun appeared only on *Erin*, and the 12in (305mm) Mk XIII aboard *Agincourt*.

Gun	Wt of shell	Muzzle velocity	Range/elevation
8in/40 Mk I	3,320lb	2,400ft/sec	28,980yd/30°
5in/42 Mk I	1,920lb	2,460ft/sec	23,730yd/20°
4in/45 Mk I	1,588lb	2,500ft/sec	24,275yd/20°
3.5in/45 Mk VI	1,400lb	2,440ft/sec	23,075yd/20°
3.5in/45 Mk V	1,400lb	2,495ft/sec	23,840yd/20°
2in/50 Mk XI	851lb	2,860ft/sec	18,900yd/20°
2in/45 Mk XIII	851lb	2,700ft/sec	20,000yd/15°
2in/45 Mk X	851lb	2,725ft/sec	18,590yd/13.5°
2in/40 Mk IX	851lb	2,560ft/sec	17,060yd/13.5°

British capital ships carried AA guns in the first year of the war and in only a few cases were these adaptations of the 47mm and 57mm weapons. Vickers had developed a 3in (76mm) 45-calibre AA weapon before the war and this was accepted by the Royal Navy in 1913 for ships under construction. Its shells reached a theoretical height of 25,600ft (7.8km) at a rate of fire of 15 rounds per minute. The Admiralty was not impressed with the gun's ballistic performance (shell weight 12.5lb, 5.7kg; muzzle velocity 2,500ft/sec, 760 m/sec) and in 1916 the 4in (102mm) 45-calibre AA gun was introduced which had a better performance at the same rate of fire. At a muzzle velocity of 2,650ft/sec (810 m/sec), the 31lb (14.1kg) shell would reach a height of over 31,000ft (9.5km). This weapon could still be found in single mountings aboard British capital ships at the beginning of the 1930s.

Note: There were naval shipyards on the south coast of Britain at Portsmouth and Devonport. The private yards on the east coast were Thames Iron Works, London, which was in liquidation in 1912; Armstrong Whitworth & Co., Elswick (abbreviated in the tables that follow as Armstrong, Elswick); and Sir W. G. Armstrong, Walker-on-Tyne (Armstrong, Newcastle). The private shipyards on the west coast were Cammell Laird & Co, Birkenhead; the Fairfield Shipbuilding & Engineering Co., Govan, Glasgow (Fairfield); John Brown & Co., Clydebank; Palmers Shipbuilding & Engineering Co., Greenock (Palmers); Scotts Shipbuilding & Ironworks, Greenock, Clyde (Scotts); Vickers, Barrow-in-Furness/Birmingham (Vickers, Barrow); W. Beardmore & Co., Dalmuir, Clyde (Beardmore); and Harland & Wolff, Belfast.

Lord Nelson/Agamemnon

Displacement: 16,350/18,100t
(*Lord Nelson*)
Dimensions: 129.5 x 24.2 x 8.2m
Machinery: 2 reciprocating
engines, 2 shafts, 16,750ihp
Fuel: 2,200t coal
Speed/range: 18.0kt; 9,180nm at
10kt
Armour: Belt 305mm, deck
51mm, main armament 305mm,
CT 305mm
Armament: 4 x 12in 45-cal, 10 x
9.2in 45-cal
Complement: 820

The *Lord Nelson* class, authorised in the 1904 Budget, were considered as an alternative to the *Dreadnought* while on the slip, particularly as regards their machinery: the two sister ships were the last British capital units with reciprocating steam engines. *Lord Nelson* reached 18.7 knots and *Agamemnon* 18.5 knots on trials, exceeding the contract speed. Completion was delayed by the transfer of the original 12in (305mm) guns to *Dreadnought*.

During the war both ships served at first in the Channel, then from February 1915 until 1918 in the Aegean. They took part in the bombardment of Turkish fortifications at the Dardanelles; the armistice with Turkey was signed aboard *Agamemnon* in November 1918.

Lord Nelson was decommissioned in 1919 and sold for scrapping at the end of 1920. *Agamemnon* was adapted as remote-controlled target ship and served as such until 1926; she was scrapped in 1927.

Ship	Builder	Laid down	Launched	Commissioned
Lord Nelson	Palmers	18.05.1905	04.09.1906	00.10.1908
Agamemnon	Beardmore	15.05.1905	23.06.1906	26.06.1908

HMS *Agamemnon* prior to the First World War.

Dreadnought

Displacement: 18,400/21,060t

Dimensions: 158.5 x 25.0 x 9.0m

Machinery: 4 Parsons turbines, 4 shafts, 23,000shp

Fuel: Up to 2,900t coal + 1,120t oil

Speed/range: 21.0kt; 6,600nm at 10kt

Armour: Belt 280mm, deck 76mm, main armament 280mm, CT 280mm

Armament: 10 x 12in 45-cal, 28 (from 1917 20) x 3in 45-cal

Anti-aircraft guns: From 1917: 4 x 3in 45-cal

Complement: 700 (810 wartime)

Builder: Portsmouth DY (laid down 02.10.1905; launched 10.02.1906; commissioned 11.12.1906)

HMS *Dreadnought* in 1913.

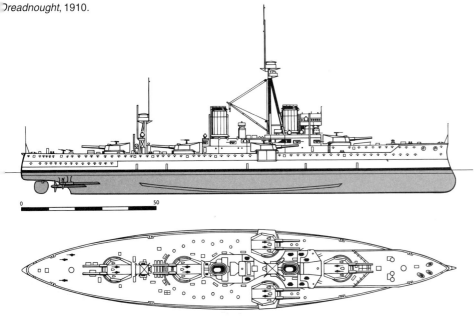

Dreadnought, 1910.

On her trials in October 1906 the world's first all-big-gun capital ship reached a speed of 21.5 knots at 24,712shp. At the outbreak of war she was the flagship of 4th Battle Squadron She rammed and sank *U29* in the North Sea on 18 March 1915. She was refitted from April 1916 on account of her poor condition and was thus absent from Jutland at the end of May 1916. She was transferred to reserve on 7 August 1917, stricken on 31 March 1920, sold for breaking up on 9 May 1921 and scrapped in 1923.

Bellerophon Class

Displacement: 18,900/22,700t
Dimensions: 159.1 x 25.1 x 9.5m
Machinery: 4 Parsons turbines, 4 shafts, 23,000shp
Fuel: 2,700t coal max. + 850t oil
Speed/range: 20.5kt; 5,700nm at 10kt
Armour: Belt 254mm, deck 76mm, main armament 280mm, CT 280mm
Weight of armour: 5,430t = 28.7% of normal displacement
Armament: 10 x 12in 45-cal, 16 x 4in 45-cal
Anti-aircraft guns: From 1915: 1 x 3in 45-cal; from 1917: also 1 x 4in 45-cal
Complement: 730 (840 wartime)

This class were slightly improved successors to *Dreadnought*, had weaker belt armour but were fitted with a torpedo bulkhead and an enhanced anti-destroyer battery of 4in (102mm) guns. All three ships were at Jutland.

Superb was the British flagship in Turkish waters and the Black Sea from 1916 until April 1919. She was transferred to reserve and was used as a target ship from December 1920. She was sold for scrapping on 12 December 1922. *Bellerophon* was in reserve from September 1919, was sold on 8 November 1921 and scrapped from the end of 1923. *Temeraire* was employed as a cadet training ship from September 1919 to April 1921. She was sold for breaking up in December 1921 and scrapped from 1922.

Bellerophon, 1910.

Bellerophon, an improved *Dreadnought*.

Ship	Builder	Laid down	Launched	Commissioned
Bellerophon	Portsmouth DY	03.12.1906	27.07.1907	20.02.1909
Temeraire	Devonport DY	01.01.1907	24.08.1907	15.05.1909
Superb	Armstrong, Elswick	06.02.1907	07.11.1907	09.06.1909

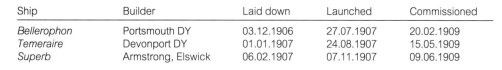

Vanguard, with torpedo nets

St Vincent Class

Displacement: 20,000/23,170t
Dimensions: 161.9 x 25.6 x 9.4m
Machinery: 4 Parsons turbines, shafts, 24,500shp
Fuel: 2,750t coal max. + 850t oil
Speed/range: 21.0kt; 6,900nm at 10kt
Armour: Belt 254mm, deck 3mm, main armament 280mm, CT 280mm
Weight of armour: 5,590t = 28.0% of normal displacement
Armament: 10 x 12in 50-cal, 18 4in 45-cal
Anti-aircraft guns: 2 x 3in 45-cal in 1915; from 1917: 1 x 4in 45-cal, 1 x 3in 45-cal
Complement: 760 (823 wartime)

This class was a further development of *Dreadnought* and was equipped with a new model 12in (305mm) gun with a longer barrel. On trials *Collingwood* achieved only 20.62 knots, but *Vanguard* and *St Vincent* exceeded the contract speed by a small margin. All three units were present at Jutland.

Vanguard blew up at Scapa Flow on 9 July 1917, probably because of the spontaneous ignition of her cordite; 804 crewmen were killed. *St Vincent* was used as a training ship from March 1919, was stricken in 1921 and sold for scrap on 1 December 1921. *Collingwood* was a gunnery training ship from October 1919 and served with the training ship *Colossus* from September 1921. She was stricken on 17 March 1922 following the Washington Treaty, sold in December 1922 and scrapped from 1923.

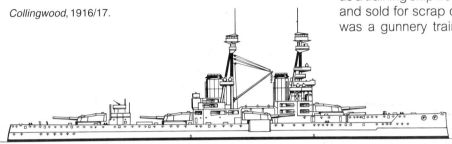

Collingwood, 1916/17.

Ship	Builder	Laid down	Launched	Commissioned
St Vincent	Portsmouth DY	30.12.1907	10.09.1908	03.05.1909
Collingwood	Devonport DY	03.02.1908	07.11.1908	19.04.1910
Vanguard	Vickers, Barrow	02.04.1908	22.04.1909	01.03.1910

Neptune

Displacement: 20,000/23,300t
Dimensions: 164.6 x 25.9 x 8.7m
Machinery: 4 Parsons turbines, 4 shafts, 25,000shp
Fuel: 2,750t coal max. + 800t oil
Speed/range: 21.0kt; 6,600nm at 10kt
Armour: Belt 254mm, deck 76mm, main armament 280mm, CT 280mm
Weight of armour: 5,790t = 29.0% of normal displacement
Armament: 10 x 12in 50-cal, 18 x 4in 50-cal
Anti-aircraft guns: 1 x 3in 45-cal; from 1917, 2 x 3in 45-cal
Complement: 760 (813 wartime)
Builder: Portsmouth DY (laid down 19.01.1909; launched 30.09.1909; commissioned 19.01.1911)

Neptune failed to reach her contractual speed on trials in September 1910 but, using best Welsh coal, achieved 21.29 knots at 25,531shp during her acceptance trials on 17 November 1910. The staggered arrangement of the wing turrets failed to meet expectations as a broadside using all five main turrets proved not to be possible without damaging the ship's superstructure. *Neptune* was present at Jutland and is reported to have scored several hits on *Lützow*. She was placed in reserve on 1 February 1919, stricken in March 1921 and sold for scrapping in September 1922.

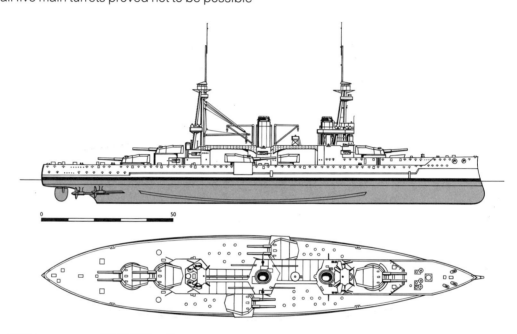

Neptune, 1911.

Neptune in 1918.

96

Colossus Class

Displacement: 20,350/23,600t
Dimensions: 165.0 x 26.4 x 9.0m
Machinery: 4 Parsons turbines,
, shafts, 25,000shp
Fuel: 2,950t coal max. + 800t oil
Speed/range: 21kt; 6,680nm at
10kt
Armour: Belt 280mm, deck
3mm, main armament 280mm,
CT 280mm
Weight of armour: 5,562t =
27.3% of normal displacement
Armament: 10 x 12in 50-cal, 16
4in 50-cal
Anti-aircraft guns: 2 x 3in 45-cal;
from 1917, 1 x 4in 45-cal, 1 x 3in
45-cal
Complement: 750 (800 wartime)

This class represented a further development of *Neptune* with certain structural modifications: for example, the tripod mainmast was discarded and the midships 305mm turrets were mounted closer together. During trials in March 1911 *Colossus* reached 21.57 knots at 29,317shp.

Both ships fought at Jutland, *Colossus* being the only battleship under Jellicoe's command to be damaged (two hits); she was repaired in June 1916. She became a cadet training ship in September 1921, was hulked from July 1923 and was sold for scrapping in August 1928. *Hercules* brought the Allied Armistice Commission to Kiel on 3 December 1918. She was placed in reserve on 1 February 1919, stricken in October 1921, sold for breaking up on 8 November 1921 and scrapped in Kiel from 1922.

Ship	Builder	Laid down	Launched	Commissioned
Colossus	Scotts, Greenock	08.07.1909	09.04.1910	08.08.1911
Hercules	Palmers	30.07.1909	10.05.1910	31.07.1911

Colossus during trials.

Orion Class

Displacement: 22,600/26,300t
Dimensions: 175.6 x 27.0 x 9.5m
Machinery: 4 Parsons turbines, 4 shafts, 27,000shp
Fuel: 3,400t coal max. + 800t oil
Speed/range: 21.0kt; 6,730nm at 10kt
Armour: Belt 305mm, deck 102mm, main armament 280mm, CT 280mm
Weight of armour: 6,560t = 29.0% of normal displacement
Armament: 10 x 13.5in 45-cal, 16 x 4in 50-cal
Anti-aircraft guns: 1 x 3in 45-cal; from 1917, 1 x 4in 45-cal, 1 x 3in 45-cal
Complement: 750 (up to 1,100 wartime)

Orion, the first British 'super-dreadnought'.

Orion, 1912.

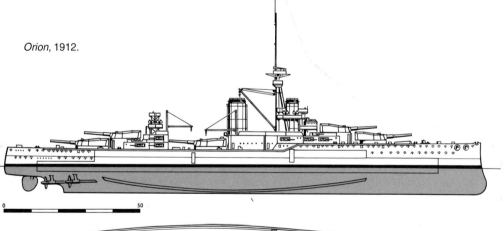

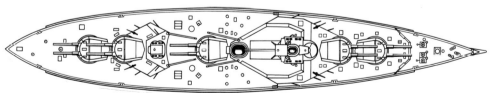

Ship	Builder	Laid down	Launched	Commissioned
Orion	Devonport DY	29.11.1909	20.08.1910	02.01.1912
Monarch	Armstrong, Elswick	01.04.1910	30.03.1911	27.04.1912
Conqueror	Beardmore	05.04.1910	01.05.1911	00.03.1913
Thunderer	Thames Ironworks	13.04.1910	01.02.1911	15.06.1912

These ships were the first 'super-dreadnoughts' in the Royal Navy, fitted with new 13.5in (343mm) guns. All four fought at Jutland. *Conqueror* experienced boiler problems during her preliminary trials in March 1912. She was provisionally commissioned at Devonport with a partial main armament in November 1912 and was fully armed by March the following year.

After 1918 all the class remained in service but were discarded under the terms of the Washington Treaty. *Orion* was stricken on 12 April 1922 and sold for scrapping on 19 December 1922. *Conqueror* was stricken in June 1922 and also sold for scrapping on 19 December 1922. *Monarch* was stricken on 5 May 1922, was employed as a gunnery target ship and was sunk by shelling in January 1925. *Thunderer* was listed for breaking up in 1922 but her place was taken by *Erin*. She was used as a cadet training ship from early 1921 to 3 August 1926. Finally sold for scrapping on 17 December 1926, she grounded en route to the breakers the following week; she was raised and broken up from April 1927.

King George V Class

Displacement: 23,400/27,000t
Dimensions: 179.7 x 27.1 x 8.4m
Machinery: 4 Parsons turbines, 4 shafts, 27,000shp
Fuel: 3,150t coal max. + 850t oil
Speed/range: 21.0kt; 6,200nm at 10kt
Armour: Belt 305mm, deck 63mm, main armament 280mm, CT 280mm
Weight of armour: 7,080t = 30.2% of normal displacement
Armament: 10 x 13.5in 45-cal, 16 x 4in 50-cal (12 x 4in from 1917)
Anti-aircraft guns: 2 x 3in 45-cal; part replaced by 4in from 1917
Complement: 870 (1,110 in 1916)

During trials in 1912 *King George V* reached 22.37 knots at 33,022shp and *Centurion* 22.87 knots at 34,530shp.

Audacious struck a mine off the coast of Northern Ireland on 27 October 1914 and sank the following day after unsuccessful salvage attempts. *King George V*, *Ajax* and *Centurion* all served at Jutland and remained in service until 1924.

King George V, 1914.

Ajax was sold for scrapping in November 1926 and *King George V* in December 1926. *Centurion* was converted to a remote controlled target ship from April 1925 to June 1927. At the outbreak of the Second World War she served as a repair ship, then as a dummy battleship (disguised as HMS *Anson*), operating on one occasion in June 1942 in Mediterranean in this role. She was run aground as a breakwater at Normandy on 9 June 1944 and was broken up *in situ* after 1945.

Ship	Builder	Laid down	Launched	Commissioned
King George V	Portsmouth DY	16.01.1911	09.10.1911	16.12.1912
Centurion	Devonport DY	16.01.1911	18.11.1911	22.05.1913
Ajax	Scotts, Greenock	27.02.1911	21.03.1912	31.10.1913
Audacious	Cammell Laird	23.03.1911	14.09.1912	15.10.1913

Audacious was mined and sunk on 27 October 1914.

Iron Duke Class

Displacement: 25,400/29,000t
Dimensions: 187.2 x 27.4 x 8.7m
Machinery: 4 Parsons turbines,
4 shafts, 29,000shp
Fuel: 3,300t coal max. + 1,050t
oil
Speed/range: 21.25kt; 8,100nm
at 10kt
Armour: Belt 305mm, deck
63mm, main armament 280mm,
CT 280mm
Weight of armour: 7,925t =
31.2% of normal displacement
Armament: 10 x 13.5in 45-cal,
12 x 6in 45-cal
Anti-aircraft guns: 2 x 3in 45-cal;
1 x 4in 45--cal + 1 x 3in 45-cal in
1917
Complement: 925–1,102 (1,012–
1,180 in 1918)

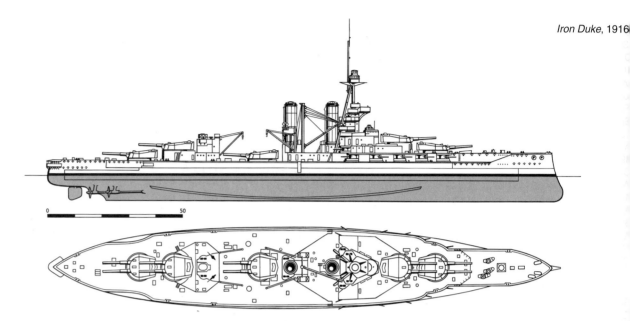

Iron Duke, 1916

Ship	Builder	Laid down	Launched	Commissioned
Iron Duke	Portsmouth DY	15.01.1912	12.10.1912	00.03.1914
Marlborough	Devonport DY	25.01.1912	24.10.1912	16.06.1914
Benbow	Beardmore	30.05.1912	12.11.1913	00.11.1914
Emperor of India	Vickers	31.05.1912	27.11.1913	00.11.1914

The fourth ship of the class, originally to be called *Delhi* was renamed *Emperor of India* one month before launching. On trials all four ships marginally exceeded their designed speed, reaching between 21.3 and 21.8 knots. All were present at Jutland. *Marlborough* was torpedoed and barely made port under tow.

All these ships were condemned for scrapping under the terms of the 1930 London Naval Treaty. *Benbow* was stricken in early 1931 and sold for breaking up in March 1931. *Emperor of India* and *Marlborough* were similarly discarded in early 1931, the former being sold in February 1932 and the latter, after being used for experiments until April that year, in May 1932. *Iron Duke* was converted to a gunnery training ship in 1931–32, her main armament being reduced to six 13.5in (343mm) guns. She was badly damaged in a German air raid and run aground on 17 October 1939 and her guns were transferred to coastal artillery batteries. Following basic repairs, she became a stationary depot ship until being scrapped in 1946.

Iron Duke in 1921, with a flying-off platform fitted atop 'B' turret.

Queen Elizabeth Class

Displacement: 29,700/33,500t (34,100–34,500t max. in 1917)
Dimensions: 193.4 x 27.6 x 10.1m
Machinery: 2 sets Parsons turbines, 4 shafts, 56,000shp
Fuel: 3,400t oil max.
Speed/range: 23.0kt; 5,000nm at 12kt, 2,500nm at 22kt
Armour: Belt 330mm, deck 89mm, main armament 330mm, CT 280mm
Weight of armour: 8,900t = 30.0% of normal displacement
Armament: 8 x 15in 42-cal, 14 x 6in 45-cal
Anti-aircraft guns: 2 x 3in 45-cal; 1917: 2 x 4in 45-cal
Complement: 950 (1,220 in 1918)

Ship	Builder	Laid down	Launched	Commissioned
Queen Elizabeth	Portsmouth DY	21.10.1912	16.10.1913	00.01.1915
Warspite	Devonport DY	31.10.1912	26.11.1913	00.04.1915
Valiant	Fairfield	31.01.1913	04.11.1914	00.02.1916
Barham	John Brown	24.02.1913	31.12.1914	00.10.1915
Malaya	Armstrong	20.10.1913	18.03.1915	00.02.1916

All the ships of this class greatly exceeded their designed displacement of 27,940/32,000t. None reached their designed speed of 25 knots at 75,000shp: during two-hour trials *Warspite* managed only 24.65 knots at 75,510shp, even at forced draught, while *Queen Elizabeth* achieved only 23.91 knots at 70,788shp.

A sixth unit, to be named *Agincourt*, was authorised in the 1914 Budget but the contract was cancelled at the end of August 1914.

All except *Queen Elizabeth* were present at Jutland, where three received serious damage: *Barham* was hit six times and was under repair for five weeks; *Malaya* was hit eight times and was under repair for eight weeks; and *Warspite* was hit by fifteen shells and was close to foundering. After the battle all ships received an extra 1in (25mm) of deck armour.

All the ships of the class survived the First World War and were twice given refits between the wars. Further career details are given later in the book.

Queen Elizabeth, 1915.

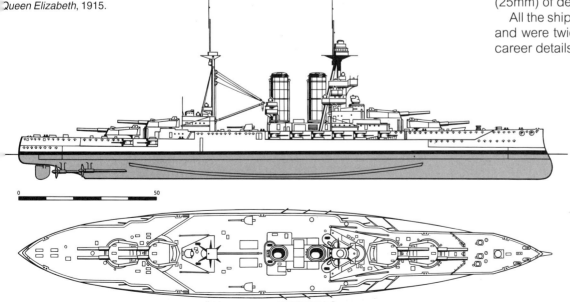

▲▲The crew of HMS *Valiant* line the decks.

Royal Sovereign Class

Displacement: 28,500/31,700t (without bulges); 30,100/33,400t (*Revenge* in 1918, with bulges)
Dimensions: 187.3 x 27.0 (31.0 over bulges) x 9.2m
Machinery: 2 sets Parsons turbines, 4 shafts, 40,000shp
Fuel: 3,400t oil max.
Speed/range: 21.5kt; 5,000nm at 10kt
Armour: Belt 330mm, deck 89mm, main armament 330mm, CT 280mm
Weight of armour: 8,380t = 29.4% of normal displacement
Armament: 8 x 15in 42-cal, 14 x 6in 45-cal
Anti-aircraft guns: 2 x 3in 45-cal
Complement: 920

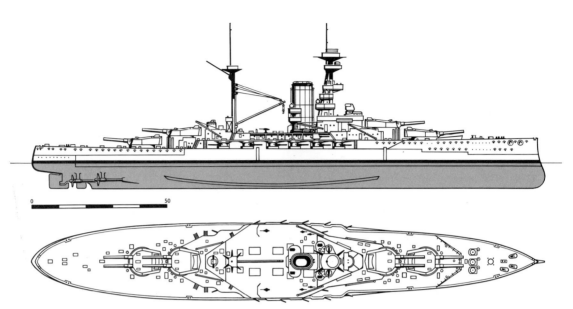

Revenge, 1916

Ship	Builder	Laid down	Launched	Commissioned
Royal Sovereign	Portsmouth DY	15.01.1914	29.04.1915	25.05.1916
Royal Oak	Devonport DY	15.01.1914	17.11.1914	01.05.1916
Revenge	Vickers	22.12.1913	29.05.1915	29.03.1916
Resolution	Palmers	29.12.1913	14.01.1915	30.12.1916
Ramillies	Beardmore	12.11.1913	12.09.1916	00.10.1917
Repulse	Palmers	30.11.1914	–	–
Renown	Fairfield	?	–	–
Resistance	Devonport DY	–	–	–

Revenge in 1918 in camouflage paintwork.

▶▼ *Royal Oak* executes a sharp turn.

Construction work on *Resistance* was halted at the end of August 1914 and on *Repulse* and *Renown* at the end of the year.

On trials, *Royal Sovereign* attained 21.8 knots a 41,112shp and *Revenge* (without bulges) 21.9 knots a 42,940shp. Units fitted with bulges in 1918 lost 0.5 knots in speed. Only *Revenge* and *Royal Oak* were present a Jutland, neither ship being damaged. All five ships saw further service in the Second World War (q.v.).

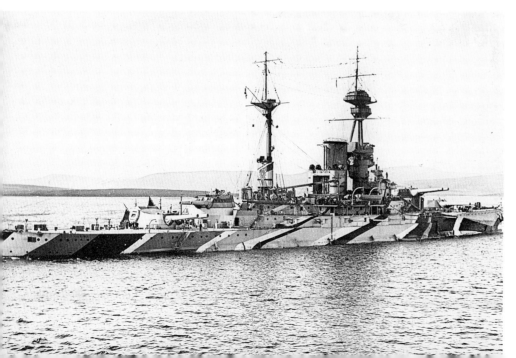

Invincible Class

Displacement: 17,000/20,450t
Dimensions: 170.7 x 23.9 x 8.0m
Machinery: Parsons turbines, 4 shafts, 41,000shp
Fuel: 3,000t coal max. + 750t oil
Speed/range: 25.0kt; 3,000nm at 22kt
Armour: Belt 152mm, deck 63mm total, main armament 178mm, CT 254mm
Weight of armour: 3,516t = 19.9% of normal displacement
Armament: 8 x 12in 45-cal, 16 x 4in 45-cal
Anti-aircraft guns: 1915: 1 x 3in 45-cal; from 1916: 2 x 4in 45-cal
Complement: 780–800

Invincible was completed on 20 March 1908 but because of breakdowns in her experimental electrically driven gun turrets she did not leave the dockyard until September; trials took place in October and November 1908. She was transferred to reserve at the end of 1908 but then attached to the 1st Cruiser Squadron, Home Fleet.

All ships exceeded their contract speed, *Invincible* making 25.64 knots at 46,500shp over the measured mile on 7 November 1908.

At the Falkland Islands on 8 December 1914 *Invincible* and *Inflexible* destroyed Admiral von Spee's Cruiser

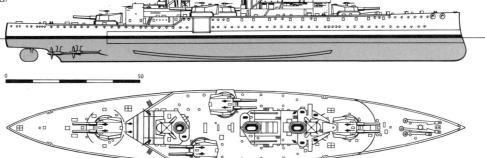

Invincible, 1909.

▼ The battlecruiser *Invincible* as completed.

Ship	Builder	Laid down	Launched	Commissioned
Invincible	Armstrong	02.04.1906	13.04.1907	20.03.1909
Inflexible	John Brown	05.02.1906	26.06.1907	20.10.1908
Indomitable	Fairfield	01.03.1906	16.03.1907	25.06.1908

Squadron, including the two armoured cruisers *Scharnhorst* and *Gneisenau*. *Indomitable* rendered assistance to the badly damaged *Lion* after the Dogger Bank action in January 1915. *Inflexible* took part in the Dardanelles

Inflexible in 1918 with raised forefunnel and a landplane carried atop 'Q' turret.

operations from 1915: mined and badly damaged on 18 March 1915, she was out of action for three months.

All three ships were present at Jutland. *Invincible* blew up and sank following a hit from *Lützow*; only six of her crew of 1,032 were saved. The two surviving ships were reduced to reserve after the war, stricken on 31 March 1920 and sold for scrapping on 1 December 1921.

Indefatigable Class

Displacement: 19,100/22,450t
Dimensions: 179.2 x 24.3 x 9.0m
Machinery: Parsons turbines, 4 shafts, 43,000shp
Fuel: 3,300t coal max. + 850t oil
Speed/range: 25.8kt; 3,350nm at 23.5kt
Armour: Belt 152mm, deck 76mm total, main armament 178mm, CT 254mm
Weight of armour: 3,795t = 19.9% of normal displacement
Armament: 8 x 12in 45-cal, 16 x 4in 45-cal
Anti-aircraft guns: 1915/16: 1 or 2 x 3in 45-cal; 1917: 1 x 4in 45-cal
Complement: 820 (850 wartime)

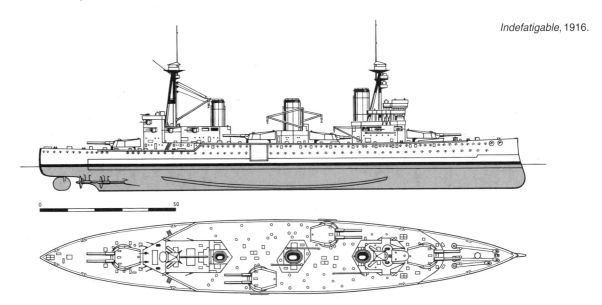

Indefatigable, 1916.

Ship	Builder	Laid down	Launched	Commissioned
Indefatigable	Devonport DY	23.02.1909	28.10.1909	24.02.1911
Australia	John Brown	23.06.1910	25.10.1911	21.06.1913
New Zealand	Fairfield	20.06.1910	01.07.1911	23.11.1912

Indefatigable prior to the Battle of Jutland.

After completion, *New Zealand* was placed at the disposal of the Royal Navy by the New Zealand Government. *Australia* was similarly transferred by the Australian Government in January 1915; she had been the flagship of the Royal Australian Navy. On trials all ships reached speeds of between 26.4 and 26.9 knots.

New Zealand in 1918.

Indefatigable, in company with *Inflexible* and *Indomitable*, took part in the pursuit of *Goeben* in the Mediterranean in August 1914. *New Zealand* collided with *Australia* on 22 April 1916. The former was badly damaged but repaired in time for Jutland; *Australia* was under repair until after Jutland. At Jutland *Indefatigable* was struck by shells from *Von der Tann* and sank so quickly that only two crew members could be rescued. *New Zealand* received slight damage.

Australia collided with *Repulse* on 12 December 1917 and was returned to the yards in need of repair. Released from the Grand Fleet on 22 April 1919, she sailed for Australia the next day. She was stricken from the RAN on 12 December 1921 and scuttled off the Australian coast on 12 April 1924. *New Zealand* was stricken on 12 April 1921, sold for scrapping on 19 December 1921 and broken up in the autumn of 1923.

Lion Class

Displacement: 26,820/30,700t (*Queen Mary* 27,200/32,000t)
Dimensions: 212.8 x 27.0 x 9.5m (*Queen Mary* 212.8 x 27.1 x 9.7m)
Machinery: Parsons turbines, 4 shafts, 70,000shp (*Queen Mary* 75,000shp)
Fuel: 3,600t coal max. (*Queen Mary* 3,700t) + 1,150t oil
Speed/range: 27.0kt (*Queen Mary* 27.5kt); 3,350nm at 20.5kt
Armour: Belt 229mm, deck 57mm (*Queen Mary* 63mm) total, CT 254mm
Weight of armour: 6,300t = 23.5% of normal displacement (*Queen Mary* 6,700t = 24.6%)
Armament: 8 x 13.5in 45-cal, 16 x 4in 50-cal
Anti-aircraft guns: 1913: 1 x 47mm (mod); 1915/16: 2 x 3in ; 1917: 2 x 4in
Complement: 1,000 (1915: 1,100; *Queen Mary* 1916: 1,275)

Over the measured mile in July 1913 *Princess Royal* reached 28.5 knots at 78,803shp. Her half-sister *Queen Mary*, fitted with more powerful machinery, attained 28.47 knots at 83,350shp.

All three units took part in Heligoland Bight action on 28 August 1914. At the Battle of the Dogger Bank in January 1915 *Lion* was badly damaged by shellfire and rendered unmanoeuvrable, and had to be towed home.

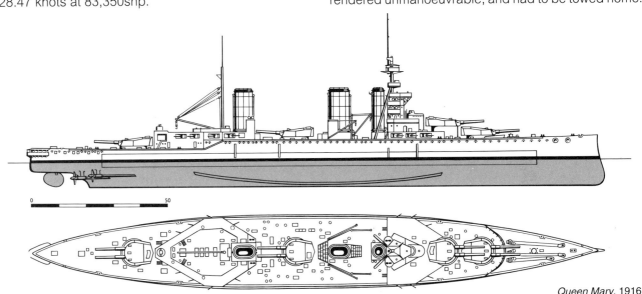

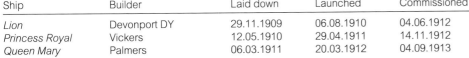

Queen Mary, 1916.

Ship	Builder	Laid down	Launched	Commissioned
Lion	Devonport DY	29.11.1909	06.08.1910	04.06.1912
Princess Royal	Vickers	12.05.1910	29.04.1911	14.11.1912
Queen Mary	Palmers	06.03.1911	20.03.1912	04.09.1913

Queen Mary in camouflage paint shortly before she was sunk.

HMS *Lion* on 8 August 1912.

All three ships fought at Jutland. *Queen Mary* blew up after receiving hits from *Seydlitz* and *Derfflinger*, only nine of her crew of 1,275 surviving. *Lion* and *Princess Royal* were badly damaged by hits, necessitating 45 days under repair. *Lion* was placed in reserve in March 1920 and stricken on 30 May 1922. She was sold for scrapping on 31 January 1924. *Princess Royal* was offered for sale to Chile but rejected in the summer 1920 and was therefore reduced to reserve. She was stricken in March 1922, sold for scrapping in December 1922 and broken up in autumn 1923.

Tiger

Displacement: 29,200/34,200t
Dimensions: 212.7 x 27.6 x 9.7m
Machinery: Brown-Curtis turbines, 4 shafts, 108,000shp (forced draught)
Fuel: 3,300t coal + 800t oil
Speed/range: 28.0kt (29.0kt forced draught)
Armour: Belt 229mm, deck 76mm total, main armament 229mm, CT 254mm
Weight of armour: 7,500t = 25.7% of normal displacement
Armament: 8 x 13.5in 45-cal, 12 x 6in 45-cal
Anti-aircraft guns: 2 x 3in; 1917: 2 x 4in 45-cal
Complement: 1,110 (1,344 in 1915)
Builder: John Brown (laid down 20.06.1912; launched 15.12.1913; commissioned 03.10.1914)

Tiger was the last battlecruiser to have mixed firing for her boilers. If necessary, the ship could accommodate up to 3,800 tons of fuel oil in her double bottom. A proposed sister-ship, reputedly to be named *Leopard*, was delayed in 1914 and then cancelled.

The ship's machinery was originally to have delivered 85,000shp, but over the measured mile on 14 October 1914 *Tiger* achieved 28.38 knots at 91,103shp and 29.07 knots at 104,635shp; even so, her speed fell short of the designed 30 knots.

Tiger was badly damaged at Dogger Bank in January 1915, to the extent that she was reported sunk by German propaganda. She was hit ten times and badly damaged at Jutland; following repairs she resumed duties with the Battle Cruiser Fleet in the North Sea.

In May 1920, in company with HMS *Hood*, she was despatched to the Baltic to attack the Bolsheviks but was recalled while in Swedish waters. She was reduced to reserve on 22 August 1921 and from February 1924 was employed as a gunnery training ship. She returned to front-line service from April 1926 to April 1931 but was again in reserve between 15 May and 26 June 1931. Finally stricken and sold for scrap in February 1932, the ship was broken up the same year.

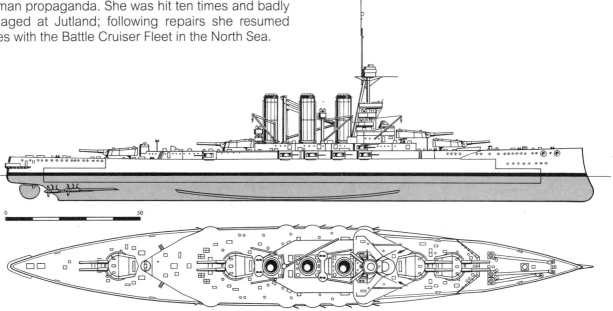

▲ A post-war photograph of *Tiger*.

Tiger, 1914.

Repulse/Renown (as in 1917)

Displacement: 27,770/32,600t; *Renown* 28,400/33,250t
Dimensions: 240.2 x 27.4 x 9.1m
Machinery: Brown-Curtis turbines, 4 shafts, 120,000shp
Fuel: 4,350t oil
Speed/range: 32.0kt; 2,570nm at 26.5kt, 4,100nm at 19kt
Armour: Belt 152mm, deck 66mm total, main armament 229mm, CT 254mm
Weight of armour: 5,360t = 19.3% (*Renown* 18.9%) of normal displacement
Armament: 6 x 15in 42-cal, 15 x 4in 44-cal
Anti-aircraft guns: 2 x 3in 45-cal
Complement: 1,050 (1919: 1,220)

Renown on completion. The ship was mockingly referred to as 'HMS Refit' in naval circles.

Ship	Builder	Laid down	Launched	Commissioned
Repulse	John Brown	25.01.1915	08.01.1916	21.09.1916
Renown	Fairfield	25.01.1915	04.03.1916	00.01.1917

Repulse was built by John Brown after it was discovered that the slip at Palmers, the original builder, was too short. On trials the ship achieved 31.73 knots at 119,025shp on 15 September 1915; her sister *Renown* reached 32.56 knots at 126,000shp on 20 September 1916. The maximum service speed was 29.7 knots at 100,800shp.

In view of the events at Jutland, both vessels had their horizontal armour strengthened at Rosyth by the addition of 550 tons of plating immediately after the ships had been commissioned; *Repulse* was in dock from 10 November 1916 to 29 January 1917 and *Renown* from 1 February 1917 to 15 April 1917. Only *Repulse* saw action in the war, taking part in the sortie into the Heligoland Bight by British battlecruisers on 17 November 1917.

After the war both ships were given a major refit, *Repulse* entering the dockyard on 17 December 1918. Both saw service in the Second World War (q.v.).

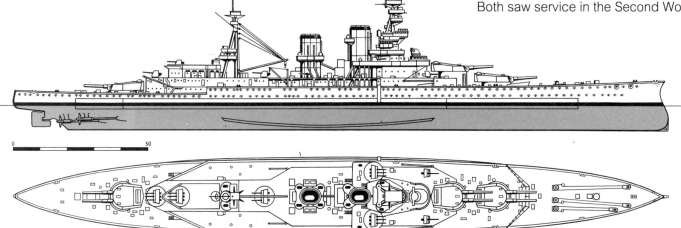

0   50

Renown, 1917

Courageous/Glorious

Displacement: 19,500/22,900t
Dimensions: 239.8 x 24.8 x 7.9m
Machinery: Parsons turbines, 4 shafts, 90,000shp
Fuel: 3,200t oil
Speed/range: 31.0kt; 6,000nm at 20kt
Armour: Belt 76mm, deck 51mm total, main armament 279mm, CT 254mm
Weight of armour: 2,953t = 15.1% of normal displacement
Armament: 4 x 15in 42-cal, 18 x 4in 44-cal
Anti-aircraft guns: 2 x 3in 45-cal
Complement: 840

HMS *Glorious* as she appeared in 1917.

Ship	Builder	Laid down	Launched	Commissioned
Courageous	Armstrong	28.03.1915	05.02.1916	00.01.1917
Glorious	Harland & Wolff	01.05.1915	20.04.1916	00.01.1917

Glorious was completed on 23 October 1916 and *Courageous* five days later. On trials in mid-November, *Courageous* reached 30.8 knots at 91,200shp; *Glorious* achieved 31.58 knots at 94,450shp over the measured mile at the end of 1916.

The ships were involved in only one action, that at the Heligoland Bight on 17 November 1917, during which their structural shortcomings were demonstrated when damage to the deck was incurred after the main armament had been fired. Both vessels were placed in reserve at Devonport in February 1919. *Glorious* was decommissioned on 4 February 1924 and *Courageous* on 29 June 1924; both ships were converted to aircraft carriers and recommissioned, the former on 10 March 1930 and the latter on 5 May 1928.

Courageous was sunk by *U29* on 17 September 1939 in the Western Approaches. *Glorious* was sunk by the German battlecruisers *Scharnhorst* and *Gneisenau* in northern waters on 8 June 1940.

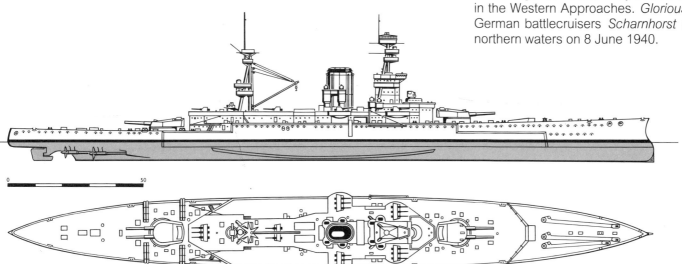

Glorious, 1918.

Furious

Displacement: 19,830/23,260t
Dimensions: 239.8 x 26.9 x 7.3m
Machinery: Brown-Curtis turbines, 4 shafts, 90,000shp
Fuel: 3,250t oil
Speed/range: 31.5kt; 6,000nm at 20kt
Armour: Belt 76mm, deck 51mm total, main armament 279mm, CT 254mm
Weight of armour: 3,958t as designed with 2 x 18in guns
Armament: 2 x 18in 40-cal (only one turret actually fitted), 11 x 5.5in 50-cal
Anti-aircraft guns: 2 x 3in 50-cal
Complement: 880
Builder: Armstrong (laid down 08.06.1915; launched 15.08.1916; commissioned 04.07.1917; converted to aircraft carrier 00.11.1917–00.03.1918)

The thickness of the main turret armour for the three 'large light cruisers' *Courageous*, *Glorious* and *Furious* is usually quoted as 9in (229mm); this was true of the turret faces, but the rear walls were 11in (279mm) in thickness.

The decision to convert *Furious* to a 'semi-carrier' was taken on 7 February 1917; work commenced in mid-March that year and the construction of the aircraft hangar on the forecastle was completed on 26 June. Contrary to original intentions, the ship carried no seaplanes but embarked eight Sopwith Pup single-seat landplanes.

After trials in the summer 1917 *Furious* had her main 18in turret aft replaced by a landing-on deck. This proved unsatisfactory, and a full conversion to an aircraft carrier proper was carried out between 1922 and 1925.

On 17 July 1918 seven Sopwith Camel aircraft armed with 55lb (25kg) bombs were launched from the ship and destroyed the hangars at the German airship base at Tondern with the Zeppelins *L54* and *L60* inside them.

Furious, showing her 18in (457mm) gun.

▶ The battlecruiser *Renown*, followed by the converted *Courageous* and *Furious*, during manoeuvres in 1935.

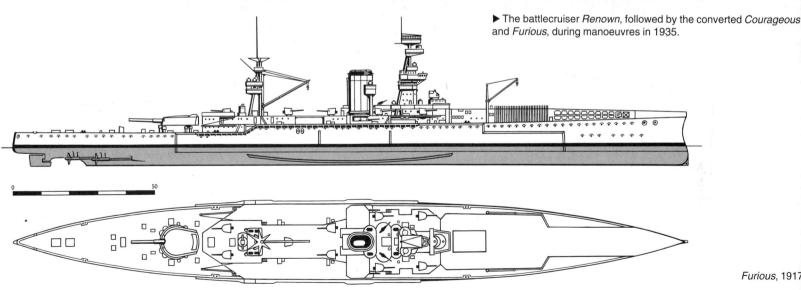

Furious, 1917

Developments up to 1945

Great Britain emerged from the First World War as a victor, but also in a weakened state economically. The doctrine known as the 'Ten Year Rule', which foresaw no major world conflict for ten years, was intended to lead to general international disarmament so as to enable the country to recover financially. An Empire that was spread across the world would have found it difficult to survive a future war on several fronts.

The stabilising factor was the presence in all oceans of the Royal Navy, but the Fleet required urgent modernisation. In a successful attempt to bring a halt to a fresh round of naval rearmament, Britain arranged with the United States and Japan a series of naval conferences with a view to agreeing a building moratorium.

Following the invasion of Manchuria by Japan, and Hitler's seizure of power in Germany, the 'Ten Year Rule' was clearly untenable, and in order to suppress tendencies towards unrestricted naval rearmament it now became British policy to seek bilateral naval agreements. The first such treaty was concluded in June 1935 with Germany, but Britain had to contend with tensions involving Italy which they had not expected, and it became obvious that Japan was no longer interested in limiting her own naval strength. Accordingly, the British budget proposals for 1936–37 included two battleships, two aircraft carriers and seven cruisers instead of the three light cruisers and one destroyer flotilla which had been the customary request in previous years.

The tempo of warship construction now increased considerably, but despite various technical problems, such as the overburdening of obsolescent shipyards with orders and a shortage of finished armour plate and guns, Britain always managed to complete her annual building programmes. The manner in which the naval budget grew in the 1930s is shown in the following table:

Year	Total budget (£ millions)	Allocated for warship construction
1931	51.6	5.3
1932	50.5	6.8
1933	53.6	8.4
1934	56.6	10.2
1935	60.0	10.5
1936	70.0	13.9
1937	78.1	28.0
1938	93.7	34.8
1939	149.5	46.1

British Battleship Construction

At the end of the First World War, HMS *Hood* was the only Royal Navy capital ship still under construction, to be completed in 1920. At the time the Director of Naval Construction (DNC) was not working on any future battleship design. It was not only Britain's financial plight that was responsible for this: the future of the battleship itself was the subject of much controversy in British military circles. However, when it became known that the United States and Japan were drawing up proposals for new and more powerful capital ships, the Admiralty instructed the DNC to prepare preliminary designs for new battleships and large battlecruisers. The Government made clear its intention to order four such ships in 1921 and four more later.

The budget of £80 million was approved in March 1921, and four battlecruisers were ordered on 26 October that year, to be followed in 1922 by contracts for four 'super-battleships', but before work had commenced the orders were rescinded as the 1922 Washington Treaty had come into force.

Although the battlecruisers authorised in August 1921 were not built their details are of interest since the design shared much in common with ships of the later *Nelson* class. The units, known only as the '1921 Battlecruisers', would have had a greater speed (up to 33.75 knots) and a stronger armament than the US *Lexington* class. Gun calibres of 18in (457mm) and 16.5in (420mm) were considered, but the final design 'G3', had 9 x 16in (406mm) 45-cal and 16 x 6in (152mm) 50-cal. The armour would have accounted for 34 per cent of the total weight of the ship, the belt armour being 14in (356mm) thick and the horizontal armour up to 8in (203mm).

Final designs for another proposed class, this time of battleships, were not available by the beginning of the Washington Conference. With belt armour increased to 15in (381mm) the units would have carried 18in (457mm) guns and have had a top speed of 23.5 knots. Outline sketches also existed of a battlecruiser 3 knots slower than the 'G3', armed with nine 16in (406mm) guns and carrying thinner armour. However, the Naval Staff, which wanted a 35,000-ton battleship with the same armament but stronger armour, was anxious about the weak protection of the battlecruisers and they were cancelled on 17 December 1921.

A final battleship design was accepted by the Admiralty on 1 September 1922, and two units were ordered on the 22nd of the following month, Britain being permitted to build two new battleships under the provisions of the Washington Treaty. *Nelson* and *Rodney* were laid down on 28 December 1922, material for their construction having been made available from the cancelled orders for HMS *Hood*'s sister ships.

Britain intended to use the enforced pause in capital ship construction primarily to modernise ships which she expected to remain in commission after 1931. The terms of the Treaty allowed modernisation of a defensive character not exceeding 3,000 tons additional displacement, and by 1930 anti-torpedo bulges had been fitted to all First World War-era British battleships.

At the London Naval Conference, which began on 21 January 1930, British representatives proposed a radical reduction in battleship size to 25,000 tons. Japan was in favour of this but the United States categorically demanded that the 35,000-ton limit be maintained. However, the moratorium agreed in 1922 was extended to the end of 1936. As Britain was proposing to decommission a number of ships armed with 13.5in (343mm) guns, the Admiralty decided on a large-scale

Battleships of the *Royal Sovereign* class in line-ahead formation. The anti-torpedo bulge is clearly visible on *Royal Oak*, the leading ship.

modernisation of the remaining ships with the exception of the *Royal Sovereign* class. A rebuilding programme was drawn up in 1933 which aimed to strengthen the ships' horizontal armour and increase their anti-aircraft batteries. Thus by the outbreak of the Second World War *Renown* and three ships of the *Queen Elizabeth* class had been reconstructed at enormous expense, the work done on *Renown* actually exceeding her original building costs 23 years previously.

In January 1934 a commission was set up to consider the future development of British battleships, and after much discussion it was agreed that two 35,000-ton units each armed with twelve 14in (356mm) guns would be built under the 1936–37 Programme. The Admiralty agreed to the recommendation on 28 November 1935 and the Government endorsed it a few days later.

From a choice of two designs, on 3 April 1936 the Naval Staff selected one with ten guns on the grounds of its better armour protection, and although the final plans would not be ready until October two ships were ordered on 29 July following approval by Parliament on 21 April. In November 1936 the Naval Staff decided to build three more ships of the same class under the 1937–38 Programme. This made possible the creation of a large number of battleships of a uniform type, the later *King George V* class. The decision was to prove hasty: Japan had no intention of respecting the 1936 London Naval Treaty limits, which made it likely that the 16in (406mm) limit on gun calibre would be exceeded on her new battleships.

The DNC began work on designs for ships carrying 16in (406mm) guns, but the weight calculations showed that a desirable layout for these weapons on a fast and well-armoured ship could only be accomplished on a minimum displacement of 36,150 tonnes. It had been learned meanwhile that Japan was planning much larger ships than this, with 16in (406mm) or even 18in (457mm) guns, and as other signatories to the 1936 Treaty were requesting an increase in the limit to 45,000 tons, a supplementary protocol to that effect was signed on 30 June 1938, although Britain was not in favour of an increase beyond 40,000 tons.

Proposals for such a ship had long been gathering dust in the drawers of the DNC, and on 26 May 1938 Design '16G' was presented ('16' representing the gun calibre). After a number of modifications this received the approval of the Naval Staff on 25 July 1938. However, although approved for the 1938–39 Programme, the building of two of these units was delayed because of pressure of work in the steel and armaments industries.

Construction plans for the *Lion* class were submitted to the Naval Staff in mid-December 1938, and two further units of the class appeared in the 1939 budget proposals; another two were earmarked for the 1940 Programme. Of all these ships, only *Lion* and *Temeraire* were eventually laid down, on 1 June and 4 July 1939 respectively, but construction was delayed for a year after September 1939. Neither of the ships ordered in the summer of 1939 were laid down, and neither *Lion* nor *Temeraire* was completed, although the orders were not cancelled until 1944.

On 19 February 1940 the newly appointed First Lord of the Admiralty, Winston Churchill, knowing of the existence of the gun turrets from the former 'large light cruisers' *Glorious* and *Courageous*, requested the DNC to prepare proposals for a large, fast battleship which might be equipped with these turrets. This proposal was approved on 20 May 1940, but the order was withheld until 14 March 1941 because of the threat of a German invasion. This battleship was envisaged for use against Japan in the Far East. *Vanguard* was not commissioned until 1946, and with her the story of British capital ship construction is brought to an end, although the intention to resume work on *Lion* and *Temeraire* on the basis of an amended 1946 design persisted for some time.

Armament

At the outbreak of war in September 1939, thirteen capital ships were equipped with a main armament of 15in (381mm) guns while only *Nelson* and *Rodney* had the 16in (406mm) weapons developed after the First World War. These did not have the accuracy of the 15in gun and were disposed in triple turrets which continually caused problems. The

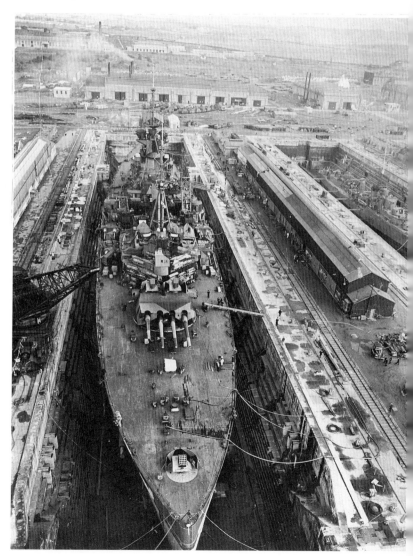

A view of HMS *King George V* in dry dock at Rosyth. Note the UP mountings at the stern and atop 'Y' turret.

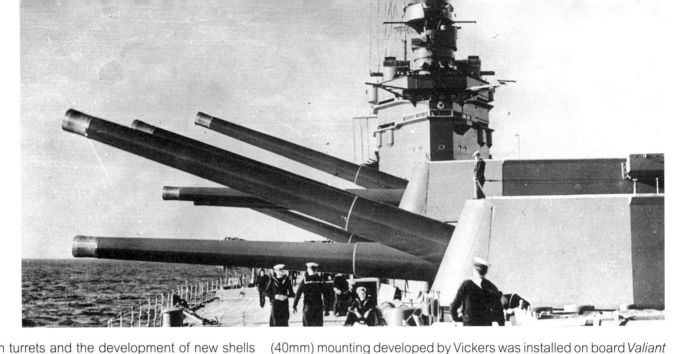

The 16in (406mm) triple turrets of HMS *Rodney*.

modernisation of the 15in turrets and the development of new shells brought good results. The last heavy gun to be introduced was the first British battleship gun of all-steel construction; despite its smaller calibre of 14in (356mm), it proved very effective.

Calibre	Model	Wt of shell	Muzzle velocity	Range/ elevation	Barrel life
16in 45-cal	Mk I	2,050lb	2,700ft/sec	39,600yd/40°	200 rds
15in 42-cal	Mk I-N	1,938lb	2,640ft/sec	32,150yd/30°	350 rds
15in 42-cal	Mk I	1,938lb	2,640ft/sec	29,525yd/20°	350 rds
14in 45-cal	Mk VII	1,665lb	2,480ft/sec	38,275yd/40°	340 rds

The standard 4in (102mm) heavy AA weapon appeared in two versions on British capital ships. The older Mk V, in a single mounting, was fitted only in *Repulse*. The Mk XVI was not developed until 1936 and was carried only by ships which had not been fully modernised.

The 4.7in (120mm) gun aboard the *Nelson* class was poorly designed. The 4.5in (114mm) and 5.25in (133mm) AA weapons were intended to serve in a dual-purpose role as medium guns but the former was unsuited to the task.

The Royal Navy had been interested in the development of small-calibre weapons for defence against dive-bombers since 1921 and needed multi-barrelled AA mountings. The prototype of the 2pdr

(40mm) mounting developed by Vickers was installed on board *Valiant* in 1930, but its poor ballistic performance suggested that further development was called for. The later 1938 model had a muzzle velocity of 2,400ft/sec (730m/sec). This pom-pom was introduced on board British capital ships until 1944 in an eight-barrelled mounting.

The well-known and efficient 40mm Bofors AA gun was received only by units refitted in the United States. All the 40mm Bofors (including a number of six-barrelled mountings) aboard *Vanguard* were produced in Britain under licence. This was also the case with the 20mm Oerlikon from 1940, though the ineffectiveness of this weapon against aircraft was quickly appreciated. The UP (unrotated projectile) anti-aircraft rocket, introduced at the beginning of 1941, was a complete failure.

Calibre	Model	Wt of shell	Muzzle velocity	Altitude	Rds/min
5.25in 50-cal	Mk I	80.5lb	2,625ft/sec	45,930ft	8
4.7in 40-cal	Mk XII	50lb	2,460ft/sec	32,150ft	8
4.5in 45-cal	Mk I	55lb	2,425ft/sec	39,700ft	12
4in 45-cal	Mk XVI	36lb	2,660ft/sec	38,710ft	18
4in 45-cal	Mk V	31lb	2,395ft/sec	31,150ft	12
2pdr 40-cal	Mk VIII	1.7lb	2,395ft/sec	4,920ft	90
40mm 60-cal	Bofors	2lb	2,800ft/sec	7,550ft	115
20mm 65-cal	Oerlikon	0.25lb	2,725ft/sec	2,950ft	450

Hood (as in 1941)

Displacement: 44,300/49,140t
Dimensions: 259.3 x 31.7 x 9.4m
Machinery: Brown-Curtis turbines, 4 shafts, 144,000shp
Fuel: 4,700t oil
Speed/range: 31.0kt (28.0kt in 1941); 8,500nm at 14kt
Armour: Belt 305mm, deck 152mm total, main armament 381mm, CT 279mm
Weight of armour: 13,870t = 31.3% of normal displacement
Armament: 8 x 15in 42-cal; up to 00.03.40 also 12 x 5.5in 50-cal
Anti-aircraft guns: 14 x 4in 45-cal, 24 x 2pdr, 5 x 20 UP launchers
Complement: 1,418 in May 1941
Builder: John Brown (laid down 01.09.1916; launched 22.08.1918; commissioned 15.05.1920)

▶▲ An aerial photograph of Hood taken on 9 October 1940.

▶▶▲ Hood in June 1939 shortly after her refit when four 4in HA guns were fitted.

▼ Hood in 1941.

Hood was the only unit of a class of three battlecruisers to be laid down. Her keel was originally laid on 31 May 1916. Three sister ships (Anson, Howe and Rodney), ordered on 7 April 1916, were never begun, and the materials allocated were used for the later battleships Nelson and Rodney (q.v.).

A refit at Portsmouth lasting from 3 June 1929 to 28 May 1931 saw her machinery overhauled, her fuel bunker capacity increased by 800 tons, a new fire control system installed and the first eight-barrelled 2pdr pom-pom batteries fitted. In her final refit, from March to May 1940, all the 5.5in (140mm) secondary guns were removed and her anti-aircraft armament was augmented by three 4in (102mm) twin mountings and five of the new UP rocket projectors. A total reconstruction approved in March 1939 was not carried out. A radical strengthening of the ship's horizontal protection had been intended together with the installation of a new dual-purpose

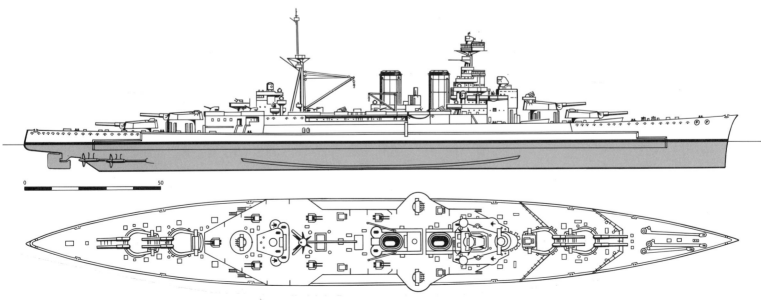

0   50

battery of sixteen 5.25in (133mm) guns; new boilers and turbines would have enabled the ship to have reached her original designed speed.

Hood operated in the North Sea in the autumn of 1939. She was hit by bomb dropped by a Ju 88 which failed to explode but caused minor damage to her anti-torpedo bulge; the German propaganda service circulated a completely fictitious report detailing the 'grave' damage done. She took part in the bombardment of the French Fleet at Mers-el-Kebir on 3 July 1940, and was in the North Sea prepared to resist the expected German invasion in September 1940.

In company with the battleship *Prince of Wales*, *Hood* intercepted and engaged the German battleship *Bismarck* and heavy cruiser *Prinz Eugen* in the Denmark Strait on 24 May 1941. After receiving heavy hits she blew up and sank with the loss of all but three of her crew.

G3 Class

Displacement: 48,400/53,909t
Dimensions: 260.9 x 32.3 x 10.0m
Machinery: Turbines, 4 shafts, 160,000shp
Fuel: 5,000t oil max.
Speed/range: 32.0–33.0kt
Armour: Belt 356mm, deck 203mm max., main armament 432mm, CT 305mm
Weight of armour: 14,700t = 30.4% of normal displacement
Armament: 9 x 16in 45-cal, 16 x 6in 50-cal
Anti-aircraft guns: 6 x 4.7in 45-cal, 40 x 2pdr
Complement: 1,716

From 1919 to 1921 a number of capital ship designs embodying war experience were prepared, and against foreign opposition from Japan and the United States Britain proposed a battlecruiser type of gigantic proportions which would easily outmatch anything planned abroad at the time. Many sketches were put forward, culminating in a design which was accepted in February 1921. The order for four ships was put out to tender, and those from John Brown, Beardmore, Fairfield and Swan Hunter were accepted on 26 October.

However, as a result of this construction and the ever-escalating naval race among the superpowers, it was

decided to call a preliminary truce to see if a naval limitation treaty could be worked out. No country wanted the great expense involved in such construction even though all wanted the ships for their fleets. The Washington Treaty resulted in the abandonment of the G3s, although, as a concession, Britain was allowed to build two ships with 16in guns, and much reduced versions of the design, *Nelson* and *Rodney*, were produced (q.v.). Had the G3 design materialised the ships would have had no equal at the time.

'G3' class battlecruisers (final design).
(Drawing by Ray Burt)

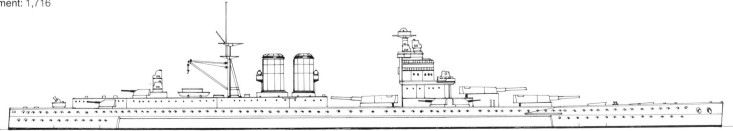

Barham (as in 1939)

Displacement: 36,600t (full operational displacement 31,350 tons standard)
Dimensions: As before
Machinery/fuel: As before
Speed/range: 22.5kt (on trials, 29.11.1933)
Armour: As before but horizontal protection over magazines increased by 102mm
Weight of armour: Deck armour heavier by 500t = 9,400t total
Armament: As before
Anti-aircraft guns: 8 x 4in 45-cal, 32 x 2pdr pom-pom
Complement: 1,260

Barham in 1941.

Barham, 1940.

During a major refit at Portsmouth from January 1931 to January 1934 *Barham* received anti-torpedo bulges (she was the last ship in the class to be so modified), her two funnels were combined into a single broad structure, the after torpedo tubes were removed and the armoured deck over the magazines was reinforced by 102mm (4in) thick plates; a new fire control system was fitted, together with an aircraft catapult and a very heavy AA defence for the period comprising four 4in (102mm) and two automatic eight-barrelled 2pdr mountings. During modernisation from February to July 1938 the single 4in AA guns were replaced by twin Mk XVI weapons of the same calibre, while at the beginning of 1941 two further pom-pom mountings were fitted.

The ship served in Mediterranean from 1935 but was attached to the Home Fleet in the autumn of 1939. She was torpedoed by *U30* on 28 December 1939 and under repair until April 1940. Returning to the Mediterranean, she took part in the bombardment of the French Fleet at Mers-el-Kebir in July 1940, the Battle of Cape Matapan in March 1941 and the bombardment of Bardia and Tripoli. She was badly damaged by a 500kg (1,100lb) bomb off Crete on 27 May 1941, but repairs were completed at Alexandria by the end of July 1941. *Barham* was sunk by *U331* off Sollum on 25 November 1941; 396 crewmen were saved out of 1,258 aboard.

Malaya (as in 1939)

Displacement: 36,000t (operational displacement 31,465 tons standard)
Dimensions: 193.4 x 31.7 x 0.3m
Machinery: As before
Fuel: 3,350t oil
Speed/range: 23.7kt (on trials, 04.11.1936)
Armour: New CT only 127mm; armour over magazines strengthened by 102mm, above machinery by 63mm
Weight of armour: Deck armour 800t more, CT 220t less
Armament: As before; all 12 x 6in guns removed 00.09.1943
Anti-aircraft guns: 8 x 4in 45-cal, 16 x 2pdr; 12 x 4in, 32 x 2pdr, 17 x 20mm from 00.12.1942
Complement: 1,300 approx.

First refitted between September 1927 and March 1929 when new anti-torpedo bulges were installed and the two funnels were trunked together, *Malaya* was reconstructed between October 1934 and December 1936, when her horizontal armour was strengthened, 4in (102mm) twin AA guns replaced the former single mountings, all underwater torpedo tubes were removed and an aircraft catapult was installed amidships above the level of the upper deck (though this was removed during the ship's 1942 refit).

Before and after her 1940 refit *Malaya* served in the Mediterranean and took part in the most important operations against the Italian Fleet; she was also used in convoy escort duties along the West African coast. During the latter operations she was torpedoed by *U106* on 20 March 1941, undergoing repairs in the USA in July 1941. From July 1941 to the summer of 1943 she was employed on convoy escort duties on the UK–Malta and Cape Town–UK routes.

She was laid up in July 1943, her machinery in poor condition, and most of her complement were transferred to other *Queen Elizabeth* class units. Her 6in (152mm) guns were removed and after urgent repairs the ship was transferred to reserve in September 1943. She was recommissioned in May 1944 in preparation for the Normandy landings and took part in coastal bombardment duties; she was returned to reserve in October 1944. *Malaya* was decommissioned in May 1945 and was then used as a training hulk; sold for scrap on 20 February 1946, she was broken up the same year.

The reconstructed *Malaya*, 1941.

Warspite (as in 1939–45)

Displacement: 36,200t (operational displacement 31,135 tons standard)
Dimensions: 193.4 x 31.7 x 10.1m
Machinery: Parsons turbines, 4 shafts, 80,000shp
Fuel: 3,600t oil
Speed/range: 23.5kt; 7,000nm at 12kt
Armour: CT only 76mm; armour over magazines strengthened by 102mm, above engine room by 63mm
Weight of armour: 9,530t = 30.1% of standard displacement
Armament: 8 x 15in 42-cal, 8 x 6in 45-cal
Anti-aircraft guns: 8 x 4in 45-cal, 32 x 2pdr

In her first refit between November 1924 and April 1926 *Warspite* received anti-torpedo bulges. She was totally reconstructed at Portsmouth between March 1934 and March 1937, when she had new boilers and machinery installed, the elevation of her main armament was increased to 30 degrees, four 6in (152mm) guns were removed, her AA defences were substantially increased and the latest fire control equipment was installed. On trials she reached 23.8 knots.

Warspite was involved in the attack on German destroyers at Narvik on 13 April 1940. Transferred to the Mediterranean at the end of April 1940, she took part in

various operations, including Cape Matapan, until April 1941 and during the Battle of Crete received a heavy bomb hit in May 1941. She served with the British Eastern Fleet from February 1942, returning to the Mediterranean in April 1943. During the landings at Salerno she was badly damaged by a German glider bomb on 16 September 1943; she was towed to Gibraltar for temporary repairs and arrived at Rosyth for full repairs in March 1944. She was deployed off Normandy in June 1944 with only three functioning 15in (381mm) turrets and no secondary battery and after bombarding land targets on 13 June 1944 was mined and seriously damaged. However, the ship continued in operation following makeshift repairs, bombarding the ports of Brest, Le Havre and Walcheren between August and November 1944. She was placed in reserve in February 1945, stricken on 31 July 1946 and sold for scrapping in early 1947. On 23 April 1947, during the voyage to the breakers, she ran aground; she was salvaged in July 1950 and gradually broken up over the next five years.

Warspite, 1939.

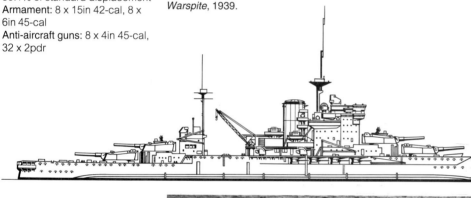

Warspite in 1938 after her final refit.

Queen Elizabeth/Valiant (after reconstruction)

Displacement: 37,150t operational displacement; (*Queen Elizabeth* 32,700 tons standard displacement)
Dimensions: 193.4 x 31.7 x 10.2m
Machinery: Parsons turbines, 4 shafts, 80,000shp
Fuel: 3,450t oil
Speed/range: 24kt; 6,000nm at 12kt
Armour: CT only 76mm; armour over magazines strengthened by 102mm, above engine room by 38mm
Weight of armour: 9,520t = 29.7% of standard displacement (*Valiant*, 1940)
Armament: 8 x 15in 42-cal, 20 x 4.5in 45-cal DP
Anti-aircraft guns: 32 x 2pdr, 47 x 20mm

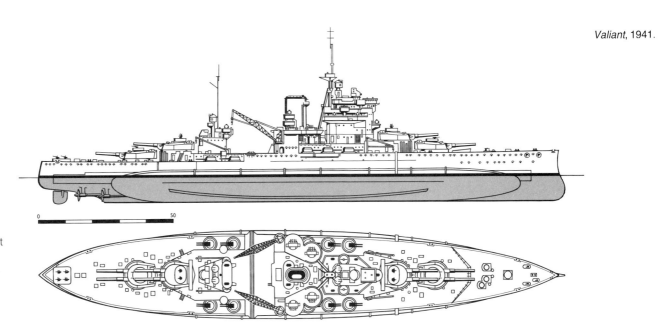

Valiant, 1941.

Ship	First reconstruction	Second reconstruction
Queen Elizabeth	00.06.1926–00.10.1927	11.08.1937–31.01.1941
Valiant	00.03.1929–00.12.1930	01.03.1937–25.11.1939

The modernised *Valiant*, in 1943.

Queen Elizabeth at Rosyth in 1941.

During their first refits both units were fitted with anti-torpedo bulges and a single funnel. Reconstruction was more comprehensive than for *Warspite*: the entire secondary battery was removed and replaced by the new 4.5in (114mm) dual-purpose guns, which were primarily heavy anti-aircraft weapons. In contrast to *Warspite*, *Queen Elizabeth* and *Valiant* had eight instead of six small-tube high-pressure boilers and the ships' maximum speed was theoretically one knot higher. The operational displacement excludes 828 tons of water in protective compartments surrounding the magazines.

Following reconstruction at Devonport *Valiant* was deployed to the Mediterranean in June 1940. *Queen Elizabeth* was reconstructed at Portsmouth, but on 12 December 1940 she was transferred to Rosyth because of the danger of air attack ; on completion in May 1941 she sailed for the Mediterranean.

Both ships were badly damaged by delayed action mines set by Italian frogmen at Alexandria on 19 December 1941. *Valiant* made for Durban, South Africa, after temporary repairs and was in dry dock from 15 April to 7 July 1942. *Queen Elizabeth* sank in shallow water, was raised and temporarily repaired in a floating dock, but her damage was so serious that she remained under repair at the US Navy Yard in Norfolk, Virginia, from 6 September 1942 to 1 June 1943. Following repairs she was transferred to the British Eastern Fleet and was joined there by *Valiant* in January 1944. Both vessels took part in carrier raids against Japanese bases in Indonesia.

Valiant was badly damaged while under refit in a floating dock at Trincomalee, Ceylon, on 8 August 1944. She arrived in Devonport on 1 February 1945 but repairs were abandoned in July 1945 and the ship was subsequently used as a training hulk for stokers until being sold for scrap in January 1948. She left Devonport for the breaker's yard on 11 August 1948. *Queen Elizabeth* was refitted at Durban in the autumn of 1944 She returned to the Eastern Fleet and took part in further operations, including that against Rangoon. She was recalled to Britain in July 1945, placed in reserve in August 1945, stricken in May 1948 and scrapped from July 1948.

Royal Sovereign Class (as in 1939–44)

Displacement: 33,500t (*Revenge*) to 35,570t (*Ramillies*) full operational displacement (1944)
Dimensions: 187.3 x 30.9 x 10.1–10.6m
Machinery: As before but with lower output
Fuel: 3,200t oil
Speed/range: 19.0–19.5kt; ,000nm at 10kt
Armour: As before, but armoured deck strengthened by 51mm in *Resolution*, *Ramillies* and *Royal Sovereign* in 1942
Weight of armour: As before (*Revenge*); 9,300t (*Royal Oak*); 8,730t (rest)
Armament: As before, but from 1942 only 8 x 6in 45-cal
Anti-aircraft guns: 8 x 4in 45-cal, 16 x 2pdr (from 1941–42: 24 x 2pdr)
Complement: 1,040–1,240

Royal Sovereign at Philadelphia in September 1943.

Royal Oak was the only unit to be rebuilt between the wars. In the first modernisations the two 6in (152mm) guns at forecastle deck level and after torpedo tubes were landed, and in the second the remaining torpedo tubes were removed and new twin 4in (102mm) twin AA guns were introduced in place of the single mountings of the same calibre.

A strengthening of the horizontal armour for *Resolution* and *Ramillies* and an increase in the elevation of the 15in (381mm) guns in all five ships were planned, but these modifications were postponed indefinitely because of the threat of war. In a string of minor refits in 1939 a new fire control system, aerials, searchlights, seaplane catapults and experimental AA weapons were fitted.

In addition to her modernised weapons *Royal Oak* was the first to receive the final AA armament and a catapult on 'X' turret. The armoured deck was increased to 5in (127mm) above the magazines and to 3.5in (89mm) above the engine room. This represented an increase in weight of 920 tons. The ship was torpedoed and sunk at Scapa Flow by *U47* on 14 October 1939. The other ships of the class took part in numerous second-line duties, mainly convoy escort.

Ramillies was torpedoed by a Japanese midget submarine off Madagascar on 30 May 1942; repairs were completed at Devonport by June 1943. She bombarded German positions on the Normandy coast and in southern France in 1944. Placed in reserve on 31 January 1945, she was stricken in December 1947, sold for scrap on 2 February 1948 and broken up from April 1948.

Ship	First modernisation	Second modernisation	Reconstruction
Royal Sovereign	00.09.1927–00.04.1928	00.06.1937–00.02.1938	–
Royal Oak	00.10.1922–00.05.1924	00.04.1926–00.06.1926	29.06.1934 to 00.07.1936
Revenge	00.01.1928–00.12 1928	00.01.1939–00.08.1939	–
Resolution	00.12.1926–00.01.1928	00.12.1935–00.09.1936	–
Ramillies	00.08.1926–00.03.1927	00.02.1933–00.08.1934	–

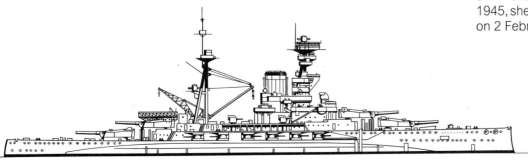

Royal Oak, 1939.

One of the last photographs taken of HMS *Royal Oak*.

Revenge was reduced to reserve on account of her poor condition on 30 September 1943. She served for a while as a depot ship before being stricken in March 1948 and sold for scrapping that July.

Resolution took part in the bombardment of the French Fleet at Mers-el-Kebir in July 1940. During the attacks on Dakar in September 1940 she was torpedoed and badly damaged by French submarine *Bévéziers* and was under repair in the United States until September 1941. She subsequently saw service in the Indian Ocean but returned home in poor condition. Consigned to reserve in October 1943, she was disarmed in June 1944, sold in February 1948 and scrapped from May 1948.

Royal Sovereign spent three years in the Mediterranean and on Atlantic convoy duty. Following a full refit in the United States, necessary because of her poor condition, that lasted from September 1942 to 14 September 1943, she spent a further month in the Indian Ocean then returned to Britain. She went into reserve on 5 November 1943 but was loaned to the Soviet Union on 30 May 1944 as a partial reparation against a promised Italian battleship; she sailed for Murmansk on 17 August as a convoy escort under name *Archangelsk* but was never employed operationally by the Soviet Navy. She returned to Rosyth on 4 February 1949 and was immediately stricken; sold in July 1949, she was scrapped after September that year.

Repulse (as in 1941)

Displacement: 38,300t operational displacement; 33,000 tons standard
Dimensions: 240.2 x 31.9 x 9.8m
Machinery: As before but only 112,400shp (1936)
Fuel: 4,940t oil maximum
Speed/range: 28.36kt (1936); 5,500nm at 18kt
Armour: Belt 229mm, deck 146mm, main armament as before
Weight of armour: Not published following 1920 and 1936 refits
Armament: 6 x 15in 42-cal, 9 x 4in 45-cal
Anti-aircraft guns: 1941: 6 x 4in 45-cal, 24 x 2pdr, 8 x 20mm
Complement: 1,300

In her December 1918–January 1921 refit *Repulse* received anti-torpedo bulges, had her belt increased from 6in (152mm) to 9in (229mm) and had up to 4in (102mm) of additional armour worked into her deck. During reconstruction from April 1933 to May 1936 her armour was increased to 5.75in (146mm) above the magazines and to 3.5in (89mm) above the machinery. The anti-torpedo bulges were also reinforced and a catapult was fitted abaft the second funnel together with a hangar for four floatplanes; the machinery was overhauled but the maximum elevation of the main armament remained at 20 degrees. During trials in March 1936 *Repulse* achieved only 28.36 knots at 112,400shp.

A further major refit planned for 1941 was postponed because of the war and never carried out, and although the AA armament was modified it remained surprisingly weak. The 4in (102mm) AA guns were in single mountings and the third eight-barrelled pom-pom and 20mm Oerlikons were installed only a few months before the ship was lost.

Repulse was employed in home waters in September 1939 and operated off Norway in April 1940. She acted as a convoy escort until summer 1941 and was transferred to the British Eastern Fleet in October 1941, docking at Singapore on 2 December that year. On 8 December she sailed in company with the battleship *Prince of Wales* and four destroyers (but without air cover) to attack Japanese naval forces in their landing areas off the Malayan coast. Both ships were overwhelmed by a massed air attack by 80 Japanese aircraft on 10 December. *Repulse* was struck by a torpedo at midday and sank at 1233 hours after a further four hits.

Repulse following the completion of her 1936 modernisation.

Repulse in September 1940.

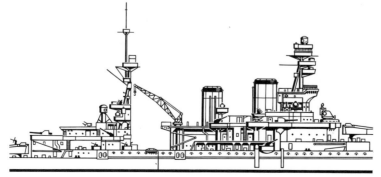

Repulse, 1936.

Renown (as in 1939)

Displacement: 36,660t operational displacement; 30,750 tons standard

Dimensions: 240.2 x 31.3 x 9.3m

Machinery: Parsons turbines, 4 shafts, 120,000shp (1936)

Fuel: 4,800t oil max.

Speed/range: 29.5kt

Armour: Belt 229mm, deck 127mm, CT 76mm, main armament as before

Weight of armour: 7,200t approx.

Armament: 6 x 15in 42-cal, 20 x 4.5in 45-cal DP

Anti-aircraft guns: 24 x 2pdr; 1944: 28 x 2pdr, 64 x 20mm

Complement: 1,300 (1945: 1,440)

In her Portsmouth refit from May 1923 to August 1926 *Renown* had her belt armour increased to 9in (229mm), mostly using plates originally intended for the Chilean battleship *Almirante Cochrane*, her horizontal armour was strengthened by from 1in (25mm) to 1.5in (38mm) and a new and lighter type of anti-torpedo bulge was added. The weight of the belt armour rose by 609 tons and that of the horizontal armour by 1,187 tons.

In reconstruction work at Portsmouth between September 1936 and August 1939 the appearance of the ship was changed and a modern conning tower containing all command and fire control equipment was fitted. New boilers and machinery were installed which was 2,800 tons lighter but gave the same performance. On trials at end of July 1939 *Renown* reached 30.1 knots at 120,560shp.

The main 15in (381mm) armament was modernised and the angle of elevation of the guns increased to 30 degrees, and all the 4in (102mm) guns were replaced by 4.5in (114mm) dual-purpose weapons in twin mountings. An aircraft catapult was added, but this was removed during repairs at Rosyth between 22 February and 9 June 1943, at which time the AA defence was augmented by four 2pdrs and 29 x 20mm guns.

During the war *Renown* was involved in naval operations in all theatres. She operated in the North Sea in September 1939 and from October conducted unsuc-

cessful searches in the Atlantic for the German 'pocket battleships' *Deutschland* and *Admiral Graf Spee*. On 9 April 1940 she exchanged fire with *Scharnhorst* and *Gneisenau* off the Norwegian coast, receiving light damage in the process. She was assigned to Force H in the Mediterranean from August 1940 to May 1941 and took part in the pursuit of *Bismarck* in May 1941. She supported the Allied landings in North Africa in November 1942. Following a refit she served with Home Fleet from August 1943 but was transferred to the British Eastern Fleet early in 1944, taking part in carrier raids in the Indian Ocean and bombarding Surabaya up to mid-October 1944. Following a three-month refit at Durban, she returned to UK waters in March 1945. She was reduced to reserve on account of her poor condition on 15 May 1945 and became a depot ship at Portsmouth and Devonport. Stricken on 1 June 1948, she was sold for scrapping the following August.

▶▶▲ *Renown* after her reconstruction, in camouflage, in late 1943.

Renown, 1939.

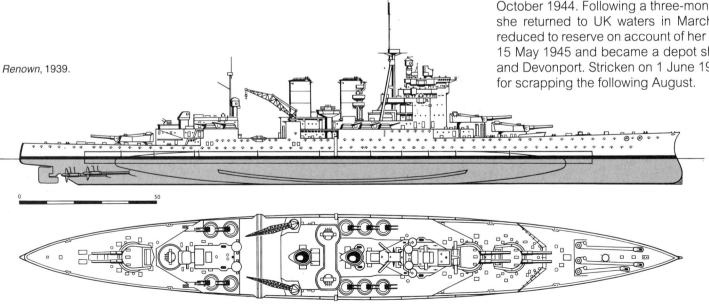

Nelson/Rodney

Displacement: 1927: 35,600/ 38,400t, 33,800 tons standard; 1942: 43,830t, operational displacement 36,000t (*Rodney*)
Dimensions: 215.0 x 32.3 x 10.8m
Machinery: Brown-Curtis turbines, 2 shafts, 45,000shp
Fuel: 3,850t oil
Speed/range: 23.0kt; 7,000nm at 16kt
Armour: Belt 356mm, deck 160mm, main armament 406mm, CT 356mm
Weight of armour: 9,750t = 27.4% of normal displacement
Armament: 9 x 16in 45-cal, 12 x 6in 50-cal
Anti-aircraft guns: 1939: 6 x 4.7in 40-cal, 24 x 2pdr; 1944: 4.7in as before but 44 x 2pdr, 68 x 20mm (*Rodney*), 48 x 2pdr, 6 x 40mm, 61 x 20mm (*Nelson*)
Complement: 1,330–1,360

On trials *Nelson* achieved 23.55 knots and at deep displacement load 23.05 knots at 45,803shp; *Rodney* made 23.8 knots at 45,614shp deep displacement.

Nelson was mined off the Scottish coast on 4 December 1939 and under repair until July 1940. She was employed in the Atlantic and Mediterranean from June 1941 and was struck by an Italian aerial torpedo on 27 September that year; returned to Rosyth, she was under repair until April 1942. She saw service in the Mediterranean until November 1943 and following a refit was employed off Normandy; mined on 18 June 1944, she was in dry dock in Philadelphia for five months, after

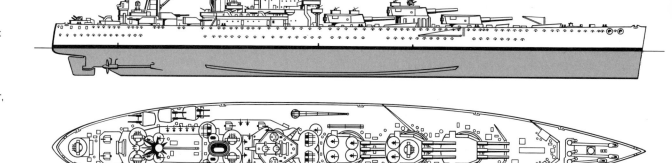

Ship	Builder	Laid down	Launched	Commissioned
Nelson	Armstrong	28.12.1922	03.09.1925	15.08.1927
Rodney	Cammell Laird	28.12.1922	17.12.1925	07.12.1927

Nelson, 1945.

The Coronation Fleet Review, with HMS *Nelson* in the foreground, 17 May 1937.

HMS *Rodney* photographed ten days before the Normandy landings.

which she was despatched to the Indian Ocean and was involved in operations off the Malayan coast. She returned home in November 1945. *Nelson* was employed as a training ship from August 1946, stricken in February 1948 and scrapped in 1949.

Rodney was in urgent need of a refit when war broke out and had to have her rudder assembly repaired in early 1940; there were further problems following two near-misses off the coast of Norway on 9 April 1940. The ship was under repair from December 1940 to January

1941. Structural weaknesses began to become apparent during Atlantic operations. *Rodney* participated in the sinking of *Bismarck* on 27 May 1941, after which she put into Boston for repairs to her machinery. A refit in the winter of 1941–42 failed to rectify her structural problems and the hull was further damaged in subsequent Atlantic operations, so much so that the ship was earmarked for reconstruction in late 1944. Flagship of the Home Fleet at Scapa Flow in November 1944, she was reduced to reserve in 1945 and sold for scrapping in 1948.

King George V Class

Displacement: 1940: 42,750t operational displacement, 36,727 tons standard; 1945: 45,000–46,000t, 39,100–40,000 tons standard
Dimensions: 226.0 x 31.4 x 10.1m
Machinery: Parsons turbines, 4 shafts, 110,000shp
Fuel: 3,750t
Speed/range: 28.0kt; 6,000nm at 13kt, 2,560nm at 28kt
Armour: Belt 381mm, deck 152mm, main armament 330mm, CT 76mm
Weight of armour: 12,612t = 33.8% of standard displacement
Armament: 10 x 14in 45-cal, 16 x 5.25in 50-cal DP
Anti-aircraft guns: 32 x 2pdr; 1945: up to 88 x 2pdr
Complement: 1940: 1,420

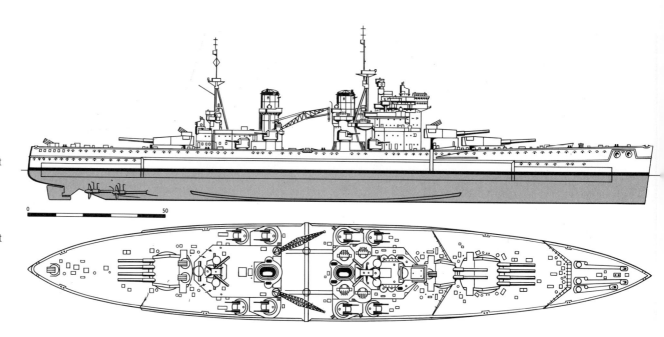

Ship	Builder	Laid down	Launched	Commissioned
King George V	Vickers, Tyne	01.01.1937	21.02.1939	11.12.1940
Prince of Wales	Cammell Laird	01.01.1937	03.05.1939	31.03.1941
Duke of York	John Brown	05.05.1937	28.02.1940	04.11.1941
Anson	Swan Hunter	20.07.1937	24.02.1940	22.06.1942
Howe	Fairfield	01.06.1937	09.04.1940	29.08.1942

King George V, 1940.

▶ A bird's-eye view of HMS King George V in 1945.

▶▼ King George V in 1941.

Howe achieved 27.7 knots at 113,457shp on trials at the end of August 1942 and 27 knots at 114,350shp in November 1944.

In company with Hood, Prince of Wales engaged Bismarck and Prinz Eugen on 24 May 1941 but broke off the engagement after receiving damage. She was at Singapore in October 1941 but in company with Repulse was sunk off the Malayan coast by Japanese torpedo aircraft on 10 December 1941.

King George V took part in the pursuit of Bismarck in May 1941 and operated off northern Norway and on the Murmansk convoy run. Following duty in the Mediterranean she underwent a long refit until July 1944. She was transferred to the Pacific Fleet in the autumn of 1944 and took part in combined operations with the US Fleet from April 1945. She was reduced to reserve in 1946, stricken in 1957 and broken up from 1958.

Duke of York remained in European waters throughout the Second World War, mostly on escort duty for the Murmansk convoys; she was involved in the sinking of the German battlecruiser Scharnhorst on 26 December 1943. Transferred to the Pacific for operations against the Japanese in August 1945, she entered reserve in 1949, was stricken in 1957 and scrapped from 1958.

Howe bore the name Beatty until 1940. After commissioning, the ship operated with the Home Fleet until April 1943 and was on duty off Sicily and in Italian waters until October 1943; she then entered refit until June 1944. She was transferred to the British Pacific Fleet and deployed off Japan from January 1945, then overhauled at Durban, returning to the Home Fleet in September 1945. She became a training ship in 1946, was stricken and sold for scrapping in 1957 and broken up from 1958.

Anson was formerly named Jellicoe. She served as a convoy escort on the Murmansk run from September 1942 and was employed with the British Pacific Fleet, but not used on operations, from March 1945. She was a guard ship at Tokyo and saw duty in Australian waters from January to July 1946. A training ship until 1956, she was stricken in 1957 and subsequently broken up.

Lion Class

Displacement: 40,500 tons standard
Dimensions: 239.3 x 31.7 x 10.1m
Machinery: Parsons turbines, 4 shafts, 130,000shp
Fuel: 3,720t oil
Speed/range: 30.0kt; 14,000nm at 10kt
Armour: Belt 381mm, deck 152mm, main armament 381mm, CT 114mm
Armament: 9 x 16in 45-cal, 16 x 5.25in 50-cal DP
Anti-aircraft guns: 48 x 2pdr
Complement: 1,680

Ship	Builder	Laid down	Launched
Lion	Vickers, Tyne	04.09.1939	–
Temeraire	Cammell Laird	01.06.1939	–
Conqueror	John Brown	–	–
Thunderer	Fairfield	–	–

In 1937 naval treaty agreements involving the USA, Britain and Japan could not be settled; in fact, the last had for all practical purposes withdrawn from the discussions altogether. Faced with this uncertainty, the Admiralty decided to draw up plans for new ships armed with 16in guns and the design was approved in June 1938.

Construction proceeded at a very slow pace, and as urgent commitment was needed elsewhere work was halted for one year to give priority to escort destroyers. Further postponement followed, and ultimately these much needed ships never did materialise.

Lion class design, 1938.
(Drawing by Ray Burt)

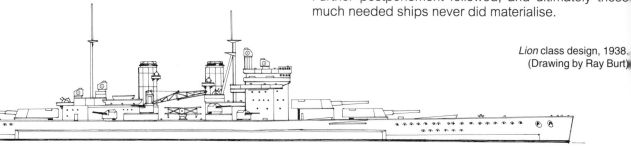

Vanguard

Displacement: 52,245t operational displacement, 44,614 tons standard
Dimensions: 243.8 x 32.9 x 10.7m
Machinery: Parsons turbines, 4 shafts, 130,000shp
Fuel: 4,500t oil + 450t diesel
Speed/range: 29.5kt; 7,150nm at 15kt, 4,400nm at 25kt
Armour: Belt 356mm, deck 152mm, main armament 330mm, CT 76mm
Weight of armour: 14,980t = 28.7% of operational displacement, 33.0% of standard displacement
Armament: 8 x 15in 42-cal, 16 x 5.25in 50-cal DP
Anti-aircraft guns: 73 x 40mm
Complement: 1,900
Builder: John Brown, Clydebank (laid down 02.10.1941; launched 30.11.1944; commissioned 09.08.1946)

Vanguard entering dock in about 1952. Note the huge flare to the bows.

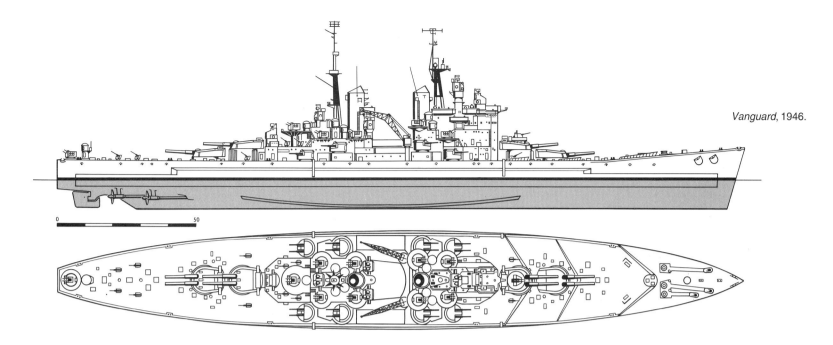

Vanguard, 1946.

On trials *Vanguard* attained 31.57 knots at 136,000shp. She was a very seaworthy vessel. Employed as a training ship in November 1949, she became the flagship of the Reserve Fleet and a NATO staff ship at Portsmouth in 1955.

She was stricken on 7 June 1960, sold for scrapping and broken up at Faslane from August 1960.

Vanguard leaving her builders on completion, 2 May 1946.

Italy

Developments up to 1918

In 1895 the Italian Fleet held third place in the world in terms of battleship tonnage. Although poorly endowed with raw materials, and with a disproportionately small industrial base still largely undeveloped, since the 1870s Italy had nevertheless managed to amass a squadron of battleships armed with the most powerful naval guns to be found anywhere. The impetus for this had been the notion of colonial expansion: amongst other things, the young monarchy had ambitions to carve for itself a slice of Africa.

Italian ships, mainly the work of the builder Benedetto Brin, excited the interest of the world but by 1906 they were hopelessly obsolete, and their huge guns were virtually useless even for harbour defence. In that year Italy's active fleet had only four battleships less than ten years of age, and two of these carried guns of only 254mm (10in) calibre.

The Italian defeat in Abyssinia in 1896, coupled with a chronic domestic economic crisis, had prevented the building of large numbers of standard battleships, and in order to maintain a strong naval presence in the Mediterranean the idea arose of devising a different type of ship. There was no shortage of gifted naval architects. With his design for *Regina Elena* in 1900, the Chief Designer of the Italian Navy, Cuniberti, created a class of fast but less heavily armed battleships which were the forerunners of the future battlecruiser. However, the building of the four ships took so long—Italian yards were dependent on imports of foreign steel—that when these interesting prototypes finally entered service in 1908 they were outclassed by HMS *Dreadnought*, which had been designed five years later, and completed two years earlier, than the Italian units.

At the beginning of 1908 Italy had no realisable design for a dreadnought-type battleship. Capital had been made available in the 1907 Budget, but there was evidently some uncertainty about whether it could be relied upon to continue, The Admiralty invited tenders for the design of a battleship early in 1908. The two prize-winning submissions were sketches of a 16,000-tonne ship with 305mm (12in) guns and a 17,000-tonne ship with 345mm (13.5in) guns in four twin turrets, but in the event the first Italian dreadnought, which was based on a design dated April 1908 (!), bore no resemblance to either of these and carried twelve heavy guns in triple turrets.

It is not now possible to say whether the design was influenced by an earlier Russian competition in which Cuniberti had participated, or by the intention of the rival Austro-Hungarian Navy only to build battleships armed with at least eight 305mm (12in) guns. Whatever the reason, Battleship 'A', for which building approval was granted in 1907, would turn out to be a much larger version of what had been originally planned.

One of the last Italian battleships: *Giulio Cesare*, pictured here under the Soviet flag as *Novorossiysk*.

Although Italy had suitable naval yards—those at La Spezia and Castellammare were state-owned and those at Ansaldo (Genoa) and Odero (Sestri Ponente) were private—she did not have at her disposal the necessary capacity in steel and armour production or the means to manufacture heavy naval guns. Armour plate imported from the United States and used in the construction of earlier battleships was of poor quality and had been delivered late. At the time, only a branch of the British Armstrong company in Pozzuoli near Naples could turn out heavy guns. A new armaments partnership comprising the firms of Terni and Vickers was established in 1910 and began a collaboration with Armstrong Pozzuoli, but the combined energies of these concerns was still insufficient to meet the demands of the Italian Navy for heavy weapons.

In the intervening years, the race in battleship construction had gathered pace and Italy, as a nascent imperialist power, now required a more powerful fleet than hitherto in order to underpin her aggressive designs in North Africa, the Aegean and the Adriatic; the last was intended to become an 'Italian lake' ('Mare Nostrum'), even though at the time the eastern coast of the Adriatic was the territory of Italy's ally Austria-Hungary. In each case the plan was for military operations to open with troop landings on the beaches. Consequently, from 1907 to 1911 the building of six major capital ships was approved (*Dante Alighieri*, three *Conte di Cavour* class and two *Andrea Doria* class vessels) but these still fell short of what the Admiralty considered desirable for its expansionist policy. Larger and, above all, more heavily gunned 'super-dreadnoughts' were required.

Because of numerous fundamental design changes, it was not until the winter of 1914–15 that work commenced on four of these battle-cruisers, but following Italy's declaration of war on the Austro-Hungarian Empire on 23 May 1915 the need for them grew less pressing and building was soon afterwards discontinued. None of the ships was completed even after the war.

During the First World War, Italian capital ships took no part in fleet operations and so it is difficult to form an opinion of their quality. The oft-repeated criticism of their lightness may well be valid, but it should be remembered that they were intended for use solely in the Mediterranean, where they represented potentially stiff opposition for both France and the Austro-Hungarian Empire. Five of the six survived the First World War—*Leonardo da Vinci* was lost in an explosion in 1916—and, of these, three went on to survive the Second World War.

Older Battleships, 1915–1918

Apart from five veteran and long-decommissioned battleships which only saw service during the First World War as depot ships or floating batteries for harbour defence, four pre-dreadnoughts were on the active list. *Ammiraglio di Saint Bon* and *Emanuele Filiberto* had been completed in 1901 and were armed with four 254mm (10in) guns, and their two 13,500-tonne sister ships *Regina Margherita* and *Benedetto Brin* had entered service in 1904–05. At the time of their design (1898) they had been immensely powerful units, carrying four 203mm (8in) and twelve 152mm (6in) guns in addition to their main armament. The first pair spent the war in the northern Adriatic, where their purpose was to defend Venice. They survived undamaged and were stricken from the

Fleet in 1920. *Benedetto Brin* was the flagship of the 3rd Battleship Division from May 1915 and was lost at Brindisi on 27 September 1915 as the result of an explosion alleged to have been caused by Austrian sabotage. *Regina Margherita* sank on 11 December 1916 off the Italian-occupied Albanian port of Valona after running on to two mines laid by the German U-boat *UC14*.

Unfulfilled Orders

In order to secure its superiority over the Austro-Hungarian Fleet in the Adriatic, the Italian Navy drew up plans for a series of 'super-dread-noughts'. These would be very heavily protected with an armament of up to fifteen guns in triple turrets. At the beginning of 1913 the first design outlines appeared, one with twelve and another with nine guns, although later the total was reduced to eight, permitting the designed speed to be increased to 28 knots. The reasoning behind the scaling-down of Italian ambitions was probably an appreciation of the situation which had arisen after the Italo-Turkish war in the Mediterranean and concern at renewed political tensions with France, for after 1914 there would have been no particular call for such large and fast battleships in confined Adriatic waters.

In April 1914 contracts for the construction of four units were awarded to different yards. The name-ship of the class, *Francesco Carraciolo*, was laid down at Castellammare on 12 October 1914 and work on her three sister ships was started between March and June 1915 at Livorno and Genoa, but soon after Italy's entry into the war construction was halted. The contracts were cancelled at the beginning of 1916. No work was done even on the most advanced hull, that of *Carraciolo*, after the spring of 1916, and the only reason that building was restarted in October 1919 was to get the hull afloat and so free the slipway. After launching on 12 May 1920 the incomplete vessel was sold for conversion to a freighter, but this project proved to be uneconomic and the hull was scrapped the following year. The final design for *Carraciolo* showed a displacement of 34,000 tonnes, dimensions of 212 x 29.6 x 9.5m and four Parsons turbines producing 105,000shp and giving a speed of 28 knots. Armour details were 300mm belt, 51mm deck, 400mm main armament and 400mm conning tower and the armament comprised eight 381mm (15in) 40-cal in four twin turrets and twelve 6in (152mm) in casemates. The 381mm guns, designed by Armstrongs in 1914 and manufactured by Pozzuoli, were eventually mounted in so-called monitors (actually artillery lighters) between 1916 and 1918 for bombarding the Isonzo front. One of these lighters, *Faà di Bruno*, was redesignated *GM194* and used in the defence of Genoa in the Second World War.

Armament

All gun patterns, with the exception of the 305mm (12in) weapons on *Da Vinci* (which were also British) were developed in Britain by either Armstrongs or Vickers and produced in their Italian subsidiary factories at Pozzuoli and La Spezia respectively. They were by no means the world's best, and the finished articles were generally considered to be no better than average. Italian cordite technology was also at a fairly primitive stage, as the loss of *Da Vinci* and *Benedetto Brin* to internal explosion would seem to confirm.

Even before the war, the Italian Navy was under no illusion regarding the quality of its ships' gunnery and even the older Austro-Hungarian *Erzherzog* class pre-dreadnoughts with their 240mm (9.45in) main armament were considered too much of a handful for *Regina Elena* to cope with. The smaller Skoda 240mm guns were built in 1901 and had a maximum range of 16km (17,500yd), whereas the 1904 Armstrong 305mm (12in) model installed in *Regina Elena* had a maximum range of only 14km (15,300yd) and a slower rate of fire.

The alleged leadership shown by the Italian Navy in the introduction of 305mm (12in) guns in triple turrets is dubious, for the two British arms manufacturers building the 1909-model turrets for the Italian dreadnoughts had tendered designs for 305mm triple turrets for the first Russian dreadnought early in 1908 and presumably had the capacity to fulfil the Italian orders, but so long were the guns and turrets in manufacture that the first Italian dreadnought, *Dante Alighieri*, was commissioned several months after the Austro-Hungarian *Viribus Unitis*, which had been laid down and launched after the Italian vessel.

The *Conte di Cavour* class were the first dreadnoughts to receive AA armament, comprising adapted Armstrong 1909 guns mounted on the main turrets and not weapons purpose-built for air defence. It was not until 1917 that Italy introduced the 76mm (3in) 45-cal AA gun which had been in service with the Royal Navy since 1914.

Details of Italian Heavy and Medium Guns

Gun	Wt of shell	Muzzle velocity	Range/elevation
305mm 46-cal	452kg	840m/sec	18km/20°
305mm 40-cal	385kg	800m/sec	14km
203mm 45-cal	113kg	770m/sec	14km

Note: Italian shipyards were as follows: Naval Yard Castellammare di Stabia (Castellammare); R. Arsenale, La Spezia (La Spezia); Cantieri Ansaldo, Genoa, Sestri Ponenta (Ansaldo); Cantieri Odero, Genoa (Odero); Cantieri del Tirreno, Genoa (CdT Genoa); and the San Marco Yard (Cantieri Riuniti dell'Adriatico) of the former Stabilimento Tecnico Triestino at Trieste (Trieste).

Regina Elena Class

Displacement: 12,750–12,860/
14,000–14,100t
Dimensions: 144.0 x 22.4 x 8.0m
Machinery: 2 triple reciprocating
steam engines, 2 shafts,
20,000ihp
Fuel: 2,000t coal max.
Speed/range: 21.5kt
Armour: Belt 250mm, deck
37mm, main armament 203mm,
CT 250mm
Armament: 2 x 305mm 40-cal,
12 x 203mm 45-cal
Anti-aircraft guns: From 1917: 3
or 4 x 76mm 40-cal
Complement: 750 (wartime)

Despite their interesting construction, the ships, designed by Cuniberti, were not especially powerful for their size, although they were on average about two knots faster than their contemporaries in other navies. Because of financial difficulties, late deliveries and, not least, problems with their machinery following their acceptance trials, they did not enter service until 1908–09, by which time they were obsolete.

In May 1915 the ships of the class formed the 2nd Battle Division which, together with the rest of the Italian battle fleet, was based at Taranto. The ships were transferred to Valona in the autumn of 1916 as the 3rd Division, and remained in the Aegean and Ionian Sea area until the end of the war.

Regina Elena was stricken on 16 February 1923, *Vittorio Emanuele* on 1 April 1923 and *Napoli* on 3 September 1923, and all three were scrapped in 1927. *Roma* was stricken on 1 September 1927 and used as a hulk until broken up in 1932.

Ship	Builder	Laid down	Launched	Commissioned
Regina Elena	La Spezia	27.03.1901	19.06.1904	00.05.1908
Vittorio Emanuele	Castellammare	18.09.1901	12.10.1904	00.10.1908
Roma	La Spezia	20.09.1903	21.04.1907	07.09.1909
Napoli	Castellammare	21.10.1903	10.09.1905	23.06.1909

A pre-First World War postcard depicting *Regina Elena*.

Dante Alighieri

Displacement: 19,550/ 21,600t
Dimensions: 165.0 x 26.6 x 8.8m
Machinery: 4 Parsons turbines,
  shafts, 32,000shp
Fuel: 2,400t coal + 600t oil
Speed/range: 23.0kt; 4,800nm at
  10kt
Armour: Belt 250mm, deck
  40mm, main armament 250mm,
  CT 280mm
Armament: 12 x 305mm 46-cal,
  20 x 120mm 50-cal
Anti-aircraft guns: From 1916: 4
  x 76mm 40-cal
Complement: 970
Builder: Castellammare (laid
  down 06.06.1909; launched
  20.08.1910; commissioned
  15.01.1913)

Dante Alighieri on trials.

Dante Alighieri, 1913.

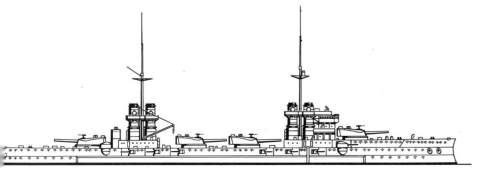

This first Italian dreadnought (designated Battleship 'A' in the 1907 Budget) was originally intended to displace 17,000 tonnes and carry eight 305mm (12in) guns in four twin turrets, the two central turrets to be arranged *en echelon*. Construction was not begun until 1909 and was then based on the plans of naval architect Masdea. The extent to which Cuniberti, Masdea's superior, influenced the project is not known, but although the design presented by Cuniberti in St Petersburg in March 1908 would have incorporated the Russian requirement for a main armament partly disposed in triple turrets amidships, it is not correct to say that the *Dante Alighieri*'s main guns were installed as per the 'Cuniberti arrangement'.

Dante Alighieri was both fast and heavily armed for her size. Trials began in November 1911 and the ship achieved 23.4 knots in the autumn of 1912; her main armament was delivered a year late by Armstrongs, in 1913. At the outbreak of war with Austria-Hungary, she was the flagship of the 1st Division at Taranto, where she remained until the Armistice in 1918. She underwent a partial modernisation in 1923 but was stricken on 1 July 1928 and scrapped the following year.

Conte di Cavour Class

Displacement: 22,900/ 24,250t; *Giulio Cesare* 23,200/24,800t
Dimensions: 176.0 x 28.0 x 9.0m
Machinery: 4 Parsons turbines, 4 shafts, 32,600shp
Fuel: 1,450t coal + 850t oil
Speed/range: 21.5kt; 4,800nm at 10kt
Armour: Belt 250mm, deck 70mm, main armament 280mm, CT 280mm
Weight of armour: 6,220t = 27.8% of normal displacement
Armament: 13 x 305mm 46-cal, 18 x 120mm 57-cal
Anti-aircraft guns: From 1916: 6 x 76mm 40-cal
Complement: 1,230

▲▶ The unlucky *Leonardo da Vinci* at the end of April 1914.

Conte di Cavour, 1915.

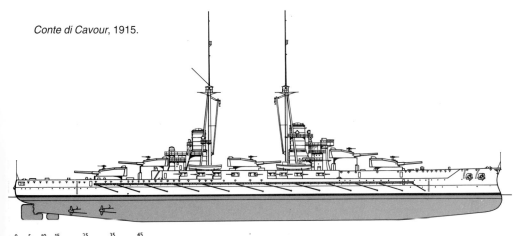

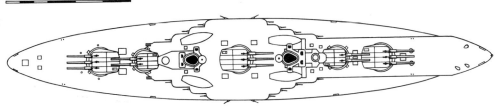

0 5 10 15   25   35   45

Ship	Builder	Laid down	Launched	Commissioned
Conte di Cavour	La Spezia	10.80.1910	10.08.1911	01.04.1915
Giulio Cesare	Ansaldo	24.06.1910	15.10.1911	14.05.1914
Leonardo da Vinci	Odero	18.07.1910	14.10.1911	17.05.1914

The 1908 Budget provided the capital for the construction of Battleship 'B', which was proposed as a sister ship to *Dante Alighieri*. The order was placed on 31 July 1908 at the naval yard at La Spezia, but what ultimately emerged was another Masdea design altogether, much larger than *Dante Alighieri* and armed with five turrets in a completely different layout. Further finance was forthcoming in the 1909 Budget for two more units of the class.

The *Cavour* class, with their unorthodox armament of thirteen heavy guns, were outstanding ships, especially for the Mediterranean. The construction period was relatively protracted due to problems with the supply of armour plating and of the 305mm (12in) guns. After her launch, work on *Conte di Cavour* was temporarily halted as a result of the war with Turkey and priority given to ship repair.

On 24 May 1915 the three *Cavour* class units plus *Dante Alighieri* formed the core of the battle fleet at Taranto, *Cavour* herself being the fleet flagship. However, the group was never deployed operationally during the First World War. *Leonardo da Vinci* sank on 2 August 1916 with the loss of 249 lives following an internal explosion. The official story blamed Austrian sabotage, but this proved to be propaganda aimed at raising the flagging morale in the Fleet. The actual cause was probably the spontaneous ignition of the propellant charges after they had become unstable. The wreck was raised and towed keel-up into dock in September 1919. Consideration was given to rebuilding the ship with ten 305mm (12in) guns but the idea was shelved in early 1921 and the hulk was sold for scrap in March 1923. The subsequent careers of *Conte di Cavour* and *Giulio Cesare* are dealt with later in the book.

Andrea Doria Class

Displacement: 23,000/24,720t
Dimensions: 176.0 x 28.0 x 9.4m
Machinery: 4 Parsons turbines, 4 shafts, 32,000shp
Fuel: 1,450t coal + 850t oil
Speed/range: 21.0kt; 4,800nm at 10kt
Armour: Belt 250mm, deck 70mm, main armament 280mm, CT 320mm
Armament: 13 x 305mm 46-cal, 16 x 152mm 45-cal
Anti-aircraft guns: From 1916: 6 x 76mm 40-cal
Complement: 1,240

Both ships were financed in the 1911 Budget and represented an improved version of the *Conte di Cavour* class. The designer, Vice-Admiral Valsecchi, placed the central 305mm (12in) turret a deck lower and increased the secondary battery by adopting the 152mm (6in) gun. After launching, the Genoese firms Cantieri Odero and Cantieri Ansaldo completed the vessels.

During the First World War it was not possible to carry out extensive trials, but it was clear that the ships were short of their designed speed. *Caio Duilio* reached only 21.3 knots at maximum output. Both vessels spent the entire war at Taranto. Subsequent career details are covered later in the book.

Ship	Builder	Laid down	Launched	Commissioned
Andrea Doria	La Spezia	24.03.1912	30.03.1913	13.03.1916
Caio Duilio	Castellammare	24.02.1912	24.04.1913	10.05.1915

Caio Duilio in 1926.

Developments up to 1945

Although Italy emerged from the First World War as one of the victorious powers, financially she was on the verge of bankruptcy. In a strategic sense, much influence had been acquired, but her demands at the Paris Peace Conference of 1919 for control of 'Mare Nostrum', i.e. the Adriatic, were not met. The old enemy, the Hapsburg monarchy, had finally been ousted from the political arena and the newly formed kingdom of Yugoslavia had no navy. A strategically favourable situation in the eastern Mediterranean was in the process of being created in the Dodecanese so that only the western rival France remained, and the French Navy had not gained in strength from the war. A precondition for the future growth of the Italian Fleet was an increase in shipyard capacity at Trieste, where battleships could be built, and also at the dockyard at Pola with its comprehensive repair facilities.

In Washington at the beginning of 1922 Italy tried to obtain parity with France in warship types, but was only successful with regard to battleships and aircraft carriers. Italy was not required to scrap any of her existing battleships and until 1931 was even at liberty to construct new units up to an aggregate displacement of 70,000 tons, as was France.

The fascists came to power in Italy on 30 October 1922, and Mussolini gave his support to the Navy, which he saw as an important instrument of policy, and from then on he skilfully used the 'fleet in being' for the purposes of propaganda. The principal aims of his foreign policy were to secure naval supremacy in the Mediterranean and to enlarge the Italian colonial empire. He was successful for a number of years in maintaining good relations with Great Britain, but, amongst other things, his naval policy helped foster an increasing antagonism with France. His attack on Ethiopia on 3 October 1935 led to a sudden deterioration in relations with Britain, and in May 1936 the British Home Fleet was transferred to the Mediterranean. This did not restrain Mussolini from involving himself in the Spanish Civil War, although he made the Italian presence conditional on the establishment of a pact with Hitler's Germany.

Building Programmes before the Second World War

The financial plight of Italy following the First World War was such that neither the repair of the salvaged *Leonardo da Vinci* at the end of 1919 nor the construction of new battleships up to the 70,000-ton limit could be afforded. In the mid-1920s, when it was deemed desirable to build two new battleships of 35,000 tons, or three of 23,333 tons, the Navy was obliged by the military-political situation of the day to apply the limited finance available to the building of new heavy cruisers instead.

The oldest dreadnought, *Dante Alighieri*, had been stricken from the Fleet and two units of the *Conte di Cavour* class placed in reserve. The Admiralty took steps to have the Naval Construction Office put forward initial designs for fast but smaller battleships following the receipt of reports about French building intentions, and in 1928 plans appeared for a ship of 23,300 tons armed with six 381mm (15in) guns, followed shortly afterwards by a rather larger design with six 406mm (16in) guns, both versions having twin turrets.

The Italian Navy did not seriously consider building such ships until 1931, when the French made known their intention of building a modern capital ship. Italian naval architects began to draw up the final designs for a 35,000-ton vessel, while orders were given to modernise the ageing battleships lying in reserve, as the United States was doing in the case of the USS *Mississippi*. As even a major rebuilding of an existing unit did not infringe the Washington Treaty, *Conte di Cavour* and *Giulio Cesare* entered the dockyards in October 1933 and returned to the Fleet four years later as essentially brand new ships. The following main alterations were carried out:

1. New turbine machinery driving only two shafts was fitted, together with new boilers. Combined with a lengthening of the hull by 32ft (10m), this resulted in a substantial increase in speed.
2. The horizontal armour was increased in thickness by a minimum of 60mm (2.4in).
3. An attempt was made to improve underwater protection by introducing the Pugliese system.
4. The midships 305mm (12) triple turret was removed and the main armament modernised. The old 305mm barrels were rebored to increase their calibre to 320mm (12.6in) and the angle of elevation was increased.
5. The anti-aircraft defence was improved and the number of barrels increased.

These changes meant that, whereas the ships were now amongst the fastest and most modern in the Mediterranean, they were not the most powerful since the weight of their broadside had decreased. The armour was inadequate and the Pugliese protection of little effect. The sinking of *Conte di Cavour* in November 1940 after a single hit by a light airborne torpedo was the first warning signal, and even the re-bored guns failed to match expectations. The rapid deterioration of the barrels demonstrated their marked inferiority compared to British heavy naval guns.

Despite the tense political situation in the Mediterranean during the period, the two remaining ships of the *Conte di Cavour* class, *Duilio* and *Doria*, entered the dockyards at the beginning of April 1937 to undergo a similar reconstruction. During the rebuilding, which lasted over three years, the same major alterations were carried out but a different secondary armament and heavy AA battery were fitted. The new 1937 model 135mm (5.3in) guns in triple turrets were favoured instead of the 120mm (4.7in) twin turrets installed in the modernised *Cavour*, and the latest 90mm single-barrelled AA guns were preferred to the unwieldy twin 100mm. The old 305mm (12in) barrels were re-bored to 320mm (12.6in) and the angle of elevation increased to 30 degrees (compared to 27 degrees in *Cavour* and *Cesare*). The completely new superstructure gave the two ships a resemblance to the *Vittorio Veneto* class, but despite the enormous financial and material expenditure lavished on them they proved to be poorly equipped for battle in comparison with new battleships in other navies.

On 28 October 1934, the anniversary of the fascists' 'March on Rome', the keel-laying ceremony was held for the first two new Italian battleships to be built since the First World War, *Vittorio Veneto* and *Littorio*. These vessels did not contravene the London or Washington agreements: Italy was permitted 175,000 tons of battleship construc tion and in 1934 she had only 90,000 tons. The extension of the moratorium in battleship building to the end of 1936 imposed by the 1930 London Naval Treaty was not binding on Italy as she had not signed it.

The design stage had begun in 1932 under the direction of the General Inspector of Warship Construction, Engineer-General Umberto Pugliese. His 35,000-ton ship sacrificed hitting power by mounting a calibre smaller than the maximum permitted 406mm (16in) for the best possible protection. The inclined belt armour was 350mm (13.8in) thick, the same as that in the Royal Navy's *Nelson* class. Great attention was paid to the horizontal armour, and the design set great store by the Pugliese system of underwater protection. In essence, this comprised a 6.5m (21ft) wide space filled with fuel oil situated beneath the belt armour and between the 40mm (1.6in) thick, semi-circular torpedo bulkhead and the inner plates of the hull. In the centre of this space was an empty cylinder 3.8m (12ft 6in) in diameter which was intended to serve as an expansion chamber to absorb the energy of an explosion. Unfortunately the system did not work. Following the Royal Navy's attack on Taranto on 12 November 1940 and the fatal damage inflicted on *Littorio*, it became clear that working the system into the new ships had been a mistake.

In the 1938 financial year two further 35,000-ton battleships were authorised and laid down. Both were generally identical to *Vittorio Veneto* though 3m (10ft) longer. For this reason the displacement of the one unit of the pair to be completed, *Roma*, was 1 per cent greater than that of her predecessors. The Italian declaration of war on the Western Allies in June 1940 brought building work on the incomplete *Impero* to a halt, the hull being towed to Brindisi for fear of a French attack on the yards at Genoa. Shortly afterwards construction was terminated because of a shortage of steel.

Italian Battleships in the Second World War

Despite their numerical superiority over the Allied units in the Mediterranean, Italian battleships obtained no successes during more than three years of war and they suffered heavy losses. The reason for this was not the poor quality of the ships, but the ill-advised tactics of the Italian High Command. Commanders were under instructions to avoid an engagement with British heavy units if outnumbered. Thus on 9 June 1940, off Punta Stilo, Calabria, *Conte di Cavour* and *Giulio Cesare* withdrew at once when confronted by three British battleships, *Cesare* receiving a 15in (381mm) hit from *Warspite* whilst doing so.

To judge from the reaction of the Italian Navy, the attack by twenty Swordfish torpedo bombers on the well-defended naval base at Taranto on the night of 11/12 November 1940 was a devastating blow to its morale. The slow biplanes scored five torpedo hits on three battleships, two of which sank in shallow water. The badly damaged *Littorio* was repairable, but *Conte di Cavour*, which received only a single hit, was out of action for the remainder of the war.

The only major offensive operation by the Italian Fleet ended in catastrophe off Cape Matapan on 26 March 1941. During the action the only battleship present, *Vittorio Veneto*, was damaged by an aerial torpedo. Later, Italian battleships escorted German-Italian convoys to Tripoli, but their presence did not deter British cruisers from attacking.

From the spring of 1942 the three older battleships were for practical purposes immobilised by the increasing fuel shortages, which also hampered the deployment of the newer units reinforced by *Roma*.

The Italians suffered their heaviest losses after the conclusion of the Armistice with the Allies, when the Fleet was ordered to Malta to be interned. On the voyage there the new battleships were set upon by the *Luftwaffe*. *Roma* was sunk by two remote-controlled glider bombs and *Italia* was badly damaged.

Armament

Italian heavy naval guns failed to sink a ship in either World War. The ballistic characteristics of the new 381mm (15in) guns, such as the imposing calibre-to-length ratio, high muzzle velocity and great range, were one side of the coin, while the rapid wearing down of the rifling in the barrels and the resultant scatter of the salvos was the other. The barrels were good for 120 rounds as compared to 200 for the French and 250 for the German guns of the same calibre. Even worse was the problem of salvo dispersal with the re-bored 320mm (12.6in) guns, which had a life of only 150 rounds. These former 305mm (12in) weapons were produced under licence from the British armaments companies Vickers and Armstrongs. The 381mm (15in) guns were manufactured by Ansaldo, but production was subcontracted to the OTO (Odero-Terni-Orlando) company which supplied the Italian Navy with both heavy and AA weapons.

Italian shipboard anti-aircraft defences in the medium calibres were ineffective and in terms of the smaller calibres not much better. The battery of guns mounted was small and during the Second World War only the numbers of 20mm AA weapons were increased, and even then insignificantly. This gun appeared in two models. The twin-mounted 1935 Breda model of 65 calibres was used almost exclusively on capital ships even though its rate of fire of 200 rounds per minute was inferior to the alternative 1940 model of 70 calibres manufactured by Isotta Fraschini. Even the small-calibre standard weapon carried on every large Italian warship, the Breda 37mm AA gun, had a low rate of fire of 120 rounds per minute. In 1939 it was offered in a single-barrelled version, with a minor improvement in performance, but it was only installed piecemeal, generally mounted on the forecastles of the newest Italian battleships.

Main Details of Italian Naval Guns

Gun	Model	Wt of shell	Muzzle velocity	Range/elevation
381mm 50-cal	1934	885kg	870m/sec	42.3km/35°
320mm 43.8-cal	1934	525kg	830m/sec	28.5km/27°
Anti-Aircraft Guns				
100mm 47-cal	1928	13.8kg	850m/sec	10,500m/85°
90mm 53-cal	1939	10.1kg	860m/sec	7,500m/75°
37mm 54-cal	1932	0.8kg	800m/sec	4,000m/80°

Conte di Cavour Class (as reconstructed)

Displacement: 28,000/ 29,032t; 25,700 tons standard
Dimensions: 181.4 (186.4 overall) x 28.0 x 10.4m
Machinery: 2 Belluzzo turbines, 2 shafts, 75,000shp
Fuel: 2,470t oil
Speed/range: 27.0kt; 3,100nm at 20kt
Armour: Belt 250mm, deck 110mm, main armament 280mm, CT 260mm
Weight of armour: 9,500t = 33.9% of normal displacement
Armament: 10 x 320mm 44-cal, 12 x 120mm 50-cal
Anti-aircraft guns: 8 x 100mm 47-cal, 12 x 37mm 54-cal (16 x 20mm 65-cal from 1940)
Complement: 1,250

Conte di Cavour was rebuilt at CRDA, Trieste, from 12 October 1933 to 1 June 1937 and *Giulio Cesare* at CdT, Genoa, from 25 October 1933 to 1 October 1937. On trials the modernised units reached a maximum speed of 28.2 knots at 93,400shp, which brought them into the ranks of the world's fastest capital ships.

Conte di Cavour was hit by a British 18in (456mm) torpedo at Taranto and sank in shallow water on 12 November 1940; salvaged and towed to Trieste for repairs in July 1941, she was still under repair at the time of the Italian capitulation. Plans to refit the ship with an improved secondary and AA battery—12 x 135mm (5.3in) 45-cal and 12 x 65mm (2.6in) 64-cal—came to

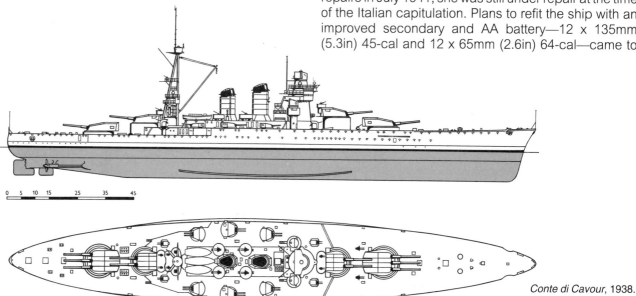

The reconstructed *Conte di Cavour* in 1938.

Conte di Cavour, 1938.

nothing and *Cavour* was scuttled in the shipyard on 10 September 1943. She was raised by the Germans but no further work was done on her and she was sunk for third time in a US air raid on 15 February 1945. She was broken up *in situ* between 1950 and 1952.

Giulio Cesare was hit by a 15in (381mm) shell from HMS *Warspite* in a skirmish off Punta Stilo on 9 June 1940. She was repaired within seven weeks but withdrawn from service in February 1942. She served at Pola as a training ship from January 1943 and escaped to Malta on 10 September 1943 after the Italian capitulation, surviving an attempt at scuttling by disaffected crew members opposed to surrendering the ship. She returned to Taranto to await delivery to the Soviet Union at the end of June 1944 but was not handed over until 3 February 1949. Renamed *Novorossiysk*, the ship was attached to the Soviet Navy's Black Sea Fleet. She sank on 28–29 October 1955 in Sevastopol harbour with the loss of 607 crew members following a mine explosion.

Caio Duilio Class

Displacement: *Andrea Doria* 28,200/ 28,900t, 25,924 tons standard; *Caio Duilio* 28,700/ 29,400t, 26,434 tons standard
Dimensions: 182.0 (186.9 overall) x 28.0 x 10.4m
Machinery: 2 Belluzzo turbines, 2 shafts, 75,000shp
Fuel: 2,550t oil
Speed/range: 26.0kt; 3,400nm at 20kt
Armour: As *Cavour* class
Weight of armour: As *Cavour* class
Armament: 10 x 320mm 44-cal, 12 x 135mm 45-cal
Anti-aircraft guns: 10 x 90mm 50-cal, 15 x 37mm 54-cal, 12 x 20mm 65-cal
Complement: 1,440

Caio Duilio was rebuilt at CdT, Genoa, between 1 April 1937 and 15 July 1940 and *Andrea Doria* at CRDA, Trieste, between 6 April 1937 and 26 October 1940. Following reconstruction both ships were slower than the modernised *Cavour* class and reached 27.1 knots at 87,415shp.

Caio Duilio was hit by an aerial torpedo at Taranto on 12 November 1940 but remained afloat. Repaired by the

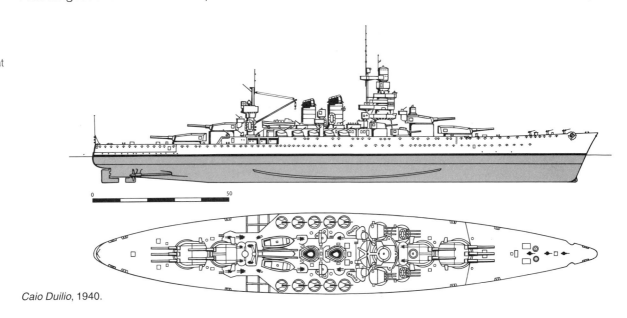

Caio Duilio, 1940.

Stern view of *Andrea Doria* in 1940, following the ship's reconstruction.

end of April 1941, she was used as distant escort for Tripoli convoys until 24 February 1942 then remained at Taranto until the capitulation, whereupon she was interned at Malta in company with *Andrea Doria*.

Both vessels were returned to the Italian Navy in June 1944. *Caio Duilio* was used as a training ship until May 1953; laid up La Spezia, she was stricken from the Fleet on 15 September 1956 and scrapped at La Spezia between 1959 and 1962. *Andrea Doria* was used as a training ship at Taranto until mid-1956 but was stricken on 1 November that year and broken up at La Spezia between 1959 and 1962.

The re-bored 320mm (12.6in) guns of *Andrea Doria*.

Roma in camouflage, 1942.

Vittorio Veneto Class

Displacement: 43,624/45,752t, 40,520 tons standard; *Roma* 44,050/46,215t, 41,000 tons standard
Dimensions: 233.0 (237.8 overall; *Roma* 235.0, 240.7 overall) x 32.9 x 10.5m
Machinery: 4 Belluzzo turbines, 4 shafts, 130,000shp
Fuel: 4,200t oil
Speed/range: 30.0kt; 3,900nm at 20kt
Armour: Belt 350mm, deck 207mm max., main armament 350mm, CT 260mm
Weight of armour: 14,023t = 32.1% of normal displacement
Armament: 9 x 381mm 50-cal, 12 x 152mm 52-cal
Anti-aircraft guns: 12 x 90mm 50-cal, 20 x 37mm 54-cal, 16 x 20mm 65-cal
Complement: 1,860

On trials *Vittorio Veneto* achieved 31.3 knots and *Littorio* 31.4 knots without difficulty and each attained a cruising speed of 28 knots. Both vessels were engaged in operations from the end of August 1940 until mid-June 1942 and received damage on several occasions.

Vittorio Veneto was hit by an aerial torpedo during the Battle of Cape Matapan on 28 March 1941 and was laid up under repair until August 1941; she was torpedoed by the British submarine *Urge* on 14 December 1941 and spent a further three months undergoing repairs. *Littorio* received three torpedo hits during the British attack on Taranto and sank in shallow water on 12 November 1940; she was salved and repaired from April 1941. After Mussolini's fall the ship was renamed *Italia* on 30 July 1943. On 9 September 1943 she was badly damaged by a German glider bomb whilst fleeing La Spezia but succeeded in reaching Malta. *Roma* was never deployed operationally. She left La Spezia for Malta to be

A midships view of *Littorio*, showing her array of 90mm weapons.

Ship	Builder	Laid down	Launched	Commissioned	In service
Vittorio Veneto	Trieste	28.10.1934	25.07.1937	06.05.1940	02.08.1940
Littorio	Ansaldo	28.10.1934	22.08.1937	06.05.1940	02.08.1940
Roma	Trieste	18.09.1938	09.06.1940	14.06.1942	00.11.1942
Impero	Ansaldo	14.05.1938	15.11.1939	–	–

interned but on 9 September 1943 was hit by two German glider bombs and sank, taking 1,254 crewmen with her.

On Italy's entry into the Second World War the incomplete *Impero* was taken to Brindisi, then to Venice and finally to Trieste, where she was requisitioned by the Germans and used as a target ship. She was sunk by US bomber aircraft on 20 February 1945, the wreck being scrapped *in situ* from 1945 to 1950.

Vittorio Veneto and *Italia* (ex-*Littorio*) were interned in the Suez Canal from 1944. They were awarded one each to Britain and the USA under the terms of the peace treaty but were stricken and returned to Italy in 1947. Both had been broken up by 1950.

Vittorio Veneto, 1943

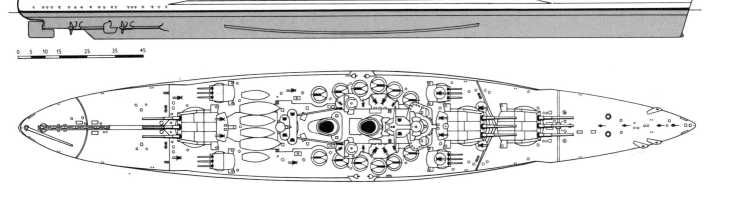

0 5 10 15   25   35   45

Japan

Developments up to 1918

In 1895, after the victory over China, the Japanese Navy was counted amongst the world's smaller fleets. However, the rapid completion of the two construction programmes of 1896 elevated Japan into the ranks of the major naval powers; after the naval victory at Tsushima in 1905 in which a number of Russian warships were seized, mostly obsolete or of doubtful military value, the Japanese came to possess one of the largest, if not one of the most powerful, navies. Two battleships closely fitting the description 'semi-dreadnoughts' were nearing completion in British shipyards and two larger units had been laid down by foreign builders in the early part of 1905, but these were effectively obsolete once HMS *Dreadnought* had been commissioned.

Following the defeat of the Czar's Fleet, only the United States Navy, with a modern, standardised battle fleet superior to the Japanese in terms of both numbers and weapons technology, represented a potential opponent in the Far East. On 4 April 1907 the Japanese Imperial Defence Council formulated its 'Principles of National Defence Policy' in which it became the objective of the Japanese Navy in the event of a future conflict with the United States to destroy the American Fleet and establish complete naval supremacy in the waters of East Asia. This was no light undertaking for the navy of a victorious but poor nation whose industrial base was not yet fully developed. In order to secure naval supremacy in the western Pacific and create the instrument by which Japan could pursue its aspirations, the future strength of the battle fleet was set down as being eight battleships and eight battlecruisers. This came to be known as the '8-8' standard, which referred not only to numbers of ships but also to the number of years before the keels of their successors should be laid down.

The realisation of such a building programme would encounter great difficulties, which were not only of a financial nature. In Japan, only the lighter types of ship had been built hitherto, and these had been of indifferent quality. The new shipbuilding industry was completely dependent on British technical assistance. Great Britain, which had been an ally of Japan since 1902, had supplied completed battleships until 1907, and for years afterwards designs, engines and weapons for warships under construction in Japanese shipyards were produced with British help. The leading Japanese firms Kawasaki and Mitsubishi obtained licences for the construction of both Curtis and Parsons turbines, and in parallel with their interest in marine engineering the Japanese also began the domestic production of heavy 305mm (12in) guns to foreign (i.e. Armstrong) patterns.

In November 1910 Vickers received an order for an exceptionally heavily armed battlecruiser, *Kongo*, on condition that the British company supplied technical assistance for the construction of three sister ships in Japanese yards. This was the last contract placed overseas for

A battlecruiser of the *Kongo* class.

a major warship for the Japanese Navy. The British supplied only the designs for the super-dreadnought (*Fuso*) approved in 1911. Her 356mm (14in) guns were manufactured in Japan from blueprints supplied to the Kure Navy Yard by Vickers in November 1910, but generally the efficiency of Japanese heavy industry was such that until the First World War the construction of capital ships took much longer than in Western shipyards.

The agreement negotiated with the former arch-enemy Czarist Russia regarding spheres of interest in Manchuria, which was contained in a secret protocol signed on 4 July 1910, enabled the Japanese formally to annexe Korea a few months later. The increasing interference of the two treaty partners in Chinese internal affairs—Japan being decidedly the more active—led to a deteriorating relationship with the United States. Between 1910 and 1912 the US Navy received eight new battleships, which drastically increased its superiority over the Japanese Navy as compared to 1908. The Japanese responded promptly with two building programmes in 1911 and 1912 which provided for four battleships and four battlecruisers equipped with a more powerful main armament than the American units. At the time the national economy of Japan was not healthy, but the country would soon skilfully manipulate the First World War for her own ends.

In order to improve her strategic position in the Pacific, Japan declared war on Germany on 23 August 1914 and occupied German possessions in the Carolines, Marianas and Marshall Islands without bloodshed. The Germans also had a naval base at Tsingtao on the Chinese mainland, and Japan eventually took this after two months' fighting. Apart from the participation of the armoured cruiser *Ibuki* in the hunt for Admiral von Spee's squadron in the autumn of 1914, the Japanese battle fleet was not involved in naval operations. Following the Battle of Jutland, Japan declined the British request for the despatch of four new battlecruisers, and the sum total of Japanese assistance rendered to Britain throughout the entire war was one detachment of twelve destroyers for anti-submarine duty in the Mediterranean.

The reasoning behind this policy lay in Japan's Pacific interests. While the major European powers were locked in a war for national survival, Japan saw the opportunity to develop her adventures in China at the beginning of 1915. An ultimatum which practically demanded the surrender of Chinese sovereignty would have been enforced had it not been for the opposition of the United States, and the August 1916 naval building programme of the latter country—ten battleships and six battlecruisers—was directly linked to Japan's increasingly aggressive political stance in Eastern Asia.

In order to achieve numerical parity with the US Navy, the implementation of the '8-8' standard had to be speeded up, for at that time Japan had only one 'super-dreadnought' while three sister ships were still building, and two of these had not yet even been launched. The Navy High Command requested more new units, but the necessary capital for four battleships and two battlecruisers was not forthcoming until July 1917. All these ships would be armed with 406mm (16in) guns and be able to outpace their American counterparts. Quality was to be replaced by quantity, but even so the '8-8' standard was not achieved.

At the end of 1917, the Japanese Navy urged approval for the two remaining battlecruisers, and although agreement was forthcoming before the end of the war they were not ordered until 1919. Meanwhile

the inventory of battleships had changed. The fleet had been strengthened by the addition of the three remaining 'super-dreadnoughts' with 356mm (14in) guns, but two large units had been lost. The large armoured cruiser *Tsukuba* blew up on 14 January 1917, and a similar tragedy overwhelmed the battleship *Kawachi* in July 1918, when 700 crew members lost their lives.

At the end of the First World War the Japanese Navy was left with only five battleships, four battlecruisers and two 'semi-dreadnoughts'. The numerous old pre-dreadnoughts and armoured cruisers contributed nothing towards altering the inferiority of the Japanese to the US battle fleet which, shortly after the Armistice, was transferred to the Pacific.

Japanese Battleships in 1914

Apart from the 21-year-old *Iki* (the former Russian *Nikolai I*), Japan possessed nine old pre-dreadnoughts, most of which served as training ships. The first group comprised *Fuji*, *Asahi*, *Shikishima* and *Mikasa*, all of which had fought at Tsushima under Admiral Togo; the second group was made up of vessels which until 1905 had sailed under the ensign of the Czar. These were *Tango* (ex *Poltava*), sister ships *Sagami* and *Suwo* (ex *Peresvet* and *Pobeda*), *Hizen* (ex *Retvizan*) and *Iwami* (the former *Orel*). In the spring of 1916 two of these ex Russian ships, the former *Poltava* and *Peresvet*, were sold back to Japan's new-found ally, Russia. In addition to these old pre-dreadnoughts there were a further two recent and four large warships under the Japanese ensign which could not be classed as front-line battleships or armoured cruisers because, although of recent construction, they were already obsolete:

Ship	Built	Disp.	Main armament
Kashima, *Katori*	1904–06	17,500t	4 x 305mm, 4 x 254mm
Tsukuba, *Ikoma*	1905–08	15,600t	4 x 305mm
Ibuki, *Kurama*	1905–11	16,250t	4 x 305mm, 8 x 203mm

Kashima and *Katori* were of British origin and essentially classical battleships with two calibres of main armament. In addition to their four 305mm (12in) guns in twin turrets they also mounted two single 254mm (10in) and can be classified as 'semi-dreadnoughts'. The other four units were of mixed type. Originally designed as armoured cruisers they were reclassified as battlecruisers on account of their size and armament in 1912. As such they were too slow (21.5 knots), were too weakly protected and carried too few 305mm (12in) guns. By 1914 when there were still few battlecruisers in the world's navies, they would nevertheless have provided somebody with doughty opposition. *Tsukuba* was lost in 1917 and the others had all been scrapped by 1924 in accordance with the terms of the Washington Treaty.

Armament

For several years after the Russo-Japanese conflict, Japan still relied on the import of heavy naval guns from Great Britain. Although a number of 305mm (12in) guns of British pattern had been cast in Japan in 1907 the armament for the battlecruiser *Kongo* in 1913 was manufactured by Vickers. The 356mm (14in) barrels for her sister ships were, however, of Japanese origin.

The First World War had been a blessing for Japanese arms manufacturers. They developed their own 410mm (16.16in) guns for the *Nagato* class battleships designed in 1916, but whether the bore was really 410mm or, as was usually the case elsewhere, only 406mm (i.e., precisely 16in), is unclear, for the Japanese quoted the calibres of their naval guns in centimetres after rounding up the last digit. For this reason it was believed for decades that the Japanese 8cm AA gun was of 80mm bore until the truth of the matter was discovered after the Second World War: it was a straightforward copy of the British 3in (76mm) weapon. Similarly, the 1908 Model J 356mm gun developed especially for the Japanese Navy by Vickers was described as a '36cm' gun.

There was also a divergence from standard practice regarding the interpretation to be put on the stated year of a particular model. Where, for example, a weapon was described as a '1914 model', in Japanese terms that meant the year when design work began and not when it was first introduced to the Fleet.

Anti-aircraft weapons appeared aboard Japanese capital ships only towards the end of the First World War, as until then they had not been necessary—no enemy aircraft visited the Asiatic theatre during the conflict. AA guns were first installed on units which had been built during the war. The standard weapon was the British Vickers 3in (76mm) 40-cal, officially designated '8cm AA' and built under licence in Japan.

Details of Japanese Heavy Guns

Gun	Wt of shell	Muzzle velocity	Range/elevation
410mm 45-cal	1,020kg	780m/sec	28.2km/30°
356mm 45-cal	674kg	770m/sec	25.8km/25°
305mm 50-cal	386kg	870m/sec	25.0km/23°
305mm 45-cal	386kg	825m/sec	21.0km/20°
254mm 45-cal	227kg	830m/sec	–

Satsuma

Displacement: 19,700/ 21,300t
Dimensions: 146.0 x 25.4 x 8.4m
Machinery: Triple-expansion reciprocating steam engines, 2 shafts, 17,300ihp
Fuel: 2,800t coal max.
Speed/range: 18.3kt; 9,000nm at 10kt
Armour: Belt 229mm, deck 51mm, main armament 229mm, CT 250mm
Armament: 4 x 305mm 45-cal, 12 x 254mm 45-cal, 12 x 120mm 40-cal
Anti-aircraft guns: 2 x 76mm 40-cal from 1918
Complement: 890
Builder: Yokosuka Navy Yard (laid down 15.05.1905; launched 15.11.1906; commissioned 25.03.1910)

Satsuma was the first capital ship built in Japan, although two-thirds of the materials used were imported. Problems procuring the 305mm (12in) guns led to a lengthy construction period. The ship was originally designed for twelve 305mm but because of financial difficulties following the war of 1904–05 the necessary purchase from Britain was not possible and therefore twelve cheaper 254mm (10in) guns were bought to replace the 305mm planned for the wing turrets. This arrangement suited Armstrongs, who were able to dis-pose of a large number of barrels for which there was no demand after HMS *Dreadnought* had entered service.

Satsuma was required to be scrapped under the terms of the 1922 Washington Treaty. She was therefore disarmed for use as target ship that year and the hulk was sunk in Tokyo Bay by gunfire from *Mutsu* and *Nagato* on 7 September 1924.

The 'semi-dreadnought' *Satsuma*.

Aki

Displacement: 20,420/ 22,150t
Dimensions: 146.9 x 25.5 x 8.4m
Machinery: Curtis turbines, 2 shafts, 24,000shp
Fuel: 3,000t coal max.
Speed/range: 20.0kt; 9,100nm at 10kt
Armour: Belt 229mm, deck 51mm, main armament 203mm, CT 250mm

Armament: 4 x 305mm 45-cal, 12 x 254mm 45-cal, 8 x 152mm 45-cal
Anti-aircraft guns: 2 x 76mm 40-cal from 1918
Complement: 930
Builder: Kure Navy Yard (laid down 15.03.1906; launched 15.04.1907; commissioned 11.03.1911)

Aki was also originally scheduled to be fitted with twelve 305mm (12in) guns and steam reciprocating engines. The long building period of the armoured cruiser *Tsukuba* delayed keel-laying, but this enabled an order to be placed in the USA for ships' turbines. Construction went ahead on an amended design, including a modified secondary battery. Like *Satsuma*, *Aki* was disarmed for use as a target ship in 1922, being sunk as such by *Kongo* and *Hyuga* in September 1924.

Settsu/Kawachi

Displacement: *Settsu* 21,800/23,000t; *Kawachi* 21,150/22,300t maximum
Dimensions: 159.3 x 25.7 x 8.5m (*Kawachi* 8.2m)
Machinery: Curtis turbines, 2 shafts, 25,000shp
Fuel: 2,500t coal + 400t oil max.
Speed/range: 20.5kt; 2,700nm at 18kt
Armour: Belt 305mm, deck 51mm, main armament 280mm, CT 254mm
Weight of armour: 5,040t = 23.2% of displacement
Armament: 12 x 305mm (wing turrets 45-cal, fore and aft 50-cal), 10 x 152mm 50-cal, 8 x 120mm 50-cal
Anti-aircraft guns: From 1917: 4 x 76mm 40-cal
Complement: 990

These vessels were improved versions of *Aki*. Although approved in 1907, they were not begun until 1909 because of the financial crisis. Economic problems influenced the choice of British 305mm (12in) gun, since those of 45 calibres length were less effective and therefore much cheaper. Twenty per cent of the building materials was imported, and turbines were produced under the Brown-Curtis licence.

Kawachi blew up with the loss of 700 lives after a magazine explosion on 12 July 1918. *Settsu* was re-quired to be scrapped under Washington Agreement, but she was disarmed, stripped of her belt armour and all but one boiler and used as target ship. She was modified for remote control operation in 1937–38; new boilers and engines were fitted in 1940 as the Japanese Navy Air Force required her to be given an extra 2 knots. She was finally sunk in shallow water off Kobe by US carrier aircraft on 24 July 1945 and was raised and broken up after the war.

Ship	Builder	Laid down	Launched	Commissioned
Settsu	Yokosuka NY	18.01.1909	30.03.1911	01.07.1912
Kawachi	Kure NY	01.04.1909	15.10.1910	31.03.1912

Settsu in 1918.

Fuso/Yamashiro

Displacement: 31,100/36,500t
Dimensions: 202.7 x 28.7 x 8.7m
Machinery: Brown-Curtis turbines, 4 shafts, 40,000shp
Fuel: 5,000t coal + 1,000t oil
Speed/range: 22.5kt; 8,000nm at 14kt
Armour: Belt 305mm, deck 75mm, main armament 305mm, CT 305mm
Weight of armour: 8,725t = 28.1% of displacement
Armament: 12 x 356mm 45-cal, 16 x 152mm 50-cal
Anti-aircraft guns: 4 x 76mm 40-cal
Complement: 1,200

Yamashiro at Yokosuka, 4 July 1917.

Ship	Builder	Laid down	Launched	Commissioned
Fuso	Kure NY	11.03.1912	28.03.1914	08.11.1915
Yamashiro	Yokosuka NY	20.11.1913	03.11.1915	31.03.1917

The first unit was requested by the Navy in 1910 but capital was not approved until 1911. The designs were drawn up by Vickers but both ships were equipped with guns and turbines manufactured in Japan. The original design was for twelve 305mm (12in) guns in four triple turrets, but an order had been placed in Britain for the battlecruiser *Kongo* and the first Japanese 'super-dreadnoughts' also received guns of 356mm (14in) calibre. Both ships were relatively fast for their size and reached 23.2 knots on trials even though 18 of their 24 boilers were coal-fired (coal was used because Japan was a net importer of oil). Both ships were modernised after the war and then reconstructed (q.v.).

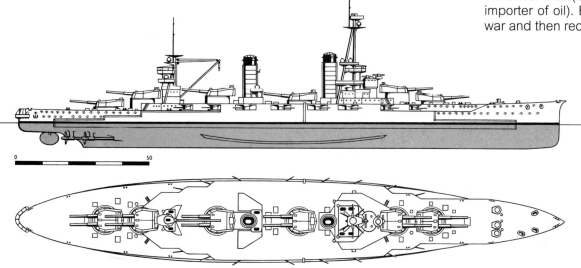

0   50

Yamashiro, 1917.

Hyuga/Ise

Displacement: 32,060/37,100t
Dimensions: 205.8 x 28.7 x 8.8m
Machinery: 4 turbines (*Hyuga* Parsons, *Ise* Curtis), 4 shafts, 45,000shp
Fuel: 4,800t coal + 1,400t oil
Speed/range: 23.0kt; 9,680nm at 14kt
Armour: Belt 305mm, deck 89mm total, main armament 305mm, CT 305mm
Weight of armour: 9,680t = 30.0% of displacement
Armament: 12 x 356mm 45-cal, 20 x 140mm 50-cal
Anti-aircraft guns: 4 x 76mm 40-cal
Complement: 1,360

The battleship *Ise* on completion.

Ship	Builder	Laid down	Launched	Commissioned
Hyuga	Mitsubishi, Nagasaki	06.05.1915	27.01.1917	30.04.1918
Ise	Kawasaki, Kobe	10.05.1915	12.11.1916	15.12.1917

Approved in November 1912 together with *Yamashiro*, both ships were first ordered in 1914 from private yards. They were an improved version of the *Fuso* class with a better arrangement for the two 356mm (14in) midships turrets. The system of horizontal armour proved superior to *Fuso*'s, while the number of medium calibre guns was greater and included the installation for the first time on a Japanese capital ship of the 140mm (5.5in) weapon developed in Japan. On trials both ships exceeded their designed speed of 24 knots. Both were rebuilt in the mid-1930s and served in the Second World War (q.v.).

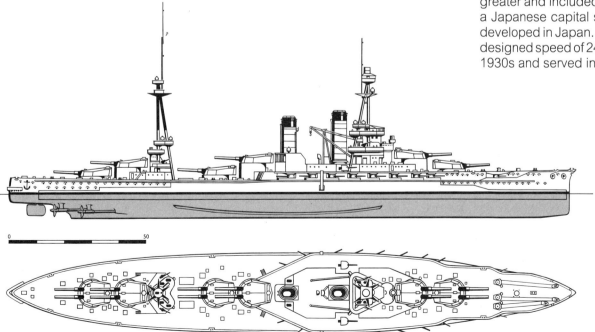

0   50

Hyuga, 1919.

Nagato/Mutsu

Displacement: 34,300/38,100t
Dimensions: 213.4 x 29.0 x 9.2m
Machinery: 4 turbines, 4 shafts, 80,000shp
Fuel: 3,400t oil + 1,400t coal
Speed/range: 26.5kt; 5,580nm at 16kt
Armour: Belt 305mm, deck 120mm total, main armament 356mm, CT 370mm
Weight of armour: 10,560t = 30.8% of displacement
Armament: 12 x 406mm 45-cal, 20 x 140mm 50-cal
Anti-aircraft guns: 4 x 76mm 40-cal
Complement: 1,330

Nagato on trials, 1920.

Ship	Builder	Laid down	Launched	Commissioned
Nagato	Kure NY	28.08.1917	09.11.1919	25.11.1920
Mutsu	Yokosuka NY	01.06.1918	31.05.1920	22.11.1921

These were the first Japanese dreadnoughts designed by a native of Japan (Captain Hiraga), and in 1916 they were also the first capital ships anywhere planned to carry 406mm (16in) guns. The heavy armour and speed were both considerable, and the latter was officially mis-stated as 23 knots. *Mutsu* had not been completed when the Washington Conference opened, and Japan was obliged to put up a fight to save her from the breakers. Further career details of these ships are given later in the book.

0   50

Nagato, 1920.

Kongo Class

Displacement: 27,950/32,500t
Dimensions: 212.0 x 28.0 x 8.4m
Machinery: 4 turbines, 4 shafts, 64,000shp
Fuel: 4,000t coal + 1,000t oil
Speed/range: 27.5kt; 8,000nm at 14kt
Armour: Belt 203mm, deck 67mm, main armament 229mm, CT 254mm
Weight of armour: 6,500t = 23.2% of displacement
Armament: 8 x 356mm 45-cal, 16 x 152mm 50-cal
Anti-aircraft guns: None in 1918
Complement: 1,200

A British photograph of *Kongo* prior to her delivery to the Imperial Japanese Navy.

Ship	Builder	Laid down	Launched	Commissioned
Kongo	Vickers, Barrow	17.01.1911	18.05.1912	16.08.1913
Hiei	Yokosuka NY	04.11.1911	21.11.1912	04.08.1914
Haruna	Kawasaki	16.03.1912	14.12.1913	19.04.1915
Kirishima	Mitsubishi	17.03.1912	01.12.1913	19.04.1915

In November 1910 Japan ordered from the Vickers yard a battlecruiser which excelled all dreadnoughts afloat or building in terms of its battleworthiness. *Kongo* was the model for three further units of the class which were constructed in Japanese shipyards. In the case of *Hiei* this objective was achieved with the aid of materials supplied by Britain, while *Haruna* and *Kirishima* were built using steel, armour and machinery of domestic origin. *Kirishima* carried no fewer than eight underwater torpedo tubes of the large 533mm (21in) type, which were removed after the First World War. All four ships were later modernised and saw service in the Second World War (q.v.).

Kongo, 1913.

Developments up to 1945

In 1918 Japan was one of the victorious powers, and her fleet had become the third largest in the world. Eight giant battleships or battlecruisers, each armed with 406mm (16in) guns, had been approved and two of them were already under construction. This building programme had its origins in the growing tensions with the United States over Japanese policy in China and East Asia, as a result of which the Americans had reacted to the threat to their interests in the area by producing their 1916 naval programme. In 1919 the US battle fleet was transferred from the Atlantic to the Pacific, and in 1920 eight further Japanese capital ships was authorised. This provoked American counter-measures in turn, and so began a new 'naval race'.

The outcome of the Washington Naval Conference was greeted with relief by Japanese political leaders, but in military circles the Japanese 60 per cent quota of US battleship tonnage was cited as proof of a Japanese 'defeat'. In fact, Japan profited by the agreement, because the four-power teaty prohibited the United States from fortifying the strategically important Philippines (as was similarly the case for Britain in respect of Hong Kong).

The Japanese Navy now concentrated its energies on building 203mm (8in) 'Washington cruisers' and began a systematic modernisation of its existing battleships, which, with the exception of the disarmed *Hiei*, had by 1937 all received new and more efficient machinery, an underwater protection system improved by the addition of anti-torpedo bulges, much stronger horizontal armour and a new AA armament. The increased elevation of the 356mm (14in) and 406mm (16in) guns gave the weapons a significantly greater range, but, as was soon to be shown, these expensive measures would be to little avail, although in the last few years before the outbreak of war the reconstructed battleships demonstrated the naval might of Japan in a most impressive manner.

In 1930 the Japanese Imperial Navy was contemplating the construction of new battleships and had ordered designs to be drawn up for units with a very powerful main armament. However, these could not have been completed before 1936, and in the intervening years circumstances changed dramatically. Japan had been condemned by the League of Nations because of her aggression in Manchuria, and in response Japan withdrew from the League in March 1933. The military were gaining increasing influence in Japanese politics and Franklin D. Roosevelt, the newly elected US President, saw the need to curb the nation's aggressive activities. This conviction found expression in the approval of more than 100 new warships by Congress in March 1934.

The Japanese Navy reacted by beginning a naval programme which included a project for a super-battleship, and on 29 December 1934 Japan repudiated the Washington agreement. By the spring of 1936 it had become clear at Military Headquarters that a war with the United States would soon be necessary. The Principles of National Defence Policy document was now supplemented by a third amendment, the basis of which was the idea that the US Fleet could be destroyed in a decisive naval battle once the Japanese Fleet attained 70 per cent of the American strength. In order to achieve this objective, a warship building programme was formulated in April 1936 that provided for four giant battleships, since (it was thought) everything hinged on the outcome of a gunnery duel between the capital ships of the respective fleets.

The advocates of the Japanese naval air arm put forward the case for building aircraft carriers in equal numbers, but they failed to convince the Naval Staff. In the text of the Fourth Completion Programme of March 1939 they also argued that the first priority was to eliminate the enemy carrier fleet by air attack before the battleships were engaged. However, the naval planners continued to regard enemy battleships as the crucial factor in any future naval war. It was therefore logical that the programme approved on 31 March 1937 should contain two battleships greater than anything the world had ever seen before—the *Yamato* class. The design for these vessels had begun in the autumn of 1934, before Japan repudiated the Washington agreement, and construction was to proceed in the greatest secrecy. The particulars of the ships remained a mystery until they were commissioned, and 'informed' opinion about them in the technical press was found to be pure speculation when the true facts came to light in 1945.

Two further units of the class appeared in the 1939 programme, and work was started on these at once. A fifth sister ship was provided for in the 1942 programme, but this vessel was never ordered, and nor were two units of the 'super-*Yamato*' class designed for 508mm (20in) guns in three twin turrets.

Design work began in 1940 on new battlecruisers of 33,000 tons standard displacement carrying nine 310mm (12.2in) guns. These ships were considered to be the answer to the American *Alaska* class. In 1942 the construction of two units with greater firepower—nine 360mm (14.12in) guns—was planned, but the defeat at Midway forced the Japanese to use their shipyard capacity for building urgently needed aircraft carriers. For that reason, work on the third 'super battleship', *Shinano*, was suspended even though the hull was well advanced, and subsequently the Japanese Navy gave no further thought to battleship construction.

Japanese Battleships in the Second World War

True to Japan's principle that battleships must be spared for the 'decisive encounter', none of them was seen in the Pacific in the first weeks of the Second World War. It was the battlecruisers that gave cover to the aircraft carriers for the attack on Pearl Harbor and for the Philippines landings, and in April 1942 it was the battlecruisers that took part in the Indian Ocean raid. Not until the massive operation at Midway did the whole Japanese battle fleet put to sea, and there no good use materialised to which the battleships could be put. In the subsequent battles for Guadalcanal, only the *Kongo* class ships and *Mutsu* were present. Two of these were lost there in October 1942, when their vulnerability, particularly in the case of *Hiei*, was clear for all to see. Two months previously the battle fleet had been reinforced for the last time by the addition of the second *Yamato* class giant, *Musashi*. Two more sister ships still building would be used later for other purposes: *Shinano* was completed as an aircraft carrier and hull No 111 was cannibalised.

In June 1943 *Mutsu* disintegrated in a magazine explosion and the same year the two oldest battleships were converted into so-called 'semi-carriers'. At Leyte they had no aircraft embarked, however, and they took part in the naval battle only as gun platforms though had no definite role. They survived, but the other pair of dreadnoughts laid down before the First World War, *Fuso* and *Yamashiro*, were caught up in the Battle of the Surigao Strait and were quickly overwhelmed by torpedoes from American destroyers and gunfire from the battleships. The duel between *Yamashiro* and American heavy units lasted only a few minutes, and this was the last gun battle in history involving capital ships.

The five remaining battleships were now assembled to form the 'Central Battle Group', which according to the *Sho-Go* (Victory) operational plan had the task of annihilating the American landing ships at the Philippines. The report that American forces had begun to land on the island of Leyte reached Vice-Admiral Kurita, commander of the Battle Group, when he was off Singapore on 18 October 1944, and on the afternoon of that day he set out for the Philippines. En route the group was attacked by submarines on 23 October, losing two heavy cruisers, and the following day the depleted force was set upon by carrier aircraft. Kurita's group had no air cover, and four waves of American aircraft inflicted serious damage on *Musashi*, while *Yamato* and *Nagato* also took multiple hits. The group steamed away, leaving *Musashi* to look after herself, and the last wave of attackers concentrated on her exclusively. After nineteen torpedo and seventeen bomb hits, the battleship capsized and sank with half her crew; she displayed tremendous durability and it was several hours before she eventually went to the bottom.

Yamato and *Nagato* ran on at full speed, reaching the operational area on the morning of 25 November 1944. Off the island of Samar, Kurita's force stumbled across a weaker American battle group consisting of six escort carriers under the protection of only three destroyers and four escort vessels. There was no quick victory, for the American commanding admiral handled his ships skilfully and the Japanese gunnery was poor. Their main error was to fire on the unarmoured escort carriers with armour-piercing shell which penetrated the carriers' thin plating but failed to explode. When American aircraft attacked, Kurita withdrew. The operation ended in a very modest victory for the Japanese battleships (the escort carrier *Gambier Bay* and three destroyers were sunk).

However, the Japanese had lost the Battle of the Philippines, and their fleet had been reduced. Theoretically they still had six battleships at their disposal, but as no fuel could be spared for them they were laid up in home waters. During the voyage to Japan, the elderly *Kongo* was torpedoed and sunk by a submarine north of Formosa on 21 November 1944, and a week later the converted *Shinano* met a similar end. On 18 November 1944 this ship had been completed as the biggest aircraft carrier in the world, and ten days later she was lying on the sea bed. Four torpedoes had been sufficient for the job. Her bulkhead doors and hatch covers had not been secured, and panic broke out amongst her inexperienced crew: she had no chance.

The last engagement involving a Japanese battleship occurred on 6 April 1945. Enough fuel had been procured to enable *Yamato* to reach the bitterly contested island of Okinawa and attempt to interdict the American landing groups there, but her kamikaze voyage ended the next morning half-way to her destination. The Japanese group (*Yamato*, *Yahagi* and eight destroyers) was sighted at 0823 hours, and at 1000

hours 280 American carrier aircraft were flown off for the attack. Nearly 80 per cent of this force found the Japanese ships. They were first seen at 1232 hours and *Yamato* was hit by two bombs nine minutes later. Over the next two hours the battleship was exposed to constant air attack without the benefit of Japanese air cover, and her AA fire was virtually ineffective. *Yamato* began to founder after six torpedo hits, and her death throes were not so protracted as had been the case with *Musashi*. After more bombs and torpedoes struck home, the ship went down at 1423 hours. Only 269 men could be saved. The Americans lost ten aircraft.

Four older battleships now took shelter in the shallow bays around the coast of Japan, where they became the focus of attacks by American carrier aircraft. After the war three were found scuttled and abandoned, while the damaged *Nagato* was still afloat. She was seized and used as a target vessel for the American atomic tests, ending her career at Bikini Atoll on 29 July 1946.

Japan's battleships, the pride of the Imperial Navy, achieved little in two world wars, and in the larger operations in which they participated they failed to play the decisive role which had been expected of them.

Armament

During the Japanese modernisation programmes the range of the guns aboard Japanese battleships was improved by increasing the angle of elevation, but during the war no opportunity presented itself in which this advantage might have been put to good use. The angle of elevation of the 356mm (14in) guns on ships of the *Kongo* class was increased from the original 25 degrees of the mid-1920s to 33 and finally, about ten years later, to 43 degrees. This extended the range from 25km (27,350yd) to a theoretical 35.5km (38,800yd). The 356mm guns were used only once in combat. This was in November 1942 at Guadalcanal in two night battles, when salvos were exchanged at short range. The Japanese fired visually with the aid of searchlights while the Americans had radar. One Japanese battleship was wrecked. Two years later a worse disaster befell *Yamashiro* in the Surigao Strait on the night of 25 October 1944. Within a few minutes of being brought to action by American battleships equipped with modern fire control radar, the ship was battered at a range of approximately 22,000yd (20km) without being able to reply because her 356mm (14in) guns could not be trained in the darkness.

The 406mm (16in) guns of *Mutsu* and *Nagato* (officially of 41cm calibre) were modernised during the ships' reconstructions, resulting in an improvement in the range from 28 to 38.4km (30,600 to 42,000yd).

The pride and joy of the Japanese gunnery officers were the huge 46cm (18.12in; not 456mm or 457mm, 18in, as often quoted) guns of the *Yamato* class, but it would seem that their sentiments were misplaced. Theoretically these monsters had a range of 42km (45,900yd) at an elevation of 45 degrees, but on trials it was found that they were hopelessly inaccurate at that range and the elevation was later reduced to 30 degrees. Theoretical calculations after the war showed that the ballistic efficiency of American and German 406mm (16in) and 380mm (15in) naval guns was better. Nevertheless giant Japanese guns were well constructed and their triple turrets very well designed, particularly the loading arrangements.

Details of Heavy Guns aboard Modernised Japanese Battleships

Gun	Wt of shell	Muzzle velocity	Range/elevation
460mm 45-cal	1,460kg	780m/sec	35.8km/30°
410mm 45-cal	1,020kg	780m/sec	38.4km/43°
356mm 45-cal	674kg	770m/sec	35.5km/43°

The anti-aircraft armament of the battleships in commission in 1941 was very poor. Eight 127mm (5in) 40-cal medium guns with short barrels constituted an inadequate battery for a modernised battleship. The weapon, which had first been introduced in 1929, had a mediocre performance—the shell weighed 23.1kg (51lb) and the muzzle velocity was 725m/sec (2,380ft/sec)—in comparison with the 5in (127mm) Mk 12 AA gun used by the US Navy. Why these guns should have been mounted on the two super-battleships, and in such miserable numbers (twelve per ship) in preference to the much better 100mm (3.9in) AA weapons, which had a longer range and at least twice the rate of fire and which had been available at the time the ships were launched, is not easy to understand. Defence against low-flying torpedo aircraft and dive-bombers was even worse, for light machine guns had been considered suitable until 1936, when the modernised ships received small-calibre automatic weapons of improved efficiency—13mm heavy machine guns in twin mountings and 25mm AA guns designed by the French Hotchkiss company, the technical documentation for which had been purchased by the Japanese Navy. It was soon appreciated, however, that heavy machine guns were inappropriate for defence against aircraft, and the 25mm AA gun was accepted as the standard weapon aboard Japanese warships for protection against low-flying aircraft. As Japanese arms manufacturers were unable to develop a more effective small-calibre AA weapon during the war, the Navy was forced to settle for this slow (only 120 rounds per minute) and unwieldy gun.

The massed batteries of 25mm guns in triple turrets to be found on all the larger capital ships were largely ineffective, as the example of Yamato shows. When commissioned she had eight triple mountings, from autumn 1943 twelve and from June 1944 thirty, plus 23 single barrels. Anti-aircraft defence was the Achilles' heel of the Japanese battleship.

Building Programmes 1918–1922

Japan built only two large battleships in 1918, although four further vessels had been authorised with a view to achieving the '8-8' standard. The situation in the Far East came to a head in 1919 with the transfer of nearly all the US Navy's battleships to the Pacific. The Japanese Admiralty responded by demanding another eight dreadnoughts.

As a result, work on the construction of two giant battleships and four even larger battlecruisers was being feverishly pursued by the time of the Washington Conference in November 1921, and orders had been placed for four more of each. The naval powers agreed very quickly to limit the size of their navies, however, and a cessation of building work on all Japanese capital ships was decreed on 5 February 1922.

The most advanced hulls were those of the 'fast battleships' of the Tosa class. With an armament of ten 41 cm (16.16in) guns, they were substantially more powerful than their immediate predecessors, but their belt armour was weaker than Nagato's although their speed was similar. Eight 609mm (24in) torpedo tubes were to have been fitted above the waterline.

Tosa's hull was used for various explosives experiments after June 1924, and the results of these tests were to play an important role in the design and construction of the Yamato class. Kaga, a sister ship, was scheduled for breaking up, but following serious damage to the original choice, Amagi, she was selected for conversion to an aircraft carrier. After her completion in March 1928 she carried 60 aircraft and an impressive fixed battery. Four of her ten 203mm (8in) guns were mounted in twin turrets on the forecastle, but a few years later these were unshipped to make room for a longer flight deck. During the conversion work, which lasted until 1936, the hull was lengthened by 10m (33ft). These alterations, in combination with new machinery, enabled the ship's top speed to be increased beyond the designed figure by two knots.

Of the four battlecruisers under construction only Akagi was ever completed, as Japan's first large aircraft carrier. As battlecruisers, Akagi and Amagi would have carried an armament similar to that of the Kaga class—ten 410mm guns of the new, longer model officially described as being 40cm in calibre. The vertical and horizontal armour was weaker than that of Tosa and Kaga, although by way of compensation the vessels would have had a top speed of 30 knots. This was three knots less than that of their potential Lexington class opponents, but the Japanese ships were clearly superior in terms of armament and protection.

Work on the battleships of the 1920 programme was not resumed. Four of these units were of a fast battleship class, corresponding to the battlecruiser Akagi but with thicker armour. Only Kii and Owari received names, the others being listed as Nos 11 and 12. Planning Nos 13 to 16 were the embryonic battlecruisers of the 1922 programme fitted with four twin turrets for the 457mm (18in) guns then under development. With a normal displacement of 47,500 tons and a length of 274m (899ft), they would have been amongst the most powerful capital ships of their time, but the Washington Treaty put an end to the concept.

Unfulfilled Programmes 1939–1945

The Fourth Completion Programme of 1939 provided for two further Yamato class ships, and these were laid down. They differed from the original pair in having a belt armour 10mm (0.4in) thinner and six fewer 155mm (6.in) guns but the AA defence was to be increased by up to sixteen new-model 100mm (3.9in) guns.

Strenuous effort was put into the two vessels until work was suspended in December 1941. The contracts were cancelled in July 1942. The first hull, some 50 per cent complete, was eventually commissioned as an aircraft carrier and the second was cannibalised. The contract for a fifth ship identified under Planning No 797, together with giant battleships 798 and 799 and battlecruisers 795 and 796, which were scheduled in the Fifth Completion Programme of 1942, was also cancelled.

Design work on the 'super-*Yamato*' battleships, for which the hitherto unheard-of armament of six 508mm (20in) guns in three twin turrets was proposed, commenced in September 1941, but nothing ever came of it. The planning of the new battlecruisers, designated 'Super-A Cruisers', began in 1940, and trials of the new 310mm (12.2) guns installed in three triple turrets, which had been specially developed for the class, were held a year later. Meanwhile the Japanese had learnt that the main armament of the new American 'super-cruisers' of the *Alaska* class corresponded to that of their projected ships, and a new project, 'B-65', was immediately produced, providing for a main armament of 360mm (14.2in) guns in three twin turrets. As the Japanese possessed no guns of this calibre, it may be surmised that they had a new or modernised version of the old Vickers 356mm gun in mind. As in the previous 'B-64'

project, there was no secondary armament, only a strong 16 x 100mm (3.9in) AA battery. After the *débâcle* at Midway, however, this design was also abandoned. Once the last touches had been applied to the *Musashi* in August 1942, the epoch of battleship building in the Empire of Japan came to its close.

Note: In accordance with the terms of the Washington agreement, the Japanese Navy introduced a trial displacement in metric tonnes in parallel with the standard displacement set by the Treaty. It differed from the normal displacement in that the formula allowed only two-thirds fuel and freshwater reserve. The trial displacement is therefore automatically greater than the normal displacement, and the values given in the following pages are approximate.

Yamato at full speed, 1942.

Tosa/Kaga

Displacement: 40,500/45,000t
Dimensions: 227.7 x 31.3 x 9.4m
Machinery: 4 Curtis turbines, 4 shafts, 91,000shp
Fuel: 3,600t oil + 1,700t coal
Speed/range: 26.5kt; 5,000nm at 16kt
Armour: Belt 280mm, deck 102–163mm, main armament 356mm, CT 356mm
Weight of armour: 14,300t = 35.3% of displacement
Armament: 10 x 410mm 45-cal, 20 x 140mm 50-cal
Anti-aircraft guns: 4 x 76mm 40-cal
Complement: 1,350 approx.

The building of these super-battleships was provided for in the 1917 programme as a progression from *Nagato* with increased side armour. Construction on both hulls was suspended on 5 February 1922. *Tosa* was used as a target ship and expended by gunfire on 9 February 1925. *Kaga* was converted to an aircraft carrier to replace *Amagi*, the latter having been destroyed in the 1923 earthquake; in a second conversion (1935–36) the hull and flight deck were lengthened to 248m (813ft 8in) and maximum displacement was increased to 43,200 tonnes. The ship participated in the attack on Pearl Harbor on 7 December 1941 and in operations against Rabaul and Port Darwin in early 1942. She was sunk by American carrier aircraft at Midway on 5 June 1942.

Ship	Builder	Laid down	Launched	Commissioned
Tosa	Mitsubishi, Nagasaki	16.02.1920	18.12.1921	–
Kaga	Kawasaki, Kobe	19.07.1920	17.11.1921	31.03.1928 (as carrier)

Kaga in 1939, after her second refit.

▼ *Kaga* as designed, 1918.

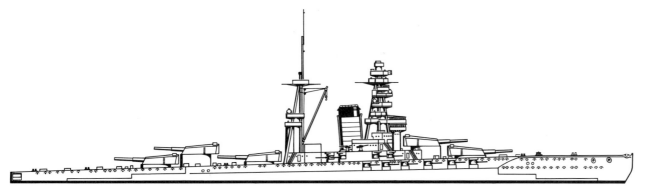

Akagi/Amagi

Displacement: 42,900/47,700t
Dimensions: 250.0 x 30.8 x 9.5m
Machinery: 4 turbines, 4 shafts, 131,200shp
Fuel: 3,900t oil + 2,500t coal
Speed/range: 30.0kt; 8,000nm at 14kt
Armour: Belt 254mm, deck 78mm, main armament ?, CT 256mm
Weight of armour: 14,300t = 33.3% of displacement
Armament: (1919 design) 10 x 410mm 45-cal, 16 x 140mm 50-cal
Anti-aircraft guns: 4 x 120mm 45-cal (designed; 6 x 120mm considered later)
Complement: ?

These battlecruisers are often incorrectly described as the *Amagi* class. *Akagi* was the first to be laid down and the only unit to be completed, albeit as an aircraft carrier. *Akagi* and *Amagi* were authorised under the July 1917 programme while *Atago* and *Takao* were not approved until 1919. Work on the latter pair was suspended on 5 February 1922 shortly after the keels had been laid down and both structures were broken up on the stocks. *Amagi* was continued as an aircraft carrier but the hull was so badly damaged during the earthquake of 1 September 1923 that it was scrapped. *Akagi* was also continued as an aircraft carrier in November 1923, and she was completed as such in March 1927. The flight deck was lengthened to accommodate a total of 90 aircraft in the 1936–38 reconstruction. The ship received heavy bomb damage from American carrier aircraft at Midway on 6 June 1942, so much so that she was torpedoed and scuttled by Japanese destroyers.

Ship	Builder	Laid down	Launched	Commissioned
Akagi	Kure NY	06.12.1920	22.04.1925	25.03.1927 (as carrier)
Amagi	Yokosuka NY	16.12.1920	–	–
Atago	Kawasaki, Kobe	22.11.1921	–	–
Takao	Mitsubishi, Nagasaki	19.12.1921	–	–

Akagi in 1939, following her modernisation.

Fuso/Yamashiro (as in 1941)

Displacement: (Trial) 39,150/
41,000t; 34,700 tons standard
Dimensions: 210.0 x 30.6 x 9.7m
Machinery: 4 turbines, 4 shafts,
75,000shp
Fuel: 5,100t oil
Speed/range: 24.7kt; 11,000nm
at 16kt
Armour: As before, but upper
deck 51mm, armoured deck
102mm
Weight of armour: 12,200t =
31.1% of trial, approx. 32.5% of
normal displacement
Armament: As before except 14
x 152mm 50-cal
Anti-aircraft guns: 8 x 127mm
40-cal, 16 x 25mm (up to 35 x
25mm in 1944)
Complement: 1,400

Ship	Reconstruction begun	Reconstruction completed
Fuso	00.05.1930	00.01.1935
Yamashiro	00.12.1930	00.02.1935

Both ships were partially modernised in the 1920s and fully rebuilt from 1930 when the hulls were extended by 7m (23ft) and fitted with anti-torpedo bulges, the horizontal armour was substantially strengthened, new turbines and boilers enabled the top speed to be increased and pure oil-firing led to an increase in the cruising range. The six underwater torpedo tubes were removed and an inadequate number of the new 127mm (5in) AA guns installed. Neither vessel was widely employed during the war, the first occasion being in support of the landings in the Aleutians and the second at the Battle of Leyte where both were sunk in the Surigao Strait on 25 October 1944: *Fuso* foundered after being torpedoed by American destroyers and *Yamashiro* was overwhelmed by gunfire from six US battleships.

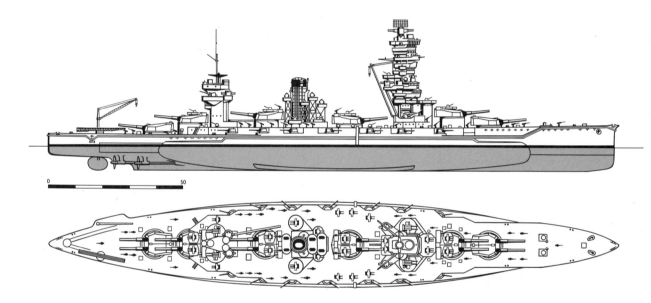

Fuso, 1944.

Fuso following her reconstruction, with a catapult on the forward midships main turret.

Hyuga/Ise (as in 1941)

Displacement: (Trial) 39,650/
42,000t; 36,000 tons standard
Dimensions: 213.4 x 31.7 x 9.2m
Machinery: 4 Kanpon turbines, 4
shafts, 80,000shp
Fuel: 5,300t oil
Speed/range: 25.3kt; 9,500nm at
16kt
Armour: As before, but upper
deck 51mm, armoured deck 96–
140mm
Weight of armour: 12,280t =
31.0% of trial, approx. 32.0% of
normal displacement
Armament: As before except 16
x 140mm 50-cal
Anti-aircraft guns: 8 x 127mm
40-cal, 20 x 25mm
Complement: 1,380

Hyuga at Kure, 4 December
1940.

Ship	Reconstructed	Rebuilt as 'semi-carrier'
Hyuga	00.11.1934–00.09.1936	00.05 1943–00.11.1943
Ise	00.08.1935–00.05.1937	00.11.1942–00.09.1943

These units were first modernised and then underwent rebuilding on a scale similar to that of *Fuso* and *Yamashiro*. Following the Japanese defeat at Midway, it was decided to convert the two ships to hybrid 'semi-aircraft carriers'; the decision was made easier after heavy damage to *Hyuga* in May 1942 when 'Y' turret blew up. Both after turrets were removed and replaced by a 60m (197ft) long hangar for 22 dive bombers. These were unable to take off from the roof of the hangar and were launched by one of two catapults; they were unable to

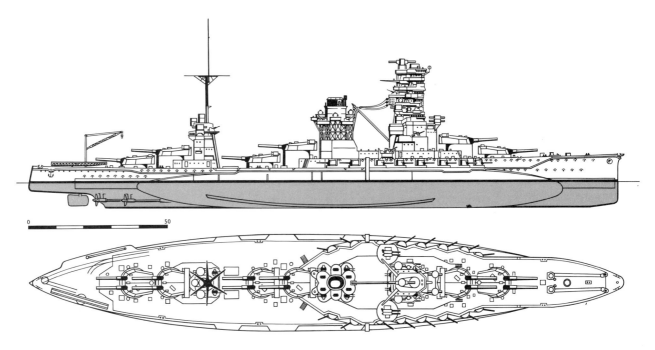

Hyuga, 1941.

Ise in August 1943 as a hybrid
battleship/carrier.

land back on board. The secondary armament was landed, but the total number of 127mm (5in) AA guns was doubled and numerous 25mm weapons were installed (by the autumn of 1944 there were 108 of these); later six launchers for primitive anti-dive-bomber rockets were added.

However, the Japanese aircraft industry was by this time unable able to supply dive-bombers and *Hyuga* and *Ise* took part in the decisive battle at Leyte without their aircraft. Neither was directly involved in the naval battle though they both sustained light bomb damage. The ships began repairs at Kobe in early 1945 but were damaged by bombing on 19 March 1945. Finally bombed and sunk in shallow water on 28 July 1945, they were salvaged and broken up from the summer of 1946.

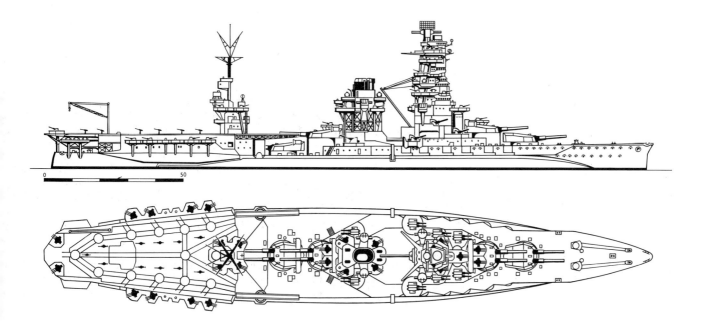

Hyuga, 194

168

Nagato/Mutsu (as in 1941)

Displacement: (Trial) 43,500/ 45,000t; 39,120 tons standard
Dimensions: 221.1 x 33.0 x 9.5m
Machinery: 4 Kanpon turbines, 4 shafts, 82,000shp
Fuel: 5,600t oil
Speed/range: 25.0kt; 8,600nm at 16kt
Armour: As before but horizontal armour 206mm
Weight of armour: 13,032t = 30.0% of trial, approx. 31.0% of normal displacement
Armament: As before except 18 x 140mm 50-cal (*Nagato* 16 x 140mm in 1944)
Anti-aircraft guns: 8 x 127mm 40-cal, 20 x 25mm (*Nagato* 68 x 25mm in 1944)
Complement: ?

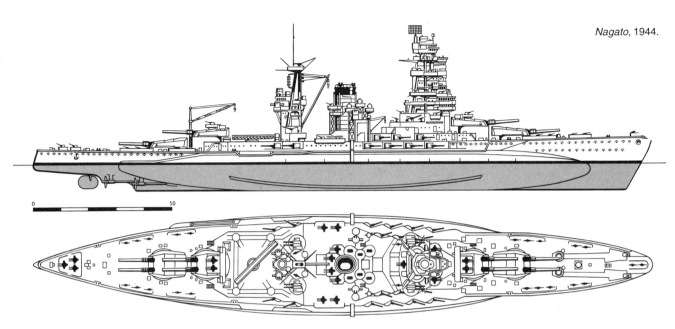

Nagato, 1944.

Mutsu in late January 1939.

Ship	Reconstruction begun	Reconstruction completed
Nagato	00.04.1934	00.01.1936
Mutsu	00.09.1934	00.09.1936

During rebuilding the ships received new turbines and modern boilers with pure oil-firing. The addition of anti-torpedo bulges approximately 3m (10ft) wide led to a reduction in speed, partly offset by the lengthening of the hull. The total of 127mm AA guns was inadequate for ships of the size. *Mutsu* was at Midway in June 1942 and was present at the Solomons in August 1942. She sank in Hiroshima Bay after a magazine explosion on 8 June 1943; there were few survivors.

Nagato was also present at Midway, and the ship distinguished herself at Leyte in October 1944, sinking the escort carrier *Gambier Bay* and three destroyers. She was in home waters for the remainder of war on account of fuel shortages. She was badly damaged by bombing at Yokosuka on 18 July 1945. Seized there by the Allies in September 1945, she was used as a target ship for the atomic tests at Bikini Atoll and was holed in the second of these tests on 25 July 1946, sinking four days later.

Kongo Class (as in 1941)

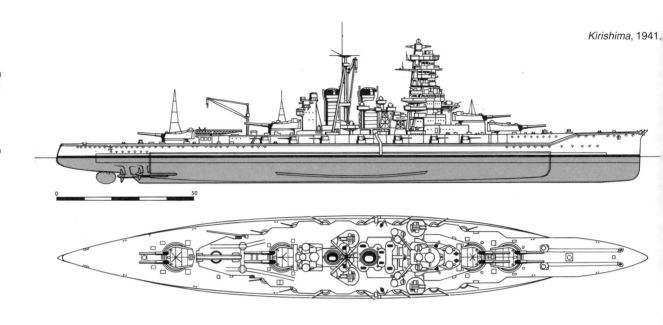

Kirishima, 1941

Displacement: (Trial) 37,000–39,000t; 31,720 tons (*Kongo*) to 32,350 tons (*Hiei*) standard
Dimensions: 219.6 x 29.0 x 9.7m
Machinery: 4 Kanpon turbines, 4 shafts, 136,000shp
Fuel: 6,300t oil
Speed/range: 30.0–30.3kt; 10,000nm at 18kt
Armour: Belt 203mm, deck up to 159mm total, main armament 229mm, CT 254mm
Weight of armour: 10,732t = 29.0% of trial, 30.0% of normal displacement
Armament: As before except 14 x 152mm 50-cal (8 x 152mm in 1944)
Anti-aircraft guns: 8 x 127mm 40-cal, 20 x 25mm (*Haruna*, *Kongo* up to 118 x 25mm from 1944)
Complement: Over 1,100

Ship	First reconstruction completed	Second reconstruction
Kongo	00.08.1931	00.11.1935–00.11.1936
Haruna	00.07.1928	00.08.1933–00.09.1934
Kirishima	00.03.1930	00.12.1934–00.06.1936
Hiei	00.12.1932 (demilitarised)	00.11.1936–00.01.1940

The battlecruiser *Haruna* following her major 1934 refit.

All units of this class were given a full refit during the mid-1920s and classified as battleships from 1930. With the exception of *Hiei*, which was disarmed in compliance with the terms of the 1930 London Naval Treaty, they were fitted for pure oil-firing, with anti-torpedo bulges and with significantly strengthened horizontal armour. The main armament was also modernised. *Hiei* was stripped of one gun turret, her armour belt and 25 boilers and as a training ship could only manage 18 knots. However, she was secretly rearmed during the second series of major refits, in which the class received new turbines and a lengthened hull, which produced an increase in maximum speed. All underwater torpedo tubes and a number of the 152mm (6in) guns were landed, the latter being replaced by new 127mm (5in) AA weapons. All units were fitted with a catapult for launching three floatplanes.

In wartime these ships were intended to provide cover for aircraft carriers, which they did successfully, but during the hard fighting around Guadalcanal their relatively thin armour proved to be the downfall of two of them. *Hiei* was badly damaged by 8in (203mm) shells from two US cruisers on 12 November 1942 and was left a drifting wreck; she was sunk by aerial torpedoes the next day. *Kirishima* was engaged in a night battle by the US battleships *Washington* and *South Dakota* on 15 November 1942 and was sunk.

Haruna and *Kongo* were fitted with primitive radar sets and had their AA battery strengthened and their secondary armament reduced in 1944. They were at Leyte as part of Vice-Admiral Kurita's battle group and contributed to the sinking of the escort carrier *Gambier Bay*. However, *Kongo* was torpedoed and sunk off Formosa by the US submarine *Sealion* on 21 November 1944. *Haruna* was laid up at Kobe but sunk in shallow water by carrier aircraft on 19 March 1945.

Yamato Class

Displacement: (Trial) 69,100t (approx. 67,500t normal), 71,500t max.; 62,315t (designed), approx. 63,000t (actual) standard
Dimensions: 256.0 x 36.9 x 10.4m
Machinery: 4 Kanpon turbines, 4 shafts, 150,000shp
Fuel: 6,300t oil
Speed/range: 27.0kt (trial 27.46kt); 7,200nm at 16kt
Armour: Belt 410mm, deck 230mm total, main armament 650mm, CT 500mm
Weight of armour: 22,900t = 33.2% of trial, 34.0% of normal displacement
Armament: 9 x 460mm 45-cal, 12 x 155mm 60-cal (6 x 155mm from 1944)
Anti-aircraft guns: 12 x 127mm 40-cal, 24 x 25mm (24 x 127mm, 98 x 25mm from June 1944)
Complement: 2,200 (2,500 from mid-1944)

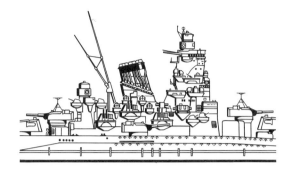

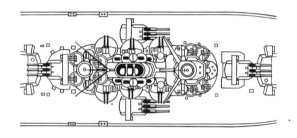

Yamato, 1942.

Ship	Builder	Laid down	Launched	Commissioned
Yamato	Kure NY	04.11.1937	08.08.1940	16.12.1941
Musashi	Mitsubishi	29.03.1938	01.11.1940	05.08.1942
Shinano	Yokosuka NY	04.05.1940	08.10.1944	19.11.1944
Kii	Kure NY	07.11.1940	–	–

The first two units were ordered in 1937, the latter pair in 1939. Design work on these giants began in the autumn of 1934 in contravention of the terms of the Washington Treaty. Even after Japan had repudiated the Treaty, construction work continued under conditions of the strictest secrecy. The two completed ships were the most powerful battleships ever built but their monster guns were never trained on an enemy vessel, and neither their thick, inclined side armour nor their 200mm thick armoured deck, nor their extensive underwater protection, could prevent their destruction when they were pitched against massive air power. *Musashi*, bombed and torpedoed by aircraft, sank south of Luzon Island on 24 October 1944. *Yamato*, despite her powerful AA armament, was sunk by bombs and torpedoes while on a one-way kamikaze mission to Okinawa on 7 April 1945.

Work on *Kii* was suspended in December 1941 and the ship was cannibalised. Work on *Shinano* was halted when she was 50 per cent complete and the ship emerged on 18 November 1944 as a huge aircraft carrier. While on trials in Japanese home waters on 28 November 1944 she was sent to the bottom by four torpedoes fired from the US submarine *Archerfish*.

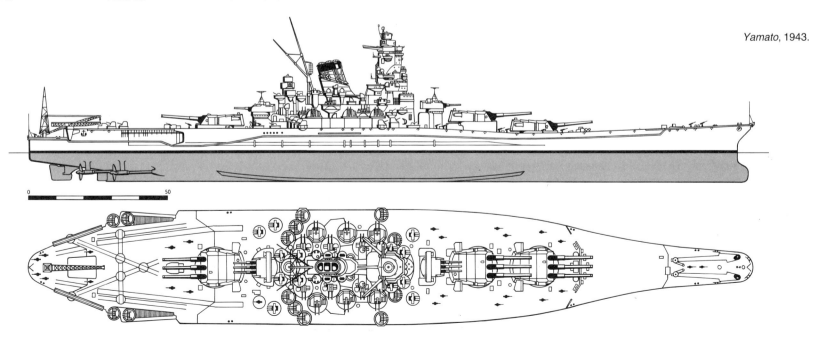

Yamato, 1943.

0   50

Austria-Hungary

The Habsburg monarchy had been a major power on the continent of Europe for several centuries, but it became a naval power only a few years before the outbreak of the First World War. The call for the acquisition of a fleet of dreadnoughts was provoked by the building of similar ships in neighbouring Italy. Italy was officially an ally in the Triple Alliance which also included Germany and Austria, but now, as previously, Italy was in reality the enemy of the monarchy and secretly laid claim to the whole of the Adriatic east coast. Ironically it was the Austro-Hungarian Navy which had a duty under the 1900 Austro-Italian Naval Agreement to protect the entire Adriatic against interference by enemy naval forces, while the Italian Navy had as its sphere of operations the western Mediterranean.

The Navy of Austria-Hungary, which since 1898 had ranked last amongst the navies of the major powers, required only a few battleships to fulfil its defensive obligations. The rocky coast, fronted by hundreds of islands and cliffs, was easy to protect, and the mountainous hinterland with its few narrow highways offered little prospect of taking decisive action against the monarchy to any attacker adept enough to get his troops ashore. The need to build a stronger fleet was therefore doubted by many; regarding the construction of battleships, for which the Navy showed a preference, there was substantial disagreement.

Battleships cost a lot of money, and the military expenditure of the monarchy had remained low in comparison to that of the other major powers. The traditionally favoured Army took the lion's share of the military budget (90 per cent in the period 1898–1904). The chronic shortage of finance and the creation of the Defensive Doctrine eventually led to designs for battleships which were about one-third smaller than those under construction elsewhere in the world, and it was only a partial justification that the specific conditions obtaining in narrow waters made possible the use of ships with a low fuel bunkerage.

Naval Construction from 1905

In October 1904 an elderly Vice-Admiral, *Graf* Montecuccoli, was nominated Commander-in-Chief of the Navy, and he came to be regarded as the creator of the small but then modern and powerful Austro-Hungarian Fleet. After just a few months in office he produced an ambitious naval construction programme which envisaged the acquisition of numerous torpedo-carrying vessels for coastal defence together with several battleships and armoured cruisers.

Design work on the battleships, which were to be of 15,000 tonnes maximum and armed with 280mm (11in) or 305mm (12in) guns), and the armoured cruisers, to be up to 10,000 tonnes, commenced in June 1905, and that same month Parliament granted to both Crown States a

A posed scene aboard the Austro-Hungarian battleship *Erzherzog Franz Ferdinand*.

generous special credit, enabling the construction programme to be speeded up.

At the end of September 1905 the designs were presented to a commission for their decision. Two of the five variations were for preferred 'all-big-gun ships' armed with eight 280mm (11in) or six 305mm (12in) guns, but because these exceeded the specification by 1,500 tonnes a variation which complied with the conditions was selected, subject to the proviso that the secondary battery of eight 190mm (7.5in) guns should be upgraded. The subsequently amended design for a 14,500-tonne battleship armed with four 305mm (12in) and eight 240mm (9.45in) guns was approved by the naval command in January 1907 after HMS *Dreadnought* had been commissioned in Britain. Therefore, in the years 1910–11, when the major naval powers had embarked upon building programmes for 'super-dreadnoughts', the Austro-Hungarian Navy took possession of three outdated 'semi-dreadnoughts'.

The final power blocs had been assembled in Europe by 1906–07. Germany was isolated, and this indirectly affected her loyal ally Austria-Hungary. The third ally, Italy, had defected, and in military circles in the capital, Vienna, it was not doubted but that a military solution would eventually have to be found for the Italians. It was for this reason that the Army High Command surprisingly urged a strengthening of the Fleet. In terms of tonnage, the superiority of the Italian Navy had risen from 2:1 in 1904–05 to 2.7:1 in 1907; moreover, the Italians had announced that they would be building two fast 'super-dreadnoughts', leaving the Austro-Hungarian Navy trailing.

The public were informed of the planned construction of dreadnoughts for Austria-Hungary on 20 February 1908 when Admiral Montecuccoli spoke of proposals for 19,000-tonne battleships, although instructions for the design of a 20,000-tonne battleship were not issued by the Admiralty until October 1908. The five outline projects submitted by the Stabilimento Tecnico Triestino (STT) shipyard in March 1909 were found to be unsatisfactory in that the ships would carry only eight or ten 305mm (12in) guns in twin turrets and have inadequate armour. On 27 April 1909 the shipyard proposed a fresh design providing for four triple turrets housing 305mm (12in) guns, and this became the basis for the later *Tegetthoff* class.

In the meantime an unusual situation had developed, taking the Commander-in-Chief by surprise. On 3 July 1909 the battleship *Radetzky* was launched at STT (the only shipyard in the monarchy capable of battleship construction). The yard, which had been modernised a short while previously, had no contracts in its order books for any large warship and, after the completion of the sister ships *Radetzky* and *Zrinyi* in 1911 would be forced to lay off hundreds of experienced craftsmen. The directors of the yard therefore pleaded with the Admiralty to place orders for two 20,000-tonne battleships, but when the 1910 Budget was debated by the deputies in September 1909, capital had not been approved for the two ships.

Admiral Montecuccoli would not admit defeat, and in a meeting with the directors and their principal suppliers (STT, Skoda Pilsen and the Witkowitz Mining, Iron and Steel Company) on 22 October 1909 it was agreed that construction would commence initially without a financial advance. The public knew nothing of this arrangement and the myth was created in the naval press that the first two Austro-Hungarian dreadnoughts were built privately as a speculative venture by STT and the two major suppliers. In fact the firms had received a guarantee in October 1909 that the Navy would purchase the vessels, and had begun at once preparing materials. This explains why *Viribus Unitis* had such an unusually short building period.

The Navy received a special credit spread over the 1911–16 financial years in respect of ships which would take the longest to build. This made possible the acquisition of four battleships, three light cruisers, six destroyers, twelve torpedo boats and five submarines, 76 per cent of the special credit having been estimated as the cost of the four battleships. Orders for three battleships would be placed with STT, but the fourth had to be built at a Hungarian yard with Hungarian materials. No such yard existed in Hungary, however, and so it was decided to convert a small yard turning out tugs and torpedo boats into a major shipbuilder.

In 1911 the rocky cliffs around the former Danubius Works were dynamited and the rubble laid on the sea bed to become the foundations for new, broader slipways. Within a year, and at great expense, two 265m (870ft) long and 35m (115ft) wide slipways had been erected, and the keel of the fourth ship, *Svent Istvàn*, was laid. The main factory of Ganz & Co, Budapest, supplied the ship's machinery, the armour plate and guns came from Witkowitz and Skoda, while the plating and most other parts were ordered from Hungarian suppliers.

The construction of the Hungarian vessel proceeded at a slow pace and was fraught with problems. Naval experts found fault with the quality of the materials, but whether this was a contributory factor in the rapid foundering of the vessel following a torpedo hit on 10 June 1918 is a question that has never been answered since the Commission of Inquiry was unable to conclude its investigation into the matter once the monarchy collapsed.

In October 1910 Admiral Montecuccoli submitted a naval programme which, if it had been realised, would have provided the Austro-Hungarian Navy with sixteen battleships by the year 1920. The imposition of an age limit of twenty years for existing ships meant that at least seven new battleships would have to have been built in the course of the next nine years: after the completion of the four *Tegetthoff* class units and the decommissioning of the *Monarch* class coast defence battleships, three further vessels would need to be built, and immediately afterwards three *Habsburg* class units also had to be replaced. In 1912 Montecuccoli was therefore requesting four 'super-dreadnoughts' within the framework of a new naval building programme.

Skoda had offered to supply the Navy with naval guns of 345mm (13.5in) calibre, but most gunnery experts preferred to stay with the 305mm (12in) calibre, though using a longer barrel. It was not until May 1912 that a decision was made in favour of fitting out the new generation of Austro-Hungarian battleships with guns of 350mm (13.8in) calibre (and not 355mm as is frequently asserted in reference books).

The plans for the first 'super-dreadnought', a 24,000-tonne ship with ten 350mm guns, was presented in January 1913. Montecuccoli wanted to order four immediately, but nothing had been authorised by the time he retired in February 1913, and his successor, Admiral Hans, was equally unsuccessful in securing finance for only two such units that year.

The two large slipways at Trieste lay vacant, and the huge workshops at Pilsen and Witkowitz, which had been modernised at great cost, were also not at full capacity. It was because of this that the three large concerns agreed amongst themselves to start work on the ships at their own risk. However, the Hungarian government was opposed to this proposal and so the slipways at Trieste and, after the launching of *Svent István*, at Fiume remained idle until the outbreak of war, even though construction work on four battleships with 350mm (13.8in) guns was finally approved on 28 May 1914. The first unit was not laid down until after the outbreak of war, when all orders already placed were cancelled with the exception of the armament for the first unit, officially designated 'Battleship VIII', under manufacture at Skoda. This order was partially fulfilled and the guns were taken over by the Army.

Unfulfilled Programmes

The 24,000-tonne ships had originally been designed in January 1913 with their heavy guns disposed in four turrets. A triple turret was to be superimposed above a twin turret both forward and aft, but this idea was discarded in fresh designs drawn up in July 1913. In the final design, which appeared twelve months later, the number of 150mm (5.9in) guns had been reduced by four, and the twenty 90mm guns projected had been reduced to seventeen, these being the numbers ordered from Skoda in August 1914. In other respects the two battleships ordered in June 1914 from STT and Danubius displaced 24,500 tonnes and had a length of 172m (564ft 4in), a beam of 28.5m (93ft 6in) and a draught of 8.4m (27ft 6in). The machinery comprised four turbines, giving 31,000shp for a speed of 21 knots. Protection consisted of a 310mm (12.2in) belt, 30mm (1.2in) and 36mm (1.4in) armoured decks, 340mm (13.4in) maximum for the main armament and 320mm (12.6in) for the conning tower. The battery comprised ten 350mm (13.8in) 45-cal and fourteen 150mm (5.9in) 50-cal, with nine 90mm (3.5in) 45-cal AA.

The Naval Budget approved on 28 May 1914 referred to four such ships of 24,500 tonnes, but it is not certain if the other two units scheduled for construction in 1916 were to be of the same dimensions. In 1913, after details relating to the planned Italian 'super-dreadnoughts' had been disclosed, critical voices were raised in naval circles about the weak armament of the so-called *Ersatz Monarch* class.

The Admiralty therefore ordered projects to be drawn up for larger ships with an armament of twelve or thirteen guns, and in January 1914 two more designs emerged, for ships of 29,600 tonnes and 32,000 tonnes. The larger vessel would have been 196.5m (644ft 8in) in length with a speed of 23 knots, and armed with thirteen 350mm (13.8in) and eighteen 150mm (5.9in) guns. With the exception of the belt armour, which was 10mm (0.4in) thicker, the protection was practically the same as for the 24,500-tonne ships. One problem with these large ships was the fact that finance was been granted in the Naval Budget only for the 24,500-tonne units.

Although the course of the naval war in the Adriatic soon showed that the narrow seas were suitable only for the operation of smaller vessels, the naval leadership blithely ignored that fact and until the end of the First World War persevered in designing giant battleships with little if any military value. On 1 August 1918, when confronted by the spectre of the fall of the monarchy within days, the Naval Technical Committee (MTK) was still delivering to the Navy Section a number of outline projects for battleships and battlecruisers with the 380mm (15in) or 420mm (16.55in) guns in twin turrets which the Admiralty wanted. The final studies, initiated in December 1917, proposed a 37,200-tonne battleship with eight 420mm guns and a 32,600-tonne battlecruiser with four 420mm guns. Skoda were still occupied with the development of the 380mm and 420mm calibre naval guns at the end of March 1917.

Austro-Hungarian Battleships in 1914

In 1914, apart from the three *Monarch* class coast defence battleships of 5,600 tonnes displacement which, for their size, carried the enormously powerful armament of four 240mm (9.45in) and six 150mm (5.9in) guns but were never considered for use with the Fleet, the Austro-Hungarian Navy possessed six other units officially classified as battleships. *Habsburg*, *Arpád* and *Babenberg* had been completed between 1902 and 1904 and were, at 8,350 tonnes and with only three 240mm (9.45in) and twelve 150mm (5.9in) guns, very small and weakly armed. Being relatively weakly armoured also, they were at best opponents for the Italian armoured cruisers, which were, however, five knots faster.

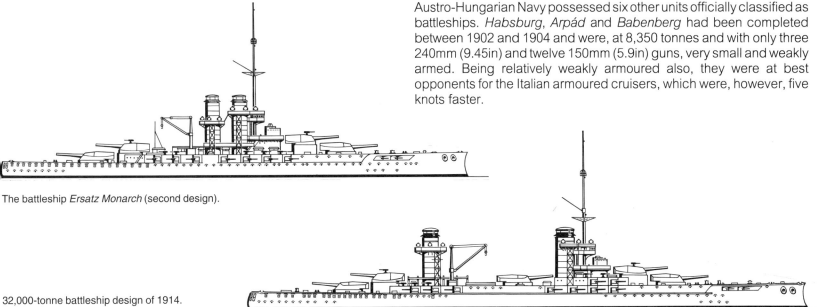

The battleship *Ersatz Monarch* (second design).

32,000-tonne battleship design of 1914.

The three 10,000-tonne *Erzherzog Karl* class units completed in 1906–07 were fine ships, but their fighting capabilities were not comparable to those of battleships in other navies. Their main armament comprised only 240mm (9.45in) weapons with the short 40-calibre barrel, and although the secondary armament was strong—twelve new 190mm (7.5in) guns with a good performance—in general they were under-armed. Only in the confines of the Adriatic, particularly against the fast Italian pre-dreadnoughts and armoured cruisers, might the *Erzherzog Karl* class ships have been able to give a good account of themselves.

Austro-Hungarian Battleships in the First World War

Austro-Hungarian battleships were never involved in a fleet action during the First World War. A group which included six of the newest battleships steamed out to render assistance to *Goeben* when she was being harassed in the early days of August 1914 but returned at once to Pola when it was learned that the German battlecruiser had succeeded in breaking through to the Dardanelles. At the time, the monarchy had not declared war on Britain. Between 22 and 27 October 1914 the battleship *Radetzky* fired salvos from her main armament against French hill batteries at Lovcen in Montenegro, putting them out of commission, after which the ship retired from Boka Kotorska and returned to Pola.

Italy declared war on Austria-Hungary on the morning of 24 May 1915 and within a few hours the entire Austro-Hungarian Fleet, including all battleships then operational, was bombarding targets along the Italian Adriatic coast. The completion of this exercise marked the final involvement of Austro-Hungarian battleships in the First World War.

Three years later, on 10 June 1918, *Svent István* was lost. Together with other *Tegetthoff* class ships, she was providing cover for an attack by a fast cruiser squadron against the Otranto barrier, and in waters off northern Dalmatia she was discovered and hit by two torpedoes fired by an Italian MTB. The weakness of her underwater protection was her downfall. Contrary to the warnings by German naval architects given in the spring of 1909, Austria's senior naval design engineer, Popper, had incorporated the so-called 'anti-mine bottom' below the ship's waterline. This was an armoured double bottom with a narrow and insufficient gap between the two protective walls. Although the torpedoes were only of 450mm (17.7in) calibre, the system failed and *Svent István* sank within a few hours.

On the morning of 1 November 1918, the first modern dreadnought in the Austro-Hungarian Navy, *Viribus Unitis*, was sunk at Pola. The previous day the ship had, together with the rest of the battle fleet belonging to the Danube monarchy, been handed over to the new Yugoslav republic with its capital at Zagreb. Upon hearing this, the Italians planned an immediate raid by saboteurs against their new potential enemy in the Adriatic. Naval swimmers penetrated the unguarded harbour and attached a mine to the bottom of the new Yugoslav flagship, and *Viribus Unitis* sank about fifteen minutes after the device went off. The majority of the Austrian complement had disembarked the previous evening, and the remnants of the crew left on board had no real opportunity to save the ship, which foundered rapidly with the loss of over 400 lives.

Armament

Whereas there is some justification for criticising Austrian naval policy and the battleship designs of the Naval Technical Committee, Skoda naval guns and Witkowitz armour plating were highly efficient.

Emil Skoda's factory began producing guns at Pilsen in 1890 after the first model, a 70mm quick-firing weapon for the Navy, had been tested on a proving range in August 1889. Naval guns represented the major part of the company's business until 1914, and, together with the later heavy mortars, these established the reputation of the Skoda works.

Babenberg, the last ship of the *Habsburg* class, received the first naval guns to be delivered by Skoda. These were a slightly improved version of the Krupp 240mm/L40K (9.45in, 40-cal) heavy guns mounted aboard *Arpád* and *Habsburg*. Firing a 215kg (474lb) shell at 725m/sec (2,380ft/sec), the Skoda 240mm/L40S guns were not particularly impressive in terms of their performance but had been installed in the ships of the *Erzherzog* class as the new long-barrelled model was still under development.

In 1905 it was made known officially that Skoda was developing a 305mm (12in) naval gun, although the company was working at the same time on a 280mm (11in) gun with three different barrel lengths. In the autumn of that year the Navy decided in favour of the first weapon, and the test model underwent trials in May 1908. A 240mm (9.45in) gun with a longer barrel was also being manufactured for the *Radetzky* class, and deliveries of both models began at the end of 1909.

A 305mm triple turret for the later *Tegetthoff* class, which had been under development for some time and which established Skoda's worldwide reputation for naval gun manufacture, owed its existence to the Russian Navy's design in December 1907 specifying a dreadnought with its main armament arranged in this way. At the beginning of January 1908 the shipbuilder STT and, a little later, Skoda, who had an office in St Petersburg, were invited to tender, but in the event neither company showed the Russians any designs for ships or turrets. However, at the end of April 1909, when the Naval Technical Committee presented the Austrian planners with the eighth version of a 20,000-tonne battleship with its main armament grouped in triple turrets, this was quickly adopted as the basis for the *Tegetthoff* class, and *Viribus Unitis* was the first battleship in the world to have its heavy guns thus disposed.

At the suggestion of the Admiralty, development work on the 305mm (12in) gun continued, although in April 1911 Skoda had proposed that a 345mm (13.6in) in twin or triple turrets was preferable. Protracted discussions about the gun calibre for the planned 'super-dreadnoughts' resulted in the choice of the 350mm (13.8in) weapon, and Skoda submitted its designs for a suitable turret in April 1912. The first gun was not tested at Pilsen until November 1914, and as it could not be fitted into any existing turret the carriage was modified and the gun was eventually used against the Italians on land. It performed so well that the French became interested in it, and after the war the French company Schneider & Co. acquired a majority shareholding in Skoda. The technical documents relating to the gun were secreted to Creusot in France without the knowledge of the Czech management and not returned. The French were also interested in the Skoda 305mm (12in) gun. They carried out tests with the guns of that calibre on the battleship

Prinz Eugen, ceded to them as a war reparation, and then presumably installed them as coastal artillery.

Details of Skoda Heavy Guns

Gun	Introduced	Wt of shell	Muzzle velocity	Range/elevation
350mm 45-cal	1914	635kg	820m/sec	25km/20°
305mm 45-cal	1908	450kg	800m/sec	20km/20°
240mm 45-cal	1909	215kg	800m/sec	16.4km/20°

Before the First World War, the design team working on the 24,500-ton battleship devised a strong AA defence for the vessel, although the weapons were described as *Ballonabwehrgeschütze* (BAG) or anti-balloon guns. Skoda supplied all AA weapons ordered by the Austro-Hungarian Navy up to the capitulation. The first model, officially designated 9cm/L45 BAG.K12, was designed in 1912 and first test-fired at the end of June 1914. The gun was heavy and unwieldy and the eight weapons delivered in the summer of 1914 for installing on board the capital ships were used instead on land for harbour defence. One and later two 66mm (2.6in) AA weapons were from 1915 mounted on the roofs of the main gun turrets aboard the *Tegetthoff* and *Radetzky* class ships. The earlier 66mm/L45 K.09 model was installed in a special 'anti-balloon' mounting, but its performance—it fired a 4.5kg (9.9lb) shell at 725m/sec (2,380ft/sec)—was meagre.

In the spring of 1916 the Navy received the first examples of an improved version of the 66mm/L50 BAG tested in 1913. Until the war's end in 1918 the Navy probably had no more than thirty of these weapons, which, in spite of their relatively small calibre, proved to have a very useful performance, firing a projectile at 830m/sec (2,725ft/sec) to a theoretical altitude of 8,000m (26,250ft). A small-calibre anti-aircraft gun ordered from Skoda in 1917 had not been fully developed by the time hostilities ceased.

Note: The displacement of all Austro-Hungarian warships was stated in metric tonnes, and the displacement of the ship 'ready to sail, with ammunition and half ship's stores' is equivalent to the normal displacement referred to in this book in respect of other vessels.

Radetzky Class

Displacement: 14,800/15,850t;
(trial) 14,460t with 500t coal
Dimensions: 137.5 x 24.6 x 8.1m
Machinery: Triple-expansion
reciprocating steam engines, 2
shafts, 20,000ihp
Fuel: 1,600t coal max.
Speed/range: 20.5kt; 1,800nm at
20kt, 4,000nm at 15kt
Armour: Belt 230mm, deck
48mm, main armament 250mm,
CT 250mm
Weight of armour: 4,697t =
31.7% of displacement
Armament: 4 x 305mm 45-cal, 8
x 240mm 45-cal, 20 x 100mm
50-cal
Anti-aircraft guns: 1916: 2 x
66mm 45-cal; 1918: up to 4 x
66mm
Complement: 890

Although *Erzherzog Franz Ferdinand* was the first unit begun and completed, these 'semi-dreadnoughts' are known as the *Radetzky* class. On trials *Erzherzog Franz Ferdinand* reached 20.57 knots at 20,888ihp.

The class formed the 2nd Division of the 1st Squadron in 1914 but were never involved in a sea battle during the First World War. At the time of the capitulation they were at Pola. After the occupation of the port by the Italians, *Radetzky* and *Zrinyi* slipped out under the Czech flag (Czechoslovakia was a partner of the Allies) and reached Split, where they came under the jurisdiction of the United States. They were awarded to the Americans in the September 1919 peace treaty and were scrapped in Italy in 1920–21. *Erzherzog Franz Ferdinand* was confiscated by Italy at Pola and interned at Venice; she was broken up in 1926.

Radetzky off Trieste in 1912.

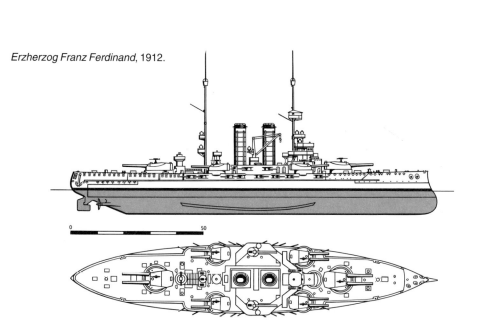

Erzherzog Franz Ferdinand, 1912.

Ship	Builder	Laid down	Launched	Commissioned
Erzherzog Franz Ferdinand	STT	12.09.1907	30.09.1908	15.06.1910
Radetzky	STT	26.11.1907	03.07.1909	15.01.1911
Zrinyi	STT	21.01.1909	12.04.1910	15.09.1911

A large G2 flying boat passes *Erzherzog Franz Ferdinand*.

Tegetthoff Class

Displacement: 20,550/21,600t;
Szent István 21,700t full load
Dimensions: 151.0 x 27.3 x 8.6m
Machinery: Parsons turbines, 4
shafts, 27,000shp; *Szent István*
AEG Curtis turbines, 2 shafts,
26,400shp
Fuel: 1,870t coal + 160t oil;
Szent István 1,845t coal + 270t
oil
Speed/range: 20.3–20.5kt;
3,500nm at 14kt (no figures
taken for *Szent István*)
Armour: Belt 280mm, deck
48mm + 30mm, main armament
280mm, CT 280mm
Weight of armour: 6,780t =
33.0% of displacement
Armament: 12 x 305mm 45-cal,
12 x 150mm 50-cal
Anti-aircraft guns: Up to 4 x
66mm 45-cal (some 50-cal)
Complement: 1,090

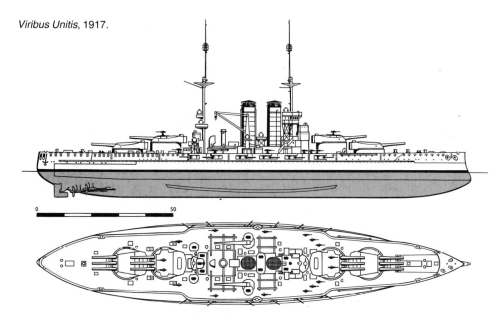

Viribus Unitis, 1917.

Ship	Builder	Laid down	Launched	Commissioned
Viribus Unitis	STT	23.07.1910	24.06.1911	06.10.1912
Tegetthoff	STT	24.09.1910	21.03.1912	14.07.1913
Prinz Eugen	STT	16.01.1912	30.11.1912	17.07.1914
Szent István	Fiume	29.01.1912	17.01.1914	13.12.1915

The first two units were ordered by the Navy in October 1909, begun in 1910 but not approved by Parliament within the terms of the new building programme until 3 March 1911, when the latter pair were also approved. The Trieste-built (STT) ships were of good quality, strongly armed and sufficiently armoured above the waterline but with poor underwater protection. Their machinery was first class and all three ships exceeded the designed top speed without difficulty. In September 1912 *Viribus Unitis* attained 20.41 knots at 27,183shp on trials; in April 1913 *Tegetthoff* reached 20.31 knots at only 24,715shp. No measurements were carried out during *Szent István's* trials and the ship was accepted 'subject to reservations'. In service her machinery was liable to break down and this led indirectly to the loss of the ship on 10 June 1918 off the island of Premuda when she was torpedoed by the Italian MTB *MAS-15*. *Viribus Unitis* was already under the Yugoslav flag when sunk by Italian saboteurs at Pola on the morning of 1 November 1918. *Tegetthoff* was awarded to Italy as a war reparation and scrapped at La Spezia in 1924–25. *Prinz Eugen* was ceded to France as a reparation, stripped of her armament and used as a target ship, in which role she was sunk off Toulon on 28 June 1922.

Szent István fires her main armament.

◀ ▲ *Viribus Unitis* carrying the bodies of the assassinated heirs to the throne to Trieste, 30 June 1914.

Russia

At the end of the nineteenth century Russia was a first-rank naval power. By the beginning of 1904 her fleet of twenty battleships and fourteen large cruisers was the third largest in the world, but within eighteen months, following its crushing defeat at the hands of the Japanese at the Battle of Tsushima, it was of paltry significance. The only battle group remaining intact, that in the Black Sea, was too small and obsolete to be useful as an instrument of power politics: Russia's total defeat in the war against Japan imbued the future path of Russian foreign policy with an air of helplessness.

The attempt by *Kaiser* Wilhelm II to enlist Russia as Germany's ally in June 1905 failed because Russia was dependent on financial aid from France. Russia was also the most important ally of France, and soon the French were acting as mediators between this old ally and their new-found friend, Great Britain. In 1906, at the instigation of France, Britain even made the Czar a handsome loan. As a consequence of the anti-German attitude of newly appointed Foreign Minister Izvolski, the way was open for a *rapprochement* with Britain, and the visit of a Russian naval group to Portsmouth in March 1907 signalled an end to the almost traditional enmity of Britain and Russia on the world's oceans.

The potential enemies of the Russian Fleet were now those of Germany, Austria-Hungary, Japan and, theoretically, Turkey, although the last was not seriously increasing in size. The Czar was presented with a choice of four naval rearmament programmes, from which he selected the least ambitious, later labelled the 'Small Building Programme', under which the Baltic Fleet would receive four new battlecruisers, eight battleships and numerous smaller units while the Black Sea Fleet would merely see its old battleships refitted. No new warships were planned for the Pacific, for the Russo-Japanese treaty signed on 30 July 1907 respecting the establishment of the two countries' spheres of interest in Manchuria virtually dissipated Russian concerns about the security of Vladivostok. Maintaining the *status quo* and the final agreement about zones of influence in Manchuria and Mongolia were the objects of further treaties in July 1910 and July 1912. Up to the time of the Revolution, the Russian Admiralty made no plans to construct heavy battle units for the Pacific, and from 1907 the Baltic came to be seen increasingly as the decisive future theatre by Russian naval planners.

The naval exercises of 1908 showed that the Russian Fleet would not have been able to prevent German landings around St Petersburg, and nine infantry and two cavalry divisions were now concentrated there. Such measures were of themselves insufficient to counter German naval supremacy in the Baltic, and in August 1907 the Czar decided to proceed with the building of four new battleships for the Baltic Fleet, although the *Duma* withheld approval for finance for some considerable time and construction did not begin until mid-1909.

Parizhskaya Kommuna at Sevastopol in 1940.

An important appointment in the strengthening of the Russian Navy was that of the energetic I. K. Grigorovich as Navy Minister. On 17 April 1911 he presented the Czar with his proposals for naval legislation and the further rebuilding of the Baltic Fleet for the period 1911–1915. This aimed to provide the Fleet with 24 battleships and twelve battlecruisers by 1930. Despite the support of the Czar, who favoured the Navy above the Army, the Navy Minister failed to obtain the approval of the *Duma* for his Bill, although on 1 June 1911 he did at least obtain authorisation to strengthen the Black Sea Fleet by building, *inter alia*, three new capital ships in order to counter the threat of Turkish supremacy there.

The *Duma* postponed its consent to the Navy Bill but approved the 'Construction Programme for Accelerated Ship Building, 1912–1916' which had been submitted to it in March 1912 and which received the Czar's assent on 6 July. The reason for the change in attitude on the part of the *Duma* had been reliable official forecasts that serious crises in international relations were likely to unfold in 1914–15. Four powerful battlecruisers for the Baltic Fleet, together with the four battleships building (plus four cruisers, 36 large destroyers and twelve submarines) were seen as a useful tool of policy in that theatre. In March, when Grigorovich informed the *Duma* of his intention to begin building four 'super-dreadnoughts' once the battlecruisers had been launched, he received the promise of the necessary finance.

In June 1912 the Russo-French Naval Treaty was signed. This provided for direct cooperation between the respective fleets, but a similar agreement with the Royal Navy had not been achieved by the outbreak of war. The Russians would have welcomed the presence of the Home Fleet in the Baltic, as this would have allowed them to transfer their capital ships to the Mediterranean in case of conflict with Turkey. The French placed Bizerta at the disposal of the Russians as a naval base, enabling the latter to make a two-pronged attack against the Turkish Narrows from the Mediterranean and the Black Sea. The Russians planned to occupy the Narrows, including Constantinople, by 1919 at the latest, and in order to give cover to such large-scale landings in the Bosphorus the three battleships just laid down would not be sufficient.

As capital ships were already building on all the slipways large enough to accommodate them at both Nikolayev and St Petersburg, Russia was forced to consider purchasing ships abroad. There was not much of a choice and negotiations with Argentina for a deal involving the sister ships *Rivadavia* and *Moreno* then building on behalf of the latter in the United States came to nothing. This left only the Russian shipbuilding industry, which was already swamped with orders. In late 1914 the Navy Minister suggested to the Government that the construction of one further battleship and two cruisers should be started at Nikolayev at once, and the battleship was ordered without waiting for approval.

A few days before the outbreak of the First World War Grigorovich notified Foreign Minister Sazonov that two 'super-dreadnoughts' armed with 406mm (16in) guns were soon to be ordered for the Black Sea Fleet. This meant that by 1919 at the latest the Russian Navy would have eighteen powerful capital ships in European waters, and this would have put Russia in fourth place in the world rankings. Of course, nothing like this actually came about, for none of the capital ships laid down after 1912 had been completed by the time of the October Revolution in 1917. Russia's economy went into such serious decline in the second year of the war that the Admiralty called a halt to the building of all large units still on the stocks in order to create capacity in the yards for the construction of urgently needed submarines and minor warships.

Developments from 1905

In October 1905, when Britain started building HMS *Dreadnought*, Russia had no similar project. At Nikolayev two hopelessly outdated battleships, *Evstafi* and *Ioann Zlatoust*, were still under construction as part of an 1896 programme. Two further ships, *Imperator Pavel* and *Andrei Pervoswanni*, were under construction in the Baltic, but these were no more than an improved version of *Borodino*, which had been sunk at Tsushima. As a result of Admiralty criticism, the design was drastically revised in 1906 to incorporate lessons learned from the war, but the resultant strengthening of the armour and medium battery led to such enormous delays in the completion dates that it was not until 1912 that these obsolete units joined the Fleet.

In the autumn of 1905 progressives in the Admiralty arranged for the British company Armstrong to design for Russia an armoured cruiser with sixteen 254mm (10in) guns and a 17,500-tonne battleship with two calibres of main armament. When the projects were assessed, however, it was accepted that future orders for capital ships should have a single main calibre. In May 1906 several firms were invited to tender for a battleship with ten 305mm (12in) guns, turbine machinery and a speed of not less than 22 knots. Within two months the Russian Navy was in receipt of three designs, one Russian and the other two from Vickers.

In the autumn of 1906 Navy Minister Birilov was refused finance for two 21,000-tonne units and was obliged to spell out a detailed building plan for the Baltic Fleet instead. In August of the following year the Naval Technical Committee drew up their specification for the Baltic battleship, which would now carry twelve 254mm (10in) guns in four triple turrets, with an belt only 203mm thick. In January 1908 six Russian and 21 foreign firms (including four German) were invited to tender designs. By the closing date, 12 March 1908, 23 projects involving 51 variants had been submitted by five Russian and eight overseas competitors, and the Naval General Staff selected nine of these for further consideration, from which a short list of five possible candidates eventually emerged.

The Naval Technical Committee decided that the design entered by the German shipyard Blohm & Voss was the winner. In second place was a Russian entry under the pseudonym '*Dalnyy Vostok*' (Far East) and third was the Ansaldo concern with drawings by the Italian naval architect Cuniberti. The Naval General Staff put Cuniberti's design first, the German second and the Russian third. As a result of joint discussions involving the two naval authorities in June and July 1908 under the chairmanship of Navy Minister Dikov, it was decided to award the contract to the German yard. However, on learning of this the French Government objected on the grounds that no part of France's financial assistance to Russia could be appropriated to pay Germany to build Russian warships. Accordingly, Blohm & Voss received half a million marks in compensation and consideration was given to Cuniberti's design instead. The Naval Technical Committee had expressed some doubts regarding the likely engine performance and the strength of the hull, and Cuniberti was invited to Russia to argue the case for his design. Subsequently it emerged that the stated displacement of 20,024 tonnes was too high by 3,000 tonnes and that in consequence the hull structure had weaknesses.

Following the elimination of Cuniberti's project the committee considered the third and last project, 'Dalnyy Vostok', submitted in fact by the Russian naval architect Coromaldi. His arrangement of 305mm (12in) turrets and the ship's machinery was similar to that of the later Sevastopol class and the hull weight of 40.6 per cent of the whole was optimal. The Navy requested detailed technical documentation for the design and placed the order at once with the Baltic shipyard whose tender had taken last place in the open competition. The yard promptly declined to build a ship to Coromaldi's plans, but suggested a compromise in which they would build their own design, amended to accommodate Coromaldi's design where appropriate. The Admiralty eventually agreed to accept this solution, further amended by having Yarrow boilers fitted instead of the original Belleville type, and Coromaldi had to be satisfied with supervising the construction of Gangut in the Admiralty Yard.

The technical documentation for the battleship's construction was undertaken, as had been the case with the first Baltic Yard design, by the British company John Brown. The four approved ships were begun, symbolically, in June 1909. The Sevastopol class—often incorrectly called the Gangut class—were considered to be battleship/battlecruiser hybrids because of their speed and light construction. The Russian Navy was not very impressed with the result, and the design was not repeated for the Black Sea capital ships.

Latterly the Russian Navy had had a preference for triple turrets, but the connection with German battleship design was indirect. In July 1907 the Russian Naval Attaché to Berlin reported that he had received confidential information from Kiel to the effect that the battleship Posen currently on the stocks was to be armed with sixteen 305mm (12in) guns in four triple and two twin turrets. As the planned Russian ships of the same tonnage were to have only ten 305mm guns, and the St Petersburg yard did not have the capacity to build larger ships, triple turrets were the only means by which the deficiency could be adjusted, and in August 1907 the Navy amended the specification and requested the Petersburg Metal Factory to produce a 305mm triple turret.

The same number and arrangement of triple turrets were prescribed for the ships approved in 1911, but otherwise there were substantial differences in the technical specifications despite their outward similarity to the Baltic units. Most importantly, for the same tonnage and armament, the Black Sea Fleet ships would be better protected, and although speed had to be sacrificed down to a maximum 21 knots in order to achieve this goal, this was not seen as a drawback in view of the distances involved in this relatively small sea area.

Of six designs, the tender submitted by the new shipbuilder AG Russud was selected. In December 1911 the yard itself was still under construction and had no drawing offices, and John Brown had the contract for the technical drafting. The consultant for the project was Colonel Coromaldi. Russud was shown preference when the orders were distributed, receiving the contracts for two ships whilst the Navy Yard received only one.

The keels of all three ships were officially scheduled to be laid at the end of October 1911, but work was not started until July 1912 as the contracts had not been placed until April that year. Building proceeded at a more rapid pace than had been the case with the Sevastopol class, and all three units were launched before the outbreak of war, but difficulties began to arise soon afterwards. Russud had placed a heavy reliance on deliveries from Britain. The turbines for the Russud ship Imperatritsa Maria arrived by sea on time but at Nikolayev, while those for her sister ship Imperator Alexander III were delayed until October 1916. The former vessel was a well-armed and well-protected ship but bow-heavy and her numerous deficiencies were compounded by poor ventilation for her magazines. Imperator Alexander III did not enter commission until two years later. On her trials she showed better seakeeping qualities than Maria as the forward 130mm (5.1in) casemate gun had been left off so as to reduce the bow-heaviness.

The Nikolayev-built ship Yekaterina II did not have this problem. Despite her outward resemblance to the Russud ships, she had been built to a Vickers design whereas the other pair were a John Brown project. In order to increase the reserve displacement, Vickers had made her longer by 1.5m (5ft), beamier by 60cm (2ft) and provided a different underwater hull form. As the machinery had been built at the Nikolayev yard's factory, the ship was commissioned in November 1915.

Three days after Yekaterina II was launched, preparations got under way to lay the keel of a fourth battleship. Although outwardly similar to Yekaterina II and carrying the same armament, Imperator Nikolai I was not a sister ship but a lengthened version with much heavier armour. Nikolai I was launched in the autumn of 1916 but towards October 1917 work on her began gradually to tail off.

At the same time there were four unfinished battlecruiser hulls at St Petersburg, whose story had begun seven years earlier in May 1910 when they had been designed to be the most powerful such ships in the world. After their unhappy experience with the Vickers-built cruiser Rurik, the Russian Naval General Staff had been unable to decide about the future construction of large armoured cruisers. In the spring of 1910 the German Blohm & Voss company, with whom the Russian Admiralty had good relations, supplied them with information concerning the new German battlecruiser Von der Tann, as a result of which St Petersburg was goaded into action. The Russian Baltic Fleet wanted to have more powerful and faster battlecruisers than the Germans: if the latter considered eight 305mm (12in) guns to be sufficient, then Russian ships would mount a 356mm (14in) armament.

On 17 April 1911 Navy Minister Grigorovich presented to the Czar not only his proposals for naval legislation but also the outline of the first stage of the 'Shipbuilding Programme for the Strengthening of the Baltic Fleet'. Within its framework, four powerful armoured cruisers (the term 'battlecruiser' was not introduced into Russian naval parlance until 1915) would be acquired, and they would mount nine 356mm (14in) guns in triple turrets. The programme was postponed, but the Navy Ministry was anxious not to lose time and at the beginning of September 1911 invited six Russian and seventeen foreign firms to tender designs. When the winner emerged in May 1912 this was again a Blohm & Voss design, for a ship with one funnel and armed with twelve 356mm (14in) guns in two triple turrets forward and aft, similar to the Austro-Hungarian Tegetthoff class battleships.

The Supreme Defence Council took the view that the German design failed to live up to 'the tradition of Russian naval construction', which thus limited the field to Russian designs. The Navy Yard at St Petersburg had submitted a design with three triple turrets, and their architects were now pressed to submit a variant with four. They did so by August 1912, and on 18 September that year contracts were placed for two units each at the Navy and Baltic shipyards.

The keels were officially due to be laid on 19 December 1912, but the slipways at both yards had to be lengthened and widened first, giving rise to financial difficulties. The capital necessary to complete the alterations at the Navy Yard was not approved by the *Duma* until July 1913; building work was not commenced there until the spring of 1913, and at the Baltic yard not until the autumn. Therefore the name-ship of the class, *Izmail*, was not launched until June 1915.

It was arranged that Vickers would develop the 356mm (14in) gun and then supply twenty-four barrels while the remainder were to be manufactured under licence at the Obuchov Works. Foreign concerns would supply the engines. Russian naval historians dispute that the turbines used by the German minelayers *Brummer* and *Bremse* were those originally intended for the battlecruiser *Navarin*, arguing that only the shafts for *Navarin* and *Borodino* were ordered from Vulcan works and that all the turbines were to be assembled in two St Petersburg factories, whilst technical assistance and supplies were being procured from Britain. Consequently the machinery for the ships (with the exception of *Izmail*) was only 30 per cent complete.

In 1915 Russia's economic situation compelled the cancellation of all costly projects and work on the three battlecruisers was abandoned; in the summer of 1917, even the attempt to get at least *Izmail* into commission was given up. This was the end of the road for Russian capital ship construction, although in the Nikolayev drawing offices work on still larger and more powerful ships continued.

From mid-1914 the Navy Ministry had thought about building 'super-dreadnoughts' armed with 406mm (16in) guns, but the outbreak of war brought an end to all their planning, although the modern shipyards at Nikolayev were commissioned to supply designs for giant vessels armed with eight to twelve 406mm guns. These were supplied in 1916, and at the beginning of 1917 the Navy Ministry concentrated on the design for a 44,000-tonne battlecruiser. This would have been a 30-knot ship 240m (787ft) in length with three triple turrets housing the 406mm guns under development. What became of the design drawings is not known; possibly they were never submitted, for in 1917 Russia had other things to worry about.

Russian Battleships in 1914

In 1914–15 it was the older battleships alone which had to face the most dangerous enemy vessel in the Black Sea, the battlecruiser *Goeben*. The oldest ship of the squadron, *Tri Svititelia*, had been completely modernised in 1911–12 and was still useful despite her age. The smallest unit, *Rostislav*, was both slow and poorly armed and owed her continued existence to the desire of the Navy Chiefs for a substantial warship for use in shallow waters.

The nucleus of the battleship squadron in the Black Sea was formed of three units of similar construction. The oldest of these was the soon-to-be-famous *Potemkin* (named *Pantelimon* until April 1917) which had been completed in December 1904 after six years' building. The sister-ships *Evstafi* and *Ioann Zlatoust* were marginally larger versions of

Potemkin, being armed with a medium battery of four 203mm (8in) and twelve 152mm (6in) guns as against the sixteen 152mm of the latter. As a result of the experience gained from the naval battles against Japan, the armour on the two larger units was more substantial, and these ships did not enter commission until 1911.

The Baltic Fleet had only two 'semi-dreadnoughts' and two old pre-dreadnoughts in commission at the outbreak of war. Only the latter were involved in naval operations after the summer of 1915. The older ship, *Tsessarevitch* (renamed *Grashdanin* in April 1917) played only a subordinate role during the war. The better protected and more modern *Slava* excelled as a 'heavy gun carrier' not only in the bombardment of German positions at Kurland but also in artillery duels with German battleships in the Gulf of Riga. (On 17 October 1917 *Slava* out-ranged the 305mm guns of the German battleships *König* and *Kronprinz* from behind a minefield, and the German dreadnoughts were forced to look on helplessly as she battered the German minesweepers.) The achievement of the Russian naval gunners was attributed to the new armament (but of the same barrel length) fitted to *Slava* in 1916.

Two of the battleships which had been sunk in the anchorage at Port Arthur were raised by the Japanese and partially rearmed. They served in the Japanese Fleet under the names *Tango* and *Sagami* until they were sold back to the Russians in March 1916. *Sagami* had her original name, *Peresviet*, restored and was re-classified as a cruiser on account of her weak armament of four 254mm (10in) guns. She did not last very long, and went down off Suez on 4 January 1917 after striking a mine laid by a German U-boat. *Tango*, ex *Poltava*, was renamed *Chesma* in April 1916, as her former name was now carried by one of the Baltic dreadnoughts. This old battleship became the flagship of the Russian North Sea Flotilla formed during the war. After putting into Kola Bay in January 1917 she was not used again and she was scrapped at Archangel in the summer of 1924.

Ship	Built	Disp. (normal)	Speed	Armament
Tri Svititelia	1891–96	12,600t	17kt	4 x 305mm, 14 x 152mm
Rostislav	1895–98	9,000t	15.8kt	4 x 254mm, 8 x 152mm
Pantelimon	1898–1903	12,600t	16kt	4 x 305mm, 16 x 152mm
Evstafi	1903–10	13,000t	16kt	4 x 305mm, 4 x 203mm, 12 x 152mm
Ioann Zlatoust	1903–10	13,000t	16kt	4 x 305mm, 4 x 203mm, 12 x 152mm
Tsessarevitch	1899–1903	13,100t	18kt	4 x 305mm, 12 x 152mm
Slava	1902–05	13,750t	18kt	4 x 305mm, 12 x 152mm
Chesma (ex *Poltava*)	1892–96	12,700t	16kt	4 x 305mm, 12 x 152mm

Armament

The performance of Russian naval artillery in the war against Japan has come in for strong criticism generally. The problem lay neither with the gunners nor their weapons, however, but was attributable to the error of the Naval Technical Committee in 1892 in introducing a 'light' shell with a high muzzle velocity. Although it had good penetration up to 4km

(4,400yd), its effectiveness was much reduced at greater ranges, and at Tsushima the range was up to 7km (7,650yd). The subsequent introduction of new gun types and armour-piercing shell with an improved ballistic performance quickly changed the situation, and in action against German battleships with guns of a similar calibre the Russian 305mm (12in) guns were found to be superior.

The Obuchov company had a monopoly for the manufacture of heavy naval guns. The 152mm (6in) naval guns built under licence from the French firm Schneider were designated the 'Canet System'. Schneider also rendered assistance in the development of the 305mm (12in) 45-cal guns ordered in 1892. Since Obuchov's technology could not cope with a barrel of this length, however, the Russian Navy had to accept the 40-calibre barrel. Although trials were carried out with this weapon in 1895, it was called the '1892 model' because development began in that year. With the exception of *Rostislav*, all Russian battleships which entered service between 1898 and 1912 were fitted with 305mm guns of this type. With the new armour-piercing shell first introduced after 1905, their performance was extremely effective in the First World War.

The new dreadnoughts were to mount 305mm (12in) guns of a new type and 50 calibres long. A 305mm 52-cal gun was also tested on the Obuchov range in December 1908. A year previously the Petersburg Metal Factory had submitted the first sketches for a triple turret for these guns, but apparently they were not to the satisfaction of the Russian Navy and tenders were sought from overseas in the spring of 1909. In July the Petersburg factory was informed that its project had won, although the personnel actually building the weapon would be British. The Metal Factory was asked to supply eight, and the Putilov and Obuchov works four each, of the turrets. The Obuchov guns ranked amongst the best in the world.

The capabilities of other large calibre guns carried on board Russian warships were not tested during the First World War. The *Izmail* class was designed to be armed with twelve 356mm (14in) guns in four triple turrets. In 1913 Vickers received a contract to manufacture and supply twelve guns and design the triple turret, while Obuchov were contracted to supply a dozen guns and a number of reserves. The Petersburg Metal Factory was to manufacture the triple turrets to Vickers' design. The upshot of this arrangement was that by the war's end one turret and three guns had been delivered complete, but even these could not be installed in *Izmail* because the turntables had been ordered from Skoda, now the enemy, before the war.

For this reason, and for other technical considerations also, the plan to fit out the fourth battleship of the Black Sea Fleet, *Imperator Nikolai I*, was abandoned, and it was decided to transfer four or five guns manufactured for the ships for installation in twin turrets and use them as coastal artillery. Two of these turrets had been completed by the autumn of 1917, but the barrels were never installed and they were eventually used by the Soviets as railway guns. Sixteen of the barrels ordered in Britain had been completed by 1919, bearing the designation 'Vickers 14-inch Mk B'. In August 1917 Vickers tested the prototype 406mm (16in) gun ordered by the Russian Navy shortly before the war, delivery of which had been stopped because of the Revolution.

The Russian Navy had recognised the possibility of attack by airships in 1909 and a number of the approved battleship designs would have carried four 'anti-balloon' guns. All Russian sources indicate that these were to have been of 63.5mm calibre, although no information exists concerning the production of such weapons in Russia up to the end of 1913. A number of 65mm AA weapons were ordered from the German firm Rheinmetall in 1913, and if these had been delivered by the outbreak of war they could well have been examples.

Adapted 75mm (2.9in) 50-cal naval guns in special small turrets and 47mm Hotchkiss quick-firing cannon were installed aboard old pre-dreadnoughts on their turret roofs. The 76mm (3in) 30-cal AA guns named after their designer, Lender, and developed in the Obuchov Works in 1915 could not be produced in sufficient quantities before the war's end. The Navy preferred the more powerful gun offered to them by Vickers in 1916. Whether any examples of this 102mm (4in) weapon had been manufactured by November 1917 is not known. In general, AA defence aboard Russian ships was relatively strong.

Gun	Model	Wt of shell	Muzzle velocity	Range/elevation
356mm 52-cal	M.1912	748kg	823m/sec	?km/20°
305mm 52-cal	M.1910	470kg	762m/sec	23.2km/25°
305mm 40-cal	M.1892	332kg	793m/sec	14.8km/15°
Anti-aircraft guns				
76mm 30-cal	M.1915	5.5kg	590m/sec	5,000m/75°
75mm 50-cal	M.1891/15	4.9kg	750m/sec	5,000m/60°

Russian Battleships in the First World War

The Baltic Fleet received its first capital ships in the winter of 1914, but they were only ever used in the role of escort for distant minelaying operations. Two old pre-dreadnoughts were involved in fighting. *Slava*, which arrived in the Gulf of Riga at the beginning of July 1915 to protect the land front, fought a gunnery duel a few days later against two German dreadnoughts, and the German advance collapsed under her withering fire. The ship was eventually brought to account in a famous action in the last phases of the German Operation 'Albion', the occupation of the Baltic islands in October 1917. *Grashdanin* (ex *Tsessarevitch*) was involved in a skirmish with German heavy units on the same day but escaped through the shallow Sound of Moon.

In contrast to the relatively peaceful existence enjoyed by the capital ships in the Baltic, Russian heavy ships in the Black Sea were very active, although they fought under markedly different conditions since their only opponent was the German-crewed Turkish battlecruiser *Goeben*. Only a week after the opening of hostilities with Turkey, all five of the older pre-dreadnoughts began a systematic bombardment of the Turkish coast, especially the coaling ports. After the second bombardment *Goeben* arrived and engaged the retiring squadron south-east of Yalta. During the exchange the older Russian 305mm (12in) guns were used to good effect, and, although the flagship *Evstafi* was damaged, *Goeben* was forced to break off after receiving several hits. The forays of the battleship squadron were brought to an end by the arrival of German U-boats at Constantinople. After the dreadnought *Imperatritsa*

Maria had entered service the Russians resumed their offensive against the Turkish coaling ports, and the old pre-dreadnoughts bombarded land targets while *Maria*, accompanied by new destroyers, covered the operation. The second dreadnought, *Yekaterina II*, joined the squadron soon afterwards and took part in the first sea battle between the new battleships and *Goeben*. On 8 June 1916 the force encountered the Turkish ship: their guns outranged hers and she was forced to withdraw.

The Russian commander-in-chief, Admiral Kolchak, now assembled a battle group consisting of a modern battleship, one or two seaplane carriers and several well-armed destroyers. These regularly undertook raids against the Turkish coast. The last battle in the Black Sea took place on 25 June 1917 when *Yekaterina II* (which had been renamed *Svobodnaya Rossia* on 29 April) pursued the faster German cruiser *Breslau* as far as the approaches to the Bosphorus.

Russian Battleships in the Civil War

All Russian Baltic battleships spent the winter of 1917–18 at Helsingfors with what remained of their crews. After the Peace Treaty of Brest-Litovsk on 3 March 1918, all Russian warships were obliged to leave Finnish waters. The icing-over of the Gulf of Finland meant that there was a danger of the ships falling into German hands, but the heavy units succeeded in escaping to Kronshtadt on 12 March, and they were laid up at St Petersburg until the end of the civil war. The exception was *Petropavlovsk*, which remained at Kronshtadt with the rump of her original crew and made a number of sorties. *Poltava* was irreparably damaged as the result of two serious fires, but the other three *Sevastopol*

class units were renamed and resumed service under the Soviet flag once the civil war had ended.

A different fate awaited the battleships in the Black Sea. *Svobodnaya Rossia* (ex *Yekaterina II*) and the incomplete *Volya* (formerly *Imperator Alexander III*) lay with the main body of old pre-dreadnoughts in the anchorage at Sevastopol. For several weeks *Volya* flew the flag of the Ukraine, and in the evening of 30 April 1918 she slipped away in company with *Svobodnaya Rossia* to avoid being handed over to Germany. Subsequently both vessels agreed to the German ultimatum to return to Sevastopol from Novorossiysk. However, *Svobodnaya Rossia*'s depleted crew could not raise sufficient steam and the ship was unable to leave the quayside. She was towed to the outer harbour and sunk by the destroyer *Kerch* on 18 June 1918.

Volya returned to Sevastopol on 19 June and raised the Imperial German ensign but the Germans did not take over the ship until October. She ran a short series of trials between 15 October and 11 November 1918, after which the ship was placed under British supervision. In October 1919 she was renamed *General Alexeyev* and took part in naval operations in the Black Sea for the White Russians. Following their defeat in the Crimea, the ship left Sevastopol crammed with thousands of refugees. Ultimately she was interned in Bizerta on 29 December 1920.

Yugoslav attempts to acquire the disputed units in December 1920 were unsuccessful. The Soviet government tried vainly to retrieve at least the former *Volya* and some of the nine destroyers from the French, but *Volya* remained at Bizerta after having been disarmed and was scrapped in 1936. A number of her 305mm (12in) guns were sold to the Finns in 1939, while another eventually reinforced the German Atlantic Wall.

Imperator Pavel/Andrei Pervoswanni

Displacement: 17,700/19,000t
Dimensions: 138.4 x 24.4 x 8.8m
Machinery: 2 triple-expansion reciprocating steam engines, 2 shafts, 17,600ihp
Fuel: 1,350t coal
Speed/range: 18.0kt; 3,300nm at 10kt
Armour: Belt 216mm, deck 90–116mm, main armament 203mm, CT 203mm
Weight of armour: 6,100t = 34.4% of displacement
Armament: 4 x 305mm 40-cal, 14 x 203mm 50-cal, 12 x 120mm 50-cal
Anti-aircraft guns: 2 x 47mm (adapted Hotchkiss)
Complement: 960

Andrei Pervoswanni in 1916, with truncated lattice masts.

Ship	Builder	Laid down	Launched	Commissioned
Imperator Pavel	Baltic Works	27.10.1904	07.09.1907	29.07.1911
Andrei Pervoswanni	Admiralty Works	11.05.1905	20.10.1906	13.05.1912

Imperator Pavel as originally completed.

Originally, i.e. from 1901, both ships had been envisaged as improved successors to the *Borodino* class. As a result of experience gained in the Russo-Japanese war, however, experts demanded many design alterations, the plans for the armament, for example, being changed on no fewer than seventeen occasions and the belt being extended. The constant variations—even the planned pole masts were replaced by American-style lattice-type masts—and problems with the machinery so delayed completion that the ships were obsolete when they were eventually commissioned. During the first major refits (for *Andrei Pervoswanni* in the summer of 1914 and for *Imperator Pavel* in the autumn of that year) the lattice masts were shortened because of excessive vibration.

Imperator Pavel was renamed *Respublika* on 29 April 1917; laid up at Kronshtadt virtually unmanned after spring 1918, she was decommissioned that August and sent for breaking up on 22 November 1923. *Andrei Pervoswanni* remained in service under the Soviet flag. She took part in the defence of Kronshtadt Bay and was torpedoed in harbour by the British *MTB31* on 18 August 1919 but was repaired by the Bolsheviks despite her age. She remained in service defending the seat of Soviet government until the end of August 1920 but was stricken on 15 December 1923 and scrapped in 1925.

Sevastopol Class

Displacement: 25,200/26,400t
Dimensions: 181.0 x 26.6 x 9.2m
Machinery: 4 Parsons turbines,
4 shafts, 42,000shp
Fuel: 1,500t coal + 700t oil max.
Speed/range: 23.0kt; 3,500nm at
10kt
Armour: Belt 225mm, deck
76mm, main armament 203mm,
CT 254mm
Weight of armour: 6,000t
approx. = 23.8% of displace-
ment
Armament: 12 x 305mm 52-cal,
16 x 120mm 50-cal
Anti-aircraft guns: 2 x 75mm 50-
cal or 2 x 76mm 30-cal
Complement: 1,120

Gangut, 1914.

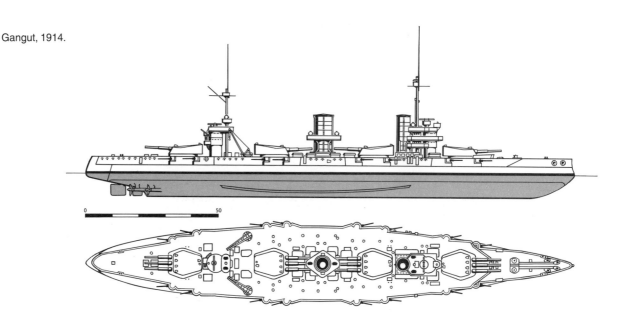

Ship	Builder	Laid down	Launched	Commissioned
Sevastopol	Baltic Works	16.06.1909	29.06.1911	17.11.1914
Poltava	Admiralty Works	16.06.1909	10.07.1911	17.12.1914
Petropavlovsk	Baltic Works	16.06.1909	09.09.1911	23.12.1914
Gangut	Admiralty Works	16.06.1909	07.10.1911	04.01.1915

The figure of 23,000 tonnes quoted in most Soviet sources is the designed displacement. All four units exceeded this by at least 2,000 tonnes; the designed speed was also exceeded, in the case of *Poltava* by as much as 1.3 knots. It is not widely realised that the ships were not genuinely battleworthy at any time during the war: some had no rangefinders and *Poltava*'s fire control facilities were not completed. The ships had many defect, the worst of which was insufficient ventilation in the magazines and shell rooms. All incidents of combustion, however, passed without disaster.

For further career details of these ships see under Soviet Union.

Petropavolvsk under her later, Soviet name *Marat*.

Imperatritsa Maria Class

Displacement: 24,000/24,800t
Dimensions: 168.0 x 27.4 x 8.9m
Machinery: 4 Brown-Curtis turbines, 4 shafts, 26,500shp
Fuel: 1,200t coal + 500t oil
Speed/range: 21.0kt; 3,000nm at 10kt
Armour: Belt 262mm, deck 76mm, main armament 250mm, CT 300mm
Weight of armour: 7,000t = 29.3% of normal displacement
Armament: 12 x 305mm 52-cal, 20 x 130mm 55-cal (*Volya* 18 x 130mm)
Anti-aircraft guns: 3 or 4 x 76mm 30-cal
Complement: 1,220

Ship	Builder	Laid down	Launched	Commissioned
Imperatritsa Maria	Russud	14.07.1912	01.11.1913	10.09.1915
Imperator Alexander III	Russud	14.07.1912	15.04.1914	28.10.1917

Imperatritsa Maria in 1916 with anti-aircraft guns atop her main turrets.

Imperator Alexander III, now renamed *General Alexeyev*, at Sevastopol in the spring of 1920.

Despite reports to the contrary, the construction of both these vessels was actually commenced in mid-July 1912: by October 1911 the proposed designs had not even been presented to the Navy Ministry. *Imperatritsa Maria* was bow-heavy and difficult to manoeuvre, for which reason the forward pair of 150mm guns was not installed on her sister ship.

Imperatritsa Maria blew up at Sevastopol on the morning of 20 October 1916. Despite rumours of sabotage, this was undoubtedly caused by the spontaneous ignition of her cordite. The capsized hull was raised in the spring of 1918, but because of the situation in Crimea it was not brought into dry dock until late May 1919. The possibility of rebuilding the ship was considered but rejected and she was broken up in 1927.

Imperator Alexander III was renamed *Volya* on 29 April 1917; this name was retained even when the ship was under the German ensign, but the White Russians renamed her *General Alexeyev* in October 1919. She was interned at Bizerta in 1920. The French refused Soviet demands to hand the ship back and she was scrapped in 1936.

Yekaterina II/Imperator Nikolai I

Displacement: 24,400/25,400t; *Nikolai* 28,200/29,600t

Dimensions: 169.8 x 27.9 x 8.7m; *Nikolai* 182.0 x 29.0 x 9.0m

Machinery: As *I. Maria* but *Nikolai* Parsons turbines, 29,700shp

Fuel: As *I. Maria*

Speed/range: As *I. Maria*

Armour: As *I. Maria* but *Nikolai* belt 270mm, deck 98mm, main armament 305mm, CT 400mm

Weight of armour: 7,036t = 29.1% of normal displacement; *Nikolai* 9,417t = 33.4%

Armament: 12 x 305mm 52-cal, 20 x 130mm 55-cal

Anti-aircraft guns: 3 x 76mm 30-cal; *Nikolai* 4 x 102mm Vickers (planned)

Complement: 1,220 (*Yekaterina*)

Whereas *Yekaterina II*'s keel was actually laid in September 1912, the date for *Imperator Nikolai I* is unknown. As the latter ship was not approved until 27 July 1914 and the shipyard received the contract one month later (on 26 August), the official keel-laying date of 22 June 1914 must mean the commencement of preparatory work on the slip. It is known that the hull was 7.7 per cent complete by mid-December 1914. The frequently quoted date of 28 January 1915 for keel-laying is incorrect, as this ceremony, in the presence of the Czar, actually took place on 28 April 1915. In comparison with *Yekaterina II*, *Imperator Nikolai I*'s armour was substantially stronger.

Imperator Nikolai I was renamed *Demokratiya* on 29 April 1917. Despite her advanced state, all work on this vessel was suspended two weeks before the October Revolution in 1917. During the civil war the hull was left uncompleted; it was towed to Sevastopol for breaking up on 28 June 1927, the armour plate being sold abroad the following year.

Yekaterina II was involved in a skirmish with the Turkish battlecruiser *Goeben* in the Black Sea on 8 June 1916. Renamed *Svobodniya Rossia* on 28 or 29 April 1917, she was in action again in the Black Sea on 25 June 1917 when she pursued the German cruiser *Breslau* to the Bosphorus. On 18 June 1918 she was sunk by six torpedoes from the destroyer *Kerch* at Novorossiysk to prevent her capture by the Germans.

Ship	Builder	Laid down	Launched	Commissioned
Yekaterina II	Naval/Nikolayev	30.10.1911	06.06.1914	13.12.1915
Imperator Nikolai I	Russud	22.06.1914	18.10.1916	–

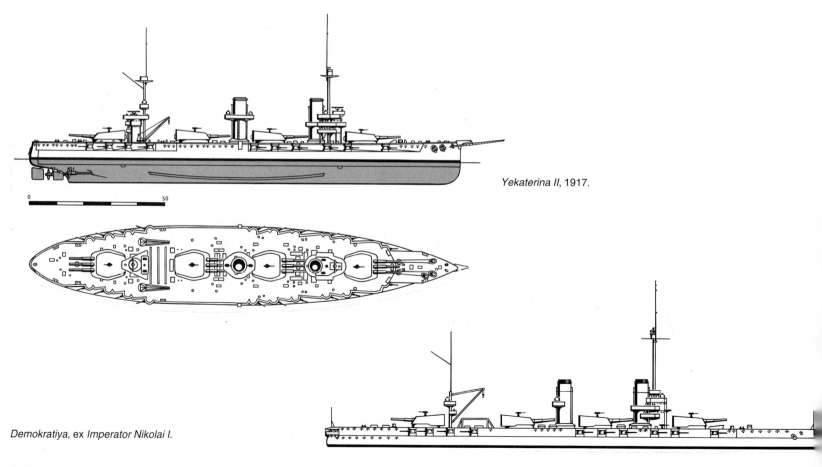

Yekaterina II, 1917.

Demokratiya, ex Imperator Nikolai I.

Izmail Class

Displacement: 30,600/33,000t
Dimensions: 222.4 x 29.9 x 10.2m
Machinery: 4 turbines, 4 shafts, 66,000shp
Fuel: 1,950t coal + 1,900t oil
Speed/range: 26.5kt; 3,800nm at 10kt
Armour: Belt 238mm, deck 75mm, main armament 305mm, CT 400mm
Weight of armour: ?
Armament: 12 x 356mm 52-cal, 24 x 130mm 55-cal
Anti-aircraft guns: 4 x 63.5mm (designed)
Complement: 1,200

The launch of *Izmail*, 22 June 1915.

Ship	Builder	Laid down	Launched
Izmail	Baltic Works	19.12.1912	22.06.1915
Kinburn	Baltic Works	19.12.1912	30.10.1915
Borodino	Admiralty Works	19.12.1912	31.07.1915
Navarin	Admiralty Works	19.12.1912	09.11.1916

The December 1912 date for keel-laying was only 'official', as the expansion programme at both St Petersburg shipyards was then still in progress and not completed until spring 1913 (Baltic) and autumn 1913 (Admiralty). The technical specifications for the ships were not supplied until the beginning of 1913. Demands for alterations of various kinds to the design were made but only those relating to the strengthening of the horizontal armour were accepted. With the exception of *Izmail*, little work was done on these ships after autumn 1915, all having been launched by November that year, although the official suspension of work was not announced until the end of October 1917. At that time *Izmail*'s hull was 65 per cent complete, *Borodino*'s 57 per cent and *Kinburn*'s 52 per cent, and *Izmail*'s machinery 66 per cent complete, *Borodino*'s 40 per cent and *Kinburn*'s 22 per cent. *Kinburn*, *Borodino* and *Navarin* were officially stricken in July 1922 and sold to Germany for scrapping between August and September 1923. Progress was made on *Izmail* with a view to placing her into service and in the mid-1920s it was suggested that she be converted to an aircraft carrier. However, the decision was taken in 1930 not to proceed. Some of the ship's boilers were removed for installation in *Oktyabrskaya Revoluciya* and the hull was scrapped in 1932.

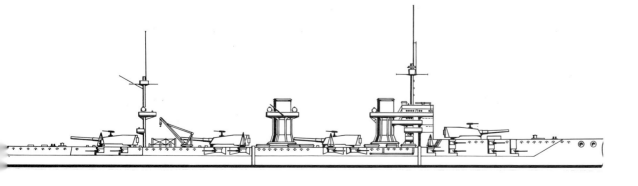

Izmail, 1915 final design (not to scale).

Soviet Union

The civil war in European Russia ended in December 1920; Vladivostok was invested by the Red Army on 25 October 1922 and the Soviet Union was proclaimed on 30 December 1922. Following the restoration of order, the Soviet government took stock of the naval situation.

The Baltic Fleet had suffered in the confusion of civil war, but most of the ships were serviceable and partly built units were theoretically available for completion as the shipbuilding industry at Petrograd (formerly St Petersburg and renamed Leningrad in 1924) had remained intact. However, there were no supplies of building materials and fuel was scarce across the entire Soviet economy. A large naval presence was not necessary in the Baltic, and it was planned to use the Baltic Fleet as a pool of ships on which naval groups in other theatres under the control of the Soviet Union could draw.

Of the Czar's Black Sea Fleet at Sevastopol only a few antiquated ships with sabotaged machinery remained. In the run-down shipyards at Nikolayev there were five partly assembled submarines at the premises of the American company Holland, together with a handful of landing ships. In the Far East, the Soviets had a few harbour vessels and in the 'unprotected' Arctic the ancient *Chesma* and some trawlers.

Before the First World War the strategic situation for Russia at sea had not been good, and it was worse for the Soviet Union after hostilities had ended, no more so than in the Baltic, where all bases had been lost to the newly independent Baltic States and Finland. What remained in Soviet hands was a strip of coast around Petrograd with the old fortification at Kronstadt. The only access to the Black Sea remained in foreign hands. Whereas there were routes to the oceans from the arctic north and the Far East, communications within the Soviet Union were poor, and the only base in the Pacific, Vladivostok, was uncomfortably close to a belligerent Japan. These were the strategic conditions which, hand in hand with a disastrous economic situation, left the USSR in no position to contemplate any continuation of the traditional expansionist policy of the Czars—nor, for that matter, the export of communist ideology.

By the mid-1920s the Soviet economy had stabilised sufficiently to allow the leadership to consider strengthening the military potential. Lenin's successor, Stalin, informed the Fifteenth Party Congress in 1927 that peaceful coexistence with capitalist societies was now at an end, but for some time the dictator avoided direct aggression.

The building up of Soviet military forces made swift progress, although the Navy was hampered in its goal of building a powerful battle fleet by the technological shortcomings of Soviet industry. It was for this reason that the first Five-Year Plan, for 1928 to 1932, required all existing shipyards at Leningrad and Nikolayev to be modernised and enlarged. In addition, new yards at Molotovsk and Komsomolsk were to be established in 1932 and new naval groups could thus be assembled in the White Sea and the Pacific respectively.

Gangut in the summer of 1915, with torpedo net booms extended.

The warship recommissioning programme was completed in 1928, by which time the Baltic Fleet had three battleships, a recently built cruiser and ten destroyers; in the Black Sea the Fleet had one new cruiser, four destroyers and five submarines. In order to give the latter group some backbone, in November 1929 the battleship *Parizhskaya Kommuna* and the new cruiser *Profintern* were transferred to Sevastopol from Kronstadt. But these ships were not the tools of power politics; on the contrary, the Soviet Union had to be careful not to become the target of aggression herself—a possibility which was brought forcefully home by the Japanese invasion of Manchuria in September 1931.

On 21 April 1932 the Far Eastern Naval Force was formed, consisting in the early years of light units, a large number of small and medium sized submarines and several dozen sea-going motor torpedo boats. At the beginning of 1933 a battle flotilla was established in the Arctic, and two weeks later the strategically important Baltic–White Sea Canal was opened, which was wide enough to be used by warships up to destroyer size. On 5 August 1933 two destroyers, two new escort ships and three submarines arrived at Murmansk.

Now began the building up of these two important Fleets as promised in the Second Naval Construction Programme (1933–37), which provided for the building of cruisers and large destroyers. The improvement in the foreign relations of the USSR was reflected in the country's admission to the League of Nations on 18 September 1934. The Franco-Soviet mutual aid treaty of May 1935 gave no help to the Soviet Navy either in matters of strategic planning or in naval development, and of much greater significance had been the non-aggression pact with Italy signed on 2 September 1933. There had been some contact previously between the Soviet Navy and Italian industry, but this agreement made it possible for a naval delegation to travel to Italy and order warships and naval armaments. The deliveries agreed at that time had a decisive influence on the future technical development of the Soviet Fleet.

Stalin succeeded in making himself absolute ruler in the USSR, and his great purge cost millions of Soviet citizens their lives, including those of many thousands of officers. The Navy was not exempt, and four of the five fleet commanders were executed in 1937–38. They had been guilty, *inter alia*, of objecting to Stalin's intention to build an enormous ocean-going fleet. Within ten years he was proposing to conjure up fifteen battleships, fifteen battlecruisers, 28 cruisers, 164 destroyers and 336 submarines. Despite several revisions this programme was never realised, and the intended number of capital ships in particular was substantially reduced: despite all the organisational measures, such as the creation of a Ministry for Naval Construction on 30 December 1937, not one of the six capital ships laid down had been launched by the time of the German invasion, 22 June 1941. The construction of Stalin's dreadnoughts was a very costly proposition, but the dictator rejected all criticism.

Stalin manipulated the deteriorating world political situation of 1938–39 for his own purposes. His successful border actions against the Japanese Army along the Soviet–Manchurian and Mongolian–Manchurian frontiers relieved many tensions in the Far East because they demonstrated that it was beyond Japan's capabilities to fight a land war alone against the Soviet Union. In Europe the Soviets spent months discussing a mutual aid package with Britain and France, but the talks were abortive because parallel negotiations for a military treaty could not be agreed. In any case, Stalin had become convinced that he could realise his global political ambitions more swiftly in partnership with Hitler.

The announcement of the Nazi-Soviet non-aggression pact came as a shock. There were clauses in a secret protocol which were important for Stalin's naval objectives, since they gave him a free hand in the Baltic states and in Finland. Within a few months the bases at Libau, Tallin and Hangö were safely under Soviet control. The pact also created the opportunity for cooperation between the respective navies and armaments industries. The Russians had in mind the purchase of three heavy cruisers currently under construction and of the design drawings of *Bismarck*, and wanted to place an order for eight 380mm (15in) twin turrets. The Germans either rejected these requirements or merely procrastinated, and ultimately the Soviets had to be content with the incomplete hull of the cruiser *Lützow*, delivered but never to be finished.

In the autumn of 1940 the spread of the European conflict prompted the Soviet naval administration to request from the shipbuilders the urgent supply of minor war vessels and submarines, and on 19 October 1940 a radical revision of the latest construction programme was ordered by the government. This led to the suspension or cancellation of several new ships under construction, including a number of battleships and cruisers.

The signing of the Neutrality Treaty with Japan on 13 April 1941 in Moscow was of great importance for the USSR as it guaranteed the security of the hinterland in the Far East and also provided the Soviet Navy with exercise areas in the North Pacific.

Large-scale building programmes could not be contemplated during the Second World War, but as soon as the military situation had begun to improve in 1944 Stalin drew up new plans for the control of the oceans. Even before the end of the war, he was demanding that a programme be devised which would provide for the building of nine 75,000-tonne battleships, twelve battlecruisers, fifteen aircraft carriers and 60 cruisers by the end of 1950—all this despite the dilapidated state of the shipyards both in the USSR and in the occupied zone of Germany.

Soviet Battleship Programmes

On 24 December 1920 the Soviet Navy approved a naval building programme for the next five years. Together with a full reconstruction of those battleships extant which were still in good condition, the completion of *Izmail*, *Kinburn* and *Demokratiya* was envisaged, while new ships were proposed for the Black Sea Fleet. By the end of 1925, however, only two battleships had been partially refurbished. In both the original and revised building programmes for the period 1926–32 it had been planned to rebuild the wrecked *Poltava* as a battlecruiser with nine 305mm (12in) guns and an increased top speed, but the detailed designs did not materialise until 1933. Stalin's concept of a powerful battle fleet involved larger and better-armed units than this, for which the entire shipbuilding capacity of the Soviet Union would be needed. The expensive conversion of an old semi-derelict like *Poltava* was unacceptable, and eventually the hull was abandoned in the harbour at Leningrad for scrap.

While the remainder of the capital ships had had refits by the end of 1926, modernisation work was not carried out until 1928. The first to enter the yards was *Marat*, to be completed by 1931. Then it was the turn of *Oktyabrskaya Revoluciya*, and at the beginning of 1934 *Parizhskaya Kommuna*, in the Black Sea. In 1940 the latter returned to the yards to have her AA armament upgraded and her machinery refitted. The modernisations included a general overhaul of the turbine plant and a changeover to pure oil-firing; the strengthening of the horizontal armour; the enlargement of the bridge structure in *Oktyabrskaya Revoluciya* and *Parizhskaya Kommuna*; the addition of a strong tubular foremast for fire control and main rangefinder equipment; the installation of additional rangefinders; and improvements to AA defence, which in the case of *Oktyabrskaya Revoluciya* and *Parizhskaya Kommuna* involved the installation of a new model 76mm AA gun. Finally the angle of elevation of the 305mm (12in) guns on all ships was increased. The last ship modernised, *Parizhskaya Kommuna*, also received anti-torpedo bulges. However, in spite of the reconstruction work and all these technical improvements, the ships still failed to meet requirements.

Apart from the conversion plan for *Poltava*, at the end of 1934 the Soviet Union had no project for building new battleships or battlecruisers, but the sharpening of the world political situation gave Stalin the impetus to change his former naval policy and strategy. For his ambitions in the Pacific, for example the occupation of the southern part of Sakhalin by 1945, he needed neither coastal submarines nor MTBs but rather a powerful battle fleet. Until then he had been focusing his attention on building super-heavy bombers and multi-turreted tanks, but now he rediscovered his interest in building 'super-dreadnoughts'.

The construction of an ocean-going battle fleet began in 1935 when the Navy's commander-in-chief, Orlov, instructed Construction Bureau CKBS-1, which specialised in warship design, to draw up a study project for battleships and heavy cruisers (the Soviet Navy did not recognise the term 'battlecruiser'). The Baltic Yard at Leningrad apparently prepared the design of a battleship on its own initiative, and by the end of 1935 Bureau CKBS-1 had supplied six study projects for ships with displacements ranging from 43,000 tonnes to 75,000 tonnes, the Baltic Yard following with its own design in February 1936. Orlov actually selected two projects, one for a ship of 57,000 tonnes and the other for one of 35,000 tonnes, and on 13 May 1936 the Research Institute for Warship Construction, which was directly subordinate to the Navy, was given the task of preparing the necessary documents.

The specifications for the Pacific units were as follows. Design 1 displaced 80,000 tonnes and had nine 508mm (20in) guns, a 500mm (19.7in) belt and a speed of between 24 and 28 knots. Design 2 displaced 55,000 tonnes and carried nine 457mm (18in) guns, with a 420mm (16.5in) belt and a speed of 30 knots. The Baltic and Black Sea ships would displace 35,000 tonnes, carry nine 406mm (16in) guns and steam at 30 knots. The two Pacific ships were in flagrant breach of the London Naval Treaty signed on 25 March 1936. Work proceeded at a rapid rate, and on 3 August 1936 Orlov decided that the Navy should continue with only two projects, designated 'A' and 'B'. By then he had seen the Italian Ansaldo Project 'UP-41' of 14 July 1936, which proposed a 42,000-tonne ship with nine 406mm (16in) guns and a speed of 32 knots, and this undoubtedly influenced the course of Soviet battleship design: the Baltic Yard, for example, was instructed to modify the previous layout of three forward turrets (as on HMS *Nelson*) in favour of the Italian version (two forward, one aft). The ineffective Pugliese

system of underwater protection was also brought into the final design of Project No 23, although turbines driving four shafts were not. Battleship 'A' in its evolutionary stage in August 1936 was almost identical to the Italian project in its principal details, having a standard displacement of 41,500 tonnes, nine 406mm (16in) and twelve 152mm (6in) guns, 380mm (15in) belt armour and a speed of 30 knots. Battleship 'B' was more a battlecruiser comparable to *Dunkerque* and *Scharnhorst* then under construction, as it provided for a 26,400-tonne ship with nine 305mm (12in) guns, only 200mm (7.9in) belt armour and a speed of 30 knots.

In November 1936 a decision was made regarding the outline projects, and Orlov, probably echoing Stalin, opted for the Baltic Yard project of 45,900 tons standard displacement. CKBS-1 was given the task of preparing the technical details for Battleship 'B', for which the displacement (quoted in metric tonnes in the Soviet Union) was 30,900 tons standard.

Eight battleships were ordered on 3 December 1936. The two Leningrad shipyards worked until the end of 1941 on two each of ships 'A' and 'B' while the two Nikolayev yards each handled two ships 'B'. These orders overrode the then current requirements of the Second Construction Programme of 1933, which had no provision for battleships at all. However, certain insoluble problems required overseas assistance and it was decided to order the heavy guns in France and Bohemia and the turbines in Switzerland. Nothing came of these negotiations and by 1937 the keels had still not been laid.

Orlov was executed in the summer of 1937 and his successor Victorov (who himself would be liquidated at the beginning of 1938) presented the Defence Committee of the Soviet Union with a new plan in September which provided for the construction of six Type 'A' units and fourteen type 'B' units within ten years. The Type 'B' ships were no longer identical to the earlier design Project 25, as the original battlecruiser had been condemned by Stalin as the work of a 'pest of the regime' and its designer, Bzezinski, had been arrested. The new ship, Project 64, would, under the directive of 15 August 1937, be equipped with nine 356mm (14in) guns as a result of the naval treaty concluded with Britain on 17 July 1937, in which the USSR had accepted the London terms of March 1936. This decision was a gesture to the British, who were advocates of the 356mm calibre.

The Soviet Government held the view that their Pacific ships should not be bound by the restrictions of the London Treaty because of the secrecy surrounding Japanese naval rearmament, and a provision to this effect was actually included in the agreement. Therefore Type 'A' ships could now be legitimately larger and better armoured, and the Project 23 vessels were scaled up to 57,825 tons.

During the planning stages of Project 64 it came to light that other naval powers were not following the British example and were arming their new capital ships without exception with a calibre larger than 356mm (14in). This meant that Type 'B' battleships would represent inferior opposition and planning was abandoned in the spring of 1938.

Attention was now concentrated on Project 23. The newly appointed Naval commander-in-chief Smirnov (in office from January to August 1938) suggested to Stalin that fifteen of the class should be built by the end of 1945. This idea was rejected, as had been other variations of the 'Great Construction Programme', but it is interesting to note the intended distribution of the new ships according to the Navy Ministry decision of August 1939, in which the Pacific Fleet would receive six units and the Baltic, Black Sea and newly constituted Northern Fleets two each.

The Soviet shipbuilding industry was not in a position to fulfil the massive programme for the year 1938–39, and by the end of 1939 only three ships of Project 23 had actually been started. None was ever finished.

The development history of the Project 69 *Kronshtadt* class battlecruiser is long and complicated. Originally, a 23,000-tonne ship armed with 254mm (10in) guns had been envisaged in 1937. Battlecruiser Type 'B', designed by Bzezinski one year earlier, was larger and more powerfully armed, and in 1937 Victorov had demanded a unit that would be superior in every respect to the German *Scharnhorst*. The Construction Office received the specifications at the end of 1937, and there is a blank period from then until the autumn of 1938 for which no information is available. Apparently the sketch designs were received by the naval administration in autumn 1938. Nothing is known of the details, although possibly the armament would have been nine 280mm (11in) guns as the development of these had been commenced at the Skoda works in Pilsen.

A variant of Project 69 at that time was for a ship of 24,450 tonnes which was 16m (52ft) shorter than the final design. The keel of the prototype was to have been laid in November 1938, but preparations were suspended after Czech cooperation became impossible. Planning work was quickly initiated for another variation displacing 32,700 tonnes and armed with nine 305mm (12in) guns produced domestically. After approval had been received for this version on 11 July 1939, the ceremonial keel-laying took place on 1 September 1939. It was technical problems at the Leningrad Yard and not the outbreak of war involving Poland that now caused a three-month delay, compounded by the discovery that the structure was too weak for a 238m (781ft) waterline length. Strengthening was necessary, as was a reinforcement of the armoured bulkheads from 260mm (10.25in) to 320mm (12.6in) forward and 275mm (10.8in) aft. The 130mm (5.1in) secondary battery in twin turrets was to be replaced by guns of 152mm (6in) calibre.

Two of these ships were on the stocks when the new technical project received approval on 12 April 1940. Navy Minister Kuznetzov ordered the replacement of the planned main armament by 380mm (15in) guns in twin turrets, which were to be imported from Germany. However, the turrets and barbettes were so large that radical alterations would have been necessary before they could be fitted. Soviet sources state that this would have led to a change in the outward appearance of the ships, as the entire forecastle would have had to be raised by one deck. The standard displacement was recalculated at 36,420 tonnes. This variant, known as Project 69-I (*Importny*), was approved on 16 October 1940. One can imagine what a hindrance these constant radical alterations to the plans must have been, and the effect they must have had on the building tempo in both yards.

It would appear that both *Kronshtadt* and *Sevastopol* were only 12 per cent complete by 22 June 1941. The latter fell into German hands in July 1941 at Nikolayev, but none of the German shipbuilding experts called in succeeded in identifying the frame as the hull of a battlecruiser.

The building of capital ships had been brought to a partial close in October 1940, although work continued at a reduced pace on a few battleships and battlecruisers. After a modification to Project 23 in the spring of 1943 the designs were given more 100mm AA guns and improved underwater protection. The Soviets expected to continue building until the end of the war and had put together two further projects for this contingency. The two units, armed with nine 406mm (16in) guns, would be faster than the *Sovietsky Soyuz* class. Project 24 envisaged 24 dual-purpose guns of 130mm calibre, while a 1945 project (no further description available) would have had the same secondary armament as Project 23 but additionally twenty-eight 85mm AA guns of a new type proved in land fighting. Nine of these ships were to be built between 1945 and 1950. The entire capacity of the nationalised Skoda weapons factory was requisitioned in mid-1945 for the manufacture of the 406mm (16in) gun barrels, but the atomic attacks against Hiroshima and Nagasaki convinced Stalin that the 75,000-tonne colossus had no future, although he took a different view of his pet ships, the three *Stalingrad* class battlecruisers (Project 82), which showed clear influences from Project 69, of which they were a further development.

These were the last capital ships with heavy guns to be commenced anywhere after the end of the war (1951). When Stalin died in the spring of 1953 the hulls were almost complete. However, Stalin's death spelt theirs also.

Overseas Collaboration

Despite what has been rumoured, the Soviets never had any intention of ordering a battleship from Italian builders, and military cooperation disintegrated once the Spanish Civil War broke out. However, after 24 November 1936 a lively relationship developed with US government offices and later with the private construction office Gibbs & Cox. The Soviet Navy received three projects from this company by the autumn of 1938 for large battleships with a flight deck and two projects for classical battleships about which no particulars are available. The following details are known about the hybrids:

Design	Disp. (std)	Armament	Aircraft/catapults
A	66,074t	8 x 457mm, 28 x 127mm AA	36/2
B	71,850t	12 x 406mm, 28 x 127mm AA	36/2
C	44,200t	10 x 406mm, 20 x 127mm AA	24/2

In late 1938 the Soviets lost all interest in the hybrids and ordered a classical battleship similar to Design C (but minus the flight deck). The Americans report that the plans were delivered in March 1939 while the Soviets confirm that the specifications of the ship ordered in the United States were approved on 5 February 1939. After extensive negotiations the US government eventually agreed to build the ship in an American yard. It is not certain if this ship was to be built to Gibbs & Cox's design D, but a comparison of the details is interesting:

Design	Disp. (std)	Speed	Armament
D	45,000 tons	31kt	10 x 406mm, 20 x 127mm AA
Soviet	45,000 tons	30kt	12 x 406mm, 24 x 127mm AA

Nothing came of the order: the signing of the non-aggression pact with Hitler and the outbreak of the Second World War provided the US government with the excuse to cancel it.

Next, the Soviets turned to the Germans for the complete technical documentation for the battleship *Bismarck*. Strangely enough, Hitler was not opposed to this request in principle, since he had no plans for sister ships of the class and was of the opinion that the Soviet shipbuilding industry was incapable of building such a vessel.

Soviet Battleships in the Second World War

The Soviet Admiralty kept their battleships well away from the fighting. The two Baltic Fleet units remained at Kronshtadt and Leningrad from the first day of the war to the last, although this failed to save them from destruction (*Marat* on 23 September 1941) or heavy damage (*Oktyabrskaya Revoluciya* on 21 and 23 September) at the hands of German Stukas.

The latter ship was repaired by November 1942 and bombarded the German lines at Leningrad in January 1943. *Marat*, which had sunk in shallow water, remained there until scrapped in 1952. The forward part of the ship, including 'A' turret, the bridge and the forefunnel, were totally destroyed but the hull was made watertight and the remaining three turrets were brought back into commission. The hulk, renamed *Petropavlovsk* in 1943, was only ever used as a stationary battery.

The only battleship of the Black Sea Fleet, *Parizhskaya Kommuna*, spent the first four months of the war idle at Sevastopol and then withdrew to Novorossiysk as the German front advanced. From there she made several sorties on 28 November 1941 to pound the German-occupied Crimean peninsula. The final deployment of the ship was the bombardment of Feodosiya on 21 March 1942, after which she was laid up at Poti on the Black Sea and underwent temporary repairs.

Eleven months before the end of the war end a fourth battleship hoisted the Soviet colours. This was HMS *Royal Sovereign*, which was loaned to the Soviets in anticipation of their receiving a surrendered Italian battleship as reparation and commissioned into the Soviet Navy as *Archangelsk* on 30 May 1944. After crew training she sailed from Rosyth on 17 August 1944 with a convoy for Murmansk, and was attached to the Northern Fleet on 24 August. She was not used operationally, although the Germans were somewhat apprehensive that she would be deployed against their supply lines. The ship was finally returned to Britain in the spring of 1949 once the Soviet Navy had taken possession of the former Italian battleship *Giulio Cesare*.

Armament

The inter-war modernisation plans for the three battleships included an armament refit. *Marat*'s 305mm (12in) 52-calibre guns had their rate of fire increased from 1.3 to 1.8 rounds per minute, but only a few years later the turrets of her two sister ships were completely rebuilt and the rate of fire of the guns improved to 2.2 rounds per minute. The weapons also outranged those installed in *Marat*; however, the range of 40km (43,750yd) claimed in Soviet sources could only be achieved with the ships heeling six degrees.

A larger calibre was required for the capital ships planned in the 'Great Construction Programme' and the orders for the heavy naval gun projects were distributed by the Ministry for Heavy Industry in March 1935 to three armaments factories. The Obuchov Works (Bolshevik) had probably been working since the beginning of 1934 on a project for a 406mm (16in) gun based on the design drawings for a Type 1712-A 16in 45-cal, but with a length of 50 calibres, which they had received from Vickers prior to the Revolution. The Leningrad Metal Factory proposed a triple turret, and the project for this installation, designated MK-1 with three B-37 pattern guns, was approved in April 1937. The guns were to be manufactured at the Stalingrad Barrikada factory and the turrets at the Leningrad Metal Factory.

At the same time, gun barrels of the same calibre were ordered abroad. Very promising negotiations with the French company Schneider were suddenly broken off at the beginning of 1937. In the autumn of 1937 the Soviet government did manage to get an order accepted by Bethlehem Steel for three triple turrets complete with 406mm (16in) guns, but even this was eventually cancelled by the Americans.

Domestic development—with the exception of the battlecruiser guns—was more successful. Intensive work was done on a project for 356mm (14in) 54-calibre guns; these had a shell weight of 750kg (1,650lb) and a muzzle velocity of up to 910 m/sec (2,985ft/sec). A prototype must have been completed, because a gun of this type was fired at the German lines from the testing range in the immediate vicinity of Leningrad. As battleship Project 64 with 356mm guns in three triple turrets was abandoned in December 1937, the order for the turrets would have been automatically cancelled.

The 406mm (16in) Type B-37 gun was completed at the beginning of 1940 and trials began at the Leningrad testing range on 6 June that year. These lasted until the beginning of October, during which period the gun fired 173 rounds. This proved the quality of the barrel, for as late as 1938 Soviet weapons manufacturers had been beset by serious problems regarding the durability of new gun barrels; for example, the life of the 180mm (7.1in) gun was only 80 rounds.

The Stalingrad factory worked flat out to produce the 406mm (16in) barrels, and by 22 June 1941 twelve pieces were reportedly available. The triple turrets ordered at LMZ had not been finished, and, with the exception of the test gun, none of the weapons was used. The test gun was successfully deployed between September 1941 and June 1944 on the Leningrad Front and fired at land targets 45km (28 miles) distant.

Development work on the heavy guns for the battlecruisers progressed less successfully. It would appear that in 1937 the Leningrad factories Bolshevik and LMZ were working on a project for a 305mm (12in) gun turret designated MK-2, apparently without much success because in June 1938 the Soviet delegation showed interest in a 280mm (11in) gun turret during talks with the Czechoslovak gun manufacturer Skoda. On 17 August it was agreed to open a Soviet-Czech Construction Office in Prague for heavy naval guns by 1 May 1939 at the latest. Its programme included the development of a 280mm 55-calibre gun and triple turret by 1942. Political events following in the wake of the Munich Agreement spelt the end of this arrangement, and the Soviet naval administration recognised the fact that the heavy turrets for the battlecruisers would also unfortunately have to be produced by the domestic armaments industry. The order in mid-1940 to convert the two battlecruisers then under construction to carry German 380mm (15in) twin turrets proves that the project for the 305mm triple turret designated MK-15 was far from being realised.

Until about 1937–38, surprisingly little attention was paid by the Soviet Navy to the question of protecting the ships against aerial attack. At the Spithead Coronation Review in May 1937 *Marat* carried only six antiquated 76mm (3in) Lender guns and a few Maxim machine guns on two main turrets, and this was still the sum total of her anti-aircraft battery when she was sunk in September 1941. Her two sister ships received a few non-automatic 45mm AA weapons from 1938, but only the new, large-calibre 12.7mm DSK machine gun was available for use against the Stukas. The year 1939 saw the introduction of the high-performance automatic 37mm AA gun, but it was 1941 before any of the ships received them.

Throughout the war the Soviet Navy generally lacked adequate AA defences. The single-mounted 76mm (3in) 55-cal AA gun of 34K pattern was fitted aboard the two modernised ships only, in insufficient numbers and not very effectively arranged. In the winter of 1939–40 the weapons became available in twin turrets of the 39K pattern. Two were set up on board *Oktyabrskaya Revoluciya* to replace the aft 120mm pair. During repairs in 1942 this ship received a further twin turret forward.

The ships of the *Sovietsky Soyuz* class were the first to receive heavy AA guns in twin mountings. These were of the same pattern as the 100mm AA weapons carried by the *Kirov* class cruisers in single mountings. In the summer of 1939 it was being proposed to fit only eight guns of the type per ship until Stalin ordered the installation of two additional twin turrets aft.

The anti-dive bomber defence of the *Sovietsky Soyuz* class was designed to comprise 37mm weapons in quadruple mountings together with heavy DSK pattern machine guns. The prototype of the quadruple 37mm in a stabilised turret designated Pattern 46-K was not completed until 1941, but its existence was still secret until long after the Second World War. It was installed behind the forward 76mm twin mounting on *Oktyabrskaya Revolutsia* and military experts in the West

were mystified for many years as to why the Soviet censor had blanked out the 'two twin heavy anti-aircraft guns mounted on the foredeck' in an aerial photograph of an old battleship taken in 1948. These quadruple mountings were intended to be fitted to the new battlecruisers then under construction.

Gun	Wt of shell	Muzzle velocity	Range/elevation
406mm 50-cal	1,105kg	830m/sec	45.5km/45°
305mm 54-cal	470kg	?	48km/45°
305mm 52-cal	470kg	762m/sec	29km/40°
Anti-aircraft guns			
100mm 56-cal	15.6kg	900m/sec	10,000m/85°
76mm 55-cal	6.6kg	813m/sec	9,300m/85°
76mm 30-cal	5.5kg	640m/sec	6,000m/75°
45mm 46-cal	1.4kg	760m/sec	6,000m/85°
37mm 67-cal	0.73	880m/sec	4,500m/85°

Note: Before the First World War, there were only four shipyards in Russia capable of building battleships. After the Revolution the names of these were changed, and they were changed again after the Second World War. These appear as numbered yards in some Soviet sources.

There were two yards at Leningrad (ex Petrograd, ex St Petersburg), *Baltiyski zavod* and *Admiralteyski zavod*. Under the Soviets these became the Ordzonikidze Shipyard (*Zavod* No 189) and the Marti Shipyard (No 194) respectively. The Nikolayev yards were Russud and Onziv (*Obscestvo Nikolayevskich zavodov*), the latter also being known as the Naval Shipyard. In the Soviet Union both yards worked officially under a common management and were run as No 198 (South Yard) and No 200 (North Yard). The yard founded in 1933 as Molotovsk was known as No 402.

Pariszkaya Kommuna, 1940.

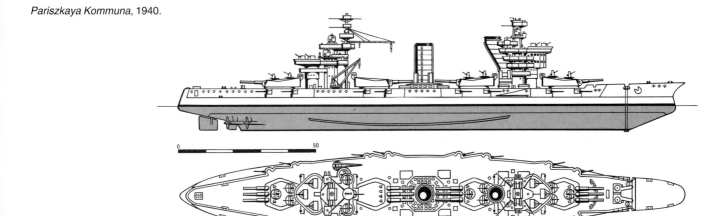

Marat/Oktyabrskaya Revolutsia

Displacement: *Marat* 25,600/ 26,170t; *Oktyabrskaya Revolutsia* 25,460/26,700t
Dimensions: As before except draught 9.5m
Machinery: As before except 60,000shp
Fuel: 2,500t oil (*Oktyabrskaya Revolutsia* 1,900t)
Speed/range: 22.5kt; 2,700nm at 14kt (*Oktyabrskaya Revolutsia* 2,500nm at 14kt)
Armour: As before except deck 75mm (*Oktyabrskaya Revolutsia* up to 125mm)
Weight of armour: Reportedly 6,500t (*Oktyabrskaya Revolutsia* approx. 7,000t)
Armament: As before except *Oktyabrskaya Revolutsia* 14 x 120mm 50-cal
Anti-aircraft guns: (1941) *Marat* 6 x 76mm 55-cal, *Oktyabrskaya Revolutsia* 10 x 76mm 55-cal, both 6 x 37mm 67-cal
Complement: *Marat* 1,300, *Oktyabrskaya Revolutsia* 1,450

Marat in 1937, with a Heinkel flying boat aboard.

Ship	Former name	Commissioned	Rebuilt
Frunze	*Poltava* (06.01.1926)	–	Planned for 1933
Marat	*Petropavlovsk* (31.03.1921)	00.09.1922	25.09.1928–06.06.1931
Oktyabrskaya Revolutsia	*Gangut* (27.06.1925)	23.07.1926	12.10.1931–04.08.1934

Frunze was badly damaged by fire in November 1919 and again in 1923; she was the last ship listed for rebuilding but was broken up in Leningrad from 1939. *Marat* and *Oktyabrskaya Revolutsia* received oil-firing during their reconstruction, the former's boilers being reduced from 25 to 22 and the latter's from 25 to 12. The cruising turbines were removed. Each ship was relieved of four 120mm guns for use by the Army, *Marat* in August 1941 and *Oktyabrskaya Revolutsia* in September 1941. During a refit in 1942 *Oktyabrskaya Revolutsia*'s AA armament was strengthened by the addition of 76mm twins and fourteen 37mm semi-automatics.

Marat was sunk off Kronshtadt by German Stukas on 23 September 1941. The forecastle, forward gun turret, bridge and forefunnel were lost, but as the ship was lying in shallow water the remainder of the hull was raised,

repaired and used as a stationary floating battery. She was named *Petropavlovsk* again on 31 May 1943. After the war she was converted into a training hulk, renamed *Volchov* in late 1950.

Oktyabrskaya Revolutsia was badly damaged by bombing off Kronshtadt on 21 September 1941 but remained afloat, and half her main armament was put out of action by three bomb hits six days later on 27 September. Repairs at Leningrad took until November 1942, but her main armament was not fully functional again until 1944. She served as a training ship from July 1954 but was condemned for scrapping on 17 February 1956.

Parizhskaya Kommuna

Displacement: 30,400/31,300t
Dimensions: (1939) 181.0 x 32.0 x 9.65m
Machinery: As before except 61,000shp
Fuel: 1,900t oil
Speed/range: 21.5kt; 2,500nm at 14kt
Armour: As before except deck 75mm
Weight of armour: ?
Armament: As before
Anti-aircraft guns: 6 x 76mm 55-cal, 16 x 37mm 67-cal
Complement: 1,550

See page 200 for drawing

Parizhskaya Kommuna (ex *Sevastopol*) was renamed on 31 March 1921. She was refitted in 1924–25, underwent a partial modernisation in 1928–29, left Kronshtadt on 22 November 1929 and arrived at Sevastopol to join the Black Sea Fleet on 18 January 1930 The ship was reconstructed from 1934 to 1938, when anti-torpedo bulges were added, resulting in a small decrease in speed, and the underwater torpedo tubes installed earlier were removed. The ship was fitted with the new 76mm AA gun from 1939. The 37mm AA gun was introduced in the winter of 1940–41 but the greater part of the ship's battery was not installed before 1942.

Following 'Barbarossa' *Parizhskaya Kommuna* was idle at Sevastopol until 30 November 1941, when she was transferred to Novorossiysk. She supported the landings at Feodosiya and Sudak in January 1942, bombarded German positions in the Crimea until 21 March 1942 and was then laid up at Poti for temporary repairs. She was renamed *Sevastopol* again on 31 May 1943. She remained in commission until July 1954 but was stricken on 17 February 1956.

Pariszkaya Kommuna (ex Sevastopol) in 1947.

Kronshtadt/Sevastopol

Displacement: 38,360/41,539t; 34,700/35,240 tons standard
Dimensions: 240.0 x 29.4 waterline (31.6 over bulges) x 8.9m
Machinery: As *Sovietsky Soyuz*
Fuel: 5,570t oil
Speed/range: 32.0kt; 8,300nm at 14.5kt, 6,900nm at 16.5kt
Armour: Belt 230mm, deck 90mm, main armament 305mm, CT 330mm
Weight of armour: ?
Armament: 9 x 305mm 54-cal, 8 x 152mm 57-cal
Anti-aircraft guns: 8 x 100mm 56-cal, 28 x 37mm 67-cal
Complement: ?

Ship	Builder	Laid down	Launch date (planned)
Kronshtadt	Leningrad No 194	30.11.1939	00.09.1942
Sevastopol	Nicolayev No 200	05.11.1939	00.09.1942

All technical details given correspond to those of the project authorised by the Soviet government on 12 April 1940. According to the ruling of the Central Committee of the Communist Party of 19 October 1940, the building of two sister ships was to be accelerated, whilst the question of the final armament was to be looked at again by the Central Committee 'around mid-November'. This did not occur, and it is not clear whether the ships were continued until July 1941 following the Soviet design of

1940 or with the German 380mm (15in) guns mounted in twin turrets (for this reason a line drawing is omitted here). Sketches published in Soviet naval periodicals in 1989 only correspond in part to the particulars above.

The 12 per cent complete hull of *Sevastopol* was captured by the Germans at Nikolayev in July 1941 and blown up when they withdrew in March 1944; the remains were scrapped by the end of 1948. *Kronshtadt* was dismantled on the stocks in 1949, the materials possibly being earmarked for use in the construction of a planned new battlecruiser.

Sovietsky Soyuz Class

Displacement: 62,000/65,150t; 58,200 tons standard
Dimensions: 261.0 x 36.4 waterline (38.9 maximum) x 10.2m
Machinery: 3 Brown-Boveri turbines, 3 shafts, 201,000–231,000shp
Fuel: 5,530t oil
Speed/range: 28.0kt; 5,580nm at 14kt, 4,300nm at 20kt
Armour: Belt 375–420mm, deck 205mm total, main armament 495mm, CT 425mm
Weight of armour: 24,000t = 38.7% of normal displacement
Armament: 9 x 406mm 50-cal, 12 x 152mm 57-cal
Anti-aircraft guns: (1940 design) 12 x 100mm 56-cal, 40 x 37mm 67-cal
Complement: (1940 design) 1,512

In the Soviet Navy it was customary to declare the standard displacement in metric tonnes. The side armour of the citadel was 420mm (16.5in) thick for 7.5 per cent of the length, 406mm (16in) for 11.8 per cent of the length and 375–390mm (14.75–15.4in) for 80.7 per cent of the length. The keel of *Sovietsky Soyuz* was in fact not laid until February 1939. The dates for the planned launchings are taken from the ruling of the Central Committee of the Communist Party of 19 October 1940.

No further work was done on *Sovietsky Soyuz* after June 1941 and the hull was scrapped in Leningrad in 1949. *Sovietskaya Ukraina* was captured undamaged by the Germans at Nikolayev in July 1941; after liberation in March 1944 the Soviets found that the condition of the damaged hull precluded further work on the ship and it was scrapped in 1946. On 19 October 1940 orders were given that building work on *Sovietskaya Belorossia* was to stop immediately and the slipway cleared, but

Sovietskaya Rossia was to be completed. However, nothing further was done about either ship until after the war. The hulls were stricken in 1947 and broken up at Molotovsk that year.

Ship	Builder	Laid down	Launch date (planned)
Sovietsky Soyuz	Leningrad No 189	15.07.1938	00.06.1943
Sovietskaya Ukraina	Nicolayev No 198	31.10.1938	00.06.1943
Sovietskaya Rossia	Molotovsk No 402	21.12.1939	00.07.1943
Sovietskaya Belorossia	Molotovsk No 402	22.07.1940	?

Sovietsky Soyuz (final design, 1940).

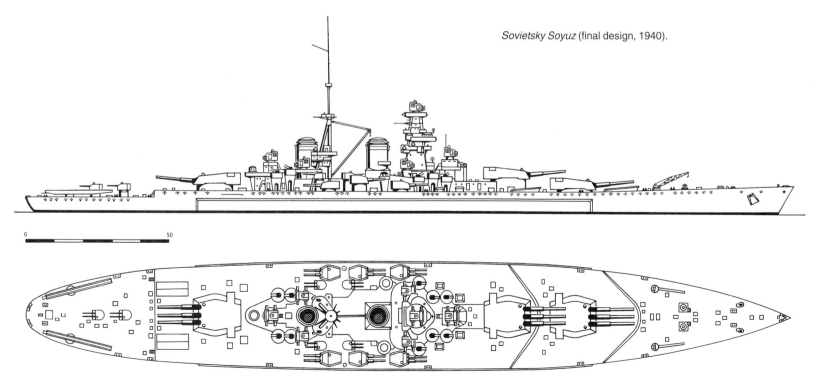

0   50

USA

Developments up to 1918

Until the outbreak of the First World War the United States was not aligned with any of the existing power blocs. The country had long pursued an imperial policy both in Latin America and the Pacific, and for this purpose a large fleet was required. However, it was not until several years after the victory over Spain in 1898 that it came into being. It was created by Theodore Roosevelt, Secretary for the Navy 1897 to 1898 and President from 1901 to 1908: it was he who first set about providing for the necessary naval construction policy. Under his Presidency a giant battle fleet was to come into existence, the second largest but most modern in the world.

In 1906 American politicians became aware of the emergence in the Far East of a new world power capable of threatening the newly acquired Philippines and US interests in China. Roosevelt responded by demonstrating the strength of the US Navy to Japan (and the rest of the world) by means of a circumnavigation by a battle group consisting of sixteen ships. The voyage took from 16 December 1907 to 22 February 1909 and highlighted the problems of organising naval operations in remote sea areas without adequate bases and coaling ports, and it led directly to the large-scale expansion of the base at Pearl Harbor. It also showed the need for a short connecting corridor between the Atlantic and the Pacific Oceans, and soon increased effort was devoted to building the Panama Canal. After the Canal was opened in August 1914 it provided the US Navy with an invaluable access route between both national coasts, although as the Fleet had no surface enemy in the Atlantic during the First World War the importance of the Canal in wartime was not fully recognised for another 27 years.

The policy of concentrating bases and shipyards along the Atlantic coast after the turn of the century was founded on the perceived threat from Germany which, along with Britain, was already considered by the United States as a rival in the struggle for world economic supremacy. A number of incidents had occurred involving Germany, for example that at Manila Bay in May 1898 and that during the Venezuelan crisis in 1902, and the German Fleet was reckoned to be the foremost potential opponent for the American Navy.

Until 1913 an operational contingency, Plan Black, existed for the possibility of war with Germany. This assumed that the German Fleet would attempt to establish an operational base on the coast of Venezuela or Columbia, or on a Caribbean island. Shortly before the outbreak of war in Europe, US naval planners came to the conclusion that the whole idea was quite impracticable. In fact, apart from the purely theoretical studies of junior naval officers, there never was a German plan for naval operations against the United States.

Missouri in 1986.

However, the size of the new and rapidly expanding German Fleet was a useful argument to employ in support of budgetary demands to Congress, and authority was obtained to build a fleet of equal strength to that of the Germans. By 1907 the US Fleet was second behind Britain in the world rankings. Yet it was not properly balanced by reason of the priority afforded to the acquisition of battleships (and, up to the 1905 naval estimates, armoured cruisers), and even in 1913 battleships and armoured cruisers outnumbered destroyers.

After the Japanese victory over the Russians at Tsushima in 1905, the danger in the Far East was clear, and the Americans became anxious about their position in the Philippines, which Japanese policy towards China in 1914–15 did nothing to allay. The US Fleet lacked the necessary superiority in modern capital ships to engage the burgeoning Japanese Navy under Plan Orange, and in 1915 the supreme naval council, the General Board, demanded a fresh naval construction policy which would have the objective of drawing level with the world's strongest fleet, the Royal Navy. President Wilson associated himself with this demand, and even declared that the United States must eventually have at its disposal 'the largest Fleet in the world'. After much debate, the proposal was finally ratified by Congress on 29 August 1916.

The successful début of the German High Seas Fleet at Jutland reinforced the view that a comprehensive expansion of the US Fleet was necessary in order to protect America against the German naval threat, and, accordingly, it was proposed that ten super-dreadnoughts be built within the next three (!) years. Only inner naval circles knew that the proposal was really the disguised response to the announced intentions of the Japanese Navy, but in the event only *Maryland* was laid down by the end of the First World War. Following the declaration of war on Germany by the United States on 6 April 1917, the construction of capital ships was shelved in favour of the mass production of destroyers, submarine-chasers and standardised merchant vessels.

US Building Programmes, 1905–18

In March 1902 a junior naval officer published in the naval periodical *USNIP* the suggestion that all the guns in the wing turrets and triple turrets forward and aft on battleships currently under construction should be of 11in (254mm) calibre rather than 12in (305mm). The idea was received with general interest, although the naval artillery lobby still recommended the installation of four twin turrets with 12in guns.

Only two months later the Bureau of Construction & Repair (C&R) submitted proposals for the '1904 Battleship' (the later BB23 and BB24 of the *Mississippi* class), one of which would have twelve 10in (254mm) guns in twin turrets. At that time the 'all-big-gun ship' with a single-calibre main armament had not gained acceptance, but in October 1903 the Navy Secretary requested C&R to develop a study project for a ship with twelve 12in (305mm) guns. President Roosevelt gave his support to the proponents of the single main calibre, but the way forward was blocked by a technical obstruction.

On 5 March 1905 Congress authorised two battleships (BB26 and BB27), subject to a maximum displacement of 16,000 tonnes. The Navy spent the next seven months fruitlessly attempting to convince Congressmen that a minimum displacement of 18,000 tonnes was neces-

sary for a ship carrying ten 12in (305mm) guns, and in mid-December 1905 the Navy Secretary received for his signature a project approved by the Navy which settled for eight 12in guns. By this time HMS *Dreadnought* had already been laid down in Britain. Some sources contend that the plans for *South Carolina* were drawn up before those of *Dreadnought*, but this is clearly not the case. The decision in favour of the design variant later to emerge as *Dreadnought* left the British Design Committee on 22 February 1905 and the Admiralty approved the building plans in March. At that time the US Navy had no idea how the 1906 Fiscal Year battleship would look, nor of the number of guns she would be carrying, since the arrangement of the 12in (305mm) guns in four triple turrets, the second and third turrets being raised above the first and fourth, forward and aft respectively, was not decided upon by the Chief Naval Architect, W. J. Capps, until April. Even in October 1905 the Navy Department still thought that future American battleships would carry an armament of at least ten 305mm guns. The completed plans for *South Carolina* were submitted to the Navy Department on 10 November 1905, approved on 23 November and signed by the Navy Minister in mid-December. Further delays ensued, and the specifications were not placed in the builders' hands until 21 March 1906. The debate over whether the ships should have conventional steam reciprocating engines or turbines rolled on until June, and by the time the keel was actually laid, in December 1906, *Dreadnought* had already been completed.

The Naval Estimates for the 1907 Fiscal Year, approved on 29 June 1906, required future battleships to be more powerful than all likely adversaries, and argued that restrictions on displacement should be done away with. Capps, *South Carolina*'s designer, submitted two projects with ten 12in (305mm) and twelve 12in guns respectively in twin turrets. A number of private corporations were also interested in the commission and tendered their own designs. However, with one exception they were of such poor quality that all US battleships subsequently were designed solely by the Bureau of Construction & Repair.

Capps' smaller variant was selected principally on account of its better armour. Procedural matters delayed the placing of the order for *Delaware* (BB28), and the yard only received the contract on 6 August 1908, fourteen months after the ship had been approved by Congress. On the same day a sister ship, *North Dakota*, which had been voted in March 1907, was ordered from another yard. In contrast to *Delaware*, it was decided that *North Dakota* should have turbines; as, in the opinion of the experts, the Parsons plant required very long machinery spaces, American Curtis turbines were chosen. This was not seen as a breakthrough for the turbine in US battleship construction. The Navy remained convinced that the oil-fired turbine was uneconomic: coal-fired battleships were easy on fuel, and did not need replenishment at sea in order to reach the strategically vital Philippines.

On 13 May 1908 Congress approved two further ships with roughly the same characteristics as the *Delaware* class but fitted with Parsons turbines to test their reliability. Work on these vessels, *Florida* (BB30) and *Utah* (BB31), would commence in March 1909.

The world cruise of the American squadron had given naval architects much to consider, particularly with regard to the sea-going qualities of the ships, the arrangement of the medium armament and the system of belt armour. Some of what had been learned was applied when the 1909 Fiscal Year ships were built, but most of it not until the later *Wyoming*.

Of still greater significance for the future development of American battleship construction was a conference organised by the Navy Ministry at Newport in July 1908 in which President Roosevelt participated. His interest in units with 14in (356mm) guns was decisive. The Bureau of Construction & Repair was directed to prepare projects for ships with eight and ten 15in guns by January 1909, but the President demanded that this period should be shortened so that preliminary details could be on his desk by mid-September 1908. Both proposed designs were so large that only two yards in the United States had the capacity to handle them. Developing the 15in gun would require two years. The naval architects had also drawn up designs for a version with twelve 12in (305mm) 50-calibre guns and the General Board, which had had jurisdiction over battleship construction since 1908, decided in favour of the latter project on 30 December 1912.

On 3 March 1909 Congress authorised two units, *Wyoming* (BB32) and *Arkansas* (BB33), although Roosevelt had asked for four. The deputies had been intimidated by the expense, for these very large ships would have a much thicker belt armour than on previous units. A few weeks after the two 1910 vessels had been authorised, the General Board began thinking about the next year's designs, which would correspond in size to the *Wyoming* class, although the questions about main armament (12in or 14in), and whether to fit turbines or steam reciprocating engines, were still unresolved. The Bureau of Construction set to work on plans for an improved *Wyoming* and a variant with ten 14in (356mm) guns; both would have turbines, although the designers were undecided between the two-shaft Curtis type or the four-shaft Parsons.

These matters were, however, soon settled. The 14in (356mm) experimental gun tested in January 1910 had proved highly successful, while the Curtis turbines installed in *North Dakota* had behaved very unreliably and were uneconomic at cruising speed. The steam machinery of the sister-ship, *Delaware*, consumed 30 per cent less coal for the same output, but vessels subsequent to the 1911 *New York* class would have turbine propulsion simply because the reciprocating engine had no further potential for development.

On 24 June 1910 Congress approved two ships with 14in (356mm) guns and reciprocating engines. They were the first US 'super-dreadnoughts' designate, but both units, *New York* (BB34) and *Texas* (BB35), suffered from weak horizontal armour, the 'disease' which afflicted the first US capital ships. It was especially serious for these new vessels, since, as gunnery ranges rapidly opened out, incoming shells fired from enemy ships would increasingly arrive in a plunging trajectory, and in practice such shells would have encountered little resistance from this thin deck armour. The shortcoming was rectified in the 1912 ships, *Nevada* (BB36) and *Oklahoma* (BB37), which were authorised on 4 March 1911.

The Navy was now in possession of two preliminary projects. When instructing the Bureau of Construction, the General Board had requested designs with an especially strong horizontal armour and, because of the worldwide trend towards larger calibres in battleship main armament, good protection for the vital areas within the ship's hull. The designers complied extraordinarily quickly by shortening the hull length by 36ft (11m) so as to reduce radically the length of the armour belt. The citadel was protected by a short expanse of very thick armour to the sides, and fore and aft by thick armoured transverse bulkheads. Two armoured decks would protect the engine room and magazines against hits by plunging shells: an incoming shell would explode on impact with the upper, thicker armour, while the lower deck served as a splinter deck. This 'all or nothing' principle of protection was later copied by other navies.

The reduction in the armoured surface also made possible the arrangement of the main armament in superimposed turrets, and *Nevada* was the first US battleship to carry 14in (356mm) guns in triple turrets. The General Board had opted for this in May 1910. In November of that year, four months before obtaining approval for the 1912 ships (*Nevada* class), the Board decided on the change to pure oil-firing for all future battleships. At the time the United States was the world's leading oil producer. Oil-firing meant a reduction in the number of boilers, a saving in both space and weight and in the number of stokers to be carried, while the loss of the former coal bunkers, which had previously provided a safety barrier, presented the designers with a major problem concerning the vertical protection. The perennial question concerning the installation of turbines or piston machinery was not resolved with the 1912 ships: only *Nevada* received improved two-stage Curtis turbines. The *Nevada* class were the first representatives of a long line of American battleships projected up to 1918, all enlarged and improved versions of the original 1912 ship.

The General Board sought four ships for 1913, but the US Senate allowed only one, *Pennsylvania* (BB38). This was a larger version of *Nevada*, with the same main armament concentrated in two triple and two twin turrets. The second unit of the class, *Arizona* (BB39), although not approved until March 1913, was ordered shortly after *Pennsylvania*, so that the vessel entered service in 1916 at almost the same time as her sister ship authorised in August 1912.

In 1913 the armament of future US battleships was energetically argued in naval circles since it was known that both the Royal Navy and the Imperial German Navy were considering fitting ships with 15in (381mm) guns and it was presumed that Japan would be likely to follow their example. The Bureau of Ordnance therefore studied projects for 16in (406mm) guns, soon to become the standard weapon aboard all US battleships, but the new Navy Secretary in the Wilson Administration, J. Daniels, ruled that as the 1915 *New Mexico* class designs did not have them, the new ships should be repeats of the *Pennsylvania* class with improvements such as the newly developed 14in (356mm) main armament with the more effective 50-calibre barrel. Two of the ships, *New Mexico* (BB40) and *Mississippi* (BB41), were authorised on 30 June 1914 and a third, *Idaho* (BB42), was added later, the cost being offset by the sale to Greece of two old pre-dreadnoughts.

New Mexico was used to test a system of turbo-electric propulsion developed by General Electric in which current produced by generators directly coupled to the turbines could drive the motors, leading to large savings in oil consumption and solving the problem of switching direct-drive turbines into reverse. The turbo-electric system survived for many years in the US Navy, but was not installed elsewhere; in 1936 it was abandoned for new vessels because of its excessive weight and bulk as compared with conventional turbine plant.

On 30 July 1914 it was decided that the successors to the *New Mexico* class would again be of similar design since the 16in (406mm) gun was still under development and was not now expected to be available until the 1917 ships.

On 3 March 1915 Congress authorised two further ships of the same size, armament and machinery as the *New Mexico*s but differing outwardly in having two funnels instead of one. This was a consequence of a rearrangement of the boiler rooms and turbine installation. A new system of underwater protection in which fuel oil served as a protective filling was copied for subsequent classes. The inner bottom was reinforced by five longitudinal bulkheads of which the middle three were armoured, the empty areas between the first and fifth bulkheads being used as oil bunkers, while the space between the hull plating and the first and fifth bulkheads was left empty. The Americans believed that this system would easily absorb the explosive energy of the contemporary torpedo.

Although the *Tennessee* class were authorised in March 1915, work was not begun on these ships for between 19 and 26 months, and neither these vessels nor the 1917 *Maryland* class, which received approval on 29 August 1916, were launched before the cessation of hostilities. All four *Maryland* units had been designed to carry the new 14in (356mm) 50-calibre guns, but in August 1916 the Navy decided to fit them instead with the long-awaited 16in (406mm) guns in twin turrets. In other respects the class resembled the *Tennessee*s. Only *Maryland* herself was laid down between the Americans' declaration of war on Germany and the end of the conflict; construction of the other three ships was begun in 1919–20.

Unfulfilled Programmes

On 29 August 1916 the US Congress passed legislation authorising the construction of six battleships and six battlecruisers for the 1918 and 1919 Fiscal Years; work on these vessels was to be commenced within three years. Despite the approval of the projects and the placing of the contracts with the shipbuilders, none of the vessels had been laid down at the time of the Armistice and none was completed to the original plans.

The designs for the *South Dakota* class would have resulted in the largest and most powerful battleships in the US Navy to that time, as the General Board had provided for twelve 16in (406mm) guns and a speed at least two knots greater than any battleship previously built. The provisional projects submitted by the Bureau of Construction & Repair provided for a top speed of 23 knots, included the new, longer-barrelled 16in guns, and broke with tradition by having a larger calibre for the secondary armament partially twin-mounted in turrets. A proposed increase in the thickness of the belt armour was forestalled by an assurance from the US steel industry that the maximum thickness of armour possible under current technology was 13.5in (343mm).

In January 1917 the Navy approved the final designs for three ships to be laid down that year, but the war with Germany brought the schedule to a halt: there were other matters far more pressing than adding to the numbers of battleships, and further construction was postponed in favour of an accelerated building programme for destroyers and submarine-chasers. Even the next three ships expected to start in 1918 were postponed until 1920–21. The 1917 *South Dakota* design

was approved by the Navy Secretary, Daniels, on 8 July 1918 after the inclusion of modifications to the armour. All six ships were begun from 1920.

As already mentioned, the 1916 legislation provided for the construction of six battlecruisers. These had been first requested by the General Board in 1912 but Congress had declined to supply the necessary capital. Battlecruisers were being constructed in increasing numbers by all the great powers, and America's potential Pacific adversary, Japan, had four of them. In 1916 the Bureau of Construction & Repair worked out the first variants of the US version. It was to be a scouting ship of considerable length with the tremendous speed (for a capital ship) of 35 knots, achieved by sacrificing armour protection. In the design variant submitted in 1917, the armour was only slightly improved. This was in contrast to the armament, which was modified from the 1916 design showing ten 15in (356mm) 50-calibre and twenty 5in (127mm) 50-calibre to one showing eight 16in (406mm) 50-calibre and fourteen 6in (152mm). A feature of the 1916 variant was the unorthodox disposal of the 24 boilers, half of which were to be fitted in an armoured box above the armour deck, resulting in the need for no fewer than seven funnels. The 1917 *Lexington* class variant had 20 boilers and only five funnels.

The involvement of the United States in the First World War from April 1917 caused the postponement of building work on the first five ships of the *Lexington* class which had been ordered during the first half of that year. The lessons of naval warfare in Europe, and particularly at Jutland, led to a thorough revision of the design in 1919 which was directly influenced by the British battlecruiser *Hood*, then nearing completion. The inward slope of the belt armour, the two armoured torpedo bulkheads and a better distribution of the magazines constituted an improvement in protection generally, but this was still inadequate for such large ships. Another improvement was the installation of sixteen efficient small-tube, oil-fired boilers and the consequent reduction in the number of funnels to two. The armament was unchanged except for the addition of two more medium-calibre guns. Six battlecruisers of the class were laid down in the second half of 1920, but only two were to be launched, and these not to the original design but as the world's largest aircraft carriers, *Lexington* and *Saratoga*.

US Battleships in the First World War

No US battleship fought in a naval battle during the First World War. In the late autumn of 1917, six units were attached to the 6th Battleship Squadron of the Royal Navy. These were all coal-fired vessels: Britain was not experiencing problems in the supply of coal, as opposed to oil, to the Fleet. After 17 December 1917 four American units were based at Scapa Flow, where they were joined later by the other two, and the group subsequently sortied into the North Sea twice with the Grand Fleet.

South Carolina and six older pre-dreadnoughts were employed in escorting American convoys eastwards across the Atlantic from September 1918. This relatively short period of cooperation with the British Fleet was of great value to the Americans, not only for tactical reasons but also with regard to fitting out their battleships.

Armament

US naval gunnery officers serving aboard the ships at Scapa Flow realised that American gunnery, particularly fire control, was far inferior to that of the Royal Navy, although the ballistic performance and longevity of the American barrels proved that the weapons ranked amongst the best in the world.

The changeover from the 12in (305mm) to a larger calibre had been decided upon in 1908, and successful trials with the 14in (356mm) gun were carried out in January 1910. Surprisingly, although developed at the fast 'American tempo', the 16in (406mm) gun, which was approved on 22 October 1912 and tested in July 1914, was not considered for actual installation until the 1916 construction programme.

The 16in (406mm) gun with the longer, 50-calibre barrel was in the process of development from 1916 and was first tested on 8 April 1918. That same month the manufacture of 88 barrels was ordered, and during 1920 that of a further 62, but none was ever installed aboard ship, although in 1939 consideration was given to the possibility of fitting out the ships of the planned *Iowa* class with some of the 50 barrels stockpiled in various naval arsenals.

In 1916 the Bureau of Ordnance had designed a gun of 18in (456mm) calibre, for which orders were later placed. The prototype was postponed until after the war as a low priority, and was still not ready by 1922 when naval guns of such calibre were outlawed by the Washington agreement. It was finally produced as a 16in (406mm) 56-calibre weapon. From 1927 many years of testing followed, but thought was not given to installing the gun aboard ship until 1938. It was quickly rejected because of its weight and short barrel life.

Principal Details of US Heavy Guns

Gun	Model	Wt of shell	Muzzle velocity	Range/elevation
16in 50-cal	Mk 2	2,240lb	2,650ft/sec	44,620yd/40°
16in 45-cal	Mk 1	2,105lb	2,600ft/sec	33,900yd/30°
14in 50-cal	Mk 4	1,400lb	2,800ft/sec	23,510yd/15°
14in 45-cal	Mk 2	1,400lb	2,600ft/sec	21,000yd/15°
12in 50-cal	Mk 7	871lb	2,900ft/sec	23,500yd/15°
12in 45-cal	Mk 6	871lb	2,750ft/sec	23,000yd/15°
12in 45-cal	Mk 5	871lb	2,700ft/sec	21,430yd/15°

AA guns appeared on US battleships in 1916, *Texas* being fitted with the first experimental weapons of 3in (76mm) 50-calibre. A year later all battleships carried two such weapons as standard, increased to four in 1918. Both the gun and its performance were good, with a shell weight of 13lb (5.9kg), a muzzle velocity of 2,700ft/sec (823m/sec) and a maximum altitude of 24,600ft (7,500m).

Note: US Navy Yards were located at New York, Norfolk and Philadelphia on the East Coast and at Mare Island on the West Coast. Private yards included W. Cramp, Philadelphia (Cramp), the New York Shipbuilding Co. (NYSB), the Fore River Shipbuilding Co., Quincy (Fore River; from 1913 Bethlehem Steel Co.) and the Newport News Shipbuilding and Dry Dock Co. (Newport News).

Nevada in the Panama Canal, 1917.

South Carolina Class

Displacement: 16,130/18,000t
Dimensions: 137.2 x 24.5.x 8.2m
Machinery: 2 reciprocating
steam engines, 2 shafts,
16,500ihp
Fuel: 2,400t coal
Speed/range: 18.0kt; 6,950nm at
10kt
Armour: Belt 305mm, deck 38–
51mm, main armament 305mm,
CT 305mm
Weight of armour: 5,025t =
31.2% of normal displacement
Armament: 8 x 12in 45-cal, 22 x
3in 50-cal
Anti-aircraft guns: From 1917: 2
x 3in 50-cal
Complement: 869 (1,100 in
1918)

Michigan and *South Carolina*,
1906–1910.

South Carolina at speed.

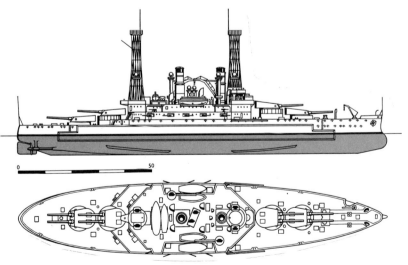

0   50

Ship	Builder	Laid down	Launched	Commissioned
South Carolina (BB26)	Cramp	18.12.1906	11.07.1908	01.03.1910
Michigan (BB27)	NYSB, Camden	17.12.1906	26.05.1908	04.01.1910

During 1917 eight of the 3in guns were removed and reallocated to mobilised vessels. Both units had very poor sea-keeping qualities. After the United States entered the war, *South Carolina* made several transatlantic crossings escorting American troop convoys to Europe.

Both ships were decommissioned in December 1921. *Michigan* was stricken in August 1923 and *South Carolina* in November 1923. The ships were sold for scrapping in 1924.

Delaware Class

Displacement: 20,140/22,230t
Dimensions: 155.5 x 26.0 x 8.2m
Machinery: 2 reciprocating steam engines (*North Dakota* 2 Curtis turbines), 2 shafts, 25,000ihp (*North Dakota* 25,000shp)
Fuel: 2,500t coal
Speed/range: 21.0kt; 9,750nm (*North Dakota* 6,560nm) at 10kt
Armour: Belt 279mm, deck 38–51mm, main armament 305mm, CT 292mm
Weight of armour: 6,130t = 30.4% of normal displacement
Armament: 10 x 12in 45-cal, 14 x 5in 50-cal
Anti-aircraft guns: From 1917: 2 x 3in 50-cal
Complement: 933 (1918: *Delaware* 1,320, *North Dakota* 1,220)

North Dakota in 1910.

Delaware and *North Dakota*, 1907–1910.

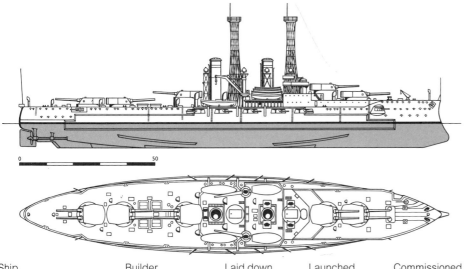

Ship	Builder	Laid down	Launched	Commissioned
Delaware (BB28)	Newport News	11.11.1907	06.02.1909	04.04.1910
North Dakota (BB29)	Fore River	16.12.1907	10.11.1909	11.04.1910

Delaware reached 21.86 knots on trials. She was detached to the British Grand Fleet at the end of November 1917. Decommissioned in November 1923 and stricken shortly afterwards, she was sold for scrapping on 5 February 1924.

North Dakota managed 21.01 knots with her troublesome engines on trials. Her Curtis turbines were completely overhauled after three years but to little avail and the ship was consigned to reserve on 1 July 1915. Parsons turbines were fitted in 1916 and she was returned to service on 27 February 1917 though was not employed on escort duties. The ship was decommissioned in November 1923 and stricken shortly afterwards, being used as a target ship until scrapped in 1931.

Florida Class

Displacement: 22,100/23,400t
(*Utah* 21,570/22,800t)
Dimensions: 155.5 x 27.0 x 9.1m
Machinery: 4 Parsons turbines,
4 shafts, 28,000shp
Fuel: 2,500t coal + 500t oil
Speed/range: 20.75kt; 5,810nm
at 10kt, 2,760nm at 20kt
Armour: Belt 279mm, deck 38–
51mm, main armament 305mm,
CT 292mm
Weight of armour: 6,210t =
28.1% (*Utah* 28.8%) of normal
displacement
Armament: 10 x 12in 45-cal, 16
x 5in 51-cal
Anti-aircraft guns: From 1917: 2
x 3in 50-cal
Complement: 940 designed
(1918: actually 1,320)

Both vessels received a new model 5in (127mm) secondary armament, but four of the sixteen guns were removed in 1917.

Florida was detached to the British Grand Fleet in December 1917. The United States was permitted to retain ships of the class under the Washington agreement and *Florida* was modernised between July 1924 and June 1926: Curtis turbines, anti-torpedo bulges and eight AA guns were fitted, and the armour was strengthened. However, the ship was required to be stricken under the terms of the 1930 London Naval Treaty and she had been scrapped by late September 1932.

Utah was employed on Atlantic convoy duty from autumn 1918. She underwent modernisation along the lines of her sister ship from August 1926 to October 1928 but in 1931 was decommissioned and converted for use as a remote controlled target ship; she recommissioned on 1 April 1932. She was used as an experimental vessel and AA crew training ship from June 1935 and refitted with 5in AA guns and a few weapons in summer 1941. *Utah* was sunk by two aerial torpedoes on 7 December 1941 at Pearl Harbor; the wreck remains *in situ*.

Ship	Builder	Laid down	Launched	Commissioned
Florida (BB30)	New York NY	19.03.1909	12.05.1910	15.09.1911
Utah (BB31)	NYSB, Camden	15.03.1909	23.12.1909	31.08.1911

A wartime photograph of *Florida*.

Wyoming Class

Displacement: 26,000/27,400t
Dimensions: 168.9 x 28.4 x 8.6m
Machinery: 4 Parsons turbines, 4 shafts, 28,000shp
Fuel: 2,700t coal + 460t oil
Speed/range: 20.5kt; 8,000nm at 10kt, 6,500nm at 12kt
Armour: Belt 279mm, deck 38–51mm, main armament 305mm, CT 292mm
Weight of armour: 8,280t = 31.8% of normal displacement
Armament: 12 x 12in 50-cal, 21 x 5in 51-cal
Anti-aircraft guns: From 1917: 2 x 3in 50-cal
Complement: 1,060 (1918: 1,520)

The number of 5in guns was reduced to sixteen in the autumn of 1917.

Wyoming was detached to the British Grand Fleet in November 1917 and returned to the USA after hostilities. She served in the Second World War (q.v.). *Arkansas* reached 21.22 knots on trials. She was detached to the Grand Fleet in July 1918 and returned to the USA after hostilities. She was employed as a training ship in the Second World War (q.v.).

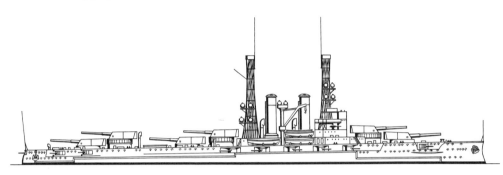

Ship	Builder	Laid down	Launched	Commissioned
Wyoming (BB32)	Cramp	09.02.1910	25.05.1911	25.09.1912
Arkansas (BB33)	NYSB, Camden	25.01.1910	14.01.1911	17.09.1912

Wyoming and *Arkansas*, 1912.

Wyoming at full speed.

New York Class

Displacement: 26,900/28,400t
Dimensions: 172.2 x 29.1 x 8.7m
Machinery: 2 reciprocating steam engines, 2 shafts, 28,100ihp
Fuel: 3,000t coal + 400t oil
Speed/range: 21.0kt; 7,700nm at 12kt
Armour: Belt 305mm, deck 51mm, main armament 356mm, CT 305mm
Weight of armour: 8,500t = 31.6% of normal displacement
Armament: 10 x 14in 45-cal, 21 x 5in 51-cal (16 x 5in from 1918)
Anti-aircraft guns: 2 x 3in 50-cal (*New York* from 1917, *Texas* from 1916)
Complement: 1,050 designed (1918: actually 1,500)

New York was detached to the British Grand Fleet from November 1917 and left European waters in December 1918. She served in the Second World War (q.v.). *Texas* was the first US battleship to carry an AA armament. Detached to British Grand Fleet from January 1918, she left European waters in December 1918. Her 5in secondary armament was reduced to 16 in autumn 1927. The ship served in the Second World War (q.v.).

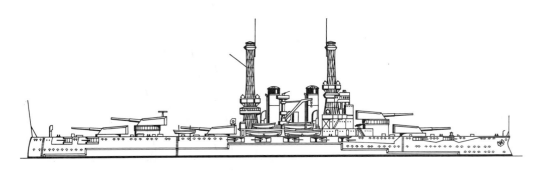

Texas, 1918.

Ship	Builder	Laid down	Launched	Commissioned
New York (BB34)	New York NY	11.09.1911	30.10.1912	15.04.1914
Texas (BB35)	Newport News	17.04.1911	18.05.1912	12.03.1914

New York as originally completed.

Nevada Class

Displacement: 28,100/29,040t
Dimensions: 175.3 x 29.1 x 8.7m
Machinery: 2 Curtis turbines (*Oklahoma* 2 reciprocating engines), 2 shafts, 26,500shp (*Oklahoma* 28,400ihp)
Fuel: 2,000t oil
Speed/range: 20.5kt; 8,000nm at 10kt, 5,200nm at 12kt
Armour: Belt 343mm, deck 114mm total, main armament 456mm, CT 406mm
Weight of armour: 11,270t = 40.1% of normal displacement
Armament: 10 x 14in 45-cal, 21 x 5in 51-cal
Anti-aircraft guns: From 1917: 2 x 3in 50-cal
Complement: 1,050 (1918: *Nevada* 1,520, *Oklahoma* 1,550)

In the winter of 1917–18 the number of 5in guns was reduced to twelve. Both vessels were based in Ireland for convoy protection duties in August–September 1918. Both served in the Second World War (q.v.).

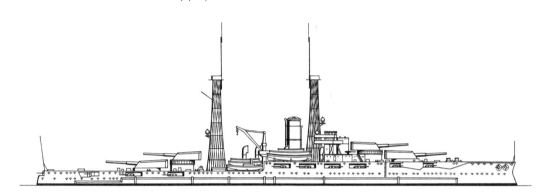

Nevada and *Oklahoma*, 1916.

Ship	Builder	Laid down	Launched	Commissioned
Nevada (BB36)	Fore River	04.11.1912	11.07.1914	11.03.1916
Oklahoma (BB37)	NYSB, Camden	26.10.1912	23.03.1914	02.05.1916

Oklahoma in dazzle camouflage.

Pennsylvania Class

Displacement: 31,400/32,430t
Dimensions: 182.9 x 29.7 x 8.8m
Machinery: 4 Curtis (*Arizona* Parsons) turbines, 4 shafts, 31,500shp
Fuel: 2,300t oil
Speed/range: 21.0kt; 8,000nm at 10kt, 6,070nm at 12kt
Armour: Belt 343mm, decks 76mm + 38mm, main armament 456mm, CT 406mm
Weight of armour: 12,135t = 38.5% of normal displacement
Armament: 10 x 14in 45-cal, 22 x 5in 51-cal
Anti-aircraft guns: From 1917: 4 x 3in 50-cal
Complement: 915 (1918: *Pennsylvania* 1,500, *Arizona* 1,550)

Arizona and *Pennsylvania*, 1917.

The number of 5in guns was reduced to fourteen at the beginning of 1918. *Pennsylvania* was earmarked as a Fleet flagship from the outset and served as flagship of the Atlantic Fleet until the end of 1918. *Arizona* was promised to the British Grand Fleet as reinforcement but did not arrive at Scapa Flow until after the Armistice. Both vessels served in the Second World War (q.v.).

Ship	Builder	Laid down	Launched	Commissioned
Pennsylvania (BB38)	Newport News	27.10.1913	16.03.1915	12.06.1916
Arizona (BB39)	New York NY	16.03.1914	19.06.1915	17.10.1916

Pennsylvania shortly after her completion.

New Mexico Class

Displacement: 32,170/33,260t
Dimensions: 182.9 x 29.7 x 9.1m
Machinery: 4 turbines, 4 shafts, 32,000shp (*New Mexico* turbo-electric drive, 4 shafts, 27,000shp)
Fuel: 2,200t oil (*Mississippi* 2,790t, *Idaho* 2,850t)
Speed/range: 21.0kt; 8,000nm at 10kt, 6,400nm at 12kt
Armour: Belt 343mm, decks 89mm + 38mm, main armament 456mm, CT 406mm
Weight of armour: 12,378t = 38.5% of normal displacement
Armament: 12 x 14in 50-cal, 14 x 5in 51-cal
Anti-aircraft guns: 4 x 3in 50-cal
Complement: 1,084 (1918: 1,485)

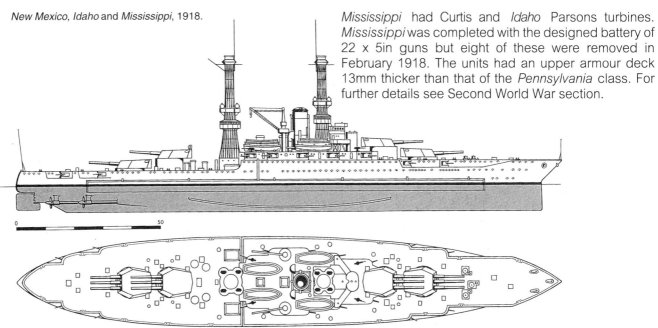

New Mexico, Idaho and *Mississippi*, 1918.

Mississippi had Curtis and *Idaho* Parsons turbines. *Mississippi* was completed with the designed battery of 22 x 5in guns but eight of these were removed in February 1918. The units had an upper armour deck 13mm thicker than that of the *Pennsylvania* class. For further details see Second World War section.

Ship	Builder	Laid down	Launched	Commissioned
New Mexico (BB40)	New York NY	14.10.1915	23.04.1917	20.05.1918
Mississippi (BB41)	Newport News	05.04.1915	25.01.1917	18.12.1917
Idaho (BB42)	NYSB, Camden	20.01.1915	30.06.1917	24.03.1919

New Mexico in 1918.

Tennessee Class

Displacement: 34,130/35,100t
(32,800/33,700t designed)
Dimensions: 182.9 x 29.7 x 9.1m
Machinery: Turbo-electric drive,
4 shafts, 28,600shp
Fuel: 1,900t oil (exceptionally
4,656t)
Speed/range: 21.0kt; 8,000nm at
10kt, 6,500nm at 12kt
Armour: As *New Mexico*, but
three armoured bulkheads
Weight of armour: 12,271t =
36.0% of normal displacement
Armament: As *New Mexico*
1918
Anti-aircraft guns: As *New
Mexico* 1918
Complement: 1,083 designed
(1,540 on completion)

Tennessee, 1922.

An aerial view of *California* with three seaplanes on her two catapults.

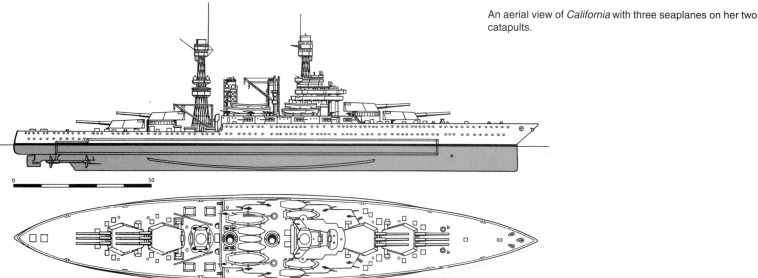

Ship	Builder	Laid down	Launched	Commissioned
Tennessee (BB43)	New York NY	14.05.1917	30.04.1919	03.06.1920
California (BB44)	Mare Island NY	25.10.1916	20.11.1919	10.08.1921

Supplementary bunkers extended the range of these ships to 20,500 miles at 10 knots. *Tennessee*'s turbines and generators were manufactured by Westinghouse, *California*'s by General Electric. During trials *Tennessee* reached 21.38 knots at 29,609shp. The 14in (356mm) guns fitted to both units elevated to 30°, compared to 15° for the same model installed in the *New Mexico* class. For further details see Second World War section.

Maryland Class

Displacement: 34,500/35,520t
(33,100/34,130t designed)
Dimensions: As *Tennessee*
Machinery: Turbo-electric drive,
4 shafts, 28,900shp
Fuel: 1,900t oil (max. 2,100t,
exceptionally 4,800t)
Speed/range: 21.0kt; 8,000nm at
10kt, 6,400nm at 12kt
Armour: As *Tennessee*
Weight of armour: 12,353t =
35.8% of normal displacement
Armament: 8 x 16in 45-cal, 14 x
5in 51-cal
Anti-aircraft guns: 4 x 3in 50-cal
(from 1923: 8 x 3in 50-cal)
Complement: 1,305 designed
(*Maryland* 1,550 in 1921)

The *Maryland* class is often described as *Colorado* class even though the latter unit was laid down and completed two years later than *Maryland*. *Colorado* and *West Virginia* carried only twelve 5in guns on completion. Under the terms of the Washington Agreement BB47 could not be completed and the ship was sunk as a target in 1924. For the further history of the three surviving units see Second World War section.

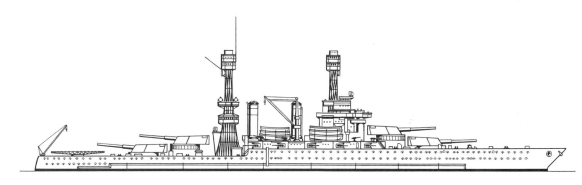

Maryland, 1923.

Ship	Builder	Laid down	Launched	Commissioned
Colorado (BB45)	NYSB, Camden	29.05.1919	22.03.1921	30.08.1923
Maryland (BB46)	Newport News	24.04.1917	20.03.1920	21.07.1921
Washington (BB47)	NYSB, Camden	30.06.1919	01.09.1921	–
West Virginia (BB48)	Newport News	12.04.1920	19.11.1921	01.12.1923

West Virginia in about 1935.

US battleships on manoeuvres off Hawaii. *Colorado* is nearest the camera

South Dakota Class

Displacement: 43,900/45,000t
Dimensions: 201.2 x 32.3 x 10.1m
Machinery: Turbo-electric drive, 4 shafts, 60,000shp
Fuel: 1,400t oil normal (max. 2,100t, exceptionally 6,600t)
Speed/range: 23.0kt; 8,000nm at 10kt
Armour: Belt 343mm, decks 121mm total, main armament 456mm, CT 406mm
Weight of armour: 14,805t = 33.7% of normal displacement
Armament: 12 x 16in 45-cal, 16 x 6in 53-cal
Anti-aircraft guns: 8 x 3in 53-cal
Complement: 1,191 designed

Ship	Builder	Laid down	% complete
South Dakota (BB49)	New York NY	15.03.1920	38.5
Indiana (BB50)	New York NY	01.11.1920	34.7
Montana (BB51)	Mare Island NY	01.09.1920	27.6
North Carolina (BB52)	Norfolk NY	12.01.1920	36.7
Iowa (BB53)	Newport News	17.05.1920	31.8
Massachusetts (BB54)	Bethlehem	04.04.1921	11.0

Under the terms of the Washington Treaty, building work on all these vessels was terminated in February 1922 and the hulls were dismantled on the slips. The completed boilers were cannibalised and used to modernise the older battleships in the mid-1920s.

Lexington (1916 outline design).

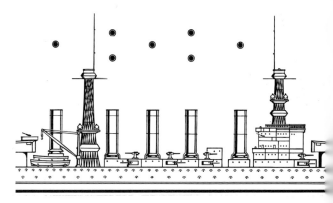

Lexington Class

Displacement: 44,200t normal, 48,500t max
Dimensions: 259.1 x 32.1 x 9.5m
Machinery: Turbo-electric drive, 4 shafts, 180,000shp
Fuel: About 5,500t oil normal (9,000t max.?)
Speed/range: 33.25kt; 12,000nm at 10kt
Armour: Belt 178mm, decks 108mm total, main armament 280mm, CT 305mm
Weight of armour: 12,580t = 28.5% approx. of normal displacement
Armament: 8 x 16in 50-cal, 16 x 6in 53-cal
Anti-aircraft guns: 6 x 3in 53-cal
Complement: 1,300 (1919 design)

Under the terms of the Washington Treaty, building work on all six units was halted in February 1922. *Lexington* and *Saratoga* were authorised for conversion to aircraft carriers on 1 July 1922. Together with the Japanese *Akagi* and *Kaga* (after their conversion), they were the world's largest capital ships of the type. The remaining four units were stricken on 17 August 1923 and sold for scrap two months later.

Lexington was commissioned on 16 November 1927 and sunk in the Pacific on 8 May 1942. *Saratoga* was commissioned on 15 December 1927. She survived the Second World War. She was employed as a target vessel for atomic bomb tests at Bikini Atoll in July 1946, being sunk in the 'Bahu' test on the 24th of that month.

Ship	Builder	Laid down	Launched	% complete
Lexington (CC1)	Bethlehem	08.01.1921	(03.10.1925)	26.7
Constellation (CC2)	Newport News	18.08.1920	–	22.7
Saratoga (CC3)	NYSB, Camden	25.09.1920	(07.04.1925)	29.4
Ranger (CC4)	Newport News	23.06.1921	–	4.0
Constitution (CC5)	Philadelphia NY	25.09.1920	–	13.4
United States (CC6)	Philadelphia NY	25.09.1920	–	12.1

Saratoga as an aircraft carrier, as originally built with 8in (203mm) turrets.

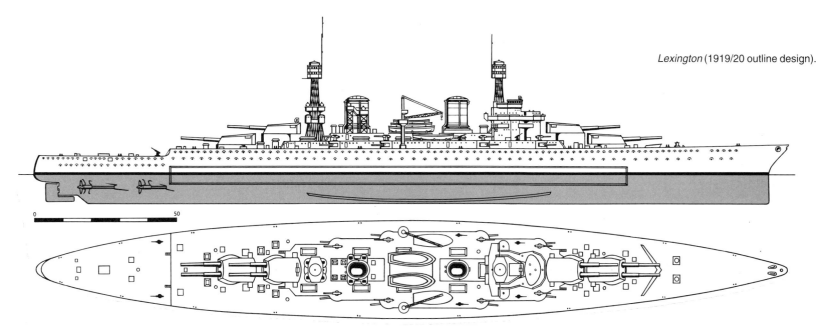

Lexington (1919/20 outline design).

Developments up to 1945

A matter of months after the Armistice, an enormous naval expansion began to loom. In Japan the unfettered build-up of the battle fleet in pursuit of the '8-8 Standard' was continuing, and, as the Peace Conference in Paris had demonstrated, Great Britain was not prepared to surrender her naval supremacy in order to achieve 'the absolute freedom to navigate the seas in peace as in war' which President Wilson had elaborated in his 'Fourteen Points'.

Wilson reacted to these circumstances with surprising alacrity. First he had the contracts distributed to lay the keels of the three *Maryland* class ships, then he reinstated the capital ships of the 1916 building programme which had been put on ice. In December 1918 he laid before Congress an even larger programme which included ten new battleships. His purpose was to entice the participants at the Peace Conference more readily to accept his plan for a League of Nations, but it had the opposite effect.

In 1920 Japan responded with a new and more comprehensive building programme. In the summer of 1921 Britain felt obliged to follow suit, even though the proposed construction of four giant battlecruisers and four equally large battleships was a lavish extravagance for a country whose finances were in a parlous state.

However, after the war, public opinion in the United States would no longer tolerate grandiose shipbuilding schemes, and even the much reduced 1919 programme barely scraped through Congress. Wilson's Democratic Party was defeated in the 1920 election, and the new Republican President, Harding, would have no truck with the idea of a League of Nations and sought instead a general disarmament amongst the world powers. At the beginning of July 1921 his Secretary of State, Hughes, invited the other four victorious powers to a disarmament conference in Washington, officially inaugurated on 12 November 1921. The resolutions passed by that Conference were encapsulated in the Washington Treaty.

After the Conference and the subsequent scrapping of outdated and newly laid down battleships and battlecruisers, the US Fleet stood in second place in the world rankings. The Americans might have the advantage in battleships, but it was their only potential adversary, Japan, which profited by the 'non-fortification' clause of the Treaty, for it forbade the United States from fortifying either the Philippines or the strategically important Pacific islands of Wake and Guam, thereby depriving the US Fleet of the opportunity to operate freely in the Far East. The transfer of the Atlantic Fleet into the Pacific made no difference to the situation.

After the agreed moratorium on battleship building, Japan switched her efforts instead to building cruisers, which had not been limited by the agreement, and particularly to cruisers with 8in (203mm) guns, the maximum calibre authorised for cruiser armament. The American reaction was the naval legislation of December 1924 providing for the construction of eight such cruisers and the modernisation of the oldest US battleships. Thus the general armaments race in battleship building was replaced by one in cruiser building, and in order to curb the latter a naval disarmament conference was convened in London at the beginning of 1930. This led to a tonnage limitation on cruisers, but the Conference also fostered the concept of 'proportionality' in battleships.

Essentially this meant that, with immediate effect, the American Fleet would contain the same number of battleships as Britain, fifteen, while the previously agreed tonnage ratio of 5:5:3 with reference to the United States, Britain and Japan remained unchanged. The Conference also took the important step of extending the moratorium on battleship building for a further five years.

The most important decision as regards the interests of the US Navy, however, was the defeat of the British proposal to reduce the maximum standard displacement for battleships from 35,000 to 25,000 tons and the maximum gun calibre from 16in (406mm) to 12in (305mm). In effect, ships built within this tonnage limitation could be successfully operated out of numerous bases in European waters or around Japan, but 25,000 tons was too small a size for US battleships intended for Pacific operations and it would have introduced a significant distortion into the 5:5:3 ratio. Subsequent developments in China were to prove the correctness of the decision: on 18 September 1931 Japan invaded Manchuria, initiating a crisis in the Far East and throwing the stability of the region into turmoil.

In 1933 Japan left the League of Nations and on 29 December 1934 gave notice of her intention to repudiate the Washington and London Treaties with effect from 31 December 1936. When the United States refused the categoric demand for the unconditional parity of Japan with the United States in all warship classes, the Japanese delegation walked out of the Second London Conference in January 1936. Meanwhile internal political developments indicated that Japan was set on further military adventures in East Asia.

Following the events in Manchuria, the US Fleet was concentrated almost permanently in the Pacific but required strengthening and modernisation, for which capital was short. The newly elected American President, Franklin D. Roosevelt (the Second Navy Secretary in the First World War) cleverly manipulated the depression in the steel industry during the world economic crisis to order 32 ships, including two aircraft carriers, aided by a national industrial assistance programme, in June 1933. Only nine months later Congress passed the first Vinson-Trammel Bill, which prescribed the replacement of all outdated units within eight years. Japanese counter-measures in naval construction resulted in the second Vinson-Trammel Bill of 17 May 1938, which provided for a 20 per cent increase in total tonnage and the building of several battleships and aircraft carriers.

The American naval leadership concentrated on plans for a future naval war in the Pacific and few gave much thought to the idea of one in the Atlantic. As the danger of war in Europe increased in 1939, the US Navy commissioned a fleet of anti-submarine vessels and fitted most of her destroyers with depth-charge equipment. An Atlantic Squadron was assembled, consisting principally of older units. When war broke out the US government declared itself 'neutral' while promising Britain and France all possible support.

In October 1939 the General Board demanded that the total warship tonnage be increased by a further one-third. A Bill was agreed in part on 14 June 1940, and only three days later Admiral Stark, the Naval Chief of Staff, requested from Congress the sum of $4 billion for the construction of a two-ocean fleet. His reason for so doing was the defeat of France and the commencement of operations by German U-boats from bases on the French Atlantic coast which ultimately threatened the United States.

Roosevelt decided that his principal enemy was Hitler, who appeared to him and to his military advisers far more dangerous than the Japanese military. What worried the Americans was the possibility that the German armaments industry might develop weapons that could bring about a German victory in Europe before the United States could mobilise there. Despite the growing hostility between Japan and the USA, therefore, the question of war in the Pacific could not be entertained for the moment.

The French capitulation and the entry of Italy into the war on the side of Germany led to the passage of the Two-Ocean Fleet legislation of 19 July 1940, which authorised the building of 1.3 million tonnes of warships, including seven battleships, six battlecruisers and thirteen aircraft carriers. This programme foreshadowed the eclipse of big-gun capital ship construction in the United States, for the naval construction acts from August 1942 took previous experience into account and forced through the building of aircraft carriers, cruisers and, primarily, destroyers, convoy escorts and submarines.

The building contracts for five units of the *Montana* class and for half of the planned programme of battlecruisers were not actually rescinded until June and July 1943 respectively, but already by October 1942 the decision had been taken not to proceed with them, for by then it had long been clear that in the aircraft carrier they had their deadliest opponent. The aircraft carrier predominated in all American building programmes from the summer of 1942 onwards, although those battleships and battlecruisers already under construction were eventually completed, as they were required for the protection of fast carrier groups on offensive operations. Older and slower battleships supported landing operations, where their heavy guns could break the resistance of the coastal batteries. While doing this, they were given air cover by carrier aircraft.

Building Programmes 1919–1945

The ships of the *South Dakota* class, although not laid down until 1920–21, had been designed and approved during the First World War. At the time work on them was begun a number of postwar sketch designs had been prepared. Towards the end of the war a new battleship type of 45,000–50,000 tons was required in order to accommodate the 18in (457mm) guns projected in 1916, but this progressed no further than the early planning stage, as was the case with the much-discussed smaller battleship of 1919. All variants of the latter had at least the installation of 16in (406mm) 50-calibre guns in triple turrets in common.

The Washington Treaty put an end to all these ideas and created the preconditions for a modernisation programme affecting all the remaining battleships of the five signatories. Only a few weeks after the signing of the agreement, the Bureau of Construction & Repair put in hand its programme, beginning with coal-fired ships on account of their poor horizontal armour. The underwater protection was also inadequate and the main armament required improvement.

The wave of cancellations and mass scrapping resulted in a huge amount of material becoming available, and this included dozens of boilers and turbine installations in various stages of completion. This modern machinery was much lighter in weight than the original engine plant and the weight saved could be used to strengthen the horizontal armour. This was particularly useful because the Washington Treaty limited conversion work to an increase of no more than 3,000 tons displacement. This limit also governed what rebuilding work authorised by Congress on 18 December 1924 might be carried out on the six battleships BB30–BB35.

All six ships received anti-torpedo bulges approximately 6ft 6in (2m) wide, while new, efficient boilers contributed indirectly to the improvement in underwater protection since the reduction in the number of boilers by half freed space which could be used to introduce new torpedo bulkheads. The space between these became bunkerage for oil fuel, the boilers having been converted to oil-firing at the same time. The horizontal protection was improved by laying armour plate 1.75–2in (45–51mm) thick over the thin armour decks. Finally, fire control equipment, catapults for the ships' aircraft and underwater torpedo tubes were installed. All the ships of this first series had been reconstructed by the end of 1927, and a start was made the following year to rebuild BB36–BB42. These units were already fitted with oil-fired boilers, but except for fitting *Nevada* (BB36) with turbines in place of her existing steam reciprocating engines the work on the *Nevada* and *Pennsylvania* class ships was broadly similar to that undertaken on the older ships. On the latter units, the angle of elevation of the main armament was increased from 15° to 30°, providing the guns with a greater range.

Reconstruction work on *Mississippi* (BB41) began in the Norfolk Navy Yard in January 1931, on *Idaho* (BB42) at the same yard later and on *New Mexico* (BB40) in the Philadelphia Navy Yard at the beginning of March 1931, so that by October 1934 the US Navy had in commission three completely different ships. In place of their lattice masts the vessels had been given a compact fighting top with the mainmast positioned on the after superstructure, but much more important than the external alterations were those inside the hull. All three ships were re-boilered and re-engined. Geared turbines replaced the turbo-electric drive in *New Mexico*, and despite the addition of anti-torpedo bulges the ships were now faster than when first commissioned. The two armour decks were strengthened by 2in (51mm) on the upper deck and 1.25in (32mm) on the lower.

Rebuilding work on the newest and most powerful vessels in the Fleet, the 'Big Five' (BB43–BB46 and BB48), scheduled for 1933, was postponed for lack of capital, and it was not until April 1939 that Congress approved a major rebuilding of these ships, although by then the rapidly deteriorating world political situation militated against having the more powerful fighting units even temporarily decommissioned and the work was postponed until October 1940. By that time the addition of anti-torpedo bulges had become essential to improve buoyancy following increases in displacement brought about by continual minor refits. All five ships were due to enter the yards consecutively during the period February 1941 to June 1942 for a three-month 'limited blistering programme', but by June 1942 only *Colorado* (BB45) and *Maryland* (BB46) had done so.

The pause in US battleship building was initially due to end on 31 December 1931 but in the summer of 1928 the Navy Secretary sought guidance on the desirable features of a future generation of battleships. The question of main calibre had been decided in 1926 when the Bureau of Ordnance became convinced that the 16in (406mm) 50-calibre gun in three triple turrets was the best arrangement for the armament, subject to the proviso that new 'super-heavy' shells would be developed for these weapons.

In October 1928 the Navy was presented with the first eight outline projects, all with 16in (406mm) guns and a speed of between 21 and 23.8 knots, but then the pause in battleship building was extended by the London Treaty for a further five years.

In the 1933 and 1934 outline projects there were designs for a 35,000-ton ship of only 22 knots and smaller, faster ships, one of which, dated May 1935, showed a 24,000-ton battlecruiser armed with six 14in (356mm) guns, capable of 30 knots and closely resembling the French *Dunkerque*. Hybrid ships were also proposed which had 12in (305mm) or 14in (356mm) guns in two triple turrets plus a flight deck and hangar for at least eight aircraft.

In mid-1935 the General Board decided in favour of the 35,000-ton ship with 14in (356mm) guns, since they were not optimistic that the London Conference would be persuaded to set the upper calibre limit at 16in (406mm).

The US Navy required four fast battleships armed with nine 14in (356mm) guns, which would allow two fast operational groups to be formed around the aircraft carriers *Lexington* and *Saratoga*. At first the naval planners were inclined to share the Navy's view, but abruptly underwent a change of heart in favour of a somewhat slower but better armoured type.

Between mid-November 1935 and August 1936 a total of 38 provisional designs were submitted. Meanwhile agreement was reached at the Second London Naval Conference for an upper limit of 14in (356mm) for the main calibre.

On 3 June 1936 the building of two new battleships was authorised although the details were unclear, but President Roosevelt postponed these 1937 Fiscal Year vessels until the following Budget because of the Presidential election of 1936. In November 1936 it was decided to proceed with the modified XVI-C design of 20 August 1936 which provided for a well-armoured ship able to make 27 knots and armed with twelve 14in (356mm) guns in three quadruple turrets capable of being replaced at a later stage by three triple turrets mounting 16in (406mm) guns. The installation of 16in guns in these new ships remained the intention of the General Board even after the construction plans had been approved, since no Board member thought it likely that Japan would respect the 14in limit. For political reasons President Roosevelt preferred to await developments, and the two ships were ordered with 14in (356mm) quadruple turrets.

In July 1937 all the signatories to the London Naval Treaty ratified the document, but as Japan had not offered a satisfactory response the 16in (406mm) calibre limit agreed in 1922 came into effect. The Navy Secretary reacted promptly and notified his agreement at once to arming the two 1938 battleships with 16in guns, although this caused some delay before work commenced and *Washington* (BB56) was not laid down until June 1938. On their trials, in the summer and autumn of 1941, the two *North Carolina* class ships were found to be good, versatile vessels with qualities more highly rated than the later *South Dakota* class, although they suffered from severe vibration which would never be entirely eliminated. The *South Dakota* ships were discussed by the General Board in July 1936 in connection with the 1938 Fiscal Year construction programme, and design work began on 30 March 1937 although orders were not placed until 1939.

Besides their slightly modified armour, the new battleships (BB57–BB60) would have a top speed of at least 27 knots. After nine months' drawing office work, a design was completed for a 35,000-ton ship which complied with all requirements with the exception of the degree of underwater protection. In order to guarantee protection against the effects of a hit by the heaviest 16in (406mm) shell, the ships were shortened and the machinery concentrated into a smaller area. The side armour was strengthened by inclining the plate 19 degrees inwards to the inner bottom, tapered in a wedge shape to 1.75in (45mm). Compared to the *North Carolina* class, the horizontal armour was stronger and consisted of an armoured bomb deck, a strongly protected main armour deck (5.1–5.3in, 130–135mm, on a 0.75in, 19mm, thick base) and a 0.6in (16mm) thick splinter deck. The shorter hull required more powerful machinery to match the speed of the *North Carolina* class, and in service the later ships proved to be slightly faster. This was achieved at the expense of manoeuvrability owing to the short hull length and the fuller hull shape.

The design was approved at the beginning of 1938 and the estimate for two ships of the class was included in the Navy Bill of 4 April 1938, but so alarmed were Congress deputies at political developments in Central Europe from March of that year that they approved four ships instead of two, limiting the displacement to 35,000 tons. Although the designers were planning a larger class than this, President Roosevelt was delighted at the prospect of receiving two unexpected additions without having to argue the case for them and therefore accepted the tonnage limitation. Ultimately this brought about an increase in the size of the US Fleet by four new battleships in a period of three months. The first three, *South Dakota* (BB57), *Indiana* (BB58) and *Massachusetts* (BB59) were ordered in December 1938 and the fourth, *Alabama* (BB60), on 1 April 1939, and all were in service by the summer of 1942 after a relatively brief period under construction. On her trials in June 1942 *Indiana* reached 27.5 knots at normal displacement, and in November 1944, more than two years after entering service, she made 27.4 knots at full load. *Massachusetts* (BB59) and *Alabama* (BB60), the two unexpected additions authorised in June 1938, had originally been intended as part of a larger class on which work had been proceeding under the Navy's construction plans since January 1938. The keel-laying was anticipated in 1939.

Contrary to previously held convictions, the US Navy now decided to sacrifice armour and armament for speed. The reasons behind this new thinking were (a) the modernisation of three Japanese *Kongo* class battlecruisers and (b) rumours current since the autumn of 1937 regarding three 46,000-tonne Japanese battleships equipped with 406mm (16in) guns and capable of 30 knots. Both the *Kongo* class vessels and the battleships would be able seriously to interfere with the movements of the slower American battle fleet throughout the Central Pacific whilst being able to avoid battle. The US Navy therefore required fast and powerful ships which could successfully engage both types. Moreover, there was at that time a call for a 'cruiser-killer'.

However, since an efficient vessel carrying nine 16in (406mm) guns at 33 knots could not be achieved on a displacement of 35,000 tons, the rumours about the Japanese programme had induced the signatories to the 1936 London Treaty to permit an increase in battleship size to 45,000 tons, and once the necessary protocol had been signed the way was open for the United States to consider building certain battleships which had been on the drawing boards since 17 January 1938. Their Senior Naval Architect had reported at the end of May 1938 that a ship with the required speed carrying 16in (406mm) 50-calibre guns in three triple turrets would displace not less than 44,560 tons.

At that time the armour system of the *South Dakota* class ships was being redeveloped. The design was ready at the end of 1938 and was quickly approved. The New York Navy Yard was given the task of working out the final details, submitting their results in November 1939. By this time the first two units of the *Iowa* class, the name ship (BB61) and *New Jersey* (BB62), had been ordered, and the contracts were passed to the Navy Yards at New York and Philadelphia on 1 July 1939. On 12 June 1940 each yard received a further order for one sister ship, *Missouri* (BB63) and *Wisconsin* (BB64).

The US Navy had now reached its target for fast battleships, but the world political situation following the fall of France was such that the United States felt compelled to take certain steps to rationalise warship construction in order to have in hand at the appropriate time the planned tonnage laid down in the 'Two-Ocean Navy' legislation passed by Congress on 19 July 1940. Accordingly, the Navy Minister arranged for work on most warships under construction to be completed against existing blueprints. This meant that the battleships *Illinois* (BB65) and *Kentucky* (BB66), which had been authorised for the 1942 Fiscal Year, would not be built to the new design currently in preparation for a still larger ship but would be completed to that of the *Iowa* class then building at the New York and Philadelphia Navy Yards.

The contracts were placed on 9 September 1941 and the keels were laid at the beginning of 1942, but neither ship was much advanced before the material was removed in order to make way for more important work on the slips. The keels were laid again in the winter of 1944–45. Work on *Illinois* (BB65) was suspended in August 1945, but *Kentucky* (BB66) survived for three years longer while consideration was given to her eventual completion as a guided missile ship. These ideas were finally abandoned in 1958, the year when the epoch of US battleship construction came to a close.

Approval for the construction of *Illinois* and *Kentucky* in September 1940 was given at the same time as that for five further battleships (BB67–BB71) and six super-heavy cruisers (CB1–CB6, the *Alaska* class), and two of the latter were actually completed. Battleship building in the United States proceeded at full speed between 1941 and 1943, although no further units were laid down after January 1941. All the *Iowa*s were completed very quickly (*Iowa* and *New Jersey* in 32 months, *Missouri* in 41 months). While the class failed to reached their projected speed on active service, they were the only battleships capable of escorting fast carriers in operational groups. Their long hulls simplified a later requirement for the installation of batteries of light automatic AA weapons, which had been found to be impracticable in the *South Dakota* class.

The *Montana* Class

Although a number of fast battleships were ordered in the 1939 Fiscal Year, the idea of the traditional, powerfully armed, well-armoured but slower ship was not yet dead. In mid-1939 the naval planners had decided with effect from FY1942 to resume building rather slower units

such as the *Iowa* which could withstand the effects of the newly introduced 2,700lb (1,225kg), 16in (406mm) shell. Such a ship was not feasible within the permissible limitation of 45,000 tons in force in 1939, even though the naval designers played with the idea of distributing the 406mm guns in three quadruple turrets.

After the outbreak of the Second World War the restrictions on ship displacement were abolished, and the Navy requested a repeat *Iowa* but with twelve 16in (406mm) guns and improved armour. At the beginning of 1940 the limitations on the size of the beam were removed, and the Army Secretary supported the Navy Secretary in his request for an enlargement of some of the Panama Canal locks. Appropriations for that purpose were made available in 1940. It was anticipated that by 1945 far beamier ships would be able to pass through the Canal.

By July 1940 C&R had produced 26 sketch designs for ships displacing at least 51,500 tons and mounting a maximum of twelve 16in (406mm) guns of an improved type on a hull capable of speeds of between 27.5 and 33 knots. However, since no decision had been taken by the time the naval legislation of 19 July 1940 was passed, the powerful but slower *Illinois* (BB65) and *Kentucky* (BB66) were ordered and constructed as vessels of the *Iowa* class and not as variants.

Due to the exigencies of the time, in August 1940 the naval designers were given a fresh specification for a ship 885ft (270m) in length and carrying twelve 16in (406mm) 50-calibre guns. Protracted discussions regarding the qualities of such a vessel ensued, even though the construction of five units had been approved months earlier and three naval yards were in receipt of orders by 9 August 1940. A decision was finally taken in March 1941 for design 'BB 67-4' as follows:

Displacement: 60,500 tons standard, 70,965 tons maximum
Dimensions: 271.3 x 36.9 x 11.2m
Machinery: 4 turbines, 4 shafts, 172,000shp
Speed/range: 28 knots; 15,000 miles at 15 knots
Armour: Belt 410mm on 25mm base; 3 decks (51mm, 158mm and 32mm on 16mm base)
Armament: 12 x 16in 50-cal, 20 x 5in 54-cal (new dual-purpose weapon)
AA: 40 x 40mm Bofors, 56 x 20mm Oerlikon

The first two units were to have been laid down in January 1941, but by then the technical documentation had still not been completed. A revised date of July 1941 was postponed for unknown reasons, and in April 1942 President Roosevelt ordered the construction to be deferred on the grounds of his preference for aircraft carriers. Accordingly all work was halted, and the orders were cancelled on 21 July 1943.

The *Alaska* Class Battlecruisers

Despite the description 'large cruisers', both ships of the *Alaska* class were true battlecruisers. For a time they were seen merely as larger versions of the standard heavy cruisers of the *Baltimore* class, but in terms of size, performance and armament the vessels clearly bore comparison with the German *Scharnhorst*.

The Japanese reacted to the first particulars of the super-cruiser, which had been under discussion in American naval circles since 1938, by preparing their own version, which went ahead once the six *Alaska* class units had been approved in July 1940. The first outline projects for a super-cruiser with 12in (305mm) guns had been worked out by the Bureau of Construction & Repair in 1938, although the original specifications provided the machinery with armour only sufficient to give protection against 8in (203mm) shells. Later the designs had to be amended to provide protection against 12in (305mm) hits.

Since the mid-1930s the classic 'Washington cruisers' with their 8in (203mm) guns had been considered too weakly armed. The US Navy was planning for the possibility of having to confront by 1939 at the latest an enemy using armoured cruisers against merchant shipping in the Atlantic. Since these armoured cruisers would be rather stronger than 'normal' heavy cruisers, the United States anticipated that they might require *Alaska* class ships for use elsewhere than in the Pacific.

Six ships of the type were approved on 19 July 1940 under the 'Two-Ocean' programme, and on 19 September 1940 all six contracts were placed with a single shipyard. Work was quickly begun on the first two, *Alaska* (CB1) and *Guam* (CB2), but a long delay ensued before the keel of the third, *Hawaii* (CB3), was laid, for reasons not connected with the urgency in building normal cruisers and light aircraft carriers. In the second half of 1943 there was a major change in the conditions of use for such ships, which were expensive to build and run, and consequently the programme was reduced from six ships to three on 24 May 1943, the contracts being cancelled exactly one month later. Work on the third hull was abandoned once the war ended, and thus *Alaska* and *Guam*, neither of which was completed until 1944, were the only representatives of the class. They were known as the 'expensive white elephants'.

US Battleships in the Second World War

Prior to the entry of the United States into the Second World War, US battleships carried out so-called 'neutrality patrols' in the North Atlantic and were involved in the occupation of Iceland in July 1941. The combat history of the ships does not really begin until 7 December 1941, when Japanese carrier aircraft attacked eight US battleships in the anchorage at Pearl Harbor and sank five (*Arizona*, *California*, *Nevada*, *Oklahoma* and *West Virginia*) and seriously damaged the other three (*Maryland*, *Pennsylvania* and *Tennessee*).

For several months afterwards the US Navy had no battleships at its disposal in the Central Pacific until the three units of the *New Mexico* class were transferred there from the Atlantic and *Colorado*, which had been undergoing a refit, was returned to the Fleet.

Following repairs to three of the Pearl Harbor casualties, a battle group was assembled to protect the American West Coast against possible Japanese raids. These old battleships saw action for the first time at the Aleutians in May 1943, where they covered the landings. From the autumn of 1943, all, with the exception of ships under refit or conversion, formed a group to be used to bombard Japanese positions on occupied islands as a 'softener' for Marine landings. This strategy was highly successful throughout the entire Pacific war, from Tarawa and Makin to Saipan and from Iwo Jima to Okinawa. The three oldest battleships played a similar role in the landings in French North Africa, Normandy and southern France. This activity tended to overshadow the battleships' convoy protection role, for by that time the danger of attack by German surface forces had passed.

Proof of the quality of the guns on board the old battleships—admittedly due in large part to their modern fire control equipment and radar—was provided in the last classical naval battle of the war, at Surigao Strait on 25 October 1944, when the Japanese *Yamashiro* was shot to pieces without having the opportunity to return fire.

The American battleships showed their ability to take punishment from enemy coastal batteries as well as from sporadic air attack. The torpedoing of *Pennsylvania* was an exception. The newer battleships were frequently used in the Atlantic in the early phases of the war, but had no encounters with enemy vessels. The duel between *Massachusetts* and the French *Jean Bart* at Casablanca demonstrated the effects of the US ship's 16in (406mm) guns, but this was another exception.

Elsewhere in the Pacific, in the Battle of Guadalcanal on the night of 14–15 November 1942, the effectiveness of *Washington*'s radar-controlled guns was demonstrated against the Japanese *Kirishima*, while the structural weakness of *South Dakota* became apparent after the failure of her radar.

For the remainder of the war no further opportunity presented itself to engage the Japanese battleships. Thus the principal task of the modernised US battleships was to act as escorts to carrier task forces, protecting them against enemy air attack with their heavy AA armament.

Armament

First World War experience had shown the US Navy that the 12in (305mm) and to some extent the 14in (356mm) American guns were inferior in ballistic performance to their British equivalents. The USN sought to enhance the effectiveness of the salvo and increase range by introducing new shells and by increasing the elevation of the barrels to 30°. Congress authorised finance for the latter measure in January 1923, but the increase in elevation and its concomitant increase in range was not given effect until the modernisation programmes of the early 1930s, and only then for guns of 14in calibre.

During the moratorium in battleship construction there was no call for heavy naval guns, although in 1925 a 16in (406mm) 56-calibre barrel was rebored to 18in (457mm) 48-calibre. It was tested in July 1927. Despite its excellent muzzle velocity of 3,000ft/sec (915m/sec), the effective life of the barrel was estimated to be only 125 rounds, compared to 180 rounds for the 16in 50-calibre gun. Accordingly, the latter was recommended as the standard weapon for US battleships. At the same time the Bureau of Ordnance initiated the development of a heavy, 2,400lb (1,088kg), 16in shell in 1929. In 1939 the Navy ordered and introduced a 16in shell of 2,700lb (1,225kg).

Improved models of the existing 14in (356mm) and 16in (406mm) guns had been manufactured for the modernisation of the 'Big Five' ships first planned before the outbreak of war, although a completely new type of gun with better ballistic performance and significantly lower weight had been developed for newer battleships. The new 16in (456mm) 45-calibre Mk 6 of 1937 weighed 87 tonnes compared to the 107 tonnes of the older Series 8 gun aboard *West Virginia*. Even the 16in 50-calibre gun of the *Iowa* class was 12 tonnes lighter than its 1918

5in (127mm) 25-calibre AA guns aboard a US battleship.

predecessor. The 12in (305mm) 50-calibre gun introduced during the Second World War was completely new.

The anti-aircraft armament of US battleships was systematically strengthened and by 1921 eight 3in (76mm) was the prescribed standard. In 1928 the 5in (127mm) 25-calibre became the new standard weapon for battleships and heavy cruisers, and on some ships remained so until the war's end. New units and those rebuilt during the war did not receive the 5in 38-calibre twin gun until the mid-1930s. Many experts consider this to have been the best AA gun of the Second World War. It had been originally developed as a dual-purpose weapon. The *Montana* class was designed to have the 5in calibre with a longer barrel, while a single-mounted version was only fitted to large aircraft carriers of the *Midway* class.

The Americans were not so fortunate with the development of a rapid-fire small-calibre weapon. A 37mm AA gun developed from 1928 was rejected by the Navy, and a quadruple 1.1in (the 'Chicago Piano'), which had been under development since the mid-1930s, had an imposing rate of fire which also rapidly wore down the barrels. In the summer of 1940 this was replaced by the well-known air-cooled 20mm Oerlikon. Production was undertaken with British assistance and the first barrels were ready by the summer of 1941. The weapon was ineffective against massed dive-bomber attack, and in June 1941 a licence was obtained from the Swedish company Bofors to produce a 40mm AA gun, which was soon installed in quadruple mountings on all battleships. The large number of small-calibre AA guns carried aboard US ships was clearly justified, particularly for protection against Japanese kamikazes.

Technical Details of Heavy Guns and AA Weapons of the US Navy 1941–45

Calibre	Model	Wt of shell	Muzzle velocity	Range	Altitude
16in 50-cal	Mk 7	2,700lb	2,500ft/sec	42,320yd/45°	–
16in 45-cal	Mk 6	2,700lb	2,300ft/sec	36,850yd/45°	–
16in 45-cal	Mk 5	2,240lb	2,520ft/sec	35,000yd/30°	–
14in 50-cal	Mk 7/11	1,500lb	2,700ft/sec	36,300yd/30°	–
14in 45-cal	Mk 8/12	1,500lb	2,600ft/sec	34,340yd/30°	–
12in 50-cal	Mk 8	1,140lb	2,500ft/sec	38,600yd/45°	–
12in 50-cal	Mk 7	871lb	2,900ft/sec	23,500yd/15°	–

Anti-Aircraft Guns

Calibre	Model	Wt of shell	Muzzle velocity	Range	Altitude
5in 54-cal	Mk 16	70lb	2,650ft/sec	25,900yd/47°	51,500ft
5in 38-cal	Mk 12	55lb	2,600ft/sec	18,150yd/45°	37,070ft
5in 25-cal	Mk 10	54lb	2,110ft/sec	14,550yd/45°	27,400ft
3in 50-cal	Mk 20	13lb	2,700ft/sec	–	29,500ft
40mm 56-cal	Mk 1/2	2lb	2,890ft/sec	–	14,750ft
1.1in 75-cal	Mk 1	0.9lb	2,700ft/sec	–	8,850ft

The rate of fire of the 5in 38-calibre gun was 20rds/min, that of the 5in 25-calibre 8rds/min and that of the 3in 50-calibre Mk 20 produced after the 1930s 15–20rds/min.

Arkansas

Displacement: 29,400/31,000t; 26,067 tons standard
Dimensions: 168.9 x 32.3 x 9.1m
Machinery: As before but only 4 boilers, 28,000ihp
Fuel: 3,800t oil (exceptionally 5,600t)
Speed/range: 21.0kt; 14,000nm at 10kt
Armour: As before but horizontal armour strengthened to 145mm
Weight of armour: 11,120t = 37.8% of normal displacement
Armament: 12 x 12in 50-cal, 16 x 5in 51-cal (from 1942: 6 x 5in)
Anti-aircraft guns: 8 x 3in 50-cal (from 1942: 10 x 3in), 16 x 1.1in
Complement: 1,242 (1,870 in 1945)

Ship	Refitted	Modernised
Arkansas (BB33)	00.09.1925–00.11.1926	00.03.1942–00.07.1942

Wyoming (BB32) was converted to a training vessel with only six 12in guns in 1931–32 and served as an AA training ship, with varying armament fits, from 1941. Her remaining 12in turrets were removed in 1943. The ship was stricken in September 1947 and scrapped in 1948.

Arkansas (BB33) received three aircraft and a catapult in 1927. Ten 5in were removed during modernisation in 1942, when the 1.1in machine guns were also replaced by 36 x 40mm Bofors in nine quadruple mountings. The ship made numerous voyages as a convoy escort between the USA and Britain from December 1941 to April 1944. She supported the Normandy landings in June 1944 and was at Iwo Jima and Okinawa in February 1945. Decommissioned in late 1945, she was sunk during atomic tests at Bikini Atoll on 25 June 1946.

Arkansas, 1944.

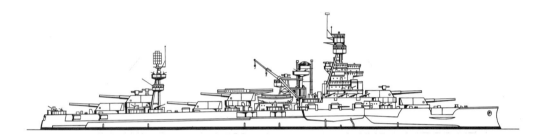

The modernised *Arkansas* in 1943.

New York/Texas

Displacement: 30,600/32,450t; 26,915 tons standard
Dimensions: 172.2 x 32.3 x 9.2m
Machinery: As before but only 6 boilers, 28,100ihp
Fuel: 2,800t oil optimum (exceptionally 4,600t)
Speed/range: 20.0kt; 15,000nm at 10kt
Armour: As before but horizontal armour strengthened to 145mm
Weight of armour: 11,526t = 37.7% of normal displacement
Armament: As before but from 1942 only 6 x 5in 51-cal
Anti-aircraft guns: 8 x 3in 50-cal (from 1942: 10 x 3in), 16 x 1.1in
Complement: 1,290 (2,264 in 1945)

Ship	Refitted	Modernised
New York (BB34)	00.10.1926–00.10.1927	00.11.1941–00.02.1942
Texas (BB35)	00.08.1925–00.11.1926	–

After their refits both units were reported to be very poor sea-keepers. Both served as training ships, *Texas* from 1936 and *New York* from 1938, and both were listed for disposal once their successors had been commissioned.

New York was first US battleship to receive experimental radar, in December 1938. The complement of light AA weapons for use against dive-bombers was steadily increased during the Second World War and by April 1945 had risen to 40 x 40mm Bofors in ten mountings and 36 x 20mm Oerlikons. Both ships were engaged in 'neutrality patrols' in the North Atlantic from May 1941 and supported the North African landings in November 1942, returning to Atlantic convoy escort duty subsequently.

New York was used as a gunnery training ship from July 1943 to June 1944 but was present at Iwo Jima and Okinawa from November 1944. She was decommissioned on 30 October 1945 and used as target ship at Bikini Atoll. However, she was little damaged after two atomic tests and was scuttled off Pearl Harbor on 8 June 1948.

Texas supported the Normandy landings on 6 June 1944. During the bombardment of Cherbourg she received numerous 280mm (11in) hits from German coastal batteries and on 25 June put into Plymouth for repairs. She also supported the invasion of southern France on 15 August 1944. The ship was transferred to the Pacific (Iwo Jima and Okinawa) in November 1944. Decommissioned on 27 October 1945, she was towed to a dredged basin at San Jacinto, Texas, and preserved as a museum.

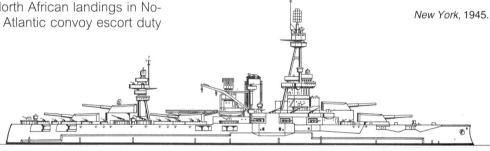

New York, 1945.

New York at the Spithead Naval Review of 1937.

Nevada/Oklahoma

Displacement: 32,200/35,570t (Nevada); 28,600 tons (Nevada 29,065 tons) standard

Dimensions: As before, but beam 32.9m

Machinery: As before, but Nevada 2 Parsons turbines, 25,000shp

Fuel: 2,300t oil (exceptionally 5,100t)

Speed/range: 20.3kt (Oklahoma 19.7kt); 15,700nm at 10kt

Armour: As before, but armour deck strengthened by 51mm

Weight of armour: 12,214t = 37.9% of normal displacement

Armament: 1941: 10 x 14in 45-cal, 12 x 5in 51-cal (1943: all 5in removed)

Anti-aircraft guns: 8 x 5in 25-cal (1943: 16 x 5in 38-cal in Nevada)

Complement: 1,400 (2,170 in 1945)

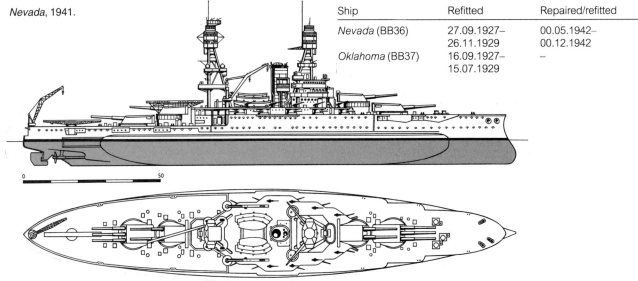

Nevada, 1941.

Ship	Refitted	Repaired/refitted
Nevada (BB36)	27.09.1927–26.11.1929	00.05.1942–00.12.1942
Oklahoma (BB37)	16.09.1927–15.07.1929	–

Nevada, 1945.

Oklahoma shortly before the outbreak of the Second World War.

During her refit Nevada received turbines originally earmarked for North Dakota and with these achieved 20.2 knots at 31,759shp on trials. Oklahoma managed only 19.68 knots at 23,599ihp with her original reciprocating machinery. In the 1942 reconstruction, Nevada's secondary battery and the old 5in single AA weapons were replaced by eight of the latest 5in AA guns in twin mountings, together with 32 x 40mm Bofors automatics in eight quadruple mountings.

Oklahoma was sunk by Japanese aerial torpedoes at Pearl Harbor on 7 December 1941. She was raised but found to be irreparably damaged in late 1943 and was sold for breaking up in December 1946. She sank en route to a San Francisco scrapyard on 17 May 1947.

Nevada was badly damaged at Pearl Harbor but was run aground in shallow water to prevent her sinking; she was raised and temporarily repaired, then refitted and modernised at Puget Sound Navy Yard. She was present at the Aleutians in May 1943 and supported the Normandy landings in June 1944 and those in southern France in August that year, Transferred to the Pacific, she saw action at Iwo Jima and Okinawa, receiving light damage from a kamikaze at Okinawa on 26 March 1945. She served with the Fleet in Japanese home waters in July and August 1945. Decommissioned on 30 October 1945, she was used in atomic tests in 1946 and although seriously damaged remained afloat. She was subsequently employed as a target and experimental vessel and was finally sunk by aerial torpedo on 31 July 1948.

Pennsylvania/Arizona

Displacement: 36,500/39,300t; 33,125 tons standard

Dimensions: 182.9 x 32.4 x 10.1

Machinery: As before, but 6 boilers, 33,375shp

Fuel: 2,200t oil optimum (exceptionally 5,700t)

Speed/range: 21.0kt; 19,000nm at 10kt (5,700t oil)

Armour: As before, but horizontal armour strengthened by 45mm

Weight of armour: 13,225t = 36.2% of normal displacement

Armament: 12 x 14in 45-cal, 12 x 5in 51-cal (1943: all 5in removed)

Anti-aircraft guns: 8 x 5in 25-cal, 8 x 1.1in (from 1943: 16 x 5in 38-cal)

Complement: 1,400 (2,550 in 1945)

Ship	Refitted	Repaired/refitted
Pennsylvania (BB38)	01.06.1929–08.05.1931	04.10.1942–05.02.1943
Arizona (BB39)	15.07.1929–01.02.1931	–

The angle of elevation of the main armament was increased to 30° in 1931. Arizona was sunk by Japanese carrier aircraft at Pearl Harbor on 7 December 1941;

1,177 crew members lost their lives. The ship broke into two parts and remains in situ. Pennsylvania received bomb damage at Pearl Harbor and spent three months undergoing repairs; she was employed as a training ship until her refit at Mare Island Navy Yard at the beginning of October 1942, when her 1.1in machine guns were replaced by 40 x 40mm Bofors in ten quadruple mountings and the 5in secondary armament and the older 'short' 5in AA weapons were removed and eight twin 5in

Arizona, 1941.

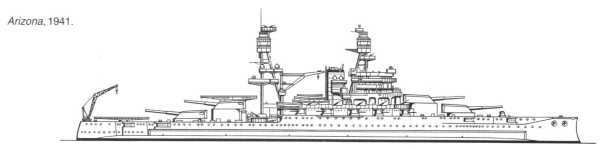

The modernised Arizona off the Californian coast.

38-calibre dual-purpose mountings installed in their place. The ship participated in Pacific island landings from May 1943 and was involved in the Battle of Surigao Strait on 24 October 1944. Further 20mm AA weapons were installed during a minor refit at Mare Island Navy Yard. *Pennsylvania* was hit aft by an aerial torpedo and came close to sinking at Wake Island on 12 August 1945. She was towed back to the USA for temporary repairs and was selected as a target ship for the atomic tests at Bikini Atoll. Slightly damaged in the atomic explosions, she continued in use as a target until destroyed by conventional aerial bombing on 10 February 1948.

A photograph of *Pennsylvania* dated 1 August 1943.

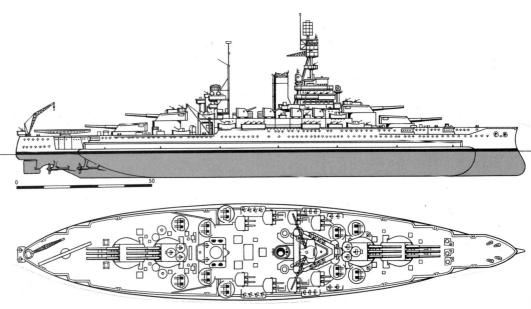

Pennsylvania, 1943.

New Mexico Class

Displacement: 36,100 (operational)/40,770t; 33,400 tons standard

Dimensions: 182.9 x 32.4 x 9.4m

Machinery: 4 Westinghouse turbines, 6 (New Mexico 4) boilers, 40,000shp

Fuel: 1,900t oil at operational displacement (exceptionally 5,400t)

Speed/range: 21.5kt; 23,000nm at 10kt (5,400t oil)

Armour: As before, but armour decks strengthened to 210mm total

Weight of armour: 14,400t = 40.0% of operational displacement

Armament: 12 x 14in 50-cal, 10 x 5in 51-cal (from 1943: 6 x 5in)

Anti-aircraft guns: 1941: 8 x 5in 25-cal, 16 x 1.1in (until 1943)

Complement: 1,440 (1,950–2080 in 1945)

In wartime operational conditions the ships carried 400t oil in excess of normal bunkerage. None of the class was further modernised during the Second World War, although the armament was changed during wartime refits; for example, *Idaho* had her 5in low-angle guns removed while the AA defence was augmented by two quadruple 40mm Bofors and in the second refit ten 5in 38-calibre were mounted to replace the 'short' 5in guns removed earlier. Eventually all three ships had a uniform ten quadruple 40mm Bofors and all had their 1.1in machine guns landed by the late autumn of 1943, while over the succeeding period to early 1945 the number of 20mm Oerlikons was increased to 40. *New Mexico* retained her short-barrelled 5in AA guns until the end of the war, but during repairs at Pearl Harbor from 3 March to 18 April 1945 *Mississippi* had a much enhanced AA defence installed, outside Navy guidelines, on the instructions of her commander: rejecting the planned new twin 5in 38-cal guns, the ship's captain doubled the battery of short-barrelled 5in AA guns to sixteen.

The three ships participated in all the important Pacific operations, and all were the targets of kamikaze bombers; *Idaho* was also hit by an aerial torpedo. *Idaho* was decommissioned on 3 July 1946 and *New Mexico* on 19 July 1946; both were sold for breaking up in November 1947. *Mississippi* was converted to a gunnery training ship in 1947 and further modified as an experimental vessel in 1952. She was decommissioned in July 1956 and scrapped from November of that year.

Ship	Reconstructed	1st refit	2nd refit
New Mexico (BB40)	05.03.1931–22.01.1933	18.08.1944–26.10.1944	–
Mississippi (BB41)	30.01.1931–31.08.1932	14.05.1944–06.10.1944	00.03–00.04.1945
Idaho (BB42)	30.09.1933–09.10.1934	14.10.1942–28.12.1942	00.10–00.12.1944

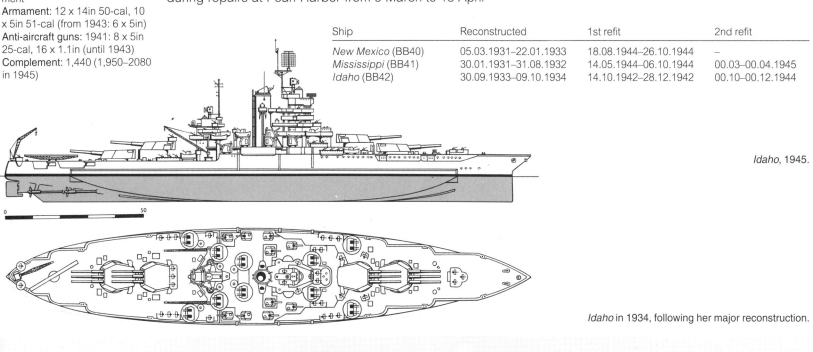

Idaho, 1945.

0   50

Idaho in 1934, following her major reconstruction.

Tennessee/California (as in 1944)

Displacement: 40,200/41,000t; *Tennessee* 34,859 tons standard
Dimensions: As before, but beam 34.75m (2.55m wide bulge each side)
Machinery: As before, but 29,500shp (*California* 30,000shp)
Fuel: 4,800t oil max
Speed/range: 20.6kt (*California* 20kt)
Armour: As before, but armour deck strengthened to 51mm (about 76mm over magazines)
Weight of armour: 13,700t = 34.1% of normal displacement
Armament: 12 x 14in 50-cal
Anti-aircraft guns: 16 x 5in 38-cal, 40 x 40mm (*California* 56 x 40mm in 1945)
Complement: 2,240 (*California* 2,370)

Ship	Repaired/refitted
Tennessee (BB43)	00.09.1942–13.05.1945
California (BB44)	07.06.1942–31.01.1944

Tennessee was damaged by two bombs at Pearl Harbor on 7 December 1941 and was under repair until the end of March 1942. *California* was sunk after numerous bomb and torpedo hits at Pearl Harbor but she was salvaged in March 1942. Following temporary repairs she proceeded to Bremerton on the West Coast for repair and modernisation. The work was not completed until late January 1944, having been accorded low priority.

The modernisation work completely altered both vessels to resemble the *South Dakota* class. Together with an increase in the horizontal armour, they were the first ships to receive the broader anti-torpedo bulges and along with *West Virginia* became the beamiest US battleships. The addition of the bulges also increased the displacement by 2,900t and the deeper draught would have had an adverse effect on the efficiency of the belt armour.

Both ships were involved in Pacific operations until the end of the war and their modern fire control equipment was principally responsible for the destruction of the Japanese battleship *Yamashiro* at Surigao Strait on 24 October 1944. *California* sustained kamikaze damage off Luzon on 6 January 1945; she returned to Bremerton for repairs at Puget Sound Navy Yard and re-joined her group on 15 February 1945. *Tennessee* was damaged by a kamikaze off Okinawa on 11 April 1945 but was repaired locally. Both ships were placed in reserve at Philadelphia in December 1945 and mothballed in 1947. Stricken on 1 March 1959, they were sold for scrapping in July 1959.

A wartime photograph of the rebuilt *Tennessee*, with twin 5in (127mm) AA guns.

Colorado/Maryland (as in late 1944)

Displacement: 39,500t operational/41,000t; about 34,700 tons standard

Dimensions: As before, but beam 33m (1.6m wide bulge each side)

Machinery: As before, but 29,500shp

Fuel: 5,200t oil max

Speed/range: 21.8kt (*Maryland* 22.6kt)

Armour: As before, but armour deck strengthened by 51mm (by 76mm over magazines)

Weight of armour: 13,730t = 34.8% of operational displacement

Armament: 8 x 16in 45-cal, 8 x 5in 51-cal

Anti-aircraft guns: 8 x 5in 25-cal, 40 x 40mm, 43–45 x 20mm

Complement: About 2,100

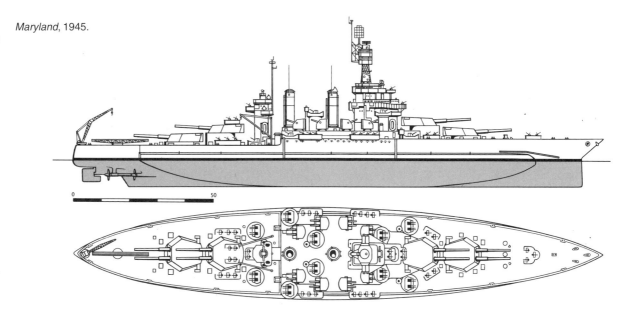

Maryland, 1945.

Ship	Refitted (bulges)	1st refit	Final refit
Colorado (BB45)	28.07.1941–26.02.1942	00.12.1942–00.01.1943	21.08.1944–09.10.1944
Maryland (BB46)	17.02.1941–01.08.1941	00.09.1943–00.10.1943	00.04.1945–00.08.1945

The modernised *Colorado*, in camouflage paintwork.

An aerial photograph of the modernised *Colorado*.

The typical basket mast aft on both ships was cut off at funnel height at the beginning of 1942 and replaced two years later by a tall turret-type structure with a simple pole mast. Until the autumn of 1943 both vessels mounted ten 5in 51-calibre and sixteen 1.1in AA guns but these were then replaced by quadruple Bofors. During her final modernisation *Maryland* received sixteen 5in 38-calibre dual-purpose guns in twin turrets to replace the old 5in short-barrelled low-angle weapons.

Maryland was damaged by two bombs at Pearl Harbor on 7 December 1941 but had been repaired by February 1942. The ship was in continuous action between November 1943 and April 1945, suffering heavy damage

on several occasions. It was whilst undergoing repair at Puget Sound Navy Yard following damage from kamikazes at Okinawa that she was fitted with her new AA suite.

Colorado was forced to undergo repairs after receiving numerous hits from coastal batteries during two bombardments of Japanese land positions, and she received light damage from kamikazes at Leyte Gulf in late November 1944. She retained all her old 5in guns until the end of the war.

Both ships were mothballed in early 1947. Stricken from the Fleet List on 1 March 1959, they were sold for breaking up in July 1959 and immediately scrapped.

West Virginia (as in September 1944)

Displacement: 39,600t operational/41,000t; about 35,400 tons standard
Dimensions: As before, but beam 34.75m (2.5m wide bulge each side)
Machinery: As before, but 29,500shp
Fuel: 4,700t oil max.
Speed/range: 21.1kt; range as before
Armour: As Colorado (strengthened in refit)
Weight of armour: 13,730t = 34.7% of operational displacement
Armament: 8 x 16in 45-cal
Anti-aircraft guns: 16 x 5in 38-cal, 40 x 40mm, 58 x 20mm
Complement: About 2,180

Ship	Repaired/refitted
West Virginia (BB43)	00.06.1942–00.09.1944

West Virginia was hit by seven aerial torpedoes and two bombs at Pearl Harbor on 7 December 1941 and sank on an even keel; raised on 30 May 1942, she was temporarily repaired and proceeded under her own steam to Bremerton for reconstruction work, which was completed by September 1944. She re-joined the Fleet for the Leyte Gulf operation and together with Tennessee and California used her modern radar to play a decisive role in the sinking of Yamashiro at Surigao Strait on 25 October 1944. She was involved in the operations at Iwo Jima and Okinawa and was damaged by kamikazes on 1 April 1945. She was hit by bombs on 17 June 1945 and following local repairs proceeded to Sagami Bay with her battle group on 27 August 1945. The ship remained in service after the war but was mothballed at Bremerton from 9 January 1947 until early 1959. Despite her poor speed she was considered a modern vessel, better suited to the fire support role even than the Iowa class ships, but she was stricken on 1 March 1959 and sold for scrapping the following September.

West Virginia, 1945.

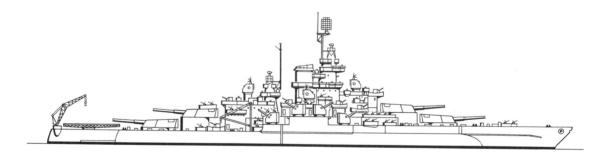

North Carolina/Washington

Displacement: 44,000/46,100t; 37,486 tons standard
Dimensions: 217.8 x 33.0 x 10.0m
Machinery: 4 turbines, 4 shafts, 121,000shp
Fuel: 5,200t oil optimum (exceptionally 7,000t)
Speed/range: 27.0kt; 13,500nm at 15kt
Armour: Belt 305mm on 19mm base, deck 197mm total, main armament 406mm, CT 406mm
Weight of armour: 15,560t = 35.4% of operational displacement
Armament: 9 x 16in 45-cal, 20 x 5in 38-cal DP
Anti-aircraft guns: 64 x 40mm, 64 x 20mm
Complement: 2,134 (2,340 in 1945)

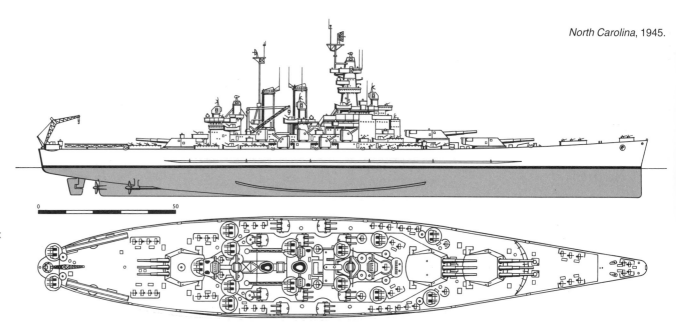

North Carolina, 1945.

Ship	Builder	Laid down	Launched	Commissioned
North Carolina (BB55)	New York NY	27.10.1937	13.06.1940	09.04.1941
Washington (BB56)	Philadelphia NY	14.06.1938	01.06.1940	15.05.1941

North Carolina in June 1942.

The horizontal armour consisted of a 37mm bomb deck (upper deck), an armour deck (105mm on a 36mm base) and a 19mm splinter deck. Until the end of 1942, the original AA armament was 16–20 x 1.1in automatics in quadruple mountings and 12–18 x 0.5in machine guns. The first 40mm Bofors guns were installed in 1942 (first six, then another four, the total of fifteen quadruples being reached in August 1943).

North Carolina made only 26.15 knots on trials and was ready for service in August 1941. Torpedoed by a Japanese submarine south-east of the Solomons on 15 September 1942, the ship was under repair until 17 November 1942 and under refit at Puget Sound from 23 June to 1 October 1944. After the war she was employed as a training ship until the end of 1946. She was decommissioned on 27 June 1947, stricken on 1 June 1960 and presented that year to the State of North Carolina as a national monument.

Washington was ready for action in March 1942. She sank the Japanese battlecruiser *Kirishima* at the Battle of Savo Island on 14–15 November 1942. The ship collided with *Indiana* at Kwajalein on 1 February 1944 and was under repair for three months at Puget Sound. After the war she was placed in reserve, decommissioned on 27 June 1947 and stricken on 1 June 1960. She was sold for scrapping on 25 May 1961.

South Dakota Class

Displacement: 43,800/45,800t; 37,700–37,800 tons standard
Dimensions: 203.0 x 33.0 x 10.7m
Machinery: 4 turbines, 4 shafts, 130,000shp
Fuel: 5,200t oil optimum (exceptionally 7,000t)
Speed/range: 27.2kt; 15,000nm at 15kt
Armour: Belt 310mm on 19mm base, deck 208mm total, main armament 456mm, CT 406mm
Weight of armour: 15,140t = 34.6% of operational displacement
Armament: 9 x 16in 45-cal, 20 x 5in 38-cal DP (*South Dakota* 16 x 5in 38-cal)
Anti-aircraft guns: Late 1942: 16–24 x 40mm (*South Dakota* also 20 x 1.1in)
Complement: 1,850 (2,350 in 1945)

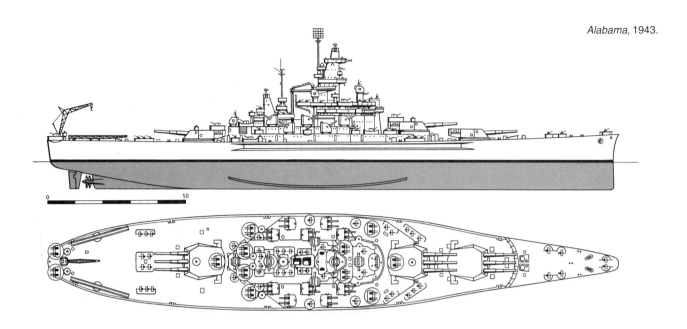

Alabama, 1943.

Alabama shortly after completing.

Ship	Builder	Laid down	Launched	Commissioned
South Dakota (BB57)	NYSB, Camden	05.07.1939	07.06.1941	20.03.1942
Indiana (BB58)	Newport News	20.11.1939	21.11.1941	30.04.1942
Massachusetts (BB59)	Bethlehem, Quincy	20.07.1939	23.09.1941	12.05.1942
Alabama (BB60)	Norfolk NY	01.02.1940	16.02.1942	16.08.1942

Despite prior doubts, all four units managed to exceed the speed requirement of 27 knots. The 1.1in automatic machine guns were removed from *South Dakota* in February 1943, while the total number of quadruple 40mm Bofors aboard each ship rose in the autumn of 1943 to 12 and by June 1944 to 17 (*South Dakota*) and 18 (*Massachusetts*). The total of 20mm Oerlikons varied among the ships of the class; in August 1945 *South Dakota* had 72.

South Dakota was ready for combat in August 1942. She received shell hits at the Battle of Savo Island on 15 November 1942 and was under repair at New York until February 1943. She was engaged in convoy escort duties in the North Atlantic from June to July 1943 but returned to the Pacific in September 1943. *Indiana* was battle-ready in October 1942 and served in the Pacific from the end of November 1942. She collided with *Washington* on 1 February 1944 and was at Pearl Harbor under repair until April 1944. *Massachusetts* was combat-ready in September 1942 and deployed off French North Africa, fighting a gunnery duel on 8 November off Casablanca with the French battleship *Jean Bart* at anchor there and receiving a number of light hits. From the autumn of 1943 the ship operated only in the Pacific theatre. *Alabama* was ready for action in November 1942 and was employed in the North Atlantic and on the Murmansk convoy run until the summer of 1943. She served in the Pacific from August 1943.

Indiana, in a photograph giving a good view of the shape of the hull.

All four units participated in the major Pacific operations and in the carrier raids against Japan during the final phases of the war. All were decommissioned between January and September 1947 and stricken on 1 June 1962. *South Dakota* was sold for breaking up in October 1962 and *Indiana* in September 1963, but the other pair are both preserved as memorials.

Iowa Class

Displacement: 57,300/59,000t; 48,804–49,066 tons standard
Dimensions: 262.1 x 33.0 x 11.0m
Machinery: 4 turbines, 4 shafts, 212,000shp
Fuel: 7,000t oil optimum (8,000t max.)
Speed/range: 32.0kt; 14,900nm at 15kt
Armour: Belt 310mm on 22mm base, deck 213mm total, main armament 406mm, CT 406mm
Weight of armour: 18,466t = 32.2% of operational displacement
Armament: 9 x 16in 50-cal, 20 x 5in 38-cal DP
Anti-aircraft guns: 80 x 40mm, 52 x 20mm
Complement: 1,921 designed (2,800–2,980 in 1945)

Missouri in 1944.

Ship	Builder	Laid down	Launched	Commissioned
Iowa (BB61)	New York NY	27.06.1940	27.08.1942	22.02.1943
New Jersey (BB62)	Philadelphia NY	16.09.1940	07.12.1942	23.05.1943
Missouri (BB63)	New York NY	16.01.1941	29.01.1944	11.06.1944
Wisconsin (BB64)	Philadelphia NY	25.01.1941	07.12.1943	16.04.1944
Illinois (BB65)	Philadelphia NY	14.01.1945	–	–
Kentucky (BB66)	Norfolk NY	06.12.1944	20.01.1950	–

Kentucky's keel was first laid on 7 March 1942 but the material was broken up on the stocks a few months later because of the pressure of orders at the shipyard and to make space for the keel of the aircraft carrier *Lake Champlain*. Following a resumption of work in 1944, building was again suspended in August 1946 but restarted in August 1948 in order to clear the slip. At that stage the ship was 73 per cent complete. There were various plans to convert the hull (first to an AA ship, then to a ballistic-missile carrier), but in the event the ship was stricken on 9 June 1958 and broken up in 1959.

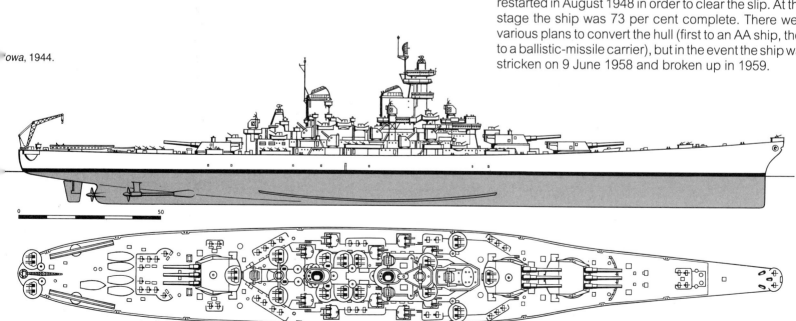

Iowa, 1944.

Iowa in Measure 22 camouflage.

Work on *Illinois* was scheduled to commence in the winter of 1941–42, but the keel-laying was postponed until January 1945. The contract for the ship was cancelled on 22 August 1945 when the hull was 22 per cent complete and she was broken up on the stocks.

None of the four surviving ships made the designed speed of 33 knots, but the actual speeds achieved were adequate for their role as carrier escorts. The horizontal armour consisted of a 38mm bomb deck, a 152–159mm on 32mm armour deck and a 19mm splinter deck.

With the exception of *Iowa* (which brought President Roosevelt to Casablanca for the Teheran Conference), all four ships served only in the Pacific theatre and were used primarily in the carrier escort role. *Missouri* was

slightly damaged by a kamikaze off Okinawa on 11 April 1945 but subsequently remained in continuous service until February 1955. The remaining three ships were transferred to reserve at the beginning of March 1949 but returned to active service following the outbreak of the Korean War.

New Jersey was decommissioned in August 1957 and *Wisconsin* in March 1958. During the Vietnam War *New Jersey* was used to bombard coastal targets, but the ship was returned to reserve in December 1969.

From 1977 there was a revival of enthusiasm in the US Navy to keep these ships in commission despite the costly modernisation programme that that would entail. Finance was eventually voted for the project for the 1981 Fiscal Year, and all four units were reactivated between 1982 and 1988.

Alaska Class

Displacement: 33,300/34,800t;
29,780 tons standard (*Alaska*)
Dimensions: 241.3 x 27.8 x 9.7m
Machinery: 4 turbines, 4 shafts,
150,000shp
Fuel: 3,700t oil
Speed/range: 31.4kt (*Guam*
31.0kt); 12,000nm at 15kt
Armour: Belt 228mm, deck
149mm total, main armament
325mm, CT 270mm
Weight of armour: 9,914t =
30.0% of operational displacement
Armament: 9 x 12in 50-cal, 12 x
5in 38-cal DP
Anti-aircraft guns: 56 x 40mm,
34 x 20mm
Complement: 2,250

Guam, the last US battlecruiser.

Ship	Builder	Laid down	Launched	Commissioned
Alaska (CB1)	NYSB, Camden	17.12.1941	15.08.1943	17.06.1944
Guam (CB2)	NYSB, Camden	02.02.1942	12.11.1943	17.09.1944
Hawaii (CB3)	NYSB, Camden	20.12.1943	03.11.1945	–

Alaska, 1945.

On 19 July 1941 six 'large cruisers' designated CB1–
CB6 were approved and on 9 September the contracts
for all six were placed at the Camden shipyard. Following
a decision to limit the programme, the orders for CB 4–

CB6 (*Philippines*, *Puerto Rico* and *Samoa*) were cancelled on 24 June 1943 before keel-laying. Work was
abandoned on *Hawaii* in August 1945 when the ship was
82 per cent complete. In 1952 some thought was given
to converting the hull, first into a ballistic missile ship and
then to a tactical command ship, but nothing came of this
and the ship was stricken on 9 June 1958 and sold for
scrapping in April 1959.

Neither of the commissioned vessels achieved their
designed speed of 33 knots. They were used from
January 1945 (*Alaska*) and March 1945 (*Guam*) as
carrier escorts. Decommissioned in December 1945
and placed in reserve on 17 February 1947, they were
stricken on 1 June 1960, *Alaska* being sold for breaking
up on 30 June 1961 and *Guam* on 24 May 1961.

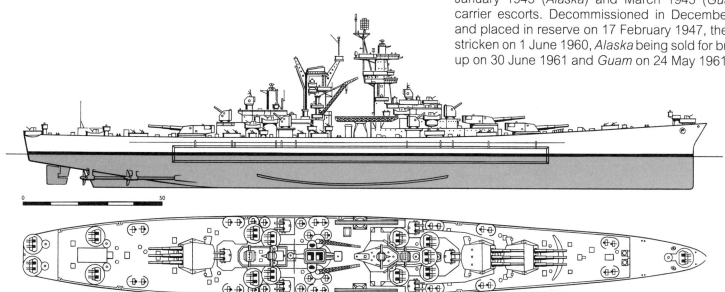

0   50

The Lesser Powers

Argentina

After the keels of two Brazilian battleships had been laid in 1907, the Argentinian Admiralty responded at once by proposing the acquisition of three similar units. Border disputes with Argentina's neighbours lent weight to these demands. However, at the end of 1908 only two units were authorised, although they were to be larger and more powerfully armed than the Brazilian ships.

Contracts were put out to tender and several British and a number of German and American firms took part. The British were confident of receiving the order, but to their surprise it was placed with US shipyards, these having submitted the most favourable tenders.

Construction began in the summer of 1910, and fifteen months later the hulls of *Rivadavia* and the *Moreno* took to the water. Some thought was given at the time to a third ship of the class, but nothing came of this.

In 1909 the *Rivadavia* class represented a cross between a battleship and a battlecruiser, for the armour protection and heavy armament corresponded to that of the most powerful battleships while the speed was actually greater.

Argentina remained neutral in the First World War and for the greater part of the Second, and her battleships never saw action. *Rivadavia* took part in the Spithead Coronation Review of 1937 and then paid a visit to Hamburg.

Sultan Yavuz Selim, the former *Goeben*, in Malta in 1936.

Rivadavia/Moreno

Displacement: 28,400/31,000t; (1939) 27,720 tons standard
Dimensions: 178.3 x 29.9 x 8.5m
Machinery: Curtis turbines, 3 shafts, 40,000shp
Fuel: 4,000t coal + 600t oil
Speed/range: 22.5kt; 10,200nm at 11kt
Armour: Belt 279mm, deck 114mm total, main armament 305mm, CT 305mm
Weight of armour: About 7,700t = 27.2% of normal displacement
Armament: 12 x 12in 50-cal, 12 x 6in 50-cal
Anti-aircraft guns: From 1926: 4 x 3in of US origin

Rivadavia in 1937 during a visit to Hamburg.

Ship	Builder	Laid down	Launched	Commissioned
Rivadavia	Fore River, Quincy	25.05.1910	26.08.1911	00.12.1914
Moreno	NYSB	09.07.1910	23.09.1911	00.03.1915

Both ships were modernised in the United States between 1924 and 1926 and converted from mixed to pure oil-firing (only 3,600t oil, range 8,500nm at 10kt). Both were stricken in 1956 and scrapped in 1957.

Moreno.

Brazil

Naval legislation of 1904 provided for Brazil's acquisition of three pre-dreadnoughts, the order for which was placed with the British shipbuilder Armstrongs on 23 July 1906. Originally the 16,000-tonne ships were to be armed with twelve 11in (254mm) guns in six turrets, but the contract signed in February 1907 required the delivery of two larger battleships carrying 12in (305mm) guns. At the time they were the most powerful capital ships in the world, and construction work began immediately. A weakness was their steam reciprocating engines, which even later were constantly troublesome.

When Brazil declared war on Germany in October 1917 she offered to detach the two battleships to the British Grand Fleet together with two light cruisers of the same age and a few destroyers, but the technical condition of the battleships was so poor that a complete refit was considered essential before they sailed. The work was carried out in the New York Navy Yard, but this began so late and proved so protracted that it was 1921 before Minas Gerais was back in service.

The third battleship authorised in the 1904 naval legislation was ordered from Armstrongs in 1907 but building was postponed until August 1910 when the Brazilian Navy surprised everybody with the announcement that it was building 'the biggest battleship in the world'. The contract with Armstrongs was signed in October 1910: the 32,000-tonne ship would be armed with twelve 14in (356mm) guns. Six weeks later mutiny broke out aboard Minas Gerais and the Navy lost much public sympathy in consequence; shortly afterwards the country was forced to review its naval construction plans following the collapse of the coffee and rubber markets.

On 3 June 1911 a fresh contract was placed with the British yard for Rio de Janeiro, a 27,500-ton ship with fourteen 12in (305mm) guns, but after it had been pointed out to them that the layout of the seven twin turrets would cause problems of instability when the ship was completed, the Brazilians decided to sell the vessel, which had by now been launched, to a third country before completion. Several nations were interested, including Russia, but eventually Turkey acquired the ship.

Having rid herself of Rio de Janeiro, Brazil now set about acquiring a true super-dreadnought for her Navy, armed with 15in (381mm) or 16in (406mm) guns, and Vickers and Armstrongs submitted a total of fourteen preliminary designs, from which Vickers Design No 781, a ship with eight 15in and fourteen 6in guns, was selected. This vessel was therefore as powerful as the British Queen Elizabeth class, although slightly slower at 22.5 knots. Armstrongs of Elswick were given the order, but the outbreak of war brought an end to the project.

After the First World War South American interest in battleships evaporated. In the early 1930s, Brazil set about modernising what had become by then the oldest battleships in the world. Minas Gerais remained in the yards from 1934 to 1938, but the planned work on São Paulo came to nothing.

In the Second World War Brazil fought on the side of the Allies from August 1942, but the two battleships served only as floating artillery batteries for the defence of the home country's main ports.

Minas Gerais/São Paulo

Displacement: 19,600/21,600t
Dimensions: 161.5 x 25.3 x 8.5m
Machinery: Steam reciprocating engines, 2 shafts, 23,500shp
Fuel: 2,350t coal + 400t oil
Speed/range: 21.0kt; 8,000nm at 10kt
Armour: Belt 229mm, deck 70mm total, main armament 305mm, CT 305mm
Armament: 12 x 12in 45-cal, 22 x 4.7in 50-cal (from 1917: 14 x 4.7in)
Anti-aircraft guns: From 1920–21: 2 x 3in of US origin

The ships were given a complete refit in New York, São Paulo in 1918–19 and Minas Gerais in 1920–21. Minas Gerais was modernised between 1934 and 1938 and converted to oil-firing; her AA armament was augmented to 4 x 4in and 4 x 40mm. In the Second World War both ships were used only as floating batteries.

Both vessels were decommissioned in 1946; São Paulo was sold for breaking up in 1951 and Minas Gerais in 1953. During her voyage to Europe to the breakers on 5 November 1951, São Paulo was lost north of the Azores when the tow parted in a heavy gale and the battleship, which had eight men aboard, was not seen again.

São Paulo prior to the First World War.

Ship	Builder	Laid down	Launched	Commissioned
Minas Gerais	Armstrong	17.04.1907	10.09.1908	06.01.1910
São Paulo	Vickers	24.09.1907	19.04.1909	22.08.1910

Chile

The Chilean Navy felt compelled to respond to the naval construction of her neighbours, particularly Argentina, but in 1908 a request for a battleship and two cruisers was rejected. Not until 1910, when Congress finally became convinced that the Fleet was obsolete, was the Navy permitted to submit a construction programme. This contained plans for the acquisition of two 'super-dreadnoughts' and a number of large, well-armed destroyers. Traditionally Chile had a very good relationship with the Royal Navy, and in 1911 the order for the whole programme was placed in Britain. The projected battleships and destroyers belonged to the most powerful of their type. The battleship had an armament of ten 14 in (356mm) guns and a speed of 23 knots but relatively weak armour. The first ship, *Almirante Latorre*, was begun at Armstrongs, Newcastle-upon-Tyne, in November 1911 but the keel

of the second, *Almirante Cochrane*, was not laid until February 1913 as the slip was occupied by *Rio de Janeiro*.

The first ship was well advanced by the outbreak of war and attracted the interest of the Royal Navy. On 9 September 1914 an agreement was reached with Chile whereby the vessel passed to Britain in return for financial compensation. *Almirante Latorre* was renamed HMS *Canada* and entered RN service in October 1915.

Work on the hull of *Almirante Cochrane* was suspended and the ship remained on the stocks until February 1918 when she was purchased by Britain for later conversion to an aircraft carrier. After the war Chile declined the offer of two *Invincible* class battlecruisers as a replacement for this ship.

In April 1920 *Almirante Latorre*, ex HMS *Canada*, was sold to Chile at a knock-down price and served as the flagship of the Chilean Navy for decades. She was finally scrapped in 1959.

Almirante Latorre Class

Displacement: 29,100/32,700t; (after 1931 refit) 28,500 tons standard
Dimensions: 199.6 x 28.1 x 8.9m (1931 beam with bulges: 31.4m)
Machinery: 2 turbines, 4 shafts, 38,000shp
Fuel: 3,300t coal + 520t oil
Speed/range: 23.0kt; 4,400nm at 10kt
Armour: Belt 229mm, deck 63mm total, main armament 254mm, CT 279mm
Weight of armour: Reportedly 7,100t = 24.4% of normal displacement
Armament: 10 x 14in 45-cal, 14 x 6in 50-cal
Anti-aircraft guns: 2 x 3in 45-cal (from 1931: 4 x 4in 45-cal)
Complement: 1,170

Almirante Cochrane remained on the stocks after the outbreak of war. She was selected for conversion to a large aircraft carrier at the end of 1917 and purchased by the Royal Navy in early 1918. Launched as HMS *Eagle* on 8 June 1918, she was completed in 1920.

Almirante Latorre was purchased by Britain on 9 September 1914 and completed and commissioned as HMS *Canada* in October 1915. Her fastest recorded

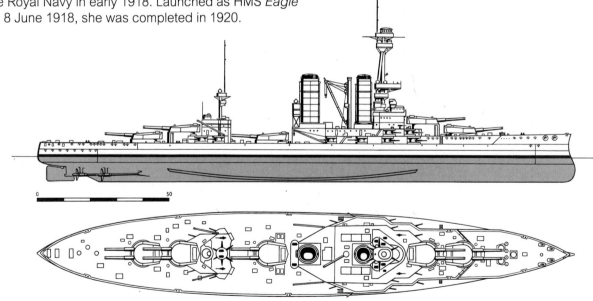

HMS *Canada*, 1916.

Ship	Builder	Laid down	Launched	Commissioned
Almirante Latorre	Armstrong, Newcastle	27.11.1911	27.11.1913	15.10.1915
Almirante Cochrane	Armstrong, Newcastle	20.02.1913	–	–

speed was 24.3 knots at 52,682shp, in May 1918. Resold to Chile in April 1920, she re-entered service under her original name on 1 August 1920. During her 1929–31 refit

Almirante Latorre served as HMS *Canada* from 1915 to 1920.

at Devonport she was re-engined with four new Parsons turbines and re-boilered from mixed- to oil-firing; anti-torpedo bulges were added and new fire control equipment and AA armament installed. In this condition, with numerous small-calibre AA guns added, she remained the flagship of Chilean Navy until decommissioned in 1958. The disarmed hulk was towed to Tokyo for scrapping in August 1959.

Greece

There were in Europe two groups of militarily weaker nations which wanted to bolster their navies by the addition of capital ships. The first group comprised states such as Greece, Portugal and Turkey, which could only order such vessels from foreign yards. The other group of nations, such as Sweden, Spain and the Netherlands, had a competent domestic shipbuilding industry and were capable of building battleships in home dockyards with the assistance of foreign companies. Of these, only Spain actually constructed true capital ships. The Swedish 1911 project for a 'ship of the line' was in fact no more than a coast defence vessel with four 283mm (11.1in) guns.

The construction of capital ships by Dutch yards was twice seriously entertained but was forestalled on both occasions by the outbreak of war, in 1914 and 1940. In 1914 planning was shelved at an early stage, and even before a decision had been taken in favour of any of the projects submitted by foreign designers. In May 1940, however, it had already been decided to start work on three battlecruisers similar to the German *Scharnhorst*. The design stage for a 32,000-tonne vessel with nine 283mm (11.1in) guns of German origin came close to completion, and in anticipation of building contracts the large national shipyards had already begun expanding their facilities when the German invasion brought about the sudden demise of the project.

The increasing tensions in the Balkans before the First World War, and the prospect of finally having the opportunity of liberating Greek populations in Turkish-occupied territories and islands, provided the Greek government with a powerful impetus to renew and strengthen the Navy. Although a large number of torpedo boats and destroyers or well-armed light cruisers would have been more useful for naval operations in the Aegean, the 1911 naval construction programme also contained proposals for two units classed as 'armoured ships'.

One of these was eventually ordered in July 1912 from the German shipbuilder Vulcan. This 23-knot vessel was designed for a normal displacement of 13,000 tonnes, with an armament of six 356mm (14in) guns of US manufacture in three twin turrets. In December 1912 Greece amended the contract and now demanded a fully fledged battleship of greater size with eight guns instead of six. The keel was laid in July 1913 and the ship was launched as *Salamis* in November 1914, after which construction was suspended. The hull remained at Hamburg until 1932, when a German-Greek court of arbitration sitting in Paris finally ruled that Greece was obliged to compensate the yard. In 1914 Greece had awarded France a contract to build a battleship to a modified *Provence* design but the project was cancelled by the French on the outbreak of war.

Despite these setbacks, between mid-1914 and April 1941 the Greek Navy possessed two ships which were still classed as battleships in the Fleet Lists of the 1930s. These were *Kilkis* (ex USS *Mississippi*) and *Lemnos* (ex USS *Idaho*), which had been purchased from the United States a few weeks prior to the First World War and in 1908 had been the last US pre-dreadnoughts to be commissioned. They carried four 12in (305mm) and eight 8in (203mm) guns. From 1932 they appeared in the Reserve List. *Kilkis* later served as an artillery training ship and *Lemnos* as an accommodation hulk. Both were sunk by German dive-bombers in April 1941.

Salamis

Displacement: 19,800 tons normal
Dimensions: 173.7 x 24.7 x 7.6m (1931 beam with bulges: 31.4m)
Machinery: AEG turbines, 3 shafts, 40,000shp
Fuel: 1,200t coal
Speed/range: 23.0kt; range not known
Armour: Belt 250mm, deck 75mm, main armament 250mm, CT 300mm
Armament: 8 x 14in 45-cal, 12 x 6in 50-cal
Complement: 710
Builder: Vulcan, Hamburg (laid down 23.07.1913; launched 11.11.1914)

Construction was suspended on 31 December 1914. As Greece declined to accept the unfinished ship after the First World War, the matter was referred to arbitration and a verdict in favour of the shipyard was delivered on 23 April 1932. On the instructions of the builder, the hull was scrapped at Bremen.

Spain

The Spanish naval programme of November 1907 provided not only for three battleships but also the large-scale development of the shipbuilding industry with British assistance together with new docks and harbour installations. The battleships were scheduled for completion by 1914. At 15,000 tonnes they were very small, and three larger units were planned in the 1913 naval programme, but nothing further was heard of these.

Work on the battleships of the original programme was commenced, but by the end of 1913, after five years, only one of them had been completed. The last of the class, *Jaime I*, was launched in September 1914, but the supply of materials from Britain gradually petered out and construction was interrupted. Spanish industry was not in a position to ensure the completion of even a single ship.

These Armstrong-designed ships were not a success. The designers succeeded in concentrating a powerful capital-ship armament on a relatively small hull with an acceptable turn of speed, but this had been achieved at the expense of stability. The *España* class were therefore the smallest and weakest battleships in the world.

In the First World War Spain remained neutral, but *España* was lost a few years later. All Spanish warships were deployed to put down the Riff rebellion in Spanish Morocco, and during this operation, in August 1923, *España* struck a reef and resisted all attempts to free her. Only the heavy guns and certain items of equipment could be salvaged before the hull broke up in a storm.

Both remaining sister ships were lost in the Spanish Civil War. *Alfonso XIII*, which had been renamed *España* on the proclamation of the Republic in 1931, was mined off the Basque coast, and *Jaime I* was almost completely destroyed by an internal explosion on 17 June 1937. This signalled the demise of the Spanish battleship, for Franco's plan to build 35,000-tonne ships with 381mm (15in) guns or a large number of 15,000-tonne coast defence battleships remained a pipe-dream: the Spanish shipbuilding industry, exhausted and financially ruined by the long civil war, was deprived of the ability to build even medium sized warships

España Class

Displacement: 15,700/16,100t; 14,224 tons standard
Dimensions: 140.0 x 24.0 x 7.8m
Machinery: Parsons turbines, 4 shafts, 15,500shp
Fuel: 1,900t coal
Speed/range: 19.5kt; 5,000nm at 10kt
Armour: Belt 203mm, deck 63mm total, main armament 203mm, CT 254mm
Weight of armour: 4,800t = 30.5% of normal displacement
Armament: 8 x 12in 50-cal, 20 x 4in 50-cal
Anti-aircraft guns: From 1926: 2 x 3in 50-cal
Complement: 850

España ran aground near Melilla and broke up during a storm on 26 August 1923 after unsuccessful efforts to salvage her.

Alfonso XIII was renamed *España* in 1931. Her crew declared for Franco on the outbreak of the Civil War in July 1936. She was mined and sunk whilst bombarding Basque positions off Santander on 30 April 1937.

Jaime I remained loyal to Republic in July 1936 and bombarded Falangist positions in southern Spain on a number of occasions. She was badly damaged by bombing at Malaga on 13 August 1936, blew up at Cartagena on 17 June 1937 and was broken up *in situ* in July 1939.

Ship	Builder	Laid down	Launched	Commissioned
España	Ferrol	05.02.1909	05.02.1912	23.10.1913
Alfonso XIII	Ferrol	23.02.1912	07.05.1913	16.08.1915
Jaime I	Ferrol	05.02.1912	21.09.1914	00.00.1921

Jaime I.

Turkey

In 1905 the Turkish Fleet possessed a considerable number of battleships of varying size, most of which were old and neglected. Twelve of them had been launched between 1864 and 1872. They were unserviceable as fighting ships, and were best employed as static training hulks.

The most recent unit, *Hamidieh*, had been built at the Constantinople Dockyard. Her keel was laid in 1872 and she took to the water twelve years later. By 1892, when she was completed, similar central-battery ships in other fleets were being scrapped as outdated. Following her commissioning *Hamidieh* rotted away for a few years at the Golden Horn (the Government shipyard at Izmir) and by 1903 was in such an appalling condition that the idea of modernising her was beyond contemplation.

The largest battleship, *Messudieh*, was built in Britain and entered service in 1877. At the turn of the century she was completely modernised, re-engined and to some degree re-armed in Italy. Her main armament of two 234mm (9.2in) guns failed to arrive, however, and so wooden gun barrels were fitted instead. Thus the fleet operated by 'the sick man of Europe' was at best a motley collection of museum pieces.

The revolt of the 'Young Turks' in July 1908 brought the possibility of change, and after the event a naval construction programme was put together providing for the acquisition of six battleships. Numerous gun boats and torpedo boats were also ordered, followed by the purchase of two old *Brandenburg* class battleships from Germany in 1910.

A British naval mission had been active in Turkey since 1909, busying itself less with training schemes for and a thoroughgoing reorganisation of the Turkish Navy than with ensuring that British shipyards obtained Turkish orders for ships. Of primary importance for Turkey were large and powerful battleships which could be deployed in the Black Sea on naval operations against Russia, although the Balkans conflict which threatened to erupt was unlikely to afford any opportunity to put the units to good use.

In 1910 the Vickers-Armstrong consortium submitted designs for a ship with ten 12in (305mm) guns, but the Turks required an altogether bigger ship than that proposed, with ten guns of larger calibre. The contract for two such units was signed in the summer of 1911, and building work began on the first unit at Vickers' Barrow yard in December 1911. The contract for the second ship placed with Armstrongs was later cancelled because of the outbreak of war in the Balkans and concern at Turkey's ability to pay. After a pause of several months, work on the first unit at Vickers was resumed and *Reshadieh* was eventually launched in September 1913, for delivery in the early summer of 1914.

The hand-over was deliberately delayed by the British, who first wanted to see what political developments would take place following Austria-Hungary's mobilisation, and the ship was then impounded. On 22 August 1914 *Reshadieh* was commissioned into the Royal Navy as HMS *Erin*.

It was not so much the growth of the Greek Fleet but rather the construction of three powerful Russian battleships in the Black Sea, the presence of which could have no other purpose than to challenge the Turkish Bosphorus Fleet, that compelled Turkey urgently to seek to acquire further capital ships.

In the spring of 1913 Armstrongs offered Turkey the unfinished *Rio de Janeiro*. Although the weak points of this ship were well known in the market, there were nevertheless a number of interested purchasers. Turkey, originally considered an outsider in the bidding, received a credit from France and acquired the ship on 28 December 1913. Building resumed under the name *Sultan Osman I*, and the ship was completed at the end of July 1914. The Turks had a crew of 500 aboard her and wanted to accept delivery, but again the British Government prevaricated and this ship, too, was confiscated, on 3 August 1914. She served in the Royal Navy until 1922 as HMS *Agincourt*. A third ship for which the order was placed in Britain in April 1914 also failed to reach the Turkish client. This was *Fatik*, an improved sister-ship of *Reshadieh*, under construction at Vickers and suspended at an early stage when war broke out.

However, a modern capital ship did eventually sail under the Turkish flag. This was the German battlecruiser *Goeben*, which put into Constantinople on 11 August 1914 and hoisted the Turkish ensign five days later under the name *Yavuz Sultan Selim*. Still with a German crew, the ship was employed operationally until 2 November 1918, when she finally passed into Turkish ownership.

Under the terms of the Armistice, Turkey was not permitted to retain large warships and accordingly was obliged to surrender *Yavuz Sultan Selim*. In fact the disabled vessel was permitted to remain in Turkish waters, and later the Allied Powers notified Turkey that they had decided not to enforce the treaty terms in this case. With French assistance the ship was refitted between 1927 and 1930, was renamed *Yavuz* in 1936 and served as the Fleet flagship until 1950. This popular battlecruiser was finally decommissioned with great ceremony in June 1973 and broken up in Turkey in 1974.

Erin  (ex *Reshadieh*)

Displacement: 23,150/25,700t, (*Fatik* 25,000t normal)
Dimensions: 168.5 x 27.9 x 8.7m (*Fatik* 170.5 x 27.4m)
Machinery: Parsons turbines, 4 shafts, 26,500shp
Fuel: 2,150t coal + 720t oil
Speed/range: 21.0kt; 5,300nm at 10kt
Armour: Belt 305mm, deck 76mm total, main armament 279mm, CT 305mm
Weight of armour: 7,000t = 30.3% of normal displacement
Armament: 10 x 13.5in 45-cal, 16 x 6in 50-cal
Anti-aircraft guns: From 1916: 2 x 3in 45-cal
Complement: 1,070

Fatik was to have been a slightly larger version of *Reshadieh* and was ordered on 29 April 1914, a specd of 22 knots and stronger armour having been requested. The hull was broken up on the stocks after the outbreak of war. An order for another ship of the class, *Reshad I. Kamis*, was placed with Armstrongs but cancelled in 1912 before the keel was laid.

Erin, 1915.

The completed *Reshadieh* was quickly fitted out after her requisition and commissioned into the Royal Navy as HMS *Erin* on 22 August 1914. She fought at Jutland in 1916 and remained on the active list until autumn 1919. She was replaced in her intended role as a training ship by HMS *Thunderer* in July 1920 and disarmed under the terms of the Washington Treaty in May 1922. She was scrapped in 1923.

Ship	Builder	Laid down	Launched	Commissioned
Reshadieh	Vickers	06.12.1911	03.09.1913	22.08.1914
Fatik	Vickers	11.06.1914	–	–

Reshadie as she might have been (from a Turkish postcard).

Agincourt (ex Sultan Osman I)

Displacement: 28,300/31,400t
Dimensions: 203.6 x 27.1 x 9.1m
Machinery: Parsons turbines, 4 shafts, 34,000shp
Fuel: 3,200t coal max. + 630t oil
Speed/range: 22.0kt; 7,000nm at 10kt
Armour: Belt 229mm, deck 114mm total, main armament 305mm, CT 305mm
Weight of armour: 7,406t = 26.2% of normal displacement
Armament: 14 x 12in 45-cal, 20 x 6in 50-cal (1918: 18 x 6in)
Anti-aircraft guns: From 1917: 2 x 3in 45-cal
Complement: 1,110 (1,270 in 1917)
Builder: Armstrong, Newcastle (laid down 14.09.1911; launched 22.01.1913; commissioned 20.08.1914)

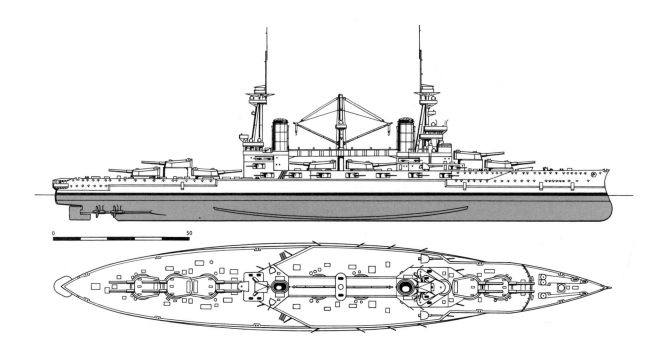

Agincourt, 1914.

Sultan Osman I was requisitioned by the Royal Navy in August 1914 and served throughout the First World War as HMS *Agincourt*.

Ordered by the Brazilian Government as *Rio de Janeiro* in June 1911 and sold to Turkey in prior to completion on 28 December 1913, this vessel ran builder's trials in July 1914 under her Turkish name, *Sultan Osman I*—complete except for a few 12in (305mm) gun barrels—and reached 22.4 knots at 40,129shp. She was requisitioned by the British at the shipyard on 3 August 1914 and provisionally accepted by the Royal Navy as HMS *Agincourt* on 7 August, being finally completed on 20 August that year. The ship was attached to the 4th Battle Squadron of the Grand Fleet and served at Jutland 1916. She was structurally altered and had her tripod mainmast removed in 1916–17 and was placed in reserve in March 1919. An offer to Brazil to repurchase the ship was declined in 1919. Work to refit the vessel as a depot ship armed with four 12in (305mm) guns, begun in April 1921, was suspended in December 1921 and the ship was sold to the breakers a year later and scrapped in 1924.

Sources

Almanach der K.u.k.-Kriegsmarine, 1904–1918 editions (Pola)

Archiv für Seewesen – Mitteilungen aus dem Gebeite des Seewesens, years to 1914 (Pola)

Besktovny, L. G., *Armiya i Flot Rossii Nacale XX Veka* (Moscow, 1986)

Breyer, S., *Schlachtschiffe und Schlachtkreuzer 1905–1970* (Munich, 1970)

Burt, R. A., *British Battleships of World War One* (London, 1986)

Buxton, I., *Big Gun Monitors* (Tynemouth, 1978)

Campbell, J., *Naval Weapons of WW2* (London, 1985)

Conway's All the World's Fighting Ships 1860–1946, 3 vols (London)

Dülffer, J., *Weimar, Hitler und die Marine* (Düsseldorf, 1973)

Evers, H., *Kriegsschiffbau* (Berlin, 1943)

Fraccaroli, A., *Italian Warships of WW1 and WW2*, 2 vols (London, 1968, 1970)

Friedman, N., *Battleship Design and Development 1905–1945* (London, 1978)

———, *US Battleships* (London)

Giorgerine-Nani, C., *Le Navl di Linea* (Rome, 1966)

Gröner, E., *Die deutschen Kriegsschiffe 1815–1945*, vol. 1 (Munich, 1982)

Hodges, P., *The Big Gun: Battleship Main Armament 1860–1945* (London, 1981)

Jane's Fighting Ships, 1901–1953 editions (London)

Jentschura, H., Jung, D., and Mickel, P., *Warships of the Imperial Japanese Navy 1869–1945* (London, 1977)

Kronenfels, *Das schwimmende Material der Seemächte* (Vienna, 1881)

Labayle-Couhat, J., *French Warships of WW1 and WW2*, 2 vols (London, 1971, 1974)

Lenton, H. T., and Colledge, J. J., *Warships of World War II* (London, 1973)

Marine-Rundschau, 1925–1990 editions

Meister, J., *Soviet Warships* (London, 1977)

Ministerstvo Oborony SSSR, *Korabli i Vspomogatelnie Suda Sovetskogo Voenno-Morskogo Flota 1917–1927 i 1928–1945*, 2 vols (Moscow, 1981, 1988)

Moisseyev, *Spisok Korabley Russkogo Flota* (Moscow, 1948)

Morskoy Sbornik, 1964–1990 editions

'Nauticus', *Jahrbuch für Deutschlands Seeinteressen*, editions to 1914, (Berlin)

Parkes, O., *British Battleships 1860–1950* (London 1958)

Potter, Nimitz and Rohwer, *Seemacht von der Antike bis zur Gegenwart* (Munich, 1974)

Preston, A., *Grosskampfschiffe des Ersten Weltkrieges* (Graz, 1976)

Raven, A., and Roberts, J., *British Battleships of World War Two* (London, 1976)

Rohwer, J., (ed.), 'The Naval Arms Race 1930–1941', *Revue Internationale d'Histoire Militaire*, No 73 (Stuttgart, 1991)

Rossiyskiy Imperatorskiy Flot, 1913–1915 editions (St Petersburg)

Schwarz, T., *Die Entwicklung des Kriegsschiffbaues*, vol. 2 (Leipzig, 1912)

Silverstone, P. H., *US Warships of WW1 and WW2*, 2 vols (London 1970, 1977)

Warship, various editions

Warship International, editions to 1991

Weyers Flottentaschenbuch, 1904–1959 editions (Bin/Munich)

Photograph credits

A Fraccaroli (5); Musée de la Marine, Paris (7); Armeemuseum, Dresden (3); Naval Records Club (12): BfZ (3); author's collection (rest)

Representatives of two eras: HMS *Dreadnought* and HMS *Victory*.

Index of Ships

The two Spanish battleships in the anchorage at Vigo, 1927.